A
GLOBAL
AGENDA

Issues Before
the 49th
General Assembly
of the
United Nations

A GLOBAL AGENDA

Issues Before the 49th General Assembly of the United Nations

An annual publication of the United Nations Association of the United States of America

John Tessitore and Susan Woolfson, Editors

University Press of America
Lanham • New York • London

Copyright © 1994 by the United Nations
Association of the United States of America, Inc.

Published by
University Press of America,® Inc.
4720 Boston Way
Lanham, Maryland 20706

3 Henrietta Street
London WC2E 8LU England

ISSN: 1057-1213
ISBN 1-880632-21-7 (cloth : alk. paper)
ISBN 1-880632-22-5 (paper : alk. paper)

Cover by Scott Rattray

 The paper used in this publication meets the minimum requirements of American National Standard for Information Sciences—Permanence of Paper for Printed Library Materials, ANSI Z39.48–1984.

Contents

Acknowledgments

A volume of this size and timeliness is not possible without the assistance of a great many people, and we wish to acknowledge their enormous contribution. First, of course, we must thank the many authors who have provided exhaustive and timely coverage of U.N. activities under the pressure of a very difficult production schedule. To these men and women—identified on the following pages—we extend both our thanks and admiration for a job so very well done.

A word must also be said of the many international civil servants working at the United Nations who graciously contributed their time and their expertise. As in past years, their helpfulness has proven a tremendous asset in the compilation of this unique volume.

Finally, a word about our Communications Interns. Providing vital assistance to the authors—and to the editors as well—was a small cadre of university students, working relentlessly throughout the spring and summer months, researching, proofreading, fact-finding, and even writing (notably within the Human Rights and Social Issues section). To these bright, energetic, and altogether delightful young people, we wish to express our special thanks and to extend our very best wishes for happy and productive careers. They are Joanna Catalano, Yvette Cuca, Aileen Hytmiah, Gretchen Kates, Whitt Orsburn, Mariana Panova, Lecia Smith, Jennifer Spiegel, and Richard Star.

John Tessitore
Susan Woolfson

New York, July 1994

Contributors

José E. Alvarez (Legal Issues) is a Professor of Law at Michigan Law School in Ann Arbor, where he teaches international law and international organizations.

Nick Birnback (Beyond Peacekeeping) is Public Affairs Coordinator for UNA-USA.

Frederick Z. Brown (Cambodia) directs Southeast Asian studies at the Paul H. Nitze School of Advanced International Studies of Johns Hopkins University and has followed the Cambodian peace process under a grant from the United States Institute for Peace.

Erika H. Burk (Human Rights) is a Program Associate at the Council on Foreign Relations.

Richard D. Caplan (The Former Yugoslavia) is New York Director of the London-based Institute for War & Peace Reporting—a conflict-monitoring organization—and Senior Editor of its bulletin, *WarReport.*

Yvette P. Cuca (Health), a UNA-USA Communications Intern, is studying for a master's degree at Columbia University's School of International and Public Affairs, with a concentration in Russian affairs.

Ivo H. Daalder (Arms Control and Disarmament, with Howard A. Moyes) is an Assistant Professor in the School of Public Affairs at the University of Maryland and Director of Research at the University's Center for International and Security Studies. He has published many works on arms control and is the co-editor (and co-author) of *Rethinking the Unthinkable: New Directions for Nuclear Arms Control.*

Jules Kagian (The Middle East and the Persian Gulf) covered the United Nations and the American scene for a number of Middle Eastern newspapers and radio and TV stations during more than two decades. He is currently U.N. correspondent for *Middle East International* (London).

Gail V. Karlsson (Environment and Sustainable Development) is a New York-based attorney specializing in international environmental law and Chair of UNA-New York's Global Policy Project.

Lee Kimball (Law of the Sea, Ocean Affairs, and Antarctica), based in Washington, D.C., is a specialist in international law and institutions dealing with environment and development issues.

Craig Lasher (Population) is a senior policy analyst and legislative assistant at Population Action International, a private nonprofit organization that works to expand the availability of voluntary family planning services worldwide.

Kathryn C. Lawler (Refugees) is a Program Associate at the Washington-based Refugee Policy Group.

Anthony Mango (Finance and Administration) worked for the U.N. Secretariat from 1960 to 1987. Between 1970 and 1983 he headed the secretariat of the Advisory Committee on Administrative and Budgetary Questions, and in the period 1983–87 he served as Secretary to the U.N. Pension Board. Since his retirement he has done consultancy work for the United Nations.

Martin M. McLaughlin (Food and Agriculture) is a consultant on food and development policy.

George H. Mitchell Jr. (Economics and Development) is an Assistant Professor of International Politics at Tufts University, where he is a member of the Department of Political Science and of the Fletcher School of Law and Diplomacy.

Howard A. Moyes (Arms Control and Disarmament, with Ivo H. Daalder), a graduate student in the School of Public Affairs at the University of Maryland, is a Research Assistant with the Project on Rethinking Arms Control conducted by the University's Center for International and Security Studies.

Mariana Panova (Aging), a UNA-USA Communications Intern, is completing a master's degree at Columbia University's School of International and Public Affairs, with a concentration in security policy.

Edmund T. Piasecki (Africa; Central America and the Caribbean; Cyprus), a Washington-based consultant to UNA-USA, is the co-author, most recently, of "The U.N. in Disarmament," a chapter-length section of the *Encyclopedia of Arms Control and Disarmament.*

Constantine V. Pleshakov (The Former Soviet Union) heads the Pacific Studies Section of the Institute for U.S. and Canada Studies of the Russian Academy of Sciences. He has spent the 1993–94 academic year as a member of the Institute for Advanced Study in Princeton.

Clare M. Sievers (The Status of Women), a Program Officer at UNA-USA, is a co-coordinator of the organization's preparatory meetings for the Beijing Conference on Women.

Lecia Renee Smith (Drug Abuse, Production, and Trafficking; Other Social Issues: Crime), a UNA-USA Communications Intern, is a graduate of Vassar College, where she majored in international studies.

Jennifer Spiegel (Other Social Issues: Children and Youth; International Year of the Family), a UNA-USA Communications Intern, is completing a master's degree in politics at New York University.

Richard J. Star (Other Social Issues: Disabled Persons; Shelter and the Homeless), a UNA-USA Communications Intern, is completing a master's degree in international politics and international business at New York University.

John Tessitore (Co-Editor) is Director of Communications at UNA-USA.

Susan Woolfson (Co-Editor) is Managing Editor of Communications at UNA-USA.

I
Making and Keeping the Peace

1. Beyond Peacekeeping
By Nick Birnback

This past year has been nothing less than a watershed in the history of the United Nations. Under the stewardship of an activist Secretary-General, the United Nations has been on the front pages and on the front lines to an extent unprecedented in its almost 50-year history. The results have been both positive and negative, with U.N. personnel alternately hailed as saviors and condemned as invaders. It was, truly, the best of times and the worst of times.

The United Nations and the End of the Cold War

During the four decades of the Cold War, the U.N.'s role in maintaining global peace and stability was marginalized by the intense competition that characterized the superpower rivalry. From 1947 to 1990, the United States and the USSR cast a combined total of 279 vetoes in the Security Council, quashing one initiative after another. Multilateralism had little place in a world dominated by the "zero-sum" realities of the Cold War. The collapse of the Soviet Union brought all-but-forgotten freedoms to millions of people, but it also triggered a resurgence of nationalism, ethnic rivalries, centuries-old religious enmities, and exclusivist and even xenophobic political entities, all previously held in check by regional Soviet hegemony. These tensions have been fueled by the lethal detritus of the Cold War: large stockpiles of conventional weapons. Such nations as Somalia, Afghanistan, and the former Yugoslavia, once considered important pawns in the superpowers' global chess game, have now turned on themselves, propagating bitter civil wars with the most modern conventional arms the West and the East have to offer.

The end of bipolarism created a power vacuum, and for the first time since the United Nations was established, nations of the world began to look to the world body and the doctrine of collective security—rather than superpower rivalry—for protection.

"An Agenda for Peace"

In June 1992, U.N. Secretary-General Boutros Boutros-Ghali issued a report entitled "An Agenda for Peace." In this document the Secretary-General offered a plan of action for a vital, actively engaged United Nations. The United Nations of the future would no longer simply maintain a post-conflict status quo but would be able actually to preempt aggression, facilitate cease-fires, and strengthen existing peace settlements. The report called for a robust and well-integrated continuum of preventive diplomacy, observer missions, sanctions, disarmament, peacekeeping operations, peacemaking, and peace enforcement. It also recommended that member states take it upon themselves to make significant contributions both financially and in terms of materials to provide the additional support necessary to propagate this more ambitious agenda. At the heart of the report was a call for member states to make military forces available to the United Nations on a standby basis—an action that would allow the United Nations to back up preventive diplomatic initiatives with the credible threat of the use of force. These arrangements would be made on a country-by-country basis in accordance with the U.N. Charter's Article 43, which states that

> All members of the United Nations . . . undertake to make available to the Security Council, on its call and in accordance with a special agreement or agreements, armed forces, assistance and facilities, including rights of passage, necessary for the purpose of maintaining international peace and security.

In a sense, "An Agenda for Peace" attempted to set out a blueprint for a "U.N. foreign policy" that would begin to address the political realities of the post-Cold War era. The past year has provided a harsh trial-by-fire for "An Agenda for Peace," and while the ideals behind the document are no less valid than they were a year ago, the United Nations has been forced to confront some very hard realities in terms of what it can and cannot do.

Peacekeeping versus Peace Enforcement

Over the course of this past year, U.N. peacekeeping forces were in more demand than at any other time in the Organization's history. The United Nations has 17 operations currently in the field, at an annual cost of over $3 billion [Office of the Spokesman for the Secretary-General, 6/94]. Just seven years ago the total peacekeeping budget was no more than $235 million ["An Agenda for Peace"]. In fact, the total amount the United Nations spent on peacekeeping operations from 1948 to 1992 totaled only $8.3 billion, compared to the roughly $30 *trillion* devoted globally to other military purposes [ibid.].

Traditional peacekeeping operations are undertaken with the con-

Table I-1
United Nations Peacekeeping Operations (as of July 1994)

Mission	Date Established
United Nations Truce Supervision Organization (UNTSO)	June 1948
United Nations Military Observer Group in India and Pakistan (UNMOGIP)	January 1949
United Nations Peacekeeping Force in Cyprus (UNFICYP)	March 1964
United Nations Disengagement Observer Force (UNDOF)	June 1974
United Nations Interim Force in Lebanon (UNIFIL)	March 1978
United Nations Iraq-Kuwait Observation Mission (UNIKOM)	April 1991
United Nations Angola Verification Mission II (UNAVEM II)	June 1991
United Nations Observer Mission in El Salvador (ONUSAL)	July 1991
United Nations Mission for the Referendum in Western Sahara (MINURSO)	September 1991
United Nations Protection Force (UNPROFOR)	March 1992
United Nations Operation in Mozambique (ONUMOZ)	December 1992
United Nations Operation in Somalia II (UNOSOM II)	May 1993
United Nations Observer Mission Uganda-Rwanda (UNOMUR)	June 1993
United Nations Observer Mission in Georgia (UNOMIG)	August 1993
United Nations Observer Mission in Liberia (UNOMIL)	September 1993
United Nations Mission in Haiti (UNMIH)	September 1993
United Nations Assistance Mission for Rwanda II (UNAMIR II)	May 1994

sent of all the parties to a conflict, and are essentially a policing and confidence-building measure designed to be employed simultaneously with diplomatic initiatives. They traditionally employ only lightly armed forces, whose job it is to monitor an existing peace settlement and help avoid any further bloodshed, not to disarm combatants or otherwise compel both sides to stop fighting. The **UNTAC mission in Cambodia** is a good example of the successful application of this type of operation. UNTAC worked to a large extent because, despite pressure to play a more active role in disarming the Khmer Rouge, the operation stuck rigidly to its mandate and stayed in the role of facilitator, monitor, and impartial observer. As former Under-Secretary-General for Peacekeeping Operations Sir Brian Urquhart has observed, whenever peacekeepers sacrifice their neutrality it "invariably leads to the peacekeepers becoming part of the conflict and therefore part of the problem" [Foreword, *U.N. Peacekeeping and the Non-Use of Force*, by F. T. Liu, Occasional Paper Series, International Peace Academy (Boulder, Colo.: Lynne Rienner Publishers, 1992)].

Unlike traditional peacekeeping missions, which derive their authority from Chapter VI of the U.N. Charter entitled "The Pacific Settlement of Disputes," **Chapter VII peace-enforcement operations** do not require consent of the parties concerned. Chapter VII missions can include humanitarian assistance, economic and military sanctions, blockades, and even direct military action, as well as efforts to further political reconciliation and restructuring. Over half of the current U.N. operations in the field are helping resolve internal conflicts [Michael Renner, *Critical Juncture: The Future of Peacekeeping*, Worldwatch Paper 114, 5/93, p. 34].

Secretary-General Boutros-Ghali has called this "new generation" of peacekeeping operations "nothing less than an effort to preserve the foundations of the state system while beginning to shape a post-Cold War structure of peace and security" [*The New York Times*, 8/20/93]. Many of these new "enforcement" operations, such as Somalia, Cambodia, and the coalition action in Iraq, are also on a much larger scale than those missions undertaken during the Cold War.

Globocop?

The end of bipolarism has also begun to change the nature of warfare itself. The vast majority of violent disputes today (and those likely to occur in the near future) are conflicts with no clearly defined battlefield and in which the distinction between soldier and noncombatant is blurred. These conflicts greatly complicate any potential peacekeeping operation. Missions of this type frequently involve at least a partial shedding of the "cloak of neutrality" that shielded U.N. peacekeepers in the past, exposing the blue helmets to charges of neoimperialism and of violating sovereignty by taking sides in an internal conflict. It was operations of this type—particularly in Somalia—that provided the most strenuous test for the United Nations over this past year.

There is no doubt that the end of the Cold War has created a greater demand for U.N. intervention abroad. At no other time have the nations of the world called on the United Nations to undertake such a diversity of security-related tasks around the globe. Unfortunately, as the scope and the mandates of the missions the United Nations chooses to undertake increase, so do the risks both to U.N. personnel in the field and to the Organization's credibility. When U.N. operations were restricted to traditional peacekeeping, the dangers to the Organization as a whole were negligible. If the situation in a host country or region became too unstable, the United Nations could simply pull out, with no loss of face or credibility. After all, the United Nations was there by direct invitation of the parties involved. As the events of 1993 proved, now that the United Nations and the international community as a whole have begun to undertake missions designed to forestall or turn back aggression (e.g., Bosnia), or to completely restructure a failed state (e.g., Somalia), the Organization puts its reputation and its credibility on the line every time it even considers coercive, punitive, or retaliatory action.

Challenges to Multilateral Action

This past year the United Nations established a number of milestones on the road to collective security. NATO forces, acting with U.N. authorization, went into combat for the first time in that organization's 40-plus-year history. In the former Yugoslavia, the United Nations presented the Bosnian Serbs with an ultimatum—backed up by a credible threat of the use of force—demanding the lifting of the siege of Sarajevo. While compliance with this ultimatum—and a similar statement regarding the town of Goražde—has been imperfect, few doubt that, by taking assertive action, the United Nations saved lives and contributed to the peace process. In Somalia, U.S.-led U.N. forces undertook a campaign to restore order to a nation that had sunk into virtual anarchy and thereby prevented the starvation of thousands, perhaps even millions of Somalis. Unfortunately, the United Nations also discovered first hand the difficulties inherent in mounting peacekeeping and enforcement operations where large segments of the population simply have no interest in keeping the peace.

The international community's greater reliance on the United Nations to settle disputes has also demonstrated the seemingly insurmountable difficulties in undertaking multilateral operations. Problems of logistics, communication, equipment, and a coherent central command structure are only some of the many pitfalls encountered on a daily basis by the U.N.'s 17 peacekeeping operations. The UNOSOM II operation in Somalia demonstrated the weaknesses of not having a clearly established chain of command, as each member state that had contributed forces felt it needed to check with its home government before accepting orders from U.N. commanders on the ground. Close coordination is a vital component of any military operation, and having national officers refuse orders from U.N. Headquarters because they feel the command is not in their unit's best interests is simply not an effective way to undertake a military operation. Unauthorized action is also as dangerous as nonaction, as witness the tragic case of the U.S. Rangers in Somalia, who were unable to summon reinforcements because the UNOSOM II central command had not been fully informed of their "snatch and grab" operation.

The large UNOSOM II operation clearly demonstrated the weakness of the ad hoc way in which peacekeeping forces are cobbled together. The United Nations is completely dependent on the contributions—of both money and manpower—of member states. Consequently the troops volunteered by member states have usually never trained together, frequently have incompatible equipment, and often do not share a common language. If governments are slow or unwilling to provide matériel for operations approved by the Security Council, the United Nations also has no coercive means of persuasion. This can stretch to unacceptable levels the lag time between when an operation is approved and when it is deployed. Boutros-Ghali has asserted that this systemic delay hampers not only the effectiveness but the viability of peacekeeping operations as a whole [Anthony McDermott, *United Nations Financing Problems and the New Generation of Peacekeeping and Peace Enforcement*, Thomas J. Watson Jr. Institute for International Studies, Occasional Paper No. 16, 11/93, p. 4].

Somalia was in many ways the most salient test of the practicality of the ideals put forward in "An Agenda for Peace." As the sole remaining superpower, the United States has a crucial role to play at the United Nations. The deaths of 18 U.S. Rangers in Mogadishu severely dampened America's enthusiasm for collective action viewed as not *directly* in the U.S. national interest. A large portion of the American public failed to take notice of the shift in the Somalia operation from a Chapter VI to a Chapter VII operation, and were shocked when the United States was taking comparatively heavy casualties. The subsequent speedy departure of the United States after having its nose bloodied sent a message of non-resolve to people all over the world. In Haiti, lightly armed U.S. forces were turned back at Port-au-Prince by dockside thugs threatening to make the Haitian city "another Somalia" if the American forces landed. Had the United States shown more resolve in the UNOSOM II operation, it is possible that Haiti's military leaders would not have risked such a crude demonstration of force. The events of this past year have also caused what the Secretary-General has referred to as "donor fatigue." Aware of the weaknesses in the current command structure of U.N. operations, member states are increasingly reluctant to donate their blood and treasure to advance multilateral goals of no direct concern to their national security. Consequently the United Nations has had tremendous difficulty recruiting the authorized number of troops for U.N. operations.

Another problem that this past year's difficulties have illustrated is the outdated composition of the Security Council, the deliberative body charged with making decisions concerning international peace and stability. The Council is the only U.N. body with the authority to make decisions binding on all member states, and many critics charge that the veto power of the five permanent members—the United States, the United Kingdom, France, China, and Russia—is obsolete and delegitimizes the Council's authority to make decisions for all 184 members. The other 179 countries, representing a large majority of the world's population and a sizable portion of its wealth, are represented by only ten rotating seats. This past year has seen renewed efforts to address this question, and there will most likely be substantive debate on the matter in the 49th General Assembly.

There is no doubt that this past year has been one of the most difficult in the U.N.'s history. The Organization has been criticized from all quarters—berated for its reluctance to act, as in the case of Rwanda, or for having an overly ambitious agenda, as in Somalia. Nonetheless, the very fact that member states continue to request U.N. intervention at a record rate indicates that the international community is actually increasingly dependent on the world body. As Robert Johansen has noted, the United Nations has suddenly "become essential before it has become effective" ["The Reagan Administration and the U.N.: The Costs of Unilateralism," *World Policy Journal,* Fall 1986]. This past year has revealed the urgent need for a more efficiently constructed mechanism for mustering and deploying peace-keeping (or peace-enforcement) operations. It has also demonstrated the importance of realistic goals when planning a peace-enforcement operation. The Secretary-General must be absolutely sure he has the full commitment of contributing states before allowing the operation to be fielded. To do otherwise would be to risk a loss of credibility similar to what occurred in the wake of the Somalia operation—a situation that could have disastrous results for the future of multilateral action.

2. The Former Yugoslavia
By Richard D. Caplan

More than two years after U.N. Secretary-General Boutros Boutros-Ghali sought to deflect world attention from the Bosnian conflict (a "rich man's war," he called it at the time), the crisis in the former Yugoslavia continues to dominate the agenda of the United Nations and to command a considerable share of the international community's resources. Indeed, to the dismay no doubt of the Secretary-General, the war in ex-Yugoslavia has come to be seen increasingly as the U.N.'s war, and the prestige of the Organization has suffered accordingly.

Over the course of 1993–94 the prospects for resolution of the Yugoslav crisis have alternately dimmed and brightened. The collapse of one and then another diplomatic initiative, renewed waves of aggression and ethnic cleansing in eastern and central Bosnia, growing frustration over continued Serb occupation of Croatia's Krajina region, and the mounting impatience of Serbia's oppressed Albanian community have augured poorly for peace in that corner of the world. And yet there have also been glimmers of hope, with the relaxation of the siege of Sarajevo, a Bosnian-Croat rapprochement, and the signing of a permanent cease-fire accord between Croats and Krajina Serbs. It was also a year that saw the use of significant U.N.-sanctioned force in ex-Yugoslavia for the first time and taught some lessons about the limitations of such force (and, indeed, of any sort of intervention) at an advanced stage of a crisis.

"The world's most difficult diplomatic problem" was U.S. Secretary of State Warren Christopher's description of the crisis in July 1993. One year later, as the United Nations prepared to convene its 49th General

Assembly, a resolution of the crisis continued to elude the world organization. The consequences are likely to be far-reaching—both for the former Yugoslavia and for the post-Cold War international order.

The U.N.'s Role in the Former Yugoslavia: An Overview

The United Nations has been actively involved in the crisis in Yugoslavia since September 25, 1991, when the Security Council adopted Resolution 713 in response to the outbreak of hostilities there, calling on all states to implement an embargo on the delivery of weapons to the region. (The resolution was adopted at the urging of the Federal Republic of Yugoslavia—now comprised of only Serbia and Montenegro—which, because of its considerable arsenal, has been able to maintain military preeminence throughout the war.) Three years and more than 50 Security Council resolutions later, the U.N.'s activities in the Balkans are arguably greater in scope than its activities anywhere else in the world.

The U.N. role in the former Yugoslavia has evolved as the nature of the crisis itself has changed, but the Organization's activities continue to fall into five broad categories: (1) delivery of humanitarian aid and refugee assistance; (2) peacekeeping; (3) monitoring and safeguarding human rights; (4) efforts at negotiating a political settlement (peacemaking); and (5) implementation and enforcement of Security Council resolutions. These activities obviously overlap but sometimes are not entirely complementary. The negotiating process, for instance, lends international legitimacy to political leaders who, in another context, are viewed as war criminals. Similarly, the need to ensure the delivery of humanitarian aid has often been invoked by the Security Council to justify its failure to take effective measures to prevent gross violations of human rights.

With each activity there is a U.N. agency or agencies assigned primary responsibility for carrying it out. The **U.N. High Commissioner for Refugees (UNHCR)**, as the designated "lead agency" with respect to humanitarian aid and refugee assistance, works closely with all the major bodies engaged in relief efforts—the World Food Programme, UNICEF, and WHO, and a number of others besides. In October 1993, UNHCR and related agencies were serving a target population of 4.26 million people in the former Yugoslavia, an increase of some 400,000 over the previous six months, at an estimated cost of $696.5 million [U.N. Department of Humanitarian Affairs, *Revised Consolidated Inter-Agency Appeal for Former Yugoslavia: January–June 1994*, GE.93-02919].

The role UNHCR is playing in the former Yugoslavia is unprecedented for the agency. As a refugee organization, UNHCR is accustomed to responding to the needs of people who have fled war zones, but in this case it is expected to operate within areas of active conflict as well, and often without the cooperation of local military and civil authorities. Indeed, the agency frequently finds its efforts obstructed by belligerent forces with little or no regard for humanitarian principles and international law. Aid convoys are routinely denied passage, hijacked, or looted. Nearly a dozen U.N. aid workers have been killed while attempting to deliver relief supplies to civilian population centers.

Responsibility for protecting humanitarian aid convoys falls to the **U.N. Protection Force (UNPROFOR)**, which in Bosnia consisted of 14,400 troops by March 15, 1994 [S/1994/300]. Resolution 770 of August 13, 1992, authorizes UNPROFOR to take "all measures necessary"— including the use of military forces—to ensure the delivery of humanitarian aid, but in virtually every instance UNPROFOR has preferred to *negotiate* safe passage when facing resistance. This practice has left some besieged enclaves, such as Maglaj in central Bosnia and Goražde in eastern Bosnia, without land shipments for months at a time.

UNPROFOR is deployed elsewhere in the former Yugoslavia as well. The original mandate (derived from Resolution 743 of February 21,

Source: Institute for War & Peace Reporting.

1992) authorized the deployment of peacekeepers to three U.N. Protected Areas (UNPAs) in largely Serb-controlled portions of Croatia, and in the adjacent "pink zones," where intercommunal tensions have erupted in the past. The already shaky cease-fire that some 14,500 UNPROFOR troops maintain in these areas threatens to collapse under a burden of mounting frustration as the Croatian government seeks the return of the roughly one-quarter of its country now in Serbian hands. Finally, in Macedonia, a much smaller UNPROFOR presence—1,050 soldiers, of whom half are American—was authorized by the Security Council on December 11, 1992, as a deterrent against the further spread of conflict in the region [S/Res/795]. This operation constitutes the first preventive deployment in the history of U.N. peacekeeping [*The United Nations and the Situation in the Former Yugoslavia*, DPI/1312/Rev. 1].

In a conflict in which massive and systematic violations of human rights are an instrument of war, the United Nations has also taken a number of steps to monitor and to safeguard those rights. The U.N. Commission on Human Rights, meeting on August 13–14, 1992, established the position of **Special Rapporteur on the Situation of Human Rights in the Territory of the Former Yugoslavia** and later named former Polish Prime Minister Tadeusz Mazowiecki to the post to investigate violations of rights and to make recommendations for action that would curb such practices. In a further effort to protect human rights, Security Council Resolutions 780 [10/6/92] and 808 [2/22/93] authorized the establishment of a **Commission of Experts** and an **International Tribunal on War Crimes,** respectively, to gather evidence and prosecute individuals alleged to have committed serious violations of international humanitarian law. UNPROFOR is also authorized to protect human rights, particularly in the UNPAs.

The U.N.'s involvement in diplomatic efforts to end the wars in the former Yugoslavia dates from the Serbo-Croat war in 1991, but the Organization stepped up its peacemaking activities when war erupted in Bosnia the following year. The **International Conference on the Former Yugoslavia,** convened in London in August 1992 and co-chaired by the European Community (now European Union) and the United Nations, has been seeking a comprehensive peace for the region. And, in fact, the parties to the conflict present at the conference, as well as the conference's sponsors, did agree to a set of governing principles—including the reversal of "ethnic cleansing" and the maintenance of a unitary Bosnian state [*Financial Times*, 8/29–30/92]—that were intended to inform any peace proposals that the mediators might put forward. The first such proposal, the Vance-Owen plan (named for the then U.N. Special Envoy Cyrus Vance and European Community representative Lord David Owen), was unveiled in January 1993 and called for the division of Bosnia and Herzegovina into ten ethnic-based cantons. It was criticized in some circles for violating the state's territorial integrity (notwithstanding signed pledges to the contrary by all three sides) and likely to lead to more forced population movements. Just prior to the rejection of the plan by Bosnian Serbs in the spring of 1993, Vance resigned his post and was replaced on May 1, 1993, by former Foreign Minister Thorvald Stoltenberg of Norway. The diplomatic initiatives of Owen and Stoltenberg, which are discussed below, are also said to contradict key principles agreed to at the London Conference.

Meanwhile, the Security Council continues the **economic and other sanctions** that, acting under Chapter VII of the U.N. Charter, it imposed on rump Yugoslavia on May 30, 1992, in reaction to Belgrade's involvement in the military campaign against Bosnia and Herzegovina [S/Res/757]. Those sanctions have been tightened progressively over the past two years. The **North Atlantic Treaty Organization (NATO)**, deputized, so to speak, by the Secretary-General, has at various moments threatened the use of force in support of U.N. resolutions—and actually carried out a military action for the first time in its history when, on February 28, 1994, it downed four Serbian planes that had violated restrictions governing the use of aircraft in Bosnia. In 1993 another U.N. agency, the **International Court of Justice (ICJ)**, heard cases brought by the government of Bosnia and Herzegovina, first against Yugoslavia under Article IX of the Genocide Convention and then against the United Kingdom for its complicity in genocide by continuing to support an arms embargo that has left Bosnian government forces at a distinct advantage throughout the conflict [Institute for War & Peace Reporting, *WarReport*, 12/93].

Humanitarian Aid and Refugee Assistance

In 1993, as the war entered its third year, the humanitarian situation in the former Yugoslavia grew steadily worse. By the end of the year there were estimates of from 140,000 to 250,000 killed or missing and an additional 60,000 to 150,000 wounded. Roughly one citizen out of five, or 4.2 million people, had been displaced by the fighting (out of a total prewar population of 22 million). And the number of people dependent on international relief assistance had grown by 10 percent. No region was untouched by the war. Even Slovenia, which had been spared for the most part, qualified to receive 5,663 metric tons of food in 1993 and had admitted more than 31,000 refugees by February 1994 [UNHCR, "Information Notes on Former Yugoslavia," 3/94]. Elsewhere, of course, conditions were much worse, notably in Bosnia and Herzegovina.

In early June 1993 the High Commissioner for Refugees, Sadako Ogata, announced that U.N. food relief to former Yugoslavia—much of it earmarked for Bosnia—would be cut in half because of a $245 million **shortfall in donor contributions.** Although donor countries would pledge a month later to make up 25 percent of the gap, intensified fighting and **deliberate efforts to obstruct aid delivery on the part of the warring parties,** especially Bosnian Serb and Croat forces, made it impossible for UNHCR to meet its delivery goals. "When I put the security and the funding problems together," U.N. Special Envoy Stoltenberg stated candidly, "the outlook for the international humanitarian effort in BiH looks bleak" [ibid., 6/93].

After a U.N. convoy was attacked on October 25, killing the driver and wounding nine others, Secretary-General Boutros-Ghali suspended convoy travel into central Bosnia for nearly four weeks. By November 1993, the U.S. State Department was warning that 2.7 million people were "at risk" in Bosnia from the fighting as well as from disease, malnutrition, and lack of adequate shelter. Two months later UNHCR announced that its aid deliveries had met less than 42 percent of Bosnia's minimum food requirements for December. UNHCR estimated that it could have delivered as much as 75 percent more food had Croats and Serbs in Bosnia not denied passage to 58 out of 128 aid convoys that month—a flagrant violation of both Security Council Resolution 859 [8/25/93], demanding the unhindered flow of humanitarian assistance, and an agreement the warring parties had signed on November 18 allowing free passage of aid convoys [Refugees International, *Bosnia Winter Watch*, No. 7, 1/18/94; *The Washington Post*, 11/19/93]. These reports prompted U.S. Ambassador to the U.N. Madeleine Albright to urge that the prosecutor for war crimes investigate the obstruction of humanitarian aid on behalf of the war crimes tribunal.

Albright's recommendation reflected a fundamental truth about the humanitarian situation in Bosnia: The crisis was not an accident of the war. Indeed, if war is the continuation of politics by other means, then the humanitarian crisis in Bosnia could be described as a continuation of war by other means. A clear pattern of activities to precipitate a humanitarian crisis emerged long ago, and ethnic cleansing, the sieges and shelling of civilian population centers, the rape of tens of thousands of women and girls, and the refusal to allow the delivery of humanitarian aid were all a part. Whether the point of these actions was to force concessions at the negotiating table or to ensure that people of different backgrounds would never want to live together again, the distinctive character of this war was readily apparent. "This is a war on populations, not armies . . . a particularly venal kind of war," a team of American public health investigators concluded after a comprehensive fact-finding mission to Bosnia in November 1993. "The hidden dimension of this conflict is an insidious, pernicious assault on the lives and well-being of the people of Bosnia" [Harvard/Einstein Study Group, "Bosnia: War and Public Health," 2/94].

Within Bosnia, the humanitarian situation was especially acute in areas outside Sarajevo, where the media were rarely on hand to record the horror. In Goražde, one of the U.N.'s so-called "safe areas" [S/Res/824, 5/6/93] (though it came under some of the fiercest shelling that any Bosnian town has experienced), aid convoys were denied entry for months on end, and the town's 65,000 residents had to rely entirely on air drops for supplies. "I have seen people gather wheat flour from the mud with spoons following an airdrop," one field worker observed, so desperate were they for food [UNHCR, "Information Notes on Former Yugoslavia," 2/94]. In **Maglaj**, encircled by Bosnian Serb and Croat forces, UNHCR reported in January that 20 to 30 percent of the town's 16,000 residents were severely malnourished. And in **Mostar,** some 50,000 people, mostly Muslims, were herded into the devastated eastern section of the city—once one of the most beautiful in Europe—where they suffered heavy shelling and other degradations by Bosnian Croat forces until a cease-fire took effect on February 23, ending ten months of fighting between erstwhile allies [Commission on Human Rights, "Fourth Periodic Report on the Situation of Human Rights in the Territory of the Former Yugoslavia," E/CN.4/1994/8].

For Sarajevans, ironically, the delivery of humanitarian aid was facilitated by a devastating event—the **February 5 mortar attack on a crowded outdoor market,** killing 68 and wounding more than 200—that galvanized world leaders into action. Until then, the city had been threatened repeatedly with "strangulation," in U.N. parlance—most notably in the summer of 1993, when Serb forces punched through Bosnian government defenses on Mount Igman and Mount Bjelašnica. With the withdrawal of most of the Serb artillery to a mandated radius of 12.4 miles outside the city in response to the **threat of NATO air strikes,** it appeared that Sarajevo's 380,000 residents would no longer have to live in the shadow of the heavy guns that, along with sniper attacks, had killed some 10,000 people in 23 months of siege. Further relief came with the signing of a **federation accord between Bosnian Croats and the Bosnian government** on March 17. As a consequence, Sarajevo gained road access to the outside world through Croatia, and this was expected to relieve the humanitarian crisis in the city [*The New York Times,* 3/23/94]. Security Council Resolution 900 [3/4/94] sought to restore all essential services to the city (vital utilities remained under Serb control), for which purpose the Secretary-General appointed U.S. diplomat William L. Eagleton to the post of Special Coordinator for Sarajevo [U.N. press release SG/A/580].

Another welcome development was the **expected opening of the Tuzla airport** to humanitarian aid shipments (a single, inaugural flight was permitted on March 22), which would help U.N. relief workers serve the 450,000 aid-dependent people in that multiethnic metropolitan region. The Bosnian Serbs had adamantly refused to allow the airport to be used for humanitarian relief flights, arguing that such flights could be transporting weapons to the Bosnian government forces. And it remains to be seen whether in fact they will allow it to be used on a permanent basis. (As of early June there had been no subsequent flights.) For the foregoing and other reasons, notably the fighting in central Bosnia,

UNHCR was able to deliver only 30 percent of the minimum monthly food requirements to Zenica and the Tuzla region in February [InterPress Service, 3/22/94]. Mazowiecki, in his sixth report, warned that unless Tuzla received its full allotment, the region could suffer intercommunal strife that heretofore it has been spared.

The humanitarian situation in other parts of the former Yugoslavia— especially Croatia and Serbia—is grave but not nearly as critical as in Bosnia. **Croatia** continues to host an extraordinarily large number of **refugees and displaced persons** (532,000 by February 1994)—a little more than half of them from Bosnia and Herzegovina and the rest largely from the Serb-occupied areas of Croatia. Some 150,000 "social cases"—the elderly, pensioners, and other vulnerable individuals—are among the beneficiaries of U.N. assistance here. Another 100,000 receive humanitarian aid within the U.N. Protected Areas, or UNPAs. Refugees continue to enter Croatia at an average rate of 1,500 a month, either in flight from fighting in Bosnia or as the victims of ethnic cleansing there [World Food Programme, "WFP in the Former Yugoslavia," 3/94].

Serbia and Montenegro's 530,000 refugees, for their part, undergo not only the usual hardships of involuntary displacement but also the effects of economic sanctions levied on rump Yugoslavia by the United Nations *and* the general indifference of the outside world to their plight because of Serbia's pariah status. (These public attitudes have had a greater impact on the work of private relief agencies and on bilateral government assistance than they have had on the activities of the United Nations [U.S. Committee for Refugees, "East of Bosnia: Refugees in Serbia and Montenegro," 9/93].)

Sanctions seem to have had little effect on the policies of the Yugoslav leadership, but there is no question that their bite has been felt by the general populace, spurring concern among relief agencies that sanctions are actually undermining the humanitarian relief effort in the region. Perhaps the greatest casualty of the sanctions regime in ex-Yugoslavia is the **health care system.** Although U.N. resolutions specifically exempt medical supplies, every item in every relief shipment must be inspected by the Sanctions Committee, leading to interminable delays and serious shortages. As a result, Yugoslavia has witnessed a rapid increase in tuberculosis, a significant drop in immunization, and an increasingly limited capacity to perform life-saving surgery. In June 1993, in an unusual appeal to the heads of their organizations, the top representatives in Yugoslavia of WHO, UNHCR, and the International Committee of the Red Cross and Red Crescent felt obliged to draw attention to "the detrimental effect of the sanctions on the health of the people and on the health care system of the country where we work." The medical situation, they said, was "catastrophic" [*The New York Times,* 8/20/93]. (Sanctions are also delivering a serious blow to the **economies of neighboring states,** which have suffered a loss of trade earnings, increased transport costs, and higher prices for imports in the absence of Yugoslav markets, supplies, and transportation routes. By June 1993, Hungary estimates, compliance with sanctions had cost the country $800 million; Albania has reported losses of $300 million to $400 million [S/26040 and Add. 1].)

The refugee crisis, like the sanctions regime, poses a serious challenge to the credibility of humanitarian relief efforts. The 1951 Geneva Convention relating to refugees requires states to provide care for individuals who have a "well-founded fear of being persecuted for reasons of race, religion, nationality, membership of a particular social group or political opinion." Yet in 1992, when UNHCR called on European governments to make provisions for the protection of refugees from former Yugoslavia, many states tightened **border controls and visa requirements** instead. Still other measures reduce the rights of refugees and asylum seekers once they enter a country—affecting the right to work and access to basic social services. Many fear that West European governments will now seek to deport refugees, as Germany has begun to do [*The Nation*, 6/13/94]. (By July 1993 an estimated 750,000 asylum-seekers had found their way to European countries.) The result of all such policies and practices is to place the United Nations in a difficult position: The European states are pressuring the Organization to contain refugee flight by providing humanitarian assistance in the crisis zone while their own lack of resolve effectively cedes the field to those who commit the acts of aggression that generate refugee flight.

These contradictory tendencies explain the decision by UNHCR and the International Committee of the Red Cross on April 2 to plan the evacuation of 7,000 Muslims and Croats (the sheer number to be moved qualified the plan as unique) from the northwest Bosnian town of Prijedor, in response to a renewed Serbian campaign of "ethnic cleansing." (The evacuation was postponed for want of sufficient security guarantees from the Bosnian Serbs.) In the past, both agencies have opposed such evacuations on the grounds that they abet the Serbs' effort to expel Muslims and Croats from Serb-controlled territories. But the agencies concluded in this case that there was no other way to save thousands from violent attacks and possibly death. The same sad fate seemed to await the U.N. "safe area" of Goražde, which came under intense Serbian shelling in early April 1994. Yet after U.S. Secretary of Defense William Perry's statement that the United States would not use force to protect the enclave—a statement many interpreted as giving a "green light" to the Bosnian Serbs—NATO bombed Serbian positions and the United Nations negotiated a partial Serbian withdrawal [*The New York Times*, 4/3, 4/4, 4/11/94].

Peacekeeping

By mid-April 1994 the United Nations had authorized the dispatch of nearly 38,500 troops to the former Yugoslavia, of which 33,300, from 34 countries, were actually deployed. (On April 27 the Security Council authorized an "increase by up to 6,550 additional troops"—plus 150 military observers and 275 civilian policy monitors—for Bosnia [S/Res/914].) Although the operational mandate of UNPROFOR extends to five former republics (excluding Slovenia), U.N. troops are deployed in only three: Croatia, Bosnia and Herzegovina, and Macedonia. It is largely in Croatia, however, that the United Nations has been conducting peace-keeping operations in the "classic" sense—that is, interposing itself between warring parties (Serbs and Croats) with their consent while a permanent political solution to the conflict is sought. Some 14,500 U.N. troops and support personnel from 16 countries are stationed in three "protected areas" (UNPAs) of Croatia in which Serbs are a majority or a substantial minority, and the adjacent "pink zones."

The Security Council first deployed peacekeeping troops in Croatia in April 1992, ten months after Croatia's declaration of independence prompted rebel Serb forces, with the support of the Yugoslav Army (JNA), to seize control of the swath of land known as **the Krajina.** The deployment, which has been renewed periodically (most recently on March 31, 1994, for six months), was meant only as an "interim arrangement" and was not to "prejudge the outcome of . . . negotiations," in the original language of the plan negotiated by U.N. Special Envoy Cyrus Vance [S/23280, annex III]. But if the presence of U.N. forces has helped to keep a relative peace, it has also created a Cyprus-like situation that serves the political purposes of the Serbs. The Secretary-General acknowledged as much on March 16, 1994, in a report to the Security Council. "The Serb side," he wrote, "has taken advantage of the presence of UNPROFOR in its efforts to freeze the status quo, under UNPROFOR 'protection,' while establishing a self-proclaimed 'State' of the 'Republic of Serb Krajina' in UNPROFOR's area of responsibility" [S/1994/300, 3/16/94].

The status quo, moreover, has meant that Croatia's Dalmatian coast has been largely cut off from the rest of the country, with serious economic and political consequences. In April 1993, determined to restore links with the coastal region, Croatian President Franjo Tudjman announced his intention to defy the Serbs and reopen the bridge over the Maslenica Gorge, east of Zadar, which he did on July 18 with much fanfare. The Serbs allowed the bridge to open and then, on August 2, destroyed it. Within a month Tudjman had opened the bridge again and launched an offensive against Serb forces in the Gospić region, to which the Serbs responded by shelling, among other targets, a Zagreb suburb. The United Nations negotiated a temporary cease-fire, which took effect on September 15. Six months later, on March 29, 1994, the United States and Russia brokered a **permanent cease-fire accord** (with which UN-PROFOR monitors compliance [S/Res/908, 3/31/94]) that led to the separation of Serb and Croat forces and the withdrawal of heavy weapons from the region.

In Bosnia and Herzegovina, UNPROFOR's functions are many and diverse, but peacekeeping, strictly speaking, is not among them, there being no peace to keep. A notable exception, however, is the ultimatum/agreement that led to the redeployment of Serb forces within and around **Sarajevo** after the February 5 shelling of the marketplace. The deployment of some 400 Russian troops to Sarajevo nine hours before the expiration of the NATO deadline on February 20 helped to persuade the Bosnian Serbs to withdraw or relinquish their heavy weapons. The Russians created a buffer zone separating predominantly Serb neighborhoods from the rest of the city.

For many people, the presence of Russian soldiers raises the specter of a permanent division of Sarajevo (which Bosnian Serb leader Radovan Karadžić favors), as happened in Berlin following World War II. Concern about Russia's pro-Serb leanings were only slightly allayed after the Bosnian Serbs had broken their pledge to Russian Special Envoy Vitaly I. Churkin that they would not storm or shell Goražde. Churkin denounced the Serbs, saying his country would not "allow a group of extremists to use the politics of great Russia for achieving its own goals" [*The New York Times*, 4/19/94].

As the disposition of the Russian soldiers might suggest, one ongoing concern of the Secretary-General and the Security Council has been the **impartiality of those who make up the U.N. forces** in Bosnia. The Organization has sometimes found itself in the awkward position of resisting offers of troops, especially from Islamic countries, at the very time it has needed more of them to implement Security Council resolutions. In his March 14 report to the Security Council, Secretary-General Boutros-Ghali appealed for 12,000 more troops for Bosnia—nearly twice the number of U.N. forces already deployed [*The Christian Science Monitor*, 3/16/94]. (In fact, the Organization had yet to meet the target of 7,600 extra troops that it had announced in June of 1993.) Boutros-Ghali has accepted troop contributions from some Islamic countries, among them Pakistan and Malaysia, but has been reluctant to accept offers from others, notably Iran, on the unstated grounds that their political agendas might interfere or compete with the U.N. agenda (notwithstanding the fact that the U.N.'s objectives are unlikely to be met absent sufficient troop support). Partly as a consequence of this dilemma, the Secretary-General has asked member states to commit a total of 100,000 troops that could be employed by the Organization as a rapid-response force upon its decision to intervene in a breaking crisis in the future. By late March 1994, more than 15 countries had pledged 54,000 troops for this purpose [*The New York Times*, 4/13/94].

UNPROFOR's role in **Macedonia** is even less like traditional peacekeeping. In fact, the 1,050 U.N. soldiers deployed here (including the only contingent of U.S. ground troops in the former Yugoslavia) are the first U.N. "blue helmets" ever dispatched for the purpose of *preventing* conflict—in this case, the spillover of conflict from the north. (Bosnian President Alija Izetbegović had requested that U.N. soldiers be deployed in his country in late 1991—before the conflict spread from Croatia—but his request was turned down.) UNPROFOR is widely viewed to be enhancing security in the southern Balkan region. In his March 16, 1994, report to the Security Council, the Secretary-General observed that "UNPROFOR's presence appears to have contributed to stability and has certainly raised the political price of any future external aggression against [Macedonia's] territorial integrity."

Human Rights Monitoring and Protection

The tragic wars in the former Yugoslavia have produced **violations of human rights** of a magnitude Europe has not seen since World War II. Since the establishment of a special rapporteur on human rights for ex-Yugoslavia in August 1992, the United Nations has sought to serve as a witness to these violations in an effort both to deter such practices and to amass evidence that could be used to prosecute offenders. A wide-ranging assessment of the human rights situation was provided by Special Rapporteur Tadeusz Mazowiecki in his fifth report to the U.N. Commission on Human Rights on November 17, 1993 [E/CN.4/1994/47]. Nor has the pattern of violations that he documented changed much since the release of these findings, as evidence his subsequent report [E/CN.4/1994/110, 2/21/94] and the reports of such nongovernmental monitoring organizations as Human Rights Watch, the International Helsinki Federation, and the Lawyers Committee for Human Rights. One is forced to conclude that the U.N. presence has had negligible deterrent effect.

This is especially true in Croatia, where the United Nations has had a **broader mandate to protect human rights** than in the other former Yugoslav republics. Under the Vance plan, discussed above, the United Nations has deployed troops and civilian police officers in the UNPAs and the "pink zones" with the aim, inter alia, of preventing the resumption of conflict, protecting individuals (particularly minorities) from armed attack and harassment, and monitoring the local police to ensure that they are carrying out their duties "without discriminating against persons of any nationality or abusing anyone's human rights" [S/23280]. UNPROFOR has also been given the mandate to facilitate the voluntary repatriation of individuals displaced by ethnic cleansing—a total of 247,000 Croatian and other non-Serbs and 254,000 Serbs by October 1993.

While Mazowiecki noted that the level of violence in Croatia has diminished in the three-month interval between his fifth and sixth reports—particularly with respect to the shelling of civilian targets in the UNPAs and surrounding areas—both parties to the conflict continue to violate human rights under the very eye of the United Nations. Mazowiecki's reports catalogue the arbitrary killing of civilians (more than 67 in the Medak "pocket" on a single day—September 9, 1993) and the systematic destruction of entire hamlets by Croatian armed forces; illegal evictions of ethnic Serbs by the Croatian military police; the arbitrary detention and trials in absentia of Croatian Serbs; the denial of citizenship to Croats of Serb or Muslim origin; and the expulsion of Bosnian Muslim refugees. Mazowiecki observed that, even in the areas under Serb control, where ethnic cleansing is largely a fait accompli, "a climate of hostility and abuse against the remaining ethnic minorities exists and they continue to leave the UNPAs." Needless to say, no ethnic Croats forcibly displaced from the so-called "Republic of Serbian Krajina" have yet been repatriated.

The difficulties the United Nations has encountered in Croatia stem, in part, from the fact that its resources have been limited and it has chosen to rely on the goodwill of local authorities to carry out its mandate. But in the UNPAs at least, the local police are often demobilized Serbian soldiers or reservists, who are seeking to accomplish a primary aim of the war—the establishment of an ethnically pure statelet—in their new guise [Lawyers Committee for Human Rights, "Protection by Presence? The Limits of United Nations Safekeeping Activities in Croatia," 9/93]. Some human rights activists contend that the United Nations should have established its own civil administration in the disputed territories, or at least have provided sufficient staff, as it did in El Salvador, rather than attempt to carry out such an ambitious agenda with nothing more than a "castrated military force," in the words of one frustrated human rights worker.

Elsewhere, notably in **Bosnia and Herzegovina,** the problem is not only that resources are few but also that the United Nations has chosen to interpret its mandate very narrowly. Although Security Council Resolution 824 [5/6/93] established six "safe areas" and Resolution 836 [6/4/93] authorizes UNPROFOR to deter attacks against them, U.N. officials have argued at times that Security Council resolutions provide for the use of force only to protect humanitarian aid delivery and ensure the safety of U.N. personnel. (Indeed, when NATO issued its ultimatum to Serbian forces ringing Sarajevo in February 1994 and bombed Serbian military positions outside Goražde two months later, it invoked this narrow mandate in support of its actions.) In the general absence of political will on the part of the international community to halt the violations of human rights in the former Yugoslavia, the abuses have continued virtually unchecked. In mid-winter 1993, for instance, Bosnian Serb forces intensified their efforts to expel Muslims and Croats from Banja Luka, Prijedor, and Goražde, using murder, beatings, bombings, and rape to achieve their ends. (More recently—and undeterred by the U.N. presence—Bosnian Serb policemen clubbed some 40 Muslim refuge-seekers just outside the UNHCR office in Banja Luka [*The New York Times*, 7/6/94]. And for months, Bosnian Croat authorities refused to allow the delivery of relief supplies to Muslims in east Mostar. But the victims of abuse have proved no less capable of abuse themselves. Mazowiecki documents numerous violations of human rights on the part of Bosnian government forces, including the summary execution of at least 120 Bosnian Croat civilians in eight villages and the arrest of over 1,000 noncombatants to be used in prisoner exchanges or as "human shields" to protect the Bosnian army's advance. It is clear, however, that human rights violations by the Bosnian loyalists have been comparatively less widespread than those of Bosnian Serb and Croat forces. It should also be said that the Bosnian government has often sought to punish human rights offenders in its own ranks.

Other Human Rights Developments

In late August 1993 the U.N. Human Rights Commission denounced the persecution of ethnic Albanians in the Serbian province of **Kosovo** [*The Christian Science Monitor*, 8/31/93]. This was the first time the United Nations had officially condemned human rights abuses in the once-autonomous province (which, with a 90 percent ethnic Albanian population under Serbian control, could be the site of the region's next violent conflict). The action followed the July 2 decision of the Belgrade authorities not to renew the mandate of 20 monitors dispatched by the **Conference on Security and Cooperation in Europe (CSCE)**. The Security Council, by a vote of 14–0 (China abstaining), urged the Federal Republic of Yugoslavia to reconsider its decision [S/Res/855, 8/9/93]. This was the first time the Kosovo question had been brought to the agenda of the Security Council. In his report of February 21, 1994, Mazowiecki recommended the establishment of an international monitoring mechanism to observe the human rights situation not only in Kosovo but in two other flashpoints within Serbia— **Sandžak** and **Vojvodina**.

It has been expected, of course, that the U.N.'s war crimes commission and war crimes tribunal will investigate and prosecute the more egregious violations of human rights perpetrated during the wars in the former Yugoslavia. In October 1992 the Security Council established the Commission of Experts to gather evidence on grave breaches of international humanitarian law [S/Res/780, 10/6/92], and eight months later established the International Tribunal on War Crimes in Former Yugoslavia [S/Res/827, 5/25/93]. In August 1993 the Security Council submitted a list of 23 candidate-judges to the General Assembly, out of which the Assembly selected 11, not a Muslim among them. (A Copt, a Hindu, a Christian, and a Pharsee were the candidates of the four predominantly Muslim countries represented: Egypt, Malaysia, Nigeria, and Pakistan.) "It seems that even Muslim countries had formed the impression that Muslim candidates were unlikely to be acceptable," noted Ian Williams, the U.N. correspondent for *WarReport* [10–11/93].

The **appointment of a prosecutor** has proved more difficult. Wrangling in the Security Council prevented the selection of one man whom many observers considered an obvious candidate: Cherif Bassiouni, the Special Rapporteur of the war crimes commission. Bassiouni had distinguished himself by establishing an extensive war crimes database with donations from financier-philanthropist George Soros and the help of volunteers. (The U.N. bureaucracy and a paucity of funds had threatened to undermine the commission's ability to gather evidence.) Bassiouni had no prosecutorial experience, however, and leading Security Council members may well have seen him as too independent. The Council settled instead on Ramón Escovar-Salom, a former Attorney-General of Venezuela [S/Res/877/, 10/21/93], but he resigned shortly afterwards to assume a government position at home. (Graham Blewitt, former director of the Australian War Crimes Prosecution Unit, was appointed deputy prosecutor in the interim.) The International Tribunal has met several times in The Hague to consider rules of evidence and procedure. It is hoping to hear its first cases some time in 1994.

Doubts have arisen about the seriousness of the U.N.'s efforts to prosecute war crimes, and some see this as a factor in Escovar-Salom's decision to resign. The U.N.'s first priority is a negotiated settlement of the Yugoslav wars, their hypothesis goes, and U.N. officials realize that it will be difficult to induce the victors to accept peace terms if they are facing criminal charges. This may explain too why the Commission was underfunded (with a budget of only $690,000 for its first nine months) and why, as a consequence, its only major investigation was the **1991 massacre at Vukovar** in Croatia. (On April 15, 1994, having seen the appointment of a prosecutor, the Commission folded its tent.) Indeed, a study by the Lawyers Committee for Human Rights concluded that "none of [the Commission's] reports contain the specific details of war crimes or evidence likely to be admissible before the Tribunal. Of 40,000 cases the Commission has compiled, perhaps 4,000 are 'usable' and about 300–400 are sufficiently detailed to send to the prosecutor's office" ["International Tribunal on War Crimes in the Former Yugoslavia: Establishment, Proceedings to Date, and Jurisdiction," 3/94]. In response to widespread skepticism about the International Tribunal, the United States has pledged that war criminals will be brought to justice and has criticized other governments for not cooperating more fully (though Washington, when asked to supply engineers for the excavation of mass graves in Vukovar, refused to do so) [*The New York Times*, 11/3/93, 1/18/94].

Special Rapporteur Mazowiecki has asserted from the start that the story of massive human rights violations in ex-Yugoslavia is one of neglect and missed opportunity by the international community. While aware of the limitations of his office, he has not hesitated to assail the major powers for their failure to act more decisively when confronted with a human tragedy of such proportions. In a concluding note to his February 1994 report, he observed darkly:

> The conflicts in the former Yugoslavia and in particular in Bosnia and Herzegovina have once again proved that human rights play a second-ary role in the context of international politics. A number of formal steps which have been undertaken may be considered as a substitute or excuse for political inertia. . . . The international community has, *de facto,* tolerated massive violations of human rights and international humanitarian law. Such a policy undermines some of the most funda-mental principles upon which international law and the system of human rights protection have been built. [E/CN.4/1994/110]

Peacemaking

The rejection of the Vance-Owen plan by the Bosnian Serbs in May 1993 dashed all hopes that a negotiated settlement of the war in Bosnia and Herzegovina was close at hand. In the year since, two new and distinctly different diplomatic initiatives have been launched to bring an end to the fighting. Although neither initiative, strictly speaking, has been the brain-child of the United Nations, each has enjoyed the blessing of the Organi-zation's negotiators.

The first plan, which eventually came to be known as the **Owen-Stoltenberg plan,** grew out of a proposal put forward jointly by Serbian President Slobodan Milošević and Croatian President Franjo Tudjman meeting in Geneva on June 16, 1993. The plan envisioned dividing Bosnia and Herzegovina into three autonomous areas, each ethnically defined, which were to be loosely federated. The plan bore strong resemblance to an earlier proposal made by the then European Community negotiator Lord Carrington in March 1992 for the division of Bosnia into "three constituent units based on national principles." (That plan, originally ac-cepted by all three parties, was subsequently rejected by Bosnian Presi-dent Alija Izetbegović with the encouragement of the United States.) Under the Owen-Stoltenberg plan, the Bosnian Muslims were to be allo-cated 30 percent of the country (up from the 10 percent the Bosnian gov-ernment controlled at the time), the Bosnian Croats 17.5 percent (down from 20 percent), and the Bosnian Serbs 52.5 percent (down from 70 per-cent) [*The Economist,* 8/28/93]. While the proposed Serb and Croat territories would have flanked Serbia and Croatia, respectively (and, it is assumed, would eventually have been annexed by their "mother" countries), the Muslim section would have consisted of four disparate areas. A corridor was to run through Croat-held territory to Ploče, giving Muslims access to the sea; and, more quixotically, a concrete flyover was to have been built across Serb-held lands to provide Muslims access to a port on the river Sava to the east. In a separate accord, the parties agreed to demilitarize Sarajevo and place it under U.N. administration for a period of two years (Mostar, for its part, would be administered by the European Community). For the international community the effect was to postpone making a choice between Izetbegović's idea of a totally open city and Bosnian Serb leader Radovan Karadžić's preference for a divided one.

Principled objections aside (among other things, the plan was said to violate Bosnia's territorial integrity and to reward aggression), there were three practical problems with the proposal. First, as with the Vance-Owen plan, there was little evidence that the international community was prepared to enforce the provisions of the plan—that is, to commit the estimated 50,000 troops that would have been needed. Yet, without such guarantees, peace was unlikely to last very long. Moreover, the fate of ethnically mixed communities remained uncertain: Guarantees that rights of minorities would be respected were not credible, and many Bosnians had little interest in living in a purely Croat, Muslim, or Serb state. (Bosnia had the highest rate of intermarriage in Yugoslavia before the wars.) Finally, it seemed unlikely that a Muslim statelet, scattered across four areas, sandwiched between hostile Croat and Serb territories, and connected by vulnerable corridors, could be economically viable. Not surprisingly, then, when the plan was put before the Bosnian Parliament on August 28, 1993, it voted a resounding "no" (65–0). However, in a separate vote one month later, the Parliament effectively conceded the principle of partition—the essence of the accord—but insisted that the Muslims be given more territory. As Izetbegović explained their thinking: "[F]uture generations should know that we are not in favor of . . . partition. It's a bad thing. We accept it as a choice between two evils. And the worse evil is to continue the war" [*The New York Times*, 8/15/93].

Yet continue the war is precisely what the Bosnian government chose to do, in the hope that successes on the battlefield would strengthen its position at the negotiating table. The decision to fight on led to a series of military gains for the Bosnian government forces at the expense of the Bosnian Croats. By mid-February 1994, the government forces had routed the Croats from roughly 40 percent of the territory they controlled ["A New Stage in the Bosnian Conflict," *RFE/RL Research Report*, 3/4/94]. These losses, together with the threat of Security Council measures against Croatia for its participation in the Bosnian war [S/PRST/1994/6, 2/3/94] and growing disaffection among Croats with Tudjman's Bosnia policy, disposed the Croatian leadership toward greater accommodation of Bosnian interests. The United States, seeking to maintain the momentum created by the withdrawal of Serb forces from Sarajevo, moved to mend and strengthen Bosnian-Croat relations, first by negotiating a cease-fire agreement, which took effect on February 23, and then by gaining acceptance from both parties for a new federal state structure.

The framework agreement, signed in Washington on March 18, 1994, provides for the establishment of a **Bosnian-Croat federation** within Bosnia and Herzegovina, which, in turn, is to be linked to Croatia in a loose **confederation.** The central government of the federation will bear most of the responsibility for defense, commerce, finance, and foreign affairs. Most of the other governmental functions devolve to cantons, designated Croat and "Bosniac" (a reference to the Bosnian Muslims)—a distinction that non-nationalist forces within Bosnia criticize as reinforcing the problem of ethnic differentiation that gave rise to war in the first place. The draft constitution envisages a complex system of power-sharing among ethnic representatives that attempts to address the concerns of the national communities in Bosnia without rendering the state inoperable. For instance, it stipulates the annual rotation of president and vice president (one Croat and the other Bosniac) and requires that each minister and deputy minister come from a different "constituent people." The larger confederation is to be governed by a Council—with Croatia and the federation equally represented—whose primary function will be the coordination of national defense and economic policies.

The door has been left open to Bosnian Serb membership in the federation. A group of Bosnian Serbs that has formed in support of a multiethnic, democratic Bosnia and Herzegovina backed the federation in a meeting in Sarajevo on March 27, but Karadžić had already rejected the idea in an interview with the German weekly *Der Spiegel* on March 7. It is hard to see why Karadžić would want to participate in a structure that, among other things, is linked to Croatia. And Tudjman has indicated that Croatia would reconsider the confederal arrangement if the Serbs joined the new Bosnian state. Obviously, Karadžić would prefer to bring his "Republika Srpska" into a confederal arrangement with Serbia; indeed, the Washington agreement could be said to legitimate such a move.

If the Serbs are left out of the federation, it will mark the end of Bosnia and Herzegovina as a community of three peoples. Yet if the Serbs can be persuaded to join the federation, they may insist on dissolving the proposed confederation with Croatia. And without the guarantees offered them by Zagreb's participation, it is noted, Bosnia's Croats might choose to opt out of the federation. The simple fact is that neither Bosnia's Serbs nor, to a lesser degree, Bosnia's Croats are inclined to accept minority status. On April 25, in an attempt to work in a more unified fashion to end the war in Bosnia, the United States, Russia, the European Union, and the United Nations announced that they were setting up a formal coordinating or **"contact" group.**

One result of that effort has been the decision among the parties in early May to seek a partition of Bosnia that would give the Bosnian Serbs 49 percent and the Muslim-Croat state 51 percent. This was followed by the French announcement (echoed by Britain) that it would withdraw peacekeepers unless there was greater progress toward a negotiated settlement. The move was widely interpreted as pressuring the Bosnian government to accept the 49–51 formula; indeed, British Foreign Secretary Douglas Hogg went so far as to say that the Bosnian government had to renounce the "military option" and recognize that it had lost the war [*The Guardian* (London), 5/20/94]. As if anticipating these developments, Kemal Kurspahić, the Editor of the Sarajevan daily *Oslobodenje,* had asked in his April 1 column: "Will the world really work for a just peace or will it just work for half a peace?" [English edition, 4/94].

On July 5 the contact group unveiled a new map reflecting the proposed division. To the surprise of many, Bosnia's Muslim president and prime minister announced just two days later that they would support the proposed division—a move that was seen to put pressure on Bosnia's Serbs. Specifically, the plan would give Muslims and Croats 49 percent of Bosnia and the Serbs 48 percent, while Serajevo—the remaining 3 percent—would be placed under U.N. administration for two years, with two-thirds going to the Muslims and the Croats and a third to the Serbs [*The Washington Post*, 7/8/94].

Other Peacemaking Fronts

The **cease-fire accord** reached by the government of Croatia and the Krajina Serbs on March 29 represents the first permanent truce signed by the two sides since the U.N.-brokered cease-fire of January 1992. The agreement calls for the separation of forces and the placing of heavy weapons under joint U.N.-Croat or U.N.-Serb control. U.N.-sponsored talks to resolve the dispute over the status of Krajina have been at a virtual standstill but may gain momentum with the cease-fire accord. Croatian President Tudjman can probably expect increased international support for his position, in light of the more conciliatory stance he has adopted toward Bosnia, while Serbian President Milošević might be willing to trade away portions of Krajina as part of a comprehensive settlement that would help consolidate Serb gains in Bosnia and end his country's pariah status. (On January 19, Zagreb and Belgrade signed agreements that signified, to Tudjman at least, Yugoslav recognition of Croatian sovereignty within its Tito-era borders [*RFE/RL News Briefs:* 1/10–21/94].)

Meanwhile in Macedonia (known in U.N. precincts as "the Former Yugoslav Republic of Macedonia," or FYROM, in deference to Greece), the United Nations has been engaged in efforts to reach an accommodation between the **majority Slav Macedonia population and the sizable**

ethnic Albanian minority. It is also engaged in helping to put an end to the **Greek-Macedonian cold war.**

Albanians, historically second-class citizens in Macedonia, are seeking status as a "constituent nation" but might settle for greater economic and other opportunities. Within the framework of the U.N.-European Union International Conference on the Former Yugoslavia (the London Conference), the Macedonian government has made a number of commitments to the Albanian community (e.g., the establishment of an Albanian-language television channel) but maintains that it does not have the resources to implement all of them.

Macedonia's economic woes have been greatly exacerbated by a **Greek economic blockade** in effect since February 1994 (wherein landlocked Macedonia is unable to gain access to the Aegean Sea through Salonika) in protest over Skopje's use of the name "Macedonia" and other "irredentist" tendencies. On April 13, the European Union, fearing further destabilization in the Balkans, announced that it would ask the European Court of Justice for an **injunction** against the two-month-old blockade. It could take well over a year, however, before a decision is reached.

Though Macedonia generally receives little media attention, most observers agree that the tense situation there, if allowed to continue, could lead to a civil war that would be regionalized very quickly, possibly drawing in Serbia, Albania, Bulgaria, Greece, and Turkey [see, for evidence, Misha Glenny's dispatches in *The New York Review of Books*, 4/7/94]. While U.N. soldiers in Macedonia may offer some protection against the spread of conflict across the border from Serbia, Kosovo, or Albania, they have no mandate to intervene in the internal situation, which is a more likely source of violence and instability.

Peace Enforcement

"If the resolution writer's pen were indeed mightier than the sword, the Balkans would be the most peaceful region in the world," one journalist noted after the Security Council had passed its 48th resolution on the former Yugoslavia in August 1993 [Ian Williams, *WarReport*, 8–9/93]. In a similar vein, Lt. Gen. François Briquemont, the U.N. commander in Bosnia, told a Reuters reporter four months later, "I don't read the Security Council resolutions anymore." They contain "beautiful words," but, "there is a fantastic gap between the resolutions of the Security Council, the will to execute those resolutions and the means available to commanders in the field" [*The New York Times*, 12/31/93]. Apparently, Briquemont's frustration was widely shared within the United Nations.

Neither will nor means have been entirely lacking. U.S. President Bill Clinton did propose air strikes against Bosnian Serb gunners in late July 1993, when Bosnian Serb forces seized two strategic positions overlooking Sarajevo (Mounts Igman and Bjelašnica) following their attack on French peacekeeping troops a few days earlier. On August 3, in what was widely viewed as a new "get-tough" policy on the part of the United States, Clinton convened an emergency meeting of NATO and won allied support to begin preparing for air attacks. NATO had already agreed in May to use air power if necessary to protect U.N. troops and relief operations in Bosnia, acting under U.N. authority [S/Res/836, 6/4/93], and in June sent additional planes to the region to strengthen allied capabilities. But the British and the French, each with sizable peacekeeping forces on the ground, had balked at any action that might invite Serb retaliation. Now, in August, with the allies willing to up the ante, the Serbs (after some dithering) ceded their positions on the two mountains.

NATO's "victory," however, was partial at best. For one thing, it did nothing to halt attacks on Sarajevo (or anywhere else, for that matter), which would continue to suffer fierce shelling. Moreover, by securing what had previously been Serbian front-line positions, U.N. soldiers in effect freed Serb forces for redeployment elsewhere—a criticism, as noted, that has been made of UNPROFOR in Croatia as well.

What the "guns of August" showdown demonstrated to many pundits and politicians was that the Serbs "understand only one language: force," in the bald words of *New York Times* columnist Anthony Lewis. Thus with the February 5 mortar attack on a crowded Sarajevan market, the NATO powers were propelled into a game of brinkmanship, threatening to bomb the Serbs unless they relinquished their heavy weapons or removed them beyond a 12.4-mile radius of the city. (A comparable ultimatum was issued to the Bosnian government forces inside Sarajevo.) Serb compliance with this ultimatum brought relief to a city that had lived under siege for 22 months, and it reinforced the view that a credible threat of force would be sufficient to exact concessions from Serbian militia elsewhere.

Three weeks later, on February 28, 1994, NATO moved beyond the threatened use of force in the Bosnian war when it downed four Serbian planes operating in violation of the **U.N. no-fly zone** near Banja Luka. (Hundreds of other violations before and since have gone unchallenged, as the Secretary-General himself dutifully notes [S/1994/300].) Even with this limited use of force, it was still unclear whether the United Nations would be willing or able to fill the "fantastic gap" that had so exasperated General Briquemont.

When, on April 9, 1994, Boutros-Ghali demanded a pullback of Serbian forces from **Goražde** (a largely Muslim town of 65,000, many of them refugees) and NATO planes bombed Serbian artillery positions outside the town, the Serbs stepped up their fierce assault and dared the alliance to do something about it.

In response, on April 22, the Security Council and NATO demanded an immediate end to the shelling and the withdrawal of Serb forces 12.4 miles from Goražde and no further shelling of the remaining unprotected **"safe areas"** of Tuzla, Srebrenica, Bihać, and Žepa as well [S/Res/913]. When the Serbs chose nonetheless to continue their attack on Goražde, NATO Secretary-General Manfred Wörner called for air strikes on April 23 but was rebuffed by **Yasushi Akashi, the senior U.N. official in the former Yugoslavia.** Akashi stated that air attacks would imperil the prospects for eventual Serbian compliance and risk the lives of U.N. personnel. (Serb forces had placed over 200 U.N. personnel in detention or under house arrest throughout Bosnia during the previous week.) The Serbs did finally accede to the U.N. ultimatum, but on their own terms: They left behind an estimated 65 soldiers to function as "policemen" [*The New York Times*, 4/29/94]. Akashi yielded again to Bosnian Serb demands in May, when he agreed to allow Serb tanks to move through the weapons-exclusion zone around Sarajevo. The agreement drew sharp criticism, and embarrassed U.N. officials abruptly cancelled it.

These events raise a number of questions, large and small, about the manner in which U.N. peacekeeping and enforcement are being conducted in the post-Cold War period. One question concerns the ultimate authority for calling air strikes and other displays of force, not to mention the practical difficulties with "dual-control steering." Moreover, as has been seen in the former Yugoslav case, political considerations may hamper enforcement efforts, particularly when the members of the Security Council and cooperating organizations have forces on the ground.

Another question concerns U.N. evenhandedness in its treatment of the warring parties, particularly when one of them—here, the Bosnian government—is also recognized as a sovereign nation. By demanding that the Bosnian government forces in Sarajevo place their heavy weapons under U.N. control or redeploy them—the same ultimatum issued the Serbs—the United Nations arguably impeded a member state's ability to defend itself. Article 51 of the U.N. Charter guarantees a state's right to self-defense "until the Security Council has taken the measures necessary to maintain international peace and security." Persuaded that the Security Council has not so acted, the General Assembly, by a sizable majority, has each year called for a lifting of the arms embargo on Bosnia, most recently on December 20, 1993 [A/Res/48/88]. ("This Organization has imposed a punishing arms embargo on the former Yugoslavia that has effectively established moral equivalence between the victim and the victimizers," Latvian Ambassador Aivars Baumanis told the General Assembly at the time [A/48/PV.84].) Following the Serbian assault on Goražde, pressure began building within the U.S. Congress for a unilateral lifting of the embargo, and on May 12, 1994, the U.S. Senate voted in favor of such a move, followed a month later by the House [*International Herald Tribune*, 5/13/94; *The New York Times*, 6/10/94].

The Bosnian government had taken its case to the **International Court of Justice,** first in August 1993 when it asked the Court to declare the arms embargo illegal (the Court announced in September that it chose not to rule on the embargo), and again in November when it charged the United Kingdom with complicity in genocide for its support of the embargo. In January the Bosnian government withdrew its charges against the British, under "duress" [*The New York Times,* 9/14/93; *WarReport,* 2/94].

The largest question, certainly, is whether the United Nations is ultimately capable of meeting the challenges represented by "non-classical" aggressions—those, in other words, that are not strictly interstate conflicts. Leaving aside the issue of resources (finances, troops), which in the case of Bosnia has been an important factor in the Organization's shortcomings, what is it that ultimately militates against the U.N.'s effectiveness there? Of course, any light that may be shed on the problem will come too late for the victims of violence in Bosnia and elsewhere in the former Yugoslavia.

3. Africa
By Edmund T. Piasecki

In the history of U.N. peacekeeping efforts, Africa holds several unfortunate records. The war in Angola continues to claim the highest casualty rate of any conflict in the world, at 1,000 deaths a day. Rwanda holds two titles: for the largest and fastest refugee flow—250,000 in 24 hours; and for the most populous refugee camp, now containing some 350,000 men, women, and children. The U.N. operation in Somalia is in danger of delivering the fewest long-term results per dollar expended—about a billion per year.

On the positive side of the ledger, the U.N.'s largest election-monitoring mission to date, about 2,300 observers, participated in officially ending white minority rule in South Africa, the culmination of more than 40 years of effort by the world body to end Pretoria's apartheid system. On a much smaller scale, the United Nations broke new ground in Liberia, cooperating with a regional organization for the first time in mounting a peacekeeping operation. The success of that experiment may rekindle interest in Chapter VIII of the U.N. Charter, which calls for extensive cooperation between regional and international organizations in the settlement of disputes.

The United Nations has tried to be similarly creative elsewhere on the continent, fielding large and complex operations with multiple mandates and employing both carrots and sticks to prod the parties toward peace. As it has imposed arms embargoes on Angola and Mozambique (while lifting one against South Africa), the world body has also raised millions of dollars in emergency humanitarian relief and established trust funds to finance special projects, such as converting the Mozambican rebel force into a mainstream political party. Such a "money for peace" approach is not without its critics, but the rewards could be invaluable if U.N.-monitored elections take place as scheduled in Liberia, Mozambique, and Western Sahara. Neither has the United Nations given up hope for performing similar tasks in Angola, Somalia, and even Rwanda. Other new ideas, such as establishing national and local police forces in Mozambique and Somalia, may help bring stability and democracy to countries too long torn apart by political and ethnic strife.

Somalia

The perceived failure of U.N. "nation building" in Somalia has become symbolic of the troubles surrounding the entire concept of peacekeeping in the post-Cold War era. Immediately following the ambush killings of 25 Pakistani peacekeepers on June 5, 1993, the United Nations and its member states were sure that an unprecedentedly forceful response to such aggression was not only justified but essential to the achievement of the international community's broader political and humanitarian goals. The very success of the ensuing disarmament campaign also strengthened the belief that the world body was capable of "restoring peaceful conditions" in war-ravaged nations while it fed the hungry, promoted economic rehabilitation and political reconciliation, and engaged in the wholesale rebuilding of societal and governmental institutions. As the events of the following 12 months suggest, however, Somalia was a poor choice as a testing ground for Boutros-Ghali's "peace-enforcement" and "peace-building" proposals and may, in fact, have set back the refinement of those ideas for years to come.

The Secretary-General reported that the attacks launched June 12–25 by the **U.N. Operation in Somalia (UNOSOM II)** against strongholds of **Gen. Mohammed Farah Aidid** in South Mogadishu were "by any measure . . . significant successes." Held personally responsible by the United Nations for the June 5 ambush, Aidid had suffered an "erosion" of his political influence as a result of the attacks, the Secretary-General said, and the United Somali Congress/Somali National Alliance (USC/SNA) militias under his control were expected to be "less of an impediment" to further efforts at disarmament, reconciliation, and rehabilitation." No progress was made, however, in executing the arrest warrant against the warlord issued on June 17 by the **Secretary-General's Special Representative, retired U.S. Admiral Jonathan Howe** [S/26022, 7/1/93].

Boutros-Ghali emphasized in his August 17 report to the Security Council that "the overall situation in Somalia has undergone a major transformation" and has "stabilized," at least in the southern part of the country. Under the Addis Ababa Agreements of January and March 1993, which provided for a cease-fire, disarmament, and political reconciliation, Somalia's clan leaders (excluding Aidid) had made meaningful progress in reestablishing governmental institutions for the proposed two-year transition period, including the formation of 21 of 92 planned district councils by the end of July. Relief and rehabilitation programs were also beginning to show results in terms of the eradication of mass starvation, the reopening of schools, and steady increases in economically significant activities like livestock export and commercial shipping. Deployment of UNOSOM II in the central and northern regions of Somalia were still pending, however, due to logistical and financial difficulties associated with fielding so large a force (20,707 on an authorized strength of 28,000), and Aidid's stronghold of South Mogadishu remained "tense" [S/26317].

While ongoing efforts to detain Aidid and locate, seize, and destroy weaponry remained an essential part of UNOSOM's activities, the Secretary-General also stressed the importance of restoring peaceful conditions through nonmilitary means. In September the Security Council approved his proposals for reestablishing Somali police, judicial, and penal systems under U.N. supervision [S/Res/865 Part B, 9/22/93]. According to the plan, interim courts and a partial prison system would begin functioning by October 31, and some 10,000 police would be trained and deployed by the end of 1994. The Secretary-General intended to assess member states an additional $10.3 million to cover the cost of the UNOSOM managers and advisors required but would seek voluntary cash or in-kind contributions to cover the $45.1 million needed to pay the salaries of Somali criminal justice officials, purchase vehicles, supply weapons and training, renovate facilities, and meet other program expenditures [S/26317].

At the same time, the Council expressed its alarm at continuing attacks on UNOSOM personnel and underlined the importance of the operation fulfilling its mandate, including the eventual monitoring of free elections, by March 1995. To help ensure that ongoing attempts to capture Aidid would not shift attention from the U.N.'s longer-term goals or delay the eventual withdrawal of U.N. forces, the Council requested the Secretary-General to develop a "future concerted strategy" for UNOSOM II to map out its humanitarian, political, and security activities over the following 18 months [S/Res/865, Part A].

The deaths of 18 U.S. servicemen on October 3 in an operation to seize a group of Aidid's senior aides placed strategic planning on the back burner and plunged UNOSOM into a deep political crisis. The 18 were elite Army Rangers, part of a detachment of 400 specially trained troops dispatched to Somalia after a command-detonated mine claimed the lives of four U.S. peacekeepers on August 8. The Rangers had captured 24 of Aidid's top lieutenants in a surprise raid on a South Mogadishu safehouse of the SNA and were transporting them to the U.N. compound in the north of the city when their 12-truck convoy was ambushed by Somali militiamen and irregulars. In the nearly 15-hour firefight that followed, one Malaysian peacekeeper was also killed and 74 Americans wounded. According to the press, the Somalis placed their own casualties at 312 killed and 814 wounded [The Washington Post, 1/30–31/94].

The raid capped three and a half months of frustration and public embarassment for Admiral Howe and the Rangers, including an August 30 attack on what turned out to be a compound of the U.N. Development Programme [ibid.]. Further firing emotions was the "despicable and humiliating manner" in which some of the dead were treated, as the Secretary-General said, including the dragging of corpses through the streets of Mogadishu. As was the case with the ambush of the Pakistanis on June 5, the Somali attackers also continued the "deplorable" practice of using woman and children as "human shields" [S/26738, 11/12/93]. From the establishment of UNOSOM I in January 1992 up to October 3, 1993, hostile action in Somalia had already claimed the lives of some 53 peacekeepers. An estimated 6,000 to 10,000 Somalis died in the June through October period alone [The Washington Post, 12/18/93].

Although the Secretary-General emphasized that the Rangers were part of the 17,700-member U.S. Joint Task Force in Somalia and were not a part of UNOSOM II and not under U.N. command or authority, public and congressional outrage over the killings prompted President Clinton to announce the complete withdrawal of all U.S. forces from Somalia by March 31, 1994. The pullout would include a 3,017-member logistical unit from UNOSOM II and the 1,100 troops of the Quick Reaction Force attached to the Joint Task Force. These troops would join some 2,200 Belgian, French, and Swedish personnel being withdrawn by their respective governments by December 31, 1993 [S/26738].

Dealing with the ramifications of so large a reduction in forces for the future of UNOSOM II had led to drastic revisions in the Secretary-General's strategic plan requested in September. On October 29, 1993, the Security Council extended the operation's mandate for an interim period through November 18 to cover the delay [S/Res/878]. In the interim, U.N. headquarters in Mogadishu marked the six-month anniversary of UNOSOM II on November 4 with a summary of achievements realized since the departure of the U.S.-led Unified Task Force in May of that year.

UNOSOM II had made good progress across a broad range of humanitarian issues. Seventy percent of all Somali children had been vaccinated against preventable diseases, and malnourishment among that population had decreased to less than 20 percent. The U.N. Children's Fund (UNICEF) was helping to reopen schools and was supplying textbooks and other assistance to 60,000 children. Curriculum guides and teacher training workshops were being provided by the U.N. Educational, Scientific, and Cultural Organization (UNESCO). The port of Mogadishu had been returned to civilian control and was employing some 1,300 Somalis under the supervision of the **U.N. Development Programme (UNDP)** and the **U.N. Conference on Trade and Development (UNCTAD)**. The **U.N. High Commissioner for Refugees (UNHCR)** was spending $4.5 million to assist some of Somalia's 1.7 million refugees and displaced persons [UNOSOM II press release, 11/4/93].

The Secretary-General reported on November 12 that the United Nations had also made significant gains toward its political goals. Working with UNOSOM advisors, the Somalis themselves had established 39 district councils by early November and the first six of 13 planned regional councils. Since June some 5,000 Somali police officers had been hired, and a U.S. contribution of $27 million in cash and equipment would facilitate the training of additional personnel. Washington was also providing $6 million for the reestablishment of the judicial and penal systems [S/26738].

Militarily, however, the situation in Somalia had become "uncertain." In his November 12 report, the Secretary-General announced that "coercive measures at disarmament had ceased," due apparently to the failure of those measures to incapacitate Aidid's militia and the number of military and civilian deaths ascribable to them. In the ensuing power vacuum, the United Nations suspected that all factions were busily rearming themselves for a renewal of full-scale warfare in 1994. "UNOSOM II," the Secretary-General said, "is now at a critical juncture."

Boutros-Ghali's "concerted strategic plan" for Somalia contained in his November 12 report consisted of three options. Under the first, the mandate, size, and cost of UNOSOM II would remain essentially unchanged. The United Nations would retain the capacity to resort to coercive disarmament and retaliation when necessary, and member states would continue to bear an annual $1 billion peacekeeping bill for UNOSOM's 29,284 troops alone. According to the second option, UNOSOM would limit the use of force to self-defense and concentrate on its humanitarian mission: the delivery and protection of relief supplies, the rehabilitation of infrastructure, repatriation, reconciliation, and the reestablishment of the criminal justice system. This alternative would require some 16,000 troops and a logistics unit to replace the departing U.S. contingent. Third, the Secretary-General suggested a 5,000-member force to bypass ongoing security problems in the city of Mogadishu and concentrate on supplying relief from the port and airport to the outlying regions. UNOSOM would continue to provide security to U.N. agency personnel and NGOs as well as training to the Somali police force.

The Security Council declined to endorse any of these options and decided simply to renew UNOSOM's mandate, again permitting the use of force under Chapter VII of the U.N. Charter, through May 31, 1994

[S/Res/886, 11/18/93]. As it has done with other peacekeeping operations, the Council also requested an interim report, including an updated strategic plan, by January 15 and promised to conduct a "fundamental review" of UNOSOM's mandate by February 1. For the first time, the Council encouraged donor countries to indirectly punish uncooperative Somali factions by channeling their assistance "to rehabilitation projects in those regions where progress on political reconciliation and security has been made."

Although the Security Council refused to make a decision on narrowing UNOSOM's mandate in response to the events of October 3, it did concede that its efforts to apprehend and prosecute Aidid and others for criminal acts against U.N. personnel had largely failed. On November 16 the Council requested the Secretary-General to suspend arrest warrants against those yet to be captured and to "deal with the situation" of the 42 Somalis—of a total 740 arrested—still jailed. Endorsing a proposal by the **Organization of African Unity (OAU),** the Council decided instead to establish a Commission of Inquiry to investigate and report on armed attacks on UNOSOM II personnel "as soon as possible" [S/Res/885, 11/16/93]. A preliminary investigation of the June 5 incident conducted by Professor Tom Farer of American University had found "clear and convincing evidence" that Aidid had authorized the attack. Farer had argued that the General's action violated Somali law and was prosecutable "before an international tribunal or the criminal courts of any State" [S/26351, 8/24/93].

The Secretary-General reported some further progress on political issues in his January 6 report. The number of district and regional councils stood at 53 and 8, respectively, and some 6,700 police had been trained and deployed. But Aidid's preference for a regional rather than an international solution and the deep rivalry between Aidid's USC/SNA faction and the factions of the **"Group of 12" that supported rival warlord Ali Mahdi** stymied all UNOSOM efforts at national reconciliation.

International donors and Somali recipients, meeting at the Fourth Coordination Meeting on Humanitarian Assistance for Somalia, emphasized that "international reserves of patience and funds are running out." In their December 1 declaration, both sides also agreed that "rehabilitation and reconstruction assistance can and will be investigated in those areas where stability and security have been attained. . . ." But banditry, inter-clan fighting, and attacks on civilian relief workers and UNOSOM personnel were on the rise, and preparations for wider conflict were continuing [*The United Nations and the Situation in Somalia,* Department of Public Information, 3/94].

Although the Secretary-General urged the Security Council to retain a U.N. presence in Somalia through the elections of March 1995, he was compelled by further troop withdrawals to recommend a narrowing of UNOSOM II's mandate. By March 31 the operation was scheduled to lose 5,510 troops from Italy, Germany, Turkey, Norway, and the United States as well as the entire Quick Reaction Force. In its Resolution 897 of February 4, the Council adopted a revised mandate comparable to the second option described in the Secretary-General's report of November 12 [ibid.].

UNOSOM II would retain its Chapter VII authorization and the capability to use force against aggressors but would rely on voluntary means to effect disarmament and enforce the cease-fire outlined in the Addis Ababa Agreements. UNOSOM II's authorized strength was to be reduced to 22,000 troops, some of which would continue to protect the supply and delivery of humanitarian relief from Mogadishu. But most of the force would concentrate on regional efforts to assist the new police force and judicial system, support repatriation, and encourage the "ongoing political process." The Council reiterated its belief that donors should also give priority to secure regions and local institutions cooperating with the international community. It urged the Secretary-General to consult with the Organization of African Unity and the League of Arab States in developing a timetable for completing the implementation of the Addis Ababa Agreements by March 1995.

As the scheduled withdrawals would leave the militarily weaker states of Pakistan, India, and Egypt to comprise two-thirds of UNOSOM's 19,000 troops, the United States leased to the United Nations armored personnel carriers, tanks, and helicopter gunships to augment the operation's firepower and mobility. The force would still be stretched very thin, however, increasing the likelihood of banditry and armed attacks on international personnel. Fears that the U.S. withdrawal would, in fact, plunge Somalia back into civil war helped the Secretary-General's new **Special Representative, Ambassador Lansana Kouyate,** broker a national reconciliation agreement between Aidid and Mahdi just two days before the last U.S. forces departed the country.

The March 24 declaration called for the convening of a National Reconciliation Conference on May 15 to elect a president and several vice presidents and to appoint a prime minister. The leaders were also to attend a preparatory meeting on April 15 to discuss the establishment of a Legislative Assembly, bypassing the Transitional National Council called for in the Addis Ababa Agreements [S/1994/16, 5/24/94]. Disputes among the various factions postponed the initial meeting at least four times, however. Moreover, large-scale fighting broke out between rival militias in April, as the sides attempted to improve their positions in the field before agreeing to talk peace. Looting and violence against humanitarian relief agencies and NGOs led to the suspension of assistance programs in several areas and reductions or withdrawals of staff.

Although the security situation was "deteriorating," the Secretary-General attempted to stress UNOSOM's accomplishments in his report of May 24. Fifty-five district councils had been established; 7,800 police recruited and trained; and 88,000 refugees and 31,000 displaced persons resettled. Arguing that "the people of Somalia deserve a last chance," Boutros-Ghali requested a further six-month extension for UNOSOM at a cost of $465 million, with periodic reviews of the military and political situation. The United States had insisted on a renewal of only 45 days should the parties fail to restart peace talks by the end of May. As a compromise, the Security Council voted on May 31 to continue the operation for up to four months at $310 million, contingent on progress toward a peaceful settlement by the end of July [*The Washington Post*, 5/13/94, 6/1/94]. At the same time, UNOSOM announced that the preparatory meeting for the National Reconciliation Conference would convene in Nairobi "in a few days' time" [UNOSOM II press release, 5/31/94].

The U.N.'s experience in Somalia has raised profound questions about the way the world body plans, establishes, and maintains peacekeeping operations. Even as UNOSOM II was breaking new ground in enforcing the cease-fire and disarmament provisions of the Addis Ababa Agreements, the Secretary-General was expressing concern over the delays in deploying troops to large peacekeeping forces caused by the "obvious obsolescence" of the U.N.'s "administrative, financial, and logistical procedures" [S/26317, 8/17/93]. Command and control of such forces have also been criticized, especially the tendency of national contingents in Somalia to consult with their respective governments before carrying out orders from the U.N. force commander [ibid.]. Similarly, the **Commission of Inquiry** investigating armed attacks on UNOSOM II reproached the United States for refusing to place its combat forces under unified command and for failing to coordinate their actions with UNOSOM personnel. While the Commission placed the blame for the attacks on Aidid and his militias, it questioned in general the appropriateness of the U.N.'s decision to abandon traditional peacekeeping neutrality in Somalia in favor of an aggressive enforcement mandate [*The Washington Post*, 3/31/94].

The United States, for its part, has codified the lessons learned from UNOSOM II in a presidential decision directive (PDD) on peacekeeping, signed by Clinton in early May after lengthy and heated debate. Once intended to map out a U.S. leadership role in pursuing multilateral military action, the PDD in its final form instead sought to limit U.S. involvement in such action. It defines increasingly rigorous criteria according to which the United States will vote for, participate in, or send combat troops to future peacekeeping operations, and it rejects the possibility of ever placing U.S. military personnel under U.N. command. The President could place U.S. forces under the "operational control" of foreign commanders, however, if he decides that such an arrangement serves "American security interests" [ibid., 5/6/94].

Rwanda and Burundi

Ethnic violence of the kind that has characterized regional conflicts in the post-Cold War world has been endemic to the small central African states of Rwanda and Burundi since both gained their independence from Belgium in 1962. Rivalry between members of the Hutu tribe (who make up 85 percent of the populations of both countries) and the minority Tutsis has resulted in hundreds of thousands of deaths and millions of refugees and internally displaced persons over the past three decades. Through military dictatorships, one tribe has generally oppressed and excluded the other: In Rwanda, Hutus have had the upper hand; in Burundi, the Tutsis have been in control.

The United Nations was first brought into this volatile mix in February 1993, when Tutsi rebels of the **Rwandan Patriotic Front (RPF)** and the government of President (and Major General) Juvenal Habyarimana requested the deployment of U.N. military observers along Rwanda's border with Uganda. Since the most recent outbreak of violence in October 1990, the RPF had used the border area as a staging ground for attacks on government-controlled areas in the north of the country. Already heavily committed to peacekeeping operations elsewhere on the continent and preferring to leave the settlement of the conflict to regional mediation, the Security Council agreed only to the dispatch of a "goodwill mission" to Rwanda and Uganda in March 1993.

That same month the RPF and the government reinstated the ceasefire of July 1992 and reopened peace negotiations under the auspices of the Organization of African Unity in Arusha, Tanzania. In response, the Security Council requested the Secretary-General to make preparations for the deployment of U.N. personnel [S/Res/812, 3/12/93]; and after the dispatch of a technical mission in April, the Council authorized the establishment of the **U.N. Observer Mission Uganda-Rwanda (UNOMUR)** in June [S/Res/846, 6/22/93]. Stationed on the Ugandan side of the border, UNOMUR's 81 military observers were to verify the compliance of the RPF with its pledge to cease the transport of weapons, ammunition, and military equipment into Rwanda. The rebels had also signed a repatriation agreement with the government on May 31, and by September, U.N. humanitarian agencies had assisted in the resettlement of 500,000 of the 900,000 Rwandans displaced by the war ["United Nations Focus: UNOMUR," U.N. Department of Public Information, 9/93].

The OAU's three-year effort to peacefully settle the Rwandan conflict culminated in the signing of the **Arusha Peace Agreement** of August 4 [A/48/824-S/26915, 12/23/93], which called for monitoring and verification capacities far beyond that of a regional organization. Although the 132 members of the **OAU Neutral Military Observer Group (NMOG)** had been monitoring compliance with the cease-fire in Rwanda since July

1992, the Arusha Agreement required the deployment of a much larger "neutral international force" to oversee the integration of the armed forces of the opposing sides. Both the government and the RPF had appealed to the United Nations in June to supply such a force.

Resolving to "make its full contribution to the implementation of the agreement," the Security Council authorized the establishment of the **U.N. Assistance Mission for Rwanda (UNAMIR)** on October 5 [S/Res/872]. Its 2,500 troops and military and police observers were to establish a weapons-free zone in the capital city of Kigali; monitor security for a "broad-based" transitional government up to elections in the fall of 1995; and oversee "demilitarization procedures," including the establishment of 26 assembly areas for concentration, disarmament, and demobilization of 43,000 rebel and government soldiers and 6,000 members of the government's "gendarmerie." UNAMIR was also mandated to monitor the training of the Integrated Rwandan Defense Forces and a National Gendarmerie, drawn from personnel of both sides. Among its nonmilitary tasks, UNAMIR was to investigate complaints against the gendarmerie, assist with mine clearance and the coordination of humanitarian relief, and monitor the repatriation of Rwandan refugees.

As cost-saving measures, observers from UNOMUR and the OAU group were to be integrated into UNAMIR. Moreover, the force was to be deployed in stages, with no more than 1,217 troops and 211 military observers arriving before the installation of the transitional government, expected by the end of 1993. The force would reach its maximum strength during the demobilization and integration phase (April–December 1994) and then gradually decrease in size through the electoral phase (January–November 1995). The Secretary-General would have to certify that satisfactory progress was being made before the Council would authorize additional deployments.

In what should have been a warning of impending trouble in Rwanda, the first Hutu president of neighboring Burundi was killed in an attempted coup on October 21. The death of Melchior Ndadaye, who was also the country's first freely elected head of state, sparked violent ethnic clashes and sent 300,000 Burundians, mostly Hutus, over the borders of Rwanda, Tanzania, and Zaire by October 25. [U.N. press release REF/1042, 10/25/93]. A Regional Summit held at Kigali on October 28 requested the United Nations to establish an "international force for stabilization and [the] restoration of confidence" in Burundi [A/48/567, 11/2/93], and in response the Secretary-General dispatched **Under-Secretary-General James Jonah as his Special Envoy to Burundi** in early November. Although he called the chances for restoring democracy without U.N. troops "very slim," Jonah reportedly informed government officials that in light of the financial and logistical burdens associated with the 16 peacekeeping operations already deployed, the Security Council "has shown no inclination to take on any new operations" [*The Washington Post*, 11/3/93].

By mid-November the conflict had produced 659,000 refugees and 150,000 internally displaced persons, some 15 percent of the population. Eighty percent were women, children, and the elderly. The **U.N. High Commissioner for Refugees (UNHCR)** was spending more than $5 million on short-term relief and seeking a total $17 million from international donors. The **World Food Programme (WFP)** estimated the cost of emergency food aid it was supplying at $14 million [U.N. press releases REF/1051, 11/12/93; WFP/928, 11/16/93]. The Security Council limited its own involvement to welcoming the appointment of Ahmedou Ould Abdallah of Mauritania as the Secretary-General's Special Representative to Burundi and encouraging the dispatch of a "small" fact-finding mission to "facilitate the efforts of the Government of Burundi and the OAU" at peaceful settlement. The Council itself would consider establishing a voluntary fund to support the possible deployment of an OAU military mission [Statement of the President of the Security Council, S/26757, 11/16/93].

Rwanda remained relatively peaceful during the fall of 1993, and the Secretary-General reported in December that UNOMUR had succeeded in appreciably decreasing "clandestine cross-border traffic" from Uganda [S/26878, 12/15/93]. Accordingly, the Security Council extended the operation's mandate for an additional six months, through June 1994 [S/Res/891, 12/20/93]. Upon the recommendation of the Secretary-General, the Council also authorized the deployment of an additional infantry battalion for UNAMIR to prepare for the demobilization process [S/Res/893, 1/6/94], although the transitional government called for in the Arusha Agreement was not yet in place.

By February 1994 the lack of a functioning government was beginning to delay the implementation of the entire peace accord and adversely affect efforts at humanitarian relief. Habyarimana had been sworn in as interim president, but other transitional arrangements, including the appointment of ethnic Tutsis as cabinet ministers and representation for the five main political parties in the National Assembly, were still being debated. The Security Council "strongly urged" the establishment of all "provisional institutions . . . without delay" and denounced rising violence in Kigali and violations of the weapons-free zone established there. "UNAMIR will be assured of consistent support," the Council said, "only if the parties implement the Arusha Peace Agreement fully and rapidly" [Statement of the President, S/PRST/1994/8, 2/17/94].

In Burundi, moderate elements in the army had put down the coup and installed a "government of national consensus" under President Ntaryamira Cyprien, another Hutu. But ethnic violence was reignited in early March after the massacre of more than 200 Hutu civilians in the capital of Bujumbura, apparently by renegade government soldiers. The

Associated Press reported that an estimated 100,000 Burundians had died in civil unrest since October 1993 [*The Washington Post*, 3/25/94]. As promised in February, the Secretary-General dispatched a two-man U.N. Preparatory Fact-Finding Mission to Burundi under the chairmanship of Ambassador Simeon Ake, which arrived in the country on March 22.

The Security Council met on April 5 to extend the mandate of UNA-MIR through July 29 but promised to "review" the operation if transitional arrangements were not completed in six weeks [S/Res/909]. To encourage President Habyarimana to finalize agreement on those arrangements—and to demonstrate support for President Cyprien's efforts to reform the army and security services—the OAU invited both leaders to another regional summit meeting, scheduled for April 6 in Dar es Salaam, Tanzania.

Rwanda became front-page news later that night, when Habyarimana and Cyprien were killed in a plane crash outside Kigali airport upon their return from the regional summit. Rwandan authorities immediately blamed rebel forces for firing the two surface-to-air missiles that reportedly brought down the presidents' plane. In apparent reprisal for the assassination of President Habyarimana, gangs of Hutus in Kigali armed with knives and machetes sought out and hacked to death thousands of Tutsi residents of the city along with ethnic Hutus considered sympathetic to the rebel cause. At the same time, the elite 700-member Presidential Guard exchanged mortar and small-arms fire with the 600 RPF soldiers encamped in Kigali as part of the Arusha peace settlement. Guard units were also implicated in the deaths of Tutsi government officials and foreigners, including the transitional prime minister, Agathe Uwilingiyimana, and 10 Belgian peacekeepers sent to investigate the plane crash. Miraculously, Burundi remained relatively calm [*The Washington Post*, 4/7, 8/94].

On April 8 the United Nations negotiated the appointment of a new president, prime minister, and five cabinet members of an interim government and arranged a limited cease-fire, permitting the International Committee of the Red Cross to retrieve bodies and transport the wounded to hospitals. But armed gangs were said to be "executing" Rwandan Tutsis employed by other relief agencies, including Doctors Without Borders, Oxfam, and UNICEF. Also on April 8, the press reported for the first time that Habyarimana may have been the victim of a coup, prompted by his willingness to honor the government's commitments under the Arusha accords [ibid., 4/9/94]. As Belgium, France, and the United States began the withdrawal of their nationals on April 11, relief workers were estimating that the death toll in Kigali had reached 10,000 [ibid., 4/12/94].

Despite pleas from the African Group at the United Nations and the Rwandan government for the expansion of UNAMIR's size and mandate [OAU press release, 4/11/94; S/1994/428, 4/13/94], the Secretary-General informed the Security Council on April 13 that contingency planning was currently under way for the withdrawal of the operation, "should this be necessary." Boutros-Ghali's announcement came one day after Belgium's decision to recall its 440-man contingent, UNAMIR's third largest [*The Washington Post*, 4/14/93]. On April 15 the **Secretary-General's Special Representative, Jacques-Roger Booh-Booh,** brought both army and rebel representatives together for their first direct negotiations on a cease-fire, but by that time the interim government had fled the capital, the Red Cross had suspended operations, and the violence had claimed some 20,000 lives [ibid., 4/15/94].

On April 19 the OAU announced its support for a peace conference to be convened by the Facilitator of the Arusha Peace Talks, President Ali Mywini of Tanzania, on April 23 [OAU press release 68/94, 4/19/94], and Ugandan President Yoweri Museveni urgently requested the United Nations to maintain its presence in Rwanda to assist in such a regional settlement [S/1994/479, 4/21/93]. As both the Red Cross and Human Rights Watch announced new estimates of 100,000 Rwandan dead and 2 million refugees [*The Washington Post*, 4/21, 22/94], the Security Council declined to either reinforce or completely withdraw UNAMIR and instead approved an "adjustment" to its mandate and size on April 21. In addition to the Belgian contingent and 341 "nonessential personnel" withdrawn earlier, the operation was to lose another 1,430 troops and observers, leaving only the Force Commander and a "support staff" of 270 to help negotiate a cease-fire, resume humanitarian operations, and report on developments in the country [S/1994/470, 4/20/94; S/Res/912, 4/21/94]. The April 23 peace conference collapsed when the government delegation failed to arrive and the RPF apparently refused to grant negotiating authority to its lone representative.

Reporting to the Security Council on April 29 that three weeks of violence in Rwanda had claimed "as many as 200,000" lives, the Secretary-General urged the Security Council to "consider again what action, including forceful action, it could take, or authorize member states to take, in order to restore law and order and end the massacres" [S/1994/518]. As if to underscore the point, some 250,000 Rwandans fled into Tanzania that same day, the largest and fastest flow of refugees ever recorded. After rebel forces resealed the border, the bodies of those unable to flee were seen floating down the Kagera River separating the two countries at a rate of 25 an hour. Human rights groups and U.N. officials quoted in the press spoke of "genocide" and "ethnic cleansing" with reference to the continued killing [*The Washington Post*, 4/30/94, 5/1/94]. UNICEF in particular implored both sides to "spare the children" after the massacre of 21 3-to-12-year-olds and 13 Red Cross workers in the southern town of Butare on May 1 [UNICEF press release PR/94/15, 5/4/94].

Also on May 1, President Mywini of Tanzania announced that both sides had agreed to new talks under his mediation, beginning May 3. Mywini took the opportunity to denounce the U.N. drawdown in

Rwanda as "one of the most unfortunate decisions" of the Security Council and an action that stood "in sharp contrast to the peacekeeping efforts of the United Nations elsewhere." He called for an immediate enlargement of UNAMIR, an arms embargo on Rwanda, and increased international assistance to refugees and displaced persons [S/1994/527, 5/2/94]. The Rwandan government echoed these requests, placing particular emphasis on cutting off the alleged flow of military assistance to the RPF by strengthening UNOMUR [S/1994/531, 5/3/94]. The United States also supported an increased international presence in May 5 talks between Assistant Secretary of State for Humanitarian Affairs John Shattuck and OAU Secretary-General Dr. Salim Salim. The two agreed that a primarily African force under U.N. command should be deployed to provide humanitarian assistance to displaced persons, protect those seeking to cross international borders, and ensure security for all humanitarian operations [OAU press release NY/OAU/BUR/75/94, 5/5/94].

The RPF opposed further U.N. intervention, arguing that UNAMIR had been unable to prevent "genocide" and that an enlarged force would only interfere with rebel efforts to end the massacres by ending the war. OXFAM reported on May 3 that "up to 500,000" may already have died, and neither side demonstrated any willingness to abide by a May 7 ceasefire worked out in peace talks in Tanzania [*The Washington Post*, 5/3, 5/94]. The United States was also qualifying its support for an enlarged U.N. presence, proposing that additional deployments be limited to 500 troops until a 150-member observer mission reported its assessment of further humanitarian and security needs. In addition, the United States questioned the practicality of U.N. plans to establish "protected zones" in the interior of the country and strongly urged that such zones be limited to border areas [ibid., 5/17/94].

Despite these concerns, the Secretary-General went forward with his plans, requested by the Security Council on May 6, to facilitate the delivery of humanitarian assistance to the 2 million Rwandans displaced by the conflict. He proposed the establishment of "UNAMIR II," a 5,500-strong force to be deployed throughout the country wherever concentrations of displaced persons were highest. The force was to establish "protected sites" at such locations, provide security to the affected populations, and facilitate access to these sites for relief workers and humanitarian convoys. UNAMIR II would also provide armed escorts for aid deliveries to the interior and security for U.N. installations there as well as "monitor" border crossings and the disposition of government and RPF forces. As if in response to U.S. concerns, the Secretary-General pointed out that displaced populations in the interior outnumbered those on the borders five to one [S/1994/565, 5/13/94].

The Security Council approved the new mandate, but, at the insistence of the United States, did so only "within the limits of the resources available." The Council permitted the establishment of secure areas "where feasible," and authorized the Secretary-General to immediately augment UNAMIR's 444 troops and observers by redeploying 179 observers previously pulled from the operation and bringing the single remaining battalion up to its full strength of 800. Further deployments would not be automatic, however, as the Secretary-General had foreseen, but contingent on his certification that several conditions had been met, including progress toward a cease-fire, sufficient contributions of troops and equipment, and a firm estimate of the duration of the operation. The Council also imposed an arms embargo on both sides and reiterated its request to the Secretary-General for a report on "serious violations of international humanitarian law" committed in the conflict. (Without using the term "genocide," the Council "recalled" that the "killing of members of an ethnic group with the intention of destroying such a group, in whole or in part, constitutes a crime punishable under international law" [S/Res/918, 5/17/94].)

The implementation of the plan hit immediate roadblocks, chief among them the RPF's capture of Kigali airport on May 22, just two days short of the date by which both sides were to have declared the site a "neutral zone" and turned control of it over to UNAMIR. Although the supply of humanitarian relief would continue by means of Red Cross truck convoys from Burundi, the United Nations would be unable to fly in the thousands of reinforcements required to guarantee the distribution of that relief. **Assistant Secretary-General for Peacekeeping Iqbal Riza** attempted to broker the transfer of the airport to U.N. control during his May 23–24 visit to Rwanda, but a temporary truce observed by both sides in Kigali expired before Riza could conclude talks. Thousands of ethnic Hutus began fleeing the city, fearing its imminent capture by rebel forces. Calling the international response to the Rwanda crisis a "failure" and a "scandal," Boutros-Ghali complained in a May 25 press conference that he had received troop commitments from only three African countries— Ghana, Ethiopia, and Senegal—totaling just 2,100 personnel. UNAMIR did succeed, however, in guiding to safety outside Kigali some 500 of the city's estimated 30,000 displaced persons on May 27, the U.N.'s "biggest breakthrough in weeks" [*The Washington Post*, 5/23, 24, 26, 27/94].

Seeking additional troops from member states as well as Security Council authority to deploy them, the Secretary-General stated flatly in a May 31 report that "There can be little doubt that [the killing of civilians in Rwanda] constitutes genocide." By June 7 the United Nations had received offers of 500 more infantrymen from Mali, Congo, and Nigeria and 800 each from Zimbabwe, Ethiopia, and Senegal [ibid., 6/8/94]. Although those contributions still left the United Nations 500 troops and about 1,300 support personnel short of its goal, the United States supported Security Council action on June 8 authorizing the "immediate" deployment of some 1,600 troops and the extension of UNAMIR's mandate through December 9, 1994 [S/Res/925]. At least a month would be required to equip and transport the troops, however [*The New York Times*, 6/10/94].

As reports of massacres increased—nine priests and 63 civilians on June 4; the Roman Catholic Archbishop of Kigali and 12 other priests on June 8 (the first confirmed killings by the RPF); 160 orphaned boys on June 10—the United States continued to refer only to "acts of genocide" in Rwanda rather than to genocide itself. The distinction was crucial, as the recognition that actual genocide was occurring might have obligated Washington to punish the perpetrators under the 1948 U.N. Convention against Genocide [*The New York Times*, 6/10/94; *The Washington Post*, 6/11/94]. The United States later conceded that the killings met the "legal definition of genocide" but argued that the convention "enabled" but did not "require" signatories to take action [*The Washington Post*, 6/17/94].

Deeply implicated in the mass slaughter by its role as chief military advisor and supplier to the Rwandan government, France began a campaign to gain international support for immediate intervention to stop the killings. **French Foreign Minister Alain Juppé** petitioned the Secretary-General on June 14 to transfer some 3,000 peacekeepers from Somalia to Rwanda, and on June 15 offered to dispatch 1,000 French troops within 24 hours as part of a combined European and African humanitarian mission [*The Washington Post*, 6/16/94; *The New York Times*, 6/17/94]. But Senegal was alone in pledging 500 additional troops to the effort, and the RPF, for its part, immediately denounced the mission as a thinly veiled attempt to prop up the government. Boutros-Ghali's June 20 announcement that the United Nations could not field an expanded UNAMIR for three months finally persuaded the United States to support reluctantly the French proposal in the Security Council on June 22 [S/Res/929]. Five members abstained (Brazil, China, New Zealand, Nigeria, and Pakistan), an uncommonly high number for the Council in recent years [*The Washington Post*, 6/21,22/94].

In the carefully worded resolution, the Council cited the "time needed to gather the necessary resources for the effective deployment of UNAMIR" and the threat to regional peace and security caused by the "magnitude of the humanitarian crisis in Rwanda." The Council stressed that the French-led mission was "strictly humanitarian" in intent and would act in an "impartial and neutral" fashion to provide "security and protection" to "displaced persons, refugees, and civilians at risk." Acting under Chapter VII of the Charter, the Council authorized the mission to operate under national command and control and to use "all necessary means" to fulfill its mandate. But the Council also set a strict two-month time limit on its activities and requested the Secretary-General to report on those activities within 15 days. The Secretary-General was also to report by August 9 on preparations to deploy UNAMIR II and on progress achieved in resuming talks toward a political settlement.

Jumping off from three bases in neighboring Zaire, some 700 French troops entered Rwanda on June 23 and quickly established a presence at the refugee camp in Cyangugu, housing 8,000 Tutsi civilians. Troops later assessed the needs of 500 Hutu refugees in two other camps, in part as a demonstration of their impartiality. France and Senegal planned to deploy some 1,000 troops between them and 1,500 more personnel to guard airports and provide logistical support [*The New York Times*, 6/24/94; *The Washington Post*, 6/26/94].

South Africa

Negotiations on ending minority white rule in South Africa took a symbolic leap forward on June 3, 1993, with the provisional decision to set April 27, 1994, as the date for the country's first all-race elections. That action by the 26-member **Multi-Party Negotiating Forum (MPNF),** established to guide South Africa from apartheid to democracy, cleared the way for further negotiations on transitional arrangements through which blacks would participate in governing the country for the first time since the arrival of Europeans some 350 years ago. Setting an election date and giving a voice in government to the 75 percent black population were crucial steps toward lifting U.N. sanctions imposed on South Africa in the 1970s [*The Washington Post*, 6/4/93].

With the support of Nelson Mandela's African National Congress (ANC) and the National party of President F. W. de Klerk, the MPNF made the election date final on July 2. Seven other MPNF members strongly opposed the move, including the **Zulu-based Inkatha Freedom Party,** representing the nominally independent black "homeland" of KwaZulu, and the white reactionary Conservative party. Both walked out of the talks in protest. Inkatha and the Conservatives were seeking assurances that the country's new constitution would grant considerable powers to regions over what was expected to be an ANC-dominated central government. Political and ethnic violence between the ANC, led by members of the Xhosa tribe, and Inkatha had already claimed the lives of some 15,000 South Africans since 1984, when major disagreements emerged between the parties on the appropriate strategy for opposing apartheid. The dramatic increase in violence in recent years—some 10,000 have died since Mandela's release from prison in February 1990—was behind the U.N.'s decision to deploy the 60-member **U.N. Observer Mission in South Africa (UNOMSA)** in September 1992 [ibid., 7/3/94].

After finalizing the election date, MPNF members reached agreement on the creation of a **Transitional Executive Council (TEC)** on September 7, 1993, which was officially approved by the South African Parliament on September 23. The country's first multiracial governing body, the TEC would provide predominantly black political parties with a limited veto over government decisions affecting the elections, including the maintenance of law and order and the activities of the security forces, through voting day [ibid., 9/8,25/94]. Although the new body would not actually begin functioning until agreement was reached on an interim consitution, its establishment meant that the process of democratic change had become irreversible. Accordingly, ANC President Nelson Mandela went before the U.N. Special Committee against Apartheid on September 24 to ask the General Assembly to lift international economic sanctions against South Africa.

In an interview with U.N. Radio, Mandela called sanctions "one of the most powerful weapons" of the anti-apartheid struggle and admitted that the ANC was abandoning its long-standing pledge to delay their repeal until white rule had been officially ended. He explained the switch with reference to the "destruction" that apartheid had wrought on the economy and hoped that lifting the sanctions while South Africa was still democratizing might remind "democratic forces throughout the world [of their] duty to help our economy to become strong, to grow, to offer job opportunities, to generate wealth" ["World Chronicle," 9/24/93]. On October 8 the General Assembly rescinded all its prohibitions or restrictions against economic relations with South Africa in the areas of trade, investment, finance, travel, and transportation. It requested member states to repeal all laws they had adopted to give effect to those sanctions but decided to leave the 1979 U.N. oil embargo in effect until the TEC became operational [A/Res/48/1]. The decision would not affect the Security Council's 1977 embargo on arms and nuclear weapons-related material.

The move was expected to do little in the short term to attract foreign investment or lower the country's 40 percent unemployment rate. The United States had already repealed its 1985 ban against new investment in 1991, and the European Community, the Organization of African Unity, and the Commonwealth had taken similar action. But the repeal resolution would allow Congress to rescind its prohibitions against loans to Pretoria from the World Bank and the International Monetary Fund and permit the 179 state and local governments that had barred investment in South Africa to reverse these rulings [The Washington Post, 9/25/93, 10/9/93].

In his September 24 address and subsequent interview, Mandela had also called on the United Nations to assist in monitoring the upcoming elections. Saying that UNOMSA had done "remarkable work" and was "putting pressure on all of us to account for our actions," the ANC leader argued that "an increase in the number of observers . . . would go a long way in ensuring that these elections are fair and free." In light of the "progress in the multi-party talks" to date, the Secretary-General petitioned the Security Council on September 29 for authorization to deploy 40 additional UNOMSA observers, bringing the mission up to its full complement of 100. The enlarged mission was to "serve as a nucleus for the anticipated United Nations role in the electoral process" [S/26558]. The Council approved the request on October 9 [S/26559]. In further recognition of the great strides blacks and whites had made together in eradicating racism and introducing democracy, the Nobel Committee awarded both Mandela and de Klerk its 1993 Peace Prize on October 15.

The leaders reached another milestone in their joint efforts on November 18, when the MPNF approved the interim constitution. Two years in the making, the constitution would enter into force on election day and serve as the supreme law of the land until a permanent constitution could be drafted by the legislature elected in April [A/48/845-S/1994/16, 1/10/94]. In deference to the rights of political minorities, the constitution provided significant powers to the regions, which could set their own policies in the areas of agriculture, education, health, housing, language, police, and welfare. It would also grant each of South Africa's nine new provinces limited powers of taxation and the right to draft and approve its own constitutional document. In addition, the interim constitution called for the establishment of the country's first constitutional court to adjudicate disputes between the regions and the central government.

The need to protect minority rights also extended to the constitutionally mandated structure of the new government. In the five-year transition period commencing with elections, the executive branch would consist of a president and two deputy presidents, at least one of whom would represent a minority party. Like the 400-member National Assembly and the 90-member Senate, the cabinet would be chosen on the basis of proportional representation. All parties receiving at least 5 percent of the vote would be included in the cabinet and the legislature [*The Washington Post*, 11/18/93]. Moreover, the MPNF also approved on November 18 the Electoral Acts, which enshrined universal suffrage in law, and the establishment of three multiracial bodies to administer the elections and certify the results: the Independent Electoral Commission (IEC), the Independent Media Commission (IMC), and the Independent Broadcasting Commission (IBC) [A/48/865].

The Security Council, for its part, "invited the Secretary-General to accelerate contingency planning for a possible United Nations role in the election process," should the South African parties request such assistance [S/26785, 11/23/93]. That request came on December 7 in the inaugural meeting of the 19-member Transitional Executive Council, which formally ended minority white rule in South Africa. In response to the convening of the TEC, the General Assembly President proclaimed the lifting of the U.N. oil embargo on December 9, according to the provisions of Resolution 48/1 [U.N. press release GA/8617], and the Secretary-General appointed a new **Special Representative for South Africa,** naming **Lakhdar Brahimi,** a former Algerian foreign minister, on December 16. Brahimi was to oversee the U.N. electoral monitoring effort and coordinate the activities of other observers from the Organization of African Unity, the European Union (E.U.), the Commonwealth, and national governments [S/26883, S/26884, 12/16/93].

The General Assembly's annual omnibus resolution on South Africa and apartheid [A/Res/159 A-D, 12/20/93] had a ring of finality about it in 1993, as the goal of a "united, democratic, and non-racial" country appeared to be finally within reach. Commenting on "international efforts" toward that goal, the General Assembly reiterated its calls for an end to political violence, rededication to the principles of the September 1991 National Peace Accord, and increased humanitarian and legal assistance to the victims of apartheid. For the first time, however, it requested the development of U.N. programs of socioeconomic assistance for "post-apartheid South Africa." The General Assembly also directed the Special Committee against Apartheid, established in 1962, to submit its "final report" as soon as possible after the installation of a democratic South African government.

The General Assembly terminated the mandate of the Intergovernmental Group to Monitor the Supply and Shipping of Oil and Petroleum Products to South Africa after 14 years but appealed for additional contributions to the U.N. Trust Fund for South Africa, which still had an "important role to play" in channeling "humanitarian, legal, and educational assistance . . . to the victims of apartheid." The General Assembly made a similar pitch for the U.N. Educational and Training Program for Southern Africa and requested that the Secretary-General include the program in the annual U.N. Pledging Conference for Development Activities [A/Res/ 48/160, 12/20/93]. For the first time since the item on apartheid was inscribed on the U.N. agenda in 1948, all five resolutions were adopted without a vote, and none requested follow-up reports to the 49th Session.

As 1993 ended with the formal approval by parliament of the interim constitution on December 22 and the posting of a record 4,200 politically motivated killings [*The Washington Post*, 12/23/93, 1/1/94], the Secretary-General presented his plan for monitoring the April elections [A/48/845-S/1994/16, 1/10/ 94]. Since its deployment, UNOMOSA had observed hundreds of political demonstrations, held thousands of meetings with some 200 nongovernmental "peace committees" and the other bodies set up under the National Peace Accord, and coordinated the activities of the 50 observers from the OAU, the E.U., and the Commonwealth.

Under the Secretary-General's plan, UNOMSA was also to monitor the activities of the electoral, media, and broadcasting commissions and the security forces; observe the electoral campaign, voter education activities, and the issuance of voting cards; and verify that voting took place free of violence and under conditions that ensured unimpeded access to polling stations and secure ballot-counting procedures. To accomplish these tasks, UNOMSA would be expanded to 500 by early April and to

1,300 by election day. The other international organizations were also expected to enlarge their own observer missions. Electoral monitors sent by various governments and nongovernmental organizations would bring the total number of observers to around 2,300 ["U.N. Fact Sheet, South Africa's Democratic Elections: the U.N.'s Observer Role," 3/94].

In approving the election-monitoring plan, the Security Council urged all political parties, including those that had boycotted the MPNF, to adhere to the agreements reached in those talks and to participate in the elections. It called for an end to violence and promised to hold accountable persons perpetrating such acts, and it welcomed the Secretary-General's proposal to set up a special trust fund to finance the participation of African states in the election-monitoring process [S/Res/894, 1/14/94]. The General Assembly reiterated these points in its own resolution and repeated an earlier call for unfettered campaigning in all ten of South Africa's violence-prone black homelands [A/Res/48/233, 1/21/94].

From January through mid-April, the ANC and the government held intensive talks with the parties of the Freedom Alliance—including Inkatha, the governments of other black homelands, and the far-right Afrikaner Volksfront—to avert a threatened electoral boycott. The coalition was holding out for amendments to the interim constitution to further expand regional powers, including a double ballot system of voting, independent taxation authority, and guarantees of ethnic self-determination for black and white minorities [South African Mission to the U.N., *News Highlights*, No. 5/94]. In February the MPNF approved separate ballots and the establishment of a parliamentary council to consider creating an autonomous Afrikaner state, and in March, Inkatha agreed to submit its remaining disputes to international mediation. Inkatha and the Volksfront "provisionally registered" for the election on March 4 [*The Washington Post*, 2/22/94, 3/4,5/94].

In mid-March civil unrest in Bophuthatswana and Ciskei forced the nominal presidents of these homelands to end their electoral boycotts, but Inkatha's continued refusal to endorse the vote led to a record 270 political killings in its stronghold of KwaZulu and throughout the surrounding province of Natal by the end of the month. President de Klerk declared a state of emergency in that region—the first in three years—on March 30 [ibid., 3/12,23/94, 4/1/94]. Finally, in what the press described as a "dramatic turnaround," Inkatha called off its boycott on April 19 and signed an agreement with the government and the ANC guaranteeing the continuation of the Zulu monarchy and further international mediation in the post-election period. Politically motivated killings fell off sharply [ibid., 4/20,21/94].

The Security Council welcomed the agreement and commended all sides for their "statemanship and goodwill." The Council also commended UNOMSA for its "positive contribution . . . to the transitional process," althought the mission had reported continuing problems with respect to the selection of voting stations, the availability of necessary equipment and materials, and the finalization of plans for electoral security [U.N. press release SC/5828, 4/19/94]. On April 23 the government and the ANC signed a second agreement, this time with "moderate" Afrikaners of the newly established Freedom Front coalition. The accord effectively isolated the Conservatives and other hard-line elements of the white right by linking the possibility of establishing a separate Afrikaner state to a "substantial" electoral showing by the Front [*The Washington Post*, 4/24/94].

Despite a last-minute bombing campaign by white extremists aimed at disrupting the elections, polls opened on April 26, a day earlier than originally planned, in the first of three scheduled days of balloting. Massive voting delays in some areas and shortages of voting materials—aggravated by the need to affix separate Inkatha stickers to each ballot to accommodate that party's late entry into the race—required de Klerk to order that polls reopen for a fourth day of voting in six tribal homelands, including KwaZulu. These problems notwithstanding, IEC Chairman Johann Kriegler declared the elections an "outstanding success" [ibid., 4/26,28,30/94].

With the ANC enjoying a commanding lead halfway through the vote-counting process, Mandela accepted victory on May 2, although the IEC was not able to complete the count and declare the elections "substantially free and fair" until May 6. On a turnout of 86 percent of all eligible voters, the ANC won the presidency with 62.6 percent of all ballots cast (just short of the two-thirds that would have allowed it to amend the constitution at will), seven of nine provinces, and 252 seats in the National Assembly. The National party finished second with 20.4 percent and 82 seats, making de Klerk one of the two deputy presidents. Inkatha placed third with 10.5 percent and 43 seats [ibid., 5/7/94]. Congratulating the President-elect, the Chairman of the Special Committee against Apartheid called him a "true statesman," capable of leading "the political process by which the new Government of National Unity will undertake the daunting tasks of reconstruction and development that now lie ahead" [U.N. press release GA/AP/2152, 5/6/94]. The Security Council's decision to drop its arms embargo against Pretoria on May 26 [S/Res/919] ensured the June 23 repeal of the 1974 resolution barring South Africa from participating in the General Assembly.

Mozambique

Delays and procrastination have characterized the compliance of the government and rebel forces in Mozambique with the General Peace Agreement they signed in October 1992, ending 16 years of civil war. President Joaquim Chissano and Alfonso Dhlakama, leader of the Resistência Nacional Moçambicana (RENAMO), were clearly committed to the cease-fire provisions of the agreement, and through June 1993 no significant violations were reported. But neither side had demonstrated much interest up to that time in honoring other major commitments, including demobilizing their forces, training a new national army, and holding elections.

The **U.N. Operation in Mozambique (ONUMOZ)** overcame delays of its own by midyear, completing in early May the full deployment of some 6,100 troops mandated to protect humanitarian aid convoys from rebel attack. ONUMOZ's 260 military oversaw the withdrawal of Zimbabwean troops in April and those of Malawi by early June, fulfilling two important provisions of the peace agreement. The observers continued to monitor compliance with the cease-fire, but were unable to discharge their verification functions with respect to the phased assembly and demobilization of the opposing forces and the collection, storage, and destruction of their weapons.

By June 1993 only six of the 49 assembly areas called for in the peace agreement (three each for government and RENAMO troops) had been opened, and both sides were proposing to abandon phased demobilization in favor of mass assembly once all 49 sites were prepared. The Secretary-General did not foresee the concentration of forces, rescheduled once for July 1, getting under way before September. Establishment of the Mozambican Defense Forces (FADM) was also being delayed by RENAMO's refusal since February to send its first contingent of troops for joint training with government forces. The rebels were no more cooperative in discussing preparations for elections, themselves already delayed a year to October 1994. RENAMO refused to attend an April 27 meeting to discuss the government's draft electoral law, presented March 26, demanding more time to study the document. Debate was not expected to begin before July.

In fact, rebel participation in all the joint implementing commissions established under the peace agreement was severely limited from March to May, when RENAMO withdrew its delegation from the Mozambican capital, Maputo, charging that the government had not provided adequate accommodations, transportation, or communications. To overcome this difficulty, the United Nations took the extraordinary step of establishing a trust fund on May 10 to finance RENAMO's political activities. Reportedly the brainchild of U.N. Special Representative Aldo Ajello, the fund received an immediate $6 million contribution from Ajello's native Italy, which played a leading diplomatic role in negotiating the peace agreement and contributed one of five infantry battalions to ONUMOZ. RENAMO returned to the capital at the end of May.

Italy has also been instrumental in arranging international humanitarian assistance for Mozambique and co-hosted with the United Nations the Follow-up Donors' Meeting on June 8–9 in Maputo. The sequel to the Donors' Conference on Mozambique, held in December 1992 in Rome, the meeting raised an additional $70 million toward the $559.6 million the United Nations estimated would be needed for assistance programs from May 1993 to April 1994. Some $450 million had already been pledged at and since the first meeting. Funds were to be channeled away from emergency relief and toward the reintegration and resettlement of some 4 million internally displaced persons, 1.5 million refugees, and 370,000 demobilized soldiers and their families [S/26034, 6/30/93].

As increased demands for U.N. peacekeeping were stretching U.N. resources to their limit, the Security Council was subjecting costly and delay-prone operations like that in Mozambique to closer scrutiny. In its Resolution 850 of July 9, the Council welcomed the progress achieved to date but stressed the importance of eliminating delays and holding elections "no later than" October 1994. It urged the sides to begin demobilization without waiting for all the assembly sites to become operational and sought to accelerate the training of the new army by approving the Secretary-General's suggestion that the United Nations chair the Joint Commission for the Formation of the Mozambican Defense Force (CC-FADM). No longer satisfied with the traditional six-month reporting period for peacekeeping operations, the Council requested the Secretary-General to keep it informed of developments and to report back by August 18.

Under U.N. chairmanship, CCFADM held its first meeting July 22, 1993, and on August 3, 100 military officers from each side had begun training as infantry instructors. Demobilization hit a new snag, however, when RENAMO announced that it would not participate until agreement was reached on extending government control over rebel-held areas. The joint oversight body involved, the National Commission for Administration, had been established but had not yet convened. Discussions of the draft electoral law also reached an impasse on August 25 after agreement on only 15 of the 284 proposed articles; talks broke down over the composition of the National Electoral Commission. Progress was similarly slow in repatriating refugees. Only 20 percent or roughly 326,000 had returned by late August, mostly from Malawi. Despite these difficulties, the Secretary-General expressed optimism that the initiation of the first direct talks between President Chissano and Mr. Dhlakama on August 21 would facilitate the "full and timely" implementation of the peace agreement [S/26385, 8/30/93].

The direct talks led to agreements on September 3 regarding state administration and a joint request for U.N. monitoring of all police activities in the country. The Security Council noted these "with satisfaction" but denounced the practice of "attach[ing] conditions to the peace process . . . to gain more time or further concessions." The Council "strongly urge[d]" both parties to sign off "without further postponement" on a timetable for implementing the peace accord in its entirety, not just the electoral provisions. As previously, the Secretary-General was to report on developments in six weeks' time [S/Res/863, 9/13/93].

After visiting Maputo and meeting with Chissano and Dhlakama in mid-October, the Secretary-General reported "new momentum" in the peace process and the signature of the revised timetable on October 22. The leaders agreed to begin concentrating their troops—including paramilitary, militia, and irregular forces—in November and to start the demobilization process in January 1994. Agreement was also reached on a rotating chairmanship between the government and RENAMO for the National Commission for Administration and on the composition of another joint body, the National Police Affairs Commission. Both were essential to the implementation of the agreements signed September 3. Chissano and Dhlakama resolved their dispute over the membership of the National Elections Commission as well, but final agreement on the draft electoral law was still pending. The count of returning refugees reached 400,000 by October, with increasing numbers from Zambia, Zimbabwe, and Swaziland. An estimated 1.2 million internally displaced persons had also been resettled [S/26666, 11/1/93].

With respect to the request for U.N. monitoring of police activities, the Secretary-General sought approval from the Security Council for the deployment of 128 police observers, pending the establishment of a full police contingent in ONUMOZ. The Council agreed in November and also renewed ONUMOZ's mandate for an additional six months, through April 1994, subject to a thorough review after 90 days. The Secretary-General was to report by January 31, 1994, and every three months thereafter on whether the parties were making "sufficient and tangible progress" complying with the revised timetable. The Council also renewed its request for further contributions to the RENAMO trust fund; the Secretary-General was seeking an additional $5 million [S/Res/882, 11/5/93].

The peace process "entered a new phase" on November 30, 1993, when both sides began concentrating their 80,000 troops. By January 24, 1994, 9,895 government soldiers and 6,714 RENAMO personnel had assembled in 35 locations. The 330 U.N. military observers overseeing the "cantonment" process collected more than 17,000 weapons. By December 20, 540 Mozambican infantry instructors had completed their training and were to begin training the first 5,000 government and RENAMO soldiers selected for the new national army on February 8. The Mozambican National Assembly finally approved the draft electoral law on December 9, and members of the National Elections Commission were appointed January 21, 1994. Refugee repatriation topped 620,000 by January, 40 percent of the total, and about half of all displaced persons had been resettled. As demand for emergency food aid declined, the United Nations was planning to devote an increasing portion of international assistance—pledges had reached their target of $560 million—to reintegration programs for demobilized soldiers, designed to identify opportunities for training and self-employment as well as to provide subsidies to public and private employers hiring former combatants.

The Secretary-General cautioned that major problems remained to be solved, primarily the initiation of actual demobilizations. The United Nations would have to work to overcome the political disagreements between the sides that prevented ONUMOZ from opening the final 14 assembly sites and transporting the weapons it had already collected to warehouses for safekeeping. The government would also have to deal more effectively with the logistical problems that held up the dismantling of its militia and paramilitary forces, which were scattered throughout the country and numbered almost 156,000. The process did not get under way until January 12, almost six weeks behind schedule. The United Nations would have to raise more money as well: at least $7.5 million, the Secretary-General now estimated, for the RENAMO trust fund, and perhaps millions more to provide adequate salaries and accommodations for the new 30,000-man army [S/1994/89, 1/28/94].

The Secretary-General nevertheless went forward with his request for 1,016 additional police monitors to implement the parties' September 3 agreement. ONUMOZ's newly formed police component (CIVPOL) was to monitor the activities and the respect for human rights of the country's 18,000 police and to provide technical assistance to the National Police Commission. CIVPOL would also assist in monitoring the election campaign [S/1994/89/Adds.1&2].

In authorizing the establishment of the police contingent, the Security Council requested the Secretary-General to make preparations for the withdrawal of U.N. personnel to offset the increased deployment and to hold costs constant. He was also to establish a timetable for the phased withdrawal of ONUMOZ in step with the peace process: military observers at the completion of demobilization; infantry troops upon the deployment of the national defense force; and the remaining personnel with the inauguration of the new government after elections. The Council welcomed the Secretary-General's informal proposal to supply RENAMO with a steady monthly stipend and encouraged the government to continue its severance payments to former soldiers to promote demobilization and reintegration [S/Res/898, 2/23/94].

On February 21 both the government and RENAMO agreed to proposals of Ambassador Ajello to open all 49 assembly points, and on March 10 actual demobilization finally got under way. Securing collected weapons at regional depots began on March 15. By April 18, U.N. observers had overseen the concentration of 55 percent of the government's troops (34,012) and 81 percent of RENAMO's forces (15,453); the demo-bilization of 12,756 combatants (mostly from the government side); and the collection of 48,746 weapons. Training the joint Mozambican Defense Force was proceeding slowly, however, and only half of the required 30,000 personnel were scheduled to complete the process by the elections of October 1994. The parties would have to agree either to complete the training after the elections or to seek additional resources from the international community to expand the training program [S/1994/511, 4/28/94].

Increased assistance seemed unlikely, as the Secretary-General was already reducing the size of ONUMOZ's military component to make room for the 1,016 additional U.N. police monitors approved in February. Two hundred seventy-eight monitors had already arrived by April 18. Of the 5,914 military and civilian police personnel in ONUMOZ, 800 infantry troops would be withdrawn by the end of April, 977 engineers and other support staff by May, and 257 more engineers in July. The Secretary-General refused, however, to cut ONUMOZ's 397 military observers until demobilization was complete, collected weapons disposed of, and a new government installed.

The process of installing a new government took a major step forward on April 11, when President Chissano announced that elections would take place on October 27 and 28. The National Elections Commission also approved an electoral timetable. According to that schedule, the training of registration "brigades" would begin on February 15, followed by the opening of actual registration on June 1. The commission would prepare final electoral rolls beginning August 16, and campaigning would commence on September 10 and run through October 24. The United Nations was helping to coordinate technical assistance to the electoral process and had already collected $47 million of the $59 million required for this purpose. The world body had also established another trust fund to channel assistance to the 14 registered political parties contesting the elections. (These funds are in addition to the monies collected exclusively for RENAMO.)

Some $18 million more was pledged to a fourth trust fund, administered by the U.N. Development Programme (UNDP), to extend severance pay to ex-soldiers for an additional 18 months. The United Nations was also coordinating with the governments of Norway, the United Kingdom, and the United States in training about 400 personnel to clear crucial roads of landmines. By mid-April, the Secretary-General reported, the United Nations had assisted in the resettlement of 3 million of Mozambique's 4 million displaced persons and 800,000 of its 1.6 million refugees.

In renewing ONUMOZ's mandate for a "final period" through November 15, 1994, the Security Council expressed its concern over delays in implementing the military aspects of the General Peace Agreement and urged the parties to complete the assembly of their forces by June 1 and demobilization by July 15. The government and RENAMO were also to "ensure that the maximum possible number of soldiers" for the new army were trained before the election. The Council would review ONUMOZ's mandate by July 15 and again by September 5 based on reports to be submitted by the Secretary-General by those dates [S/Res/916, 5/5/94].

Liberia

The United Nations had originally intended to stay out of the civil war in Liberia, touched off in December 1989 when guerrilla forces under Charles Taylor invaded the country from the Côte d'Ivoire and toppled the corrupt regime of President Samuel Doe. A subregional organization, the Economic Community of West African States (ECOWAS), had undertaken peacekeeping responsibilities in the conflict, dispatching a seven-nation Military Observer Group (known as ECOMOG) in the summer of 1990 that reestablished order in the capital of Monrovia and installed an interim government. Taylor's National Patriotic Front of Liberia (NPFL) continued to control 90 percent of the country, however.

Violating a June 1991 peace agreement, Taylor attacked Monrovia in October 1992, unleashing full-scale warfare with ECOMOG and former Doe supporters in the United Liberation Movement for Democracy in Liberia (ULIMO). After a U.N.-imposed arms embargo [S/Res/788, 11/19/92] and significant military gains by ECOWAS and ULIMO, Taylor sued for peace. The war had already killed 150,000 Liberians and created 750,000 refugees, a third of the population and the largest per capita refugee flow in the world [*The Washington Post*, 11/3/93].

ʼThe United Nations became more deeply involved in Liberia when it cooperated with ECOWAS and the Organization of African Unity in negotiating a comprehensive settlement among the Interim Government of National Unity of Liberia (IGNU) of Amos Sawyer and the two guerrilla movements. The Peace Agreement [S/26272] signed July 25, 1993, in Contonou, Benin, mandated an August 1 cease-fire, the installation of a coalition government for a seven-month interim period, disarmament and demobilization of combatants, and free elections. ECOWAS was to ensure that the agreement was fully implemented, while the United Nations would monitor the implementation process to verify its impartiality.

In preparation for the dispatch of the **U.N. Observer Mission in Liberia (UNOMIL),** the Secretary-General sent a technical team to Liberia in August 1993 along with 30 military observers to assist the Joint Ceasefire Monitoring Committee set up under the Agreement. The Security Council approved these actions on August 10 [S/Res/856]. Noting that the United Nations would be "treading on fresh ground" in launching a peacekeeping operation with another organization, the Secretary-General recommended the dispatch of an additional 303 military observers, primarily to verify ECOMOG's enforcement of the arms embargo and the demobilization process. The Security Council approved the new mission on September 22 for a seven-month period, including in its mandate the monitoring of the electoral process and the provision of humanitarian relief. The Council also welcomed the establishment of a trust fund to facilitate the deployment of the 4,000 additional ECOMOG troops required to implement the agreement [S/Res/866, 9/22/93].

The parties to the Contonou Agreement had agreed in August on the composition of the five-member Council of State, the executive authority in the new Liberia National Transitional Government, but the distribution of 17 cabinet posts remained outstanding as of December. This delay prevented the scheduled start of the disarmament process and the swearing-in of the Council. Additional troops to ECOMOG were also not forthcoming, although a $20 million voluntary contribution to the Liberian trust fund from the United States elicited pledges of more personnel from Tanzania, Uganda, and Zimbabwe. The United Kingdom, for its part, made a $1 million contribution to the fund to facilitate humanitarian assistance and voluntary repatriation. Although the Joint Elections Commission was in place by December, voting was not considered possible before May 1994, two months later than scheduled [S/26868, 12/13/93].

Progress on military and political matters picked up after a meeting of the parties on February 15, 1994, in Monrovia. With the assistance of the Secretary-General's **Special Representative for Liberia, Trevor Gordon-Somers,** the interim government and the rebel factions agreed to supply ECOMOG and UNOMIL with information they had requested to facilitate disarmament—numbers and locations of troops, numbers of weapons and artillery, and the like. The United Nations and ECOWAS announced plans to complete the deployment of their respective forces and commence disarmament by March 7, and the parties agreed to swear in the Council of State on that date. Elections were set for September 7 [S/1994/187, 2/17/94].

By April, cabinet selections remained incomplete, but demobilization had begun and the Council of State was installed as scheduled on March 7. The two other governmental bodies authorized under the Contonou Agreement, a Transitional Legislative Assembly and a reconstituted supreme court, became operational within the week. The Secretary-General estimated that the demobilization of the 60,000 combatants from all sides would require two months, but several expert teams he had recently dispatched reported that organizing elections could take a year. Voting was also dependent on the receipt of some $5 million in international assistance. U.N. humanitarian agencies continued to provide relief to most of the 1.4 million Liberians in need, and the U.N. High Commissioner for Refugees (UNHCR) had assisted in the return of half of the

60,000 refugees already repatriated. UNHCR expected that an additional 414,000 would request assistance [S/1994/463, 4/18/94; press release SC/5829, 4/21/94].

The Security Council approved an extension of UNOMIL's mandate through October 22, 1994, dependent on the completion of the cabinet selection process by May 18 and sufficient progress in the demobilization and electoral processes by June 30 [S/Res/911, 4/21/94]. The Liberians met the first deadline, after intensive negotiations between the parties and the Council of State and the personal involvement of the Secretary-General. Appointment of the last cabinet member was made on May 11, and the cabinet held its first meeting on May 13. With the resolution of the dispute, the Secretary-General expected demobilization to accelerate. By mid-April only 2,900 combatants had surrendered their weapons. The Secretary-General was also dispatching another team of electoral experts, who would examine possibilities for changing Liberia's single-constituency voting system to a more easily managed system based on proportional representation.

The peace process was "finally yielding some positive results," Boutros-Ghali wrote in his May 18 report, which "provide a reasonable basis for optimism" [S/1994/588]. Should cooperation between the United Nations and ECOWAS succeed in bringing lasting peace in Liberia, it might serve as a model for effective peacekeeping efforts elsewhere.

Western Sahara

The Secretary-General began the process of voter registration in 1993 for the long-awaited referendum on self-determination in Western Sahara despite his failure to completely resolve disagreements over voter eligibility. Morocco and the guerrilla forces of the Popular Front for the Liberation of Saguia el-Hamra and Rio de Oro (POLISARIO) ended their 15-year war for control over the former Spanish colony in 1990, but POLISARIO has yet to fully accept the criteria for eligibility to vote put forward by former Secretary-General Javier Pérez de Cuéllar in December 1991. Although registration is going forward on the basis of compromise criteria proposed by Boutros-Ghali in April 1993, the role of the **U.N. Mission on the Referendum in Western Sahara (MINURSO)** continues to be limited to monitoring the cease-fire in effect since September 1991.

The proposal of April 1993 was designed to break the deadlock between the parties on interpreting the voting provisions of the 1990 Settlement Plan, which stipulated only that all Western Saharans counted in the Spanish census of 1974 and aged 18 years or older at the time of the referendum would be permitted to participate in it. Because the census underrepresented the number of nomadic tribespeople present in the territory at the time, both sides agree that the list of potential voters should be expanded, but they differ sharply on the method for doing so. Morocco has advocated extending suffrage to all those who can demonstrate any "tribal link" to the territory, but POLISARIO would allow additions only to those "family groups" or "tribal subfractions" that had a majority of its members counted in 1974 [S/26797, 11/24/93, par. 26]. This limitation was designed to exclude nonindigenous tribes, most of whose members resided outside the territory.

In his compromise solution, the Secretary-General accepted Morocco's more liberal position regarding the inclusion of all "tribal units" as well as POLISARIO's restriction that they have representation in the 1974 census. He suggested that the potential electorate encompass those who could claim membership in any of Western Sahara's tribal subfractions counted in 1974, "regardless of the number of individuals . . . counted." There was, the Secretary-General emphasized, no clear definition of "Western Saharan" based on tribal affiliation [ibid., par. 27].

Working out a practical agreement on the matter, however, is crucial to interpreting and applying the voter eligibility criteria, which are themselves quite straightforward. Pérez de Cuéllar proposed five categories of eligible voters: persons whose names are included in a revised 1974 census list; persons who were living in the territory as members of a Saharan tribe at the time of the census but who were not counted; immediate family members of the first two groups; persons born of a Saharan father born in the territory; and persons who are members of a Saharan tribe belonging to the territory and who have resided in Western Sahara for six years consecutively or for 12 years intermittently before December 1, 1974 [S/26185, 7/28/93, Annex I].

In a breakthrough of sorts, POLISARIO dropped its objections to some of these criteria in June 1993 and accepted all five for the first time. Equally significant was POLISARIO'S acceptance in principle of "oral testimony" from tribal chiefs, confirming individual membership in a given subfraction. The Popular Front had previously insisted that only written evidence and "authentic" documents were valid forms of identification. POLISARIO sought significant changes in the Secretary's compromise interpretation of the criteria, however, to limit the influence of tribal chiefs and guarantee that voters had tighter tribal links to the territory. Morocco, for its part, had previously accepted the criteria and "acquiesced" to compromise interpretation [ibid., par. 6–7].

Although agreement on the compromise was still not in reach, the Security Council had recommended on March 2 [S/Res/809] that preparations for the referendum get under way to allow voting to begin before the end of 1993. In June the Secretary-General appointed the chairman of the Identification Commission, the body mandated to verify the eligibility of applicants for voter cards and to officially register those found to meet the necessary criteria. But disagreements over the timetable for registration and the registration form itself delayed the start of the process to early November. The Commission published a revised list of the 1974 census on November 22, deleting the names of persons who had since died and adding those of persons recently turned 18. Registration forms were to be distributed by the end of November and would be accepted for processing beginning December 8. The Commission would start taking testimony from tribal chiefs on January 8, 1994. The Secretary-General concluded that voting could not take place before mid-1994 [S/26797, 11/24/93].

By the end of March 1994 the parties had still not agreed to the compromise interpretation of the voting criteria, and the work of the Identification Commission had fallen even further behind schedule. In its Resolution 907 of March 29, the Security Council declared simply that the compromise remained a "sound framework for determining eligibility" and directed the Commission to use it in completing its analysis of applications for voter cards. The Council further directed the Commission to begin the process of identifying eligible voters and actually registering them by June 30. The Secretary-General was to submit a progress report by July 15, and voting was to take place by the end of 1994. Should the referendum be further delayed, the Council would reconsider the mandate and the continued operations of MINURSO.

Angola

The guarded optimism that surrounded the resumption of peace talks in Arusha, Côte d'Ivoire, between Angolan President José Eduardo dos Santos and rebel leader Jonas Savimbi quickly dissipated once negotiations broke off May 21, 1993. Eight months after its defeat in U.N.-monitored elections and its decision to reopen Angola's 17-year civil war, Savimbi's National Union for the Total Independence of Angola (UNITA) was again on the offensive, capturing the oil and diamond-producing centers of Soyo and Cafunfo and pressing its siege of the provincial capitals of Cuito/Bie, Malange, and Menongue. The rebels had already occupied four of the 18 capitals and controlled up to three-quarters of the country's territory. The United Nations estimated that some 2 million of Angola's 12 million people were at risk of starvation and disease and dependent on emergency humanitarian assistance.

Following the breakup of the talks she had chaired, the Secretary-General's **Special Representative to Angola, Joan Antsee,** resigned May 27 and was replaced on June 28 by **Alioune Blondin Beye,** a former minister of foreign affairs of Mali. Beye reported on July 9 that both sides were willing to resume talks and facilitate the delivery of humanitarian relief. In June, UNITA had denied the World Food Programme access to cities under siege, leading the government to suspend implementation of a one-month emergency relief plan [S/26060, 7/12/93].

In extending the mandate of the 68 military and police observers of the **U.N. Mission in Angola (UNAVEM II)** through September 15, the Security Council reiterated earlier appeals for both sides to abide by the rules of international humanitarian law. It repeated its demands that UNITA accept the election results, cease military operations, withdraw from newly occupied territory, and resume peace negotiations. To force compliance, the Council threatened the rebels with a mandatory arms embargo for the first time but also promised once again to significantly expand the U.N.'s presence in the event of significant progress in the peace process [S/Res/851, 7/15/93].

Despite U.N. carrots and sticks, fighting intensified through July and August. Savimbi proposed an "immediate ceasefire without preconditions" and renewed talks on August 11, but the government rejected the overture, insisting that UNITA accept in writing the principles of the draft Abidjan Protocol negotiated in May before talks could resume. UNITA repeated its offer on September 3, and the government rejected it again, this time claiming that an unconditional cease-fire did not conform to the provisions of the original peace agreement and relevant resolutions of the Security Council. The Secretary-General reported that the humanitarian tragedy had already reached "catastrophic" proportions by July: 3 million people were at risk and 1,000 were dying every day, "the highest fatality rate of any conflict in the world." U.N. emergency relief flights to secure areas resumed on July 15 with the agreement of both parties, but UNITA did not approve access to areas considered "unsafe" or to "zones of active conflict" until September 3 [S/26434, 9/15/93].

In a three-part resolution adopted September 15, the Security Council made good on its threat to impose mandatory sanctions on UNITA. In part A of Resolution 864, the Council extended the mandate of UNAVEM II through December 15, 1993, reiterated its readiness to expand the operation, and restated demands for UNITA cooperation in the peace process. Part B directed states to prevent the sale or supply of both arms and petroleum to Angola other than through government-controlled points of entry, beginning September 25. The Council threatened UNITA with additional "trade measures" and travel restrictions unless it agreed by November 1 to an effective cease-fire and the full implementation of the peace agreement and the Council's resolutions. By part C, the Council would "review" the embargo in the event of a cease-fire agreement and "substantial progress" in restarting the peace process.

In an effort to stave off sanctions, UNITA announced its intention to declare a unilateral cease-fire, effective September 20, and called for immediate talks on, among other things, the establishment of a national army; the formation of national, state, and local police forces; and the decentralization of governmental authority. Labeling the proposed cease-fire a mere cessation of hostilities rather than the bilateral agreement required, Special Representative Beye called on UNITA to reaffirm its support for the peace accords, accept the election results, and agree to abide by the Abidjan Protocol and the relevant U.N. resolutions. The rebels generally honored their cease-fire pledge, and the intensity of fighting in Angola decreased after September 21, but international sanctions took hold on September 25 as scheduled [S/26644, 10/27/93].

UNITA presented a new peace package on October 6, revised along the lines suggested by Beye but with significant qualifications. Although the rebels affirmed the "validity" of the peace accords and reiterated their "acceptance" of the election results, they claimed that the accords "should be updated" and that the election results were "fraudulent." UNITA supported the Abidjan Protocol "as a serious basis for negotiations" but only "took note" of the Security Council resolutions on Angola. The rebels also pledged to maintain the unilateral cease-fire and requested U.N. verification of it. Beye welcomed these statements but asked for clarification on UNITA's view of the U.N.'s resolutions. On the humanitarian front, the agreement of both sides to unimpeded access for U.N. relief personnel allowed the World Food Programme to double its deliveries of food aid between July and September and to reach the hardest hit populations for the first time. Nevertheless, the Secretary-General called his earlier announcement of 1,000 deaths a day in Angola a "conservative estimate" [ibid.].

UNITA's acceptance of the "general legal framework" of the peace process led to exploratory talks between government and rebel representatives, October 25–31, in the Angolan capital of Lusaka. Although the parties were unable to negotiate a cease-fire agreement by the Security Council's November 1 deadline, the Council agreed to postpone the threatened trade and travel restrictions on UNITA at the recommendation of the Secretary-General. In the course of the talks, UNITA identified the provisions of the peace accords it sought to update and explained that its characterization of the election results as "fraudulent" was "political in nature and without legal import." The rebels also gave their written acceptance of the "principle" of troop withdrawal from territory occupied since the resumption of fighting, as demanded by the Security Council.

Formal peace talks commenced November 15, and the parties adopted a seven-point agenda on November 19. As required by the first two agenda items, the government reaffirmed its acceptance of the peace accords and all relevant U.N. resolutions. The rebels agreed only to a compromise formulation put forward by Beye that held out the possibility of amending the accords and stated that Security Council resolutions were mandatory and enforceable. By early December the sides had reached agreement on the third agenda item covering military questions related to the implementation of the peace accords. On December 10 the parties adopted "general and specific principles" and a timetable to govern a renewed cease-fire; the withdrawal, concentration, and disarmament of UNITA forces; and the demobilization of government and rebel troops and armed civilians. The Secretary-General called agreement on these issues a "significant accomplishment" [S/26872, 12/14/93].

The Security Council welcomed these developments and again postponed the imposition of additional sanctions against UNITA. It agreed to extend UNAVEM's mandate through March 16, 1994, and supported the Secretary-General's contingency planning for a significantly expanded peacekeeping mission in the event of a breakthrough in the talks. The Council also urged both sides to "stop immediately all military actions" and agree to procedures for implementing the cease-fire they had agreed to in principle [S/Res/890, 12/15/93].

UNITA suspended its participation in the talks on December 13, however, charging that the government had attempted to kill Savimbi by bombarding the city of Cuito/Bie, where he was known to be meeting with his local military commanders. Based on a December 20 report from a U.N. fact-finding mission, which found "no credible and conclusive evidence" of such a plot, talks resumed the next day but were suspended again on December 23 by mutual agreement. Combat intensified along with preparations on both sides for further military action in the event the talks would fail. Despite the increase in military activity, the U.N.'s ability to deliver humanitarian relief and gain access to affected populations continued to improve through January 1994. The World Food Programme conducted regular airlifts to 23 locations (up from 13 in November), as well as the first deliveries by road to Malange and Cuito/Bie, though the total number of Angolans at risk increased by 300,000 to 3.3 million [S/1994/100, 1/29/94].

Under political pressure from the heads of neighboring states to continue negotiations, the parties resumed talks on January 5, 1994, and reached agreement by January 31 on the fourth agenda item, police matters. They also approved general principles related to the fifth item, national reconciliation, on February 17, but talks stalled on specific points, including UNITA's representation in senior government posts. The military situation remained "volatile" through early March, with fighting in the provinces of Bie, Huambo, and Malange disrupting humanitarian relief operations there. Nevertheless, the U.N. Department of Humanitarian Affairs was already looking forward to assisting the troop demobilization process and was emphasizing nonfood aid (health, nutrition, agriculture, water, and sanitation) in its appeal for an additional $179 million in Angolan relief through July 1994. The Secretary-General stated that the negotiations had taken a "decisive turn" with the agreement on police matters and were "proceeding toward the conclusion of a comprehensive peace agreement" [S/1994/282, 3/9/94].

Although the future mandate of the United Nations in Angola remained an outstanding agenda item in the talks, the Security Council extended UNAVEM's mandate through May 31 and expressed readiness "in principle" to authorize expanding the mission to its original size (475 military and police observers) upon the successful conclusion of negotiations. The Council urged the parties to conclude work on the other two items (national reconciliation and the completion of the electoral process) and reach a peaceful settlement "without procrastination." Reaffirming earlier decisions, the Council also demanded an immediate cessation of hostilities and unimpeded delivery of humanitarian assistance and declined to impose additional sanctions on UNITA for the duration of the talks [S/Res/903, 3/16/94].

The Secretary-General reported that by the end of March the parties had agreed to 12 of 18 specific principles relating to national reconciliation, including pardon and amnesty for UNITA supporters and freedoms of association, speech, and the press in postwar Angola [S/1994/611, 5/24/94]. But differences remained on the harder questions of troop withdrawal ("the reestablishment of state administration" throughout the country) and power sharing (UNITA's seating in the National Assembly and especially its "participation in the management of [S]tate affairs," i.e., the apportionment of senior government posts to rebel leaders). At the suggestion of Ambassador Beye, the parties went on to consider the sixth agenda item, completion of the electoral process, and on May 5 reached full agreement on it. By the end of May, the fifth and seventh items (national reconciliation and the future mandate of the United Nations) remained outstanding.

As talks dragged on, UNITA kept up its shelling of besieged cities and launched ambushes and small-scale attacks against government forces, mostly in the southern and central regions of the country. Both sides continued to reposition, reinforce, and resupply their troops, anticipating the failure of negotiations. The United Nations, on the other hand, accelerated its contingency planning for enlarging UNAVEM once a comprehensive agreement was reached.

Despite the fighting, U.N. humanitarian relief officials were able to evaluate emergency needs in several previously restricted areas. Ground access to affected populations remained difficult, however, due to poor roads and security concerns. The World Food Programme airdropped the required supplies in mid-April, the first time it had conducted such an operation in Angola. The Secretary-General also reported that donors had contributed only 27 percent of the $179 million in humanitarian assistance sought through July. He warned that delays in disbursing sufficient aid would hamper the U.N.'s ability to initiate demobilization, social reintegration, and mine clearance programs in the crucial period immediately following a final peace accord.

Intent on forcing a quick conclusion to the peace talks, the Security Council disregarded the Secretary-General's request for a three-month extension for UNAVEM and agreed to reauthorize the mission only through June 30. The Council promised to "reconsider the role of the United Nations in Angola" should the parties fail to reach agreement by that date and "strongly deplore[d]" the continued fighting and its effect on the humanitarian situation. While it again demanded an immediate cessation of hostilities and condemned restrictions on the movement of humanitarian relief and relief workers, the Council implied that the United Nations would maintain its presence in Angola as long as both sides continued to demonstrate the "political will" to achieve a lasting peace [S/Res/922, 5/31/94].

4. The Former Soviet Union
By Constantine V. Pleshakov

Armenia and Azerbaijan

The conflict between Armenia and Azerbaijan, which began in 1988 when both were part of the Soviet Union, has escalated since and resisted various international efforts at settling it. At issue originally was the status of Nagorno Karabakh, situated on Azerbaijan territory and populated largely by Armenians. By 1993, Armenian guerrilla warfare in "Karabakh" had ripened into direct confrontation between Armenia and Azerbaijan, now two sovereign states, and the fighting had spread outside the borders of Karabakh itself. Armenia and the leaders of "the Republic of Nagorno Karabakh," who are supported by Armenia with all the means at the disposal of the government in Yerevan, have been attempting to gain control over the **areas separating Nagorno Karabakh from Armenia.** It remains to be seen whether the final goal of these military operations is to build a corridor between the Armenian enclave and Armenia, to seize enough territory to exert strategic pressure on Azerbaijan if the conflict drags on for years without a settlement, or simply to force Azerbaijan to yield to Armenian demands for Karabakh's independence (and inevitable incorporation into the Armenian state).

Two southern neighbors with an interest in the outcome of the conflict between Armenia and Azerbaijan are **Turkey,** with ethnic kin in Azerbaijan and its own record of conflict with Armenians, and **Iran,** with an Azerbaijani minority of 20 million and thus a potentially explosive situation on its hands, and with links to post-Soviet Azerbaijan through a shared Shiism. **Russia,** for its part, is concerned that the conflict will inspire similar moves by **Muslim separatists** in its own northern Caucasus. Russia's leaders, not wanting to be accused of "imperialist intervention" in any form, tried to gain the West's acceptance of its role in the region. On January 3, 1993, then-U.S. President George Bush and Russian President Boris Yeltsin issued a joint statement calling for an immediate end to the bloodshed in Nagorno Karabakh and an early convocation of the "Minsk Group" of the Conference of Security and Cooperation in Europe (CSCE) [S/25148, 1/23/93]. A similar statement was issued by Yeltsin and French President François Mitterrand on March 16 [S/25499, 3/31/93].

Nineteen ninety-three brought significant victories for the Armenians, changing the geostrategic landscape of the Caucasus as well as undermining the stability of already shaky Azerbaijan. The first weeks of that year saw an Armenian offensive in southwestern Azerbaijan, and with it the flight of more than 20,000 Azerbaijanis into northern Iran [*The Christian Science Monitor*, 11/1/93]. That influx raised the anxiety level in Teheran, fearful that Iranian Azerbaijanis might be moved to demand revenge for the humiliation of independent Azerbaijan by Armenia. Driven by ethnic pressure from within, a sense of religious duty, and suspicion about Turkey's intentions in having already shaken Baku's hand, Iran lent reluctant support to Azerbaijan.

By this time the conflict between Armenia and Azerbaijan had become an international issue, attracting the rather permanent attention of the **U.N. Security Council** and of the **CSCE**, whose **Minsk Group** (Germany, the United States, Belarus, France, Italy, Russia, Sweden, the Czech Republic, and Turkey) was attempting to bring peace to the region. If, prior to 1993, the guilt for heightening tensions was often split between Yerevan and Baku, the new Armenian offensive brought a reassessment. On April 30, 1993, following the invasion of Azerbaijan's Kelbadjar district by Armenian-backed forces, the Security Council voted to demand the immediate cessation of all hostilities, withdrawal of all occupying forces from the Kelbadjar district and other areas of Azerbaijan, and the resumption of negotiations to resolve the conflict [S/Res/822].

The success of an offensive by Armenian forces in Karabakh in June led to Armenian control over the disputed enclave [*The New York Times*, 6/29/93], which precipitated a domestic crisis in Azerbaijan and brought a **coup d'état by the former Communist leader of Azerbaijan, Heydar Aliev**. The **ousting of elected President Abulfez Elchibey**, scapegoat for the military defeat, failed to alter the strategic balance in the area, however, and Azerbaijani troops retreated from Azerbaijan's southwestern region between Armenia and Karabakh once again [ibid., 8/24/93].

U.N. Security Council Resolution 853 of July 29, occasioned by the seizure of the Azerbaijani district of Agdam and the displacement of large numbers of civilians, reaffirmed the sovereignty and territorial integrity of the Azerbaijan Republic "and of all other States in the region." Reaffirming too the inviolability of international borders and the inadmissibility of the use of force to acquire territory, the Security Council condemned outright the seizure of Agdam and other areas occupied by Armenia, endorsed the efforts of the Minsk Group, and urged the Armenian government to exert its influence over the Armenians of Nagorno Karabakh in bringing about their compliance with April's Resolution 822 [S/Res/853].

In August, Armenian-backed forces launched yet another successful offensive against the southwestern areas of Azerbaijan, capturing the towns of Fizuli and Djebrail, among others [S/26381, 8/30/93]. The war had now spread to the triangle between Karabakh, Armenia, and Iran. According to Azerbaijani sources, 17 percent of Azerbaijan's territory was occupied by this time, and 1 million people had become refugees. The Armenian side seemed unconcerned about the international efforts to terminate the conflict—and, in fact, conducted the August offensive even as the Minsk Group was meeting in Rome [S/26382, 8/30/93].

The **large numbers of refugees** now gathered along the **Azerbaijan-Iran frontier** caused a good deal of concern in Iran, which demanded from Armenia agreement to a cease-fire and a withdrawal of Armenian-backed forces to internationally recognized borders [S/26387, 8/31/93]. The Armenian side countered that Nagorno Karabakh (which it referred to as the **"Nagorno Karabakh Republic"**) was subject to military attacks and blockades by Azerbaijani forces and that "any action in response by the Defense Force of Nagorno Karabakh meets with severe condemnation by the United Nations" [S/26386, 8/31/93]. It seemed to be saying that the U.N.'s negative attitude toward the violent secession of Nagorno Karabakh from Azerbaijan supplied part of the justification for the Armenian offensive against Azerbaijan. And despite Yerevan's references to the "Nagorno Karabakh Republic," Armenia actually looked upon the enclave as an area in which to extend its territory and raise its own flag.

On August 31, 1993, the authorities of Azerbaijan and Nagorno Karabakh, after mediation efforts by the Russian Federation, did reach agreement on a cease-fire [S/26394, 9/1/93], and "Nagorno Karabakh" announced the withdrawal of its forces from the Kubatli region "at the request of the President of the Republic of Armenia" [S/26408, 9/7/93], Armenia having denied any direct involvement in the fighting. The European Community (soon to be European Union) now made clear that it regarded the so-called "Republic of Nagorno Karabakh" as a mere projection of Armenian might [S/26417, 9/8/93].

Armenian President Levon Ter-Petrosyan visited Moscow on September 15, where he reportedly failed to get a sympathetic hearing: The Russian side echoed Azerbaijani statements that thousands of civilians were being victimized and forced to flee [*The Christian Science Monitor*, 9/21/93]. Not many days earlier, Turkish Prime Minister Tansu Ciller had paid a call on Russian President Yeltsin and Prime Minister Victor S. Chernomyrdin to discuss the situation in the Caucasus [*The New York Times*, 9/10/93], a visit that coincided with the arrival in Moscow of Azerbaijan's President Aliyev. Aliyev had come to request Russian mediation of the conflict and to demonstrate his willingness to tilt toward Russia, casting off the anti-Russian prejudices of his predecessor. And, indeed, on September 20, Azerbaijan's parliament voted to rejoin the Commonwealth of Independent States (CIS), which Russia regarded as the only—if not yet efficient—international framework available for organizing cooperation among the former Soviet republics.

On October 1, 1993, Mario Raffaelli, Chairman of the CSCE Conference on Nagorno Karabakh, reported to the President of the U.N. Security Council on the status of the Minsk Group's efforts at settling the conflict. The Group had held unofficial consultations in Moscow from September 9 to 11 and again in Paris from September 22 to 28; and, at its instigation, the parties to the conflict had met face to face in Moscow. As a result, the cease-fire was extended from August 31 to October 5. To keep the peace process going, the Minsk Group believed, it was urgent to implement Security Council Resolutions 822 [4/30/93] and 853 [8/29/93] calling for withdrawal from recently occupied territories and a permanent cessation of all military activities [S/26522, 10/1/93], and it made public an **"Adjusted Timetable of urgent steps to implement United Nations Security Council resolutions 822 and 853."**

On October 10, while Armenia and Azerbaijan were discussing the "Timetable," Armenian-based forces launched a new attack on the Djebrail district of Azerbaijan [S/26575, 10/13/93], which helped to strengthen their military position. These brought a strong reaction from several nations, among them Russia, which both Armenia and Azerbaijan saw as a major candidate for the role of mediator [*The New York Times*, 10/26/93]. Security Council Resolution 874 of October 14 reaffirmed the sovereignty and territorial integrity of Azerbaijan and the inviolability of international borders, and it welcomed the "timetable" introduced by the Minsk Group.

Meanwhile Azerbaijan, in a desperate attempt to strengthen its armed forces, had begun **hiring Afghan *mojahedin*** to fight against Armenia in the zone of the latest offensive [*The Christian Science Monitor*, 11/16/93]. On October 23 came a new Armenian offensive, during which Armenian troops occupied a number of Azerbaijani settlements and reached the frontier between Azerbaijan and Iran. The President of Azerbaijan requested an urgent meeting of the Security Council [S/26647, 10/27/93], and Armenia's southern neighbors, Turkey and Iran, expressed their anger at the internationalization of the conflict.

On November 9, the Minsk Group vigorously condemned the behavior of "the parties" to the recent hostilities and requested the withdrawal of occupying Armenian forces from the city of Goradiz and the Zangelan district and the immediate restoration of the cease-fire [S/26718,

11/10/93]. The European Union, issuing a statement on the same date, stressed the importance it attaches to the territorial integrity and sovereignty of the Republic of Azerbaijan [S/26728, 11/12/93]. Security Council Resolution 884 of November 12 expressed "alarm" at the Armenian occupation of these two areas and repeated the major points of Resolution 874, issued a month previously. Russian-mediated talks between the Armenian and Azerbaijani Presidents at a meeting of the heads of state of the CIS, held in Ashkhabad on December 24, also failed to influence the situation. A U.N. General Assembly resolution on "Emergency international assistance to refugees and displaced persons in Azerbaijan," bearing a December date, calls attention to the "acute problems" now facing those who had fled their homes and appeals to member states and U.N. bodies for help in alleviating a situation that "has continued to deteriorate seriously" [A/Res/48/114].

On December 26 the Armenian offensive resumed, and the two sides remained locked in combat throughout the early months of 1994. In February the Azerbaijanis claimed that 20 percent of their territory was under Armenian occupation and was the object of "ethnic cleansing" [S/1994/155, 2/11/94]. Although **a shaky cease-fire was introduced on March 1,** all attempts to mediate the dispute itself have failed, including talks involving the Ministers of Defense of Azerbaijan, Armenia, and Russia.

Tajikistan

The same political and intraregional disputes that launched a civil war in Tajikistan in 1992 are causing unrest today, a year and a half after the fighting ended. Among those with a stake in the settlement of these disputes are **Afghanistan** (with ties to the opposition coalition, which includes both Islamic and democratic groups), **Russia,** and the **other Central Asian republics.** Tajikistan has the highest proportion of Muslims of all the former Soviet republics in the region, and the Central Asian group continues to fear that Tajikistan, with considerable help from Afghanistan, could provide a gateway for Islamic fundamentalism. Moscow is also wary of such a development, believing that Islamic fundamentalism would pose a threat to Russians who make their home in Central Asia and a geopolitical threat to the Russian Federation itself.

This **view of the Tajik-Afghan border as a frontier between stability and instability** is what led to Moscow's intervention in 1992 on behalf of a politically conservative, anti-Islamic faction in Tajikistan. Although Moscow (with the participation of **Uzbekistan**) did manage to bring the critical stage of the civil war under control through political and military intervention, it could not impose a political settlement on rival factions. By early 1993, the conservative Tajik government, which proved unwilling to enter into serious negotiations with the Islamic opposition (now with headquarters in Afghanistan), had begun to irritate the Russians. Moscow had hoped to assume the role of peacemaker—a neutral party with no direct connection to the central government in Tajikistan—and in this way enhance its maneuverability as it sought to maintain stability in the region. It had also hoped that some of the Central Asian republics would share the political—and, if possible, the military—burden of keeping Tajikistan out of the Islamic fundamentalist orbit.

When the fighting in Tajikistan came to an end late in 1992, conditions in the Republic were such that **the United Nations launched an Urgent Preliminary Appeal** for $20.4 million in humanitarian assistance [U.N. press release IHA/470, 1/11/93], and the U.N. Secretary-General appointed a **Special Envoy for Tajikistan,** naming **Ismat Kittani.** On August 16 the Security Council extended Kittani's three-month mandate for three more months, until October 31, and on August 24, the Council made its first appeal to the Tajik government to "accept as soon as possible the need for an overall political solution," including a cease-fire and national reconciliation [*Far Eastern Economic Review,* 9/16/93].

Kittani spent the period August 17–26 visiting Pakistan, Tajikistan, Iran, and Afghanistan. In Kabul he met various Afghan leaders as well as leaders of the Tajik opposition. **Emomali Rakhmonov, Chairman of the Supreme Council of the Republic of Tajikistan,** visited Kabul too in an attempt to reduce tension along the Tajik-Afghan border [S/26744, 11/15/93].

By the fall of 1993 the conflict in Tajikistan had taken the lives of some 50,000 people and rendered another 500,000 homeless. At least 90,000 Tajiks fled to Afghanistan during the critical stage of civil war in 1992, and another 486,000 were classified as displaced persons [*The Christian Science Monitor,* 8/3/93]. Now, months after the large-scale fighting had ended, Russia continued its support of the government in Dushanbe, and the **20,000 Russian troops remaining in the Republic** were given the job of preventing the entry of fighters, weapons, and drugs from Afghanistan [*The New York Times,* 10/13/93]. On July 13, 25 Russian troops guarding the border were killed by Tajik Islamic fundamentalists. There was a public outcry in Russia and concern about the cost to the Russian Federation of supporting the central government in Dushanbe.

On August 9, meeting in Moscow with the leaders of Central Asia, Russian President Yeltsin said that his government supported a political solution to the Tajikistan civil war. The Tajik opposition, however, regarded the policy of Russia (and Uzbekistan) as supporting an unpopular government by force of arms and eliminating any possibility that the opposition forces could win a popular election [*Far Eastern Economic Review,* 9/16/93]. Reportedly, Yeltsin did urge Chairman Rakhmonov to "establish direct dialogue with the opposition, with all its elements" [*The New York Times,* 8/8/93].

During the 48th General Assembly in 1993 the **Secretary-General** discussed the problem of Tajikistan with, among others interested in the situation, Tajikistan's Rakhmonov and Uzbeki President Islam A. Karimov and had an exchange of correspondence with President Burhanuddin Rabbani of Afghanistan. Reporting to the Security Council, Boutros-Ghali stressed that the current situation in Tajikistan, especially on the Tajik-Afghan border, gave grounds for serious concern. Fighting between opposing factions was intensifying once again; incursions across the Afghan border by armed opposition groups brought daily clashes between the guerrillas and government and CIS forces; fighting inside the country (especially in Khatlon and Gorno-Badakhshan) was on the upsurge too; and economic life had come to a halt in many areas. In late fall the U.N. Secretary-General decided to extend the mandate of Special Envoy Kittani until March 31, 1994 [S/26743, 11/14/93].

For most of this period not a single Central Asian republic—not even Uzbekistan, despite its deep political involvement in Tajikistan—had been willing to share the military burden with Russia. Now Moscow, faced with growing concern at home about current and future Russian casualties, made a concerted effort to "orientalize" the support of the central government in Dushanbe. On September 24, 1993, Kazakhstan, Kyrgyzstan, the Russian Federation, Tajikistan, and Uzbekistan agreed to establish a **collective peacekeeping force,** the purpose of which was to stabilize the situation in Tajikistan [S/26610, 10/21/93]. On March 14, 1994, Tajikistan asked the Security Council to confer U.N. peacekeeping status on the CIS forces (still mainly Russian) on its territory on the grounds that clashes on the Tajik-Afghan border threatened regional security [U.N. Daily Highlights, DH/1601, 3/14/94].

In June, with no letup in the pace of infiltration from Afghanistan or in the daily clashes between government forces and the opposition, two new dimensions of disarray emerged. Fighting between Uzbeks and Tajiks in both Tajikistan and Afghanistan was one of them. A campaign to assassinate Russian military personnel in Tajikistan was the other, and by June 15, seven Russian officers had been killed in Dushanbe alone [S/1994/715, 6/16/94]. The very deployment of the Russian 201st Motorized Rifle Division, even as a peacekeeping force deployed at the request of the Tajik government [*The New York Times*, 5/23/94], was causing unease in Ankara, which saw the Russian presence as a challenge to Ankara's influence in the post-Soviet Turkic states [ibid., 6/19/94].

The first meeting of a new **"Joint Commission"** on problems relating to refugees and displaced persons from Tajikistan was held in Moscow on June 1. The Commission, under the chairmanship of the Office of the U.N. High Commissioner for Refugees, worked out its rules of procedure and identified three objectives for future activities: enumeration and registration of the Tajik refugees, the provision of humanitarian assistance, and cooperation with the immigration services of the CIS and other states [S/ 1994/716, 6/16/94].

In mid-May 1994, preparing for a second round of inter-Tajik talks, Ambassador **Ramiro Piriz-Ballon, the current Special Envoy of the U.N. Secretary-General,** had visited Teheran for consultations with the leaders of the Tajik opposition and Iranian authorities. U.N. Under-Secretary-General for Political Affairs Marrack Goulding spent May 27–28 in Dushanbe discussing the preparations for these inter-Tajik talks with the Tajik leadership. A cessation of hostilities was the goal of this second round of talks, beginning in Teheran on June 18, and the Secretary-General extended until the end of September the mandate of his Special Envoy and of the group of U.N. officials currently in Tajikistan [*ibid.*].

Georgia

During the Soviet era, **Abkhazia** was an autonomous republic within Georgia, and the **Abkhaz themselves were only a minority in their own republic.** It was for the reason of small numbers and little power that, when the Abkhaz secessionist struggle chalked up some successes, observers began to suspect that the insurgents were receiving military support from Russia.

Fighting broke out in Abkhazia in August 1992 and quickly became an international issue, largely due to the international reputation of **Georgian President Eduard Shevardnadze,** Foreign Minister of the Soviet Union under the presidency of Mikhail Gorbachev and a firm opponent of Abkhaz secession. In September 1992 and again in October, the **U.N. Secretary-General** dispatched a U.N. fact-finding mission to Georgia and Abkhazia. After the second mission, with Security Council endorsement, two U.N. staff remained in Georgia to supply the initial U.N. presence, and early in 1993 the Department of Humanitarian Affairs organized a U.N. interagency mission that visited every area of Georgia. At the end of March 1993 the **United Nations issued a consolidated appeal** for $21 million to cover the needs of the affected population in Abkhazia, in government-controlled areas of Georgia, and to a small extent, in **South Ossetia** (where a relatively minor separatist movement was also making itself felt). In May 1993 the Secretary-General appointed **Edouard Brunner** as his **Special Envoy to Georgia** with a mandate to revive the peace process [Secretary-General Boutros-Ghali, *Report on the Work of the Organization,* 9/ 93, pp. 115–16].

The situation in Georgia was very complicated, and remains so. Those with an insider's knowledge of the Russian military establishment maintain that the Abkhaz bid for secession *did* have the **support of the Russian military, working independently of the Yeltsin administration,** and that the chaotic situation in Russia allowed for such a decentralized political arrangement. According to this hypothesis, the military gave its assistance to the Abkhaz insurgents for the purpose of defeating Shevardnadze, who the new nationalists consider one of the "traitors of the USSR." And it might be added that during September 1993, President Yeltsin, preparing to disband the Russian parliament and badly needing the support of the military, could easily have taken a laissez-faire attitude toward the Abkhaz issue. To make things worse for Shevardnadze, his predecessor—the **deposed (but duly elected) President of Georgia, Zviad Gamsakhurdia**—had been able to **retain a power base in Western Georgia.** Thus the central government in Tbilisi was confronted by two threats simultaneously: the Abkhaz secession and civil war.

(Several attempts had already been made to bring the fighting in Abkhazia to an end. Early on Russia had declared its intention to mediate any conflict that might develop on its borders; and at a meeting in Moscow on September 3, 1992, the Republic of Georgia, the leadership of Abkhazia, and the Russian Federation reached agreement on the terms of a cease-fire, which stipulated that "the territorial integrity of the Republic of Georgia shall be ensured." The agreement was never fully implemented and on October 1, 1992, collapsed entirely.)

On July 9, 1993, the Security Council adopted Resolution 849 requesting the Secretary-General to send his Special Envoy to the region to assist in reaching agreement on the implementation of a cease-fire and to prepare to dispatch 50 military observers to Georgia once it had been implemented. A **cease-fire agreement,** mediated by the personal representative of the President of Russia, Boris Pastukhov, was signed on **July 27, 1993,** by the Georgian and Abkhaz sides. **Russia pledged to act as guarantor** of the peace between the two.

On August 6, 1993, the Security Council welcomed the signing of the agreement and approved the Secretary-General's proposal to deploy a team of up to ten U.N. military observers to the region as soon as possible [S/Res/854]. Resolution 858 of August 24 established the **U.N. Observer Mission in Georgia (UNOMIG).**

On September 15, forces loyal to deposed President Gamsakhurdia began a new offensive in **Mingrelia in the western area of Georgia** and on September 16 the Abkhaz separatists violated the Russian-guaranteed cease-fire of July 27.

Independent observers are certain that during this last, victorious leg of the war, the Abkhaz separatists were supported not only by some elements of the Russian military but also by **Cossack mercenaries and Muslim paramilitary units from the Russian northern Caucasus** [*The New York Times*, 10/3/93]. The measure of the **Moscow establishment's involvement** in this stage of war in Abkhazia remains unknown, however, and the Russian Foreign Ministry categorically denies that the Russian Federation and its armed forces had any role, on either side, in the bloody clashes in Abkhazia in September 1993 [*The New York Times*, 9/28/93].

The siege of Sukhumi, capital of the former autonomous republic, lasted from September 16 to September 27. Though Shevardnadze himself led the defense of the city, the Abkhaz separatists prevailed, Sukhumi fell, and by the end of September, Abkhaz separatists had routed Georgian government soldiers from the last corner of Abkhazia [*The New York Times*, 10/1/93].

In **mid-October,** after the defeat of government troops in Abkhazia and when the supporters of Gamsakhurdia had begun an ultimately successful offensive, **Shevardnadze appealed to Moscow for help,** at least against these "Zviadists." The Russian Army had not been directly involved previously in the fighting against the deposed President's forces (although there were occasional clashes [*The New York Times*, 11/2/93]), but it now helped the government troops regain control over communications in the western areas of Georgia captured by the Zviadists. By the end of October the government troops had entered the rebel stronghold and were beginning to gain control of the situation everywhere in Georgia but the province of Abkhazia. In March 1994, Shevardnadze publicly acknowledged the role Russian troops had played in supporting his government troops during the insurgency of deposed President Gamsakhurdia [*The New York Times*, 3/6/94].

Throughout the fall of 1993 the United Nations gave its firm support to Shevardnadze and, reserving judgment about the nature of the Russian involvement in the Abkhaz conflict, referred to Russia as a mediator between the parties. On September 17 the Security Council expressed extreme concern at the renewed outbreak of fighting in Abkhazia, mentioning attacks by the Abkhaz forces on the towns of Sukhumi and Ochamchira, and "demanded" that the Abkhaz leadership end the hostilities immediately and withdraw all its forces to the cease-fire lines agreed upon the previous July [S/PV.3279, 9/17/93]. A month later, on October 19, the Council adopted a resolution expressing extreme concern about the situation in Abkhazia, affirming the sovereignty and territorial integrity of the Republic of Georgia, and strongly condemning the grave violation of the July cease-fire agreement by the Abkhaz side [S/Res/876].

Security Council Resolution 881 of November 4 welcomed the **efforts of the Secretary-General and his Special Envoy, in cooperation with the Conference on Security and Cooperation in Europe (CSCE) and the Russian Federation,** to "carry forward" the peace process with the aim of achieving an overall political settlement. On December 23 the General Assembly decided, "on an exceptional basis," to authorize the Secretary-General to spend a designated sum on UNOMIG, "should the Security Council extend the mandate beyond 31 January 1994" [A/Res/48/475].

By the winter of 1993, Russia had begun to take a more active role in terminating the conflict in Abkhazia. After all, despite the benefits Moscow might derive from better relations with the nationalist military, the Georgian cause did have the support of the United Nations; and Moscow had begun to realize that Georgia is the Russian Federation's only ally in the Caucasus against the Muslim separatists in the Russian northern Caucusus, for both nations faced the same threat of separatist movements.

Collaborative efforts between the United Nations and the Russian Federation finally bore fruit, and on **December 1** the Georgians and Abkhazians signed a **Memorandum of Understanding.** In Resolution 892, adopted on December 22, the Security Council welcomed the signing of the Memorandum and authorized the **phased deployment of up to 50 additional U.N. military observers** to UNOMIG, as recommended by the Secretary-General.

On January 31, 1994, the Security Council adopted Resolution 896 welcoming the progress of the second round of peace negotiations between the Georgian and Abkhaz sides, stressing the role of the Russian Federation as facilitator, and urging the parties to demonstrate a greater willingness to reach a comprehensive political settlement.

On March 4 the Security Council extended the mandate of UNOMIG until March 31 [S/Res/901; U.N. press release SC/5801, 3/4/94]. Shevardnadze had a meeting with U.S. President Bill Clinton three days later and, hoping to reduce the Russian presence in the Caucusus (and Russian influence on the Georgian domestic political scene), asked the United States to contribute to a peacekeeping force that would help to end Georgia's civil war [*The New York Times*, 3/8/94]. The *Times* commented that this was the last thing the U.S. President wanted to hear from Shevardnadze. Meeting on March 25, the Security Council extended UNOMIG's mandate until June 30 [S/Res/906]. (By May the number of military observers stood at 22 [S/1994/529, 5/3/94].) In mid-June the Secretary-General recommended a further extention of UNOMIG's mandate through July 31 [S/1994/725, 6/16/94].

Meanwhile, the **U.N.-sponsored Georgian-Abkhaz peace negotiations** continued in Geneva, New York, and Moscow, facilitated by Moscow and with the participation of representatives of the CSCE and the U.N. High Commissioner for Refugees. On April 4, 1994, the Georgian and Abkhaz sides signed a **"Declaration on measures for a political settlement of the Georgian/Abkhaz conflict"** and committed themselves to the non-use of force or threat of the use of force, establishing a "strict formal cease-fire." They requested the early deployment of a U.N. peacekeeping operation, whose peacekeeping forces would include a Russian military contingent. According to the Declaration, Abkhazia would have its own constitution and "legislation." The actual "distribution of powers" will be part of a more comprehensive settlement, which must await a "final solution to the conflict." (The Security Council did not commit itself to supplying such forces, merely stating that it supports a further increase in the deployed strength of UNOMIG if the Secretary-General believes that conditions on the ground make it appropriate [S/PRST/1994/17, 4/8/94].) Along with the Declaration, the two sides signed an agreement on the voluntary return of refugees and displaced persons.

Negotiations on the establishment of a U.N. peacekeeping operation between the Georgian and Abkhaz sides were held in Geneva, April 12–15, under the chairmanship of the U.N. Secretary-General's Special Envoy and in the presence of representatives of the U.N. Secretariat, the Russian Federation, and the CSCE. The Russian Federation indicated its readiness to deploy an advance contingent of a U.N. force in the area of conflict, although the parties continued to disagree on a number of key issues relating to the cease-fire, the security zone, and the nature of U.N. deployments in the zone and throughout Abkhazia [S/1994/529, 5/3/94].

The formal signing of an **Agreement on a Cease-Fire and Separation of Forces** between Georgia and Abkhazia took place in Moscow on May 14 as representatives of the United Nations, the Russian Federation, and the CSCE looked on. The agreement creates a 24-kilometer-wide security zone on both sides of the Inguri River and bars all armed forces and heavy military equipment from that zone. Heavy military equipment would also be barred from a restricted-weapons zone in the area right outside the security zone. A peacekeeping force of the Commonwealth of Independent States (CIS) and the U.N.'s military observers would be deployed in the security zone to monitor compliance with the agreement, investigate violations, and work toward the resettlement of refugees and displaced persons—requiring the Security Council to broaden the observers' present mandate. Meanwhile and until a political agreement has been signed and sealed, a **Georgian-Abkhaz Coordinating Commission** will discuss practical matters of mutual interest, such as energy, transport, communications, and ecology [S/1994/583, 5/17/94].

In meetings between the U.N. Secretariat and representatives of Russia and the Georgia and Abkhaz sides during May and June it was noted that under any such plan the CIS peacekeeping force would function as a "separate and independent operation" under its own command but would coordinate its actions with the U.N. military observers [S/1994/529/Add.1, 6/6/94]. On June 6, the Secretary-General recommended that the strength of UNOMIG be increased to about 150 observers (with appropriate support staff) to fulfill the role the United Nations was assigned in the May cease-fire agreement, that the UNOMIG forces be increased to 55 as a first step (to be taken in consultation with the parties), and that the Security Council give speedy consideration to the recommendation [ibid.].

A continuing problem was the makeup of the CIS peacekeeping

force in the security zone. There seemed to be no practical alternative to a large Russian contingent, but the prospect caused apprehension among former Soviet republics. Some believed that the Security Council was likely to "take note of" Russia's intention to send in peacekeepers rather than to "authorize" it [*The New York Times*, 5/27/94].

The actual reintegration of Abkhazia into Georgia has yet to begin, and the fighting—though formally terminated—could escalate once again, with or without the participation of other groups or countries. As for the civil war, it seems to have been halted, at least for a time, by **the defeat of the Zviadists** in western Georgia and the **suicide of Zviad Gamsakhurdia** himself.

5. The Middle East and the Persian Gulf
By Jules Kagian

Iraq

Iraq's formal acceptance in November 1993 of Security Council Resolution 715 (October 1991), which calls for long-term monitoring of its industries with potential military use, was hailed as a "breakthrough" by Swedish diplomat Rolf Ekeus, Head of the U.N. Special Commission charged with overseeing the elimination of Iraq's capacity to produce weapons of mass destruction. Ekeus described this acceptance as an important development relating to the implementation of the cease-fire resolution [S/Res/687 (April 1991)], which calls for, among other things, the dismantling of Iraq's weapons of mass destruction [*The New York Times*, 11/27/93]. Iraq informed the Security Council of its decision in a letter delivered November 26 to the Council's President. "I should like to inform you of the decision of the Government of Iraq to accept the obligations stated in Resolution 715 (1991)," wrote Foreign Minister Mohammed Said al-Sahaf, "and to comply with the provisions of the plans for monitoring and verification in accordance with said resolution."

Specifically, Resolution 715 calls for Iraq to provide a full inventory of plants and other sites with the potential for making weapons of mass destruction, as well as all machinery, chemicals, and other materials that might be devoted to such activity, including "dual capability plans"—that is, facilities used for permitted purposes but which could be used for prohibited purposes. Under the terms of the resolution, U.N. inspectors are empowered to travel anywhere within Iraq and to enter any area they choose.

Following high-level talks in Baghdad in February 1994, a joint statement was issued by Iraq's Deputy Prime Minister, Tariq Aziz, and Ambassador Ekeus. The two sides expressed their readiness to expedite the process of establishing ongoing monitoring and verification in a spirit of goodwill in order to achieve their joint objective, namely, for the Commission and the **International Atomic Energy Agency (IAEA)** to report to the Security Council at the earliest feasible time that Iraq had taken all the actions called for by **paragraph 22** of Security Council Resolution 687. The significance of the paragraph is that it stipulates that the **ban on foreign purchases of Iraqi oil** "shall have no further force or effect" once the Security Council is satisfied that Baghdad has fully complied with its obligation to give up its weapons of mass destruction and agreed to the long-term monitoring regime. The United Nations approved the oil embargo on August 6, 1990, as part of a larger package of economic sanctions that also barred Iraq from importing other goods.

The Security Council in Resolutions 706 (August 1991) and 712 (September 1991) did authorize Iraq to sell $1.6 billion in oil, with the proceeds to be put in an escrow account and used for U.N. activities in Iraq and for the purchase of foodstuffs, medicines, and other civilian necessities. The United Nations would monitor the sale of the oil as well as the equitable distribution of the supplies among the population—including the Kurds. Iraq, however, has always asserted that U.N. monitoring of its limited oil sales was too intrusive, and has refused to sell oil under such conditions.

In his most recent report on the status of the implementation of the plan for the ongoing monitoring and verification of Iraq's compliance [S/1994/489], the Secretary-General noted that during the latest round of high-level talks between the Commission and Iraq, held in New York in March 1994, Iraq expressed a **lack of confidence in the impartiality of the Commission** and implied that, unless the Special Commission reported immediately under paragraph 22 of Resolution 687, cooperation might be withdrawn. In light of these statements, the Commission viewed with great concern an incident in which a crowd threw stones at one of its helicopters as it was taking on board two injured soldiers from the U.N. Guards Contingent for medical evacuation. Baghdad was reminded that it is required to ensure the safety and security of Special Commission personnel and property. Iraq's failure to provide adequate security was strongly protested by the Commission to Iraqi authorities in both Baghdad and New York.

In response, the Iraqi government has strongly denied any involvement in the attack. The Commission has noted Iraq's assurances that this incident should not be seen as being in any way politically motivated and that the government was taking steps to prevent similar incidents from occurring. Notwithstanding this incident, Rolf Ekeus believes that Iraq is finally on the right track toward compliance with U.N. resolutions demanding both the elimination of all weapons of mass destruction and the perpetual inspections to ensure that these weapons are not amassed again.

Diplomats have said that even if Iraq receives positive and final certification from the Special Commission, there is no likelihood of an immediate lifting of the embargo on oil [*The Washington Post*, 11/27/93]. The **Gulf allies appear to differ on how to deal with Iraq.** For example, **France** favors a narrow reading of Resolution 687 that would assess Iraq's compliance only on arms-related matters. But **Britain** and the **United States** keep open the possibility of requiring Iraq to improve its human rights performance and to formally recognize the U.N.-delineated Iraq-Kuwait border. At the sanctions review in March, Deputy Prime Minister Tariq Aziz demanded an immediate relaxation, warning that otherwise Iraq may "reassess its position and act in a manner that protects the people of Iraq against the harm to which it is being subjected" [*The New York Times*, 4/15/94].

At that review, the U.S. Representative to the United Nations, Madeleine Albright, reported that President Saddam Hussein was moving new troops north toward the Kurdish areas he is already blockading in possible preparation for an attack. But the tough warning to President Hussein to keep his hands off the Kurdish safe haven came at a time of growing divisions within the Security Council over easing the embargo, as members contemplated the prospect of winning new and lucrative Iraqi contracts.

The March 1994 sanctions review by the Security Council, its eighteenth, was the first at which the Security Council failed to issue a statement of its conclusion—this because members were so divided over whether to say a positive word about Iraq for its cooperation with Rolf Ekeus [*Middle East International*, 4/1/94]. Ekeus himself concedes that a strictly legal reading of the weapons resolution suggests that the oil embargo should be lifted when the job is done. He has long told Iraq that weapons cooperation is the surest ticket to renewed oil sales [*The Christian Science Monitor*, 4/27/94]. However, he believes that before the embargo is lifted, any longterm weapons monitoring mechanism should be in operation for six months or more to be sure that it works and to establish that Iraqi cooperation will continue. The decision on when to lift the embargo, however, is a political one for the Security Council alone to make, he says [ibid.]. But sanctions against Iraq constitute a basic component of the Clinton administration's policy of isolating the Iraqi government of President Hussein. Washington believes that as long as sanctions are in place, Iraq's ability to rearm itself substantially is limited.

U.S. Secretary of State Warren Christopher assured Arab Gulf States during his trip to the region in late April that **maintaining sanctions was vital to press Iraq to comply with all U.N. resolutions**—a position clarified in an article written by Mr. Christopher for *The New York Times* [4/29/94]. His views contradict Iraq's expectations that full implementation of Security Council resolutions relating to armaments should pave the way to lifting the oil embargo. Writing that the international community must continue to insist that Iraq meet all its obligations, Mr. Christopher said that Iraq is not in compliance with any of the obligations the Security Council imposed at the end of the Gulf War—not even those it accepted as a condition of the cease-fire. It remains to be seen whether this position will eventually lead to U.S. confrontation with China, France, and Russia, which have indicated that the oil embargo should be eased because Iraq has made sufficient progress in eliminating its weapons of mass destruction.

In another development, **the United States has accepted Jordan's request for land-based inspection of cargo** destined for Iraq via the Jordanian port of Aqaba rather than sea-based inspections, which Jordan said were hurting its economy. This removed a major stumbling block to Jordan's full participation in Middle East talks with Israel, which King Hussein had threatened not to resume unless the marine blockade on Aqaba is lifted.

The downing of two American helicopters by friendly fire in northern Iraq on April 14, 1994, killing 26 people, refocused world attention on **Operation Provide Comfort,** which was initiated in April 1991 shortly after the Gulf War when Iraqi forces used brutal measures to put down an uprising by Kurds in the north [for background, see *A Global Agenda: Issues/ 48*]. Kurds fled to the mountainous border with Turkey and into Iran; and world outrage caused the United States, France, and Britain to step in. A no-fly zone prohibiting Iraqi flights was established above the 36th parallel. Consequently, Kurds were able to return to their homes. Six months later a similar no-fly zone was established south of the 32nd parallel to protect Shiite Muslims.

The United Nations reacted swiftly to the downing of the two helicopters. A U.N. spokesman stated that they were neither on a U.N. mission nor acting under U.N. authority. He added that the missions in northern Iraq fall under the jurisdiction of a military coordination center established by Operation Provide Comfort, which is a joint effort of the United States, Britain, France, and Turkey [*Financial Times*, 4/15/94]. The confusion regarding this effort on behalf of the Kurds arises from **conflicting interpretations of Resolution 688** (April 1991), which was adopted following attacks by the Iraqi army against the Kurds. Unlike most resolutions adopted against Iraq, Resolution 688 was not adopted under Chapter VII of the Charter (which provides for enforcement measures) because China threatened to use the veto. Furthermore, the resolution does not refer to an air-exclusion zone or military measures. A number of legal experts, including the U.N. Legal Department, hold the view that the resolution is not enforceable. However, the United States and its allies maintain that the no-fly zones permit the monitoring of Iraq's compliance with Security Council Resolutions 687 and 688.

The **Special Rapporteur of the U.N. Commission on Human Rights, Max van der Stoel,** reported in November 1993 [A/48/600] on Iraq's repression of civilian populations, devoting most of the report to Iraq's Marsh Arabs in the south. The Special Rapporteur previously addressed the situation in the marsh area in his report to the General Assembly at its 47th Session and to the Commission on Human Rights at its 49th session. His initial alarm related to reports of military attacks on civilian settlements, forced relocation of the indigenous tribal people, and the imposition of an effective internal economic environment through the drainage and destruction of the marshes. While the Special Rapporteur has received reports and specific allegations of summary and arbitrary executions within the marsh area, the most consistent violations of the right to life are said to stem from the continuing bombardment of civilian settlements, resulting in the death of large numbers of people, including women, children, and the elderly. The Special Rapporteur indicated that despite the imposition at the end of August 1992 of a no-fly zone against Iraqi aircraft flying south of the 32nd parallel, allegations indicate continuing and even intensifying assaults by means of ground-to-ground artillery. The Special Rapporteur concluded that **Iraq is in violation of Resolution 688.**

Iraq's **Ambassador to the United Nations, Nizar Hamdoon,** presented his government's rebuttal in a special report to the General Assembly [A/48/875]. In December 1993 the General Assembly adopted the Special Rapporteur's report and **expressed its strong condemnation of the massive violations of human rights** for which the government of Iraq is responsible. The General Assembly called on Iraq to allow unhindered access of U.N. humanitarian agencies throughout the country, including ensuring the safety of U.N. personnel and humanitarian workers through the continued implementation of the Memorandum of Understanding signed by the United Nations and the government of Iraq. On April 14 the United States, Britain, and France warned President Saddam Hussein that he faces "serious consequences" if his forces fire at or otherwise harass military reconnaissance convoys they plan to resume in northern Iraq [*The New York Times*, 4/15/94].

Iraq still has not met its obligations **concerning Kuwait's and third-country nationals it detained during the war,** and it has refused to cooperate fully with the International Committee of the Red Cross as required by Security Council Resolution 687, although it has received more than 600 files on missing individuals.

Acting on the Secretary-General's report [S/26520], the Security Council agreed in October 1993 **to maintain for a further six-month period the U.N. Iraq-Kuwait Observation Mission (UNIKOM).** The observer unit, to take position in the demilitarized zone (DMZ) along the Iraq-Kuwait border, was established by Security Council Resolution 689 of

April 1991 to monitor the Khawr Abd Allah waterway, to deter violations of the boundary, and to observe any potentially hostile action mounted from the territory of one state into the other. The authorized strength of the unit is 300; and in 1993–94 it continued to provide technical support to other U.N. missions in Iraq and Kuwait, such as the **U.N. Iraq-Kuwait Boundary Demarcation Commission** and the **U.N. Coordinator for the Return of Property from Iraq to Kuwait.** UNIKOM also provides movement control in respect to all U.N. aircraft operating in the area. The Secretary-General noted to the Security Council that the UNIKOM area of operations has been calm during the six months covered by his report. He cautioned, however, that the **present calm along the Iraq-Kuwait border should not obscure the fact that tensions persist** and full peace has yet to be restored to the area. The government of Kuwait has decided to defray two-thirds of the UNIKOM budget, which will considerably ease the burden on member states of maintaining the mission.

By adopting Resolution 833 on May 27, 1993, the Security Council unanimously endorsed the international boundary between Iraq and Kuwait. Acting under Chapter VII of the Charter, the Council demanded that the two countries respect the "inviolability" of the boundary as approved by the Boundary Demarcation Commission and the right to navigational access. However, the Iraqi government continues to refer publicly to Kuwait as a "province" and "governorate" of Iraq. The Security Council is not expected to modify or lift the sanctions imposed on Iraq before Iraq formally renounces its territorial claims and recognizes Kuwait's sovereignty.

Libya

U.N. sanctions imposed against Libya for its refusal to surrender two Libyans accused of blowing up **Pan Am Flight 103** over Scotland in December 1988 have so far **failed to alter Libya's defiant stance.** In its latest maneuver, Libya proposed to have the suspects tried at the International Court of Justice in The Hague before Scottish judges. The offer was rejected by Britain, the United States, and France. They insisted that Libya must comply with Security Council Resolutions 731 and 748 [1/21/92, 3/31/92] by surrendering the two suspects for trial in Scotland or the United States [*Middle East International*, 4/15/94]. The Security Council reviews the situation every 120 days (or sooner, if necessary). When the Council held consultations on April 8, 1994, it decided to maintain the sanctions regime. However, when the Council tightened its sanctions in November 1993, it did not impose a total ban on oil exports as it did with Iraq. Washington continues to accept its allies' assertion that they depend on Libyan oil and therefore cannot go along with U.S. requests for a U.N.-imposed oil embargo [*The Wall Street Journal*, 2/28/94].

Clinton administration officials have made it clear that the United States will press again for a full oil embargo, if the present sanctions do not force Libya to hand over the suspects. On the other hand, Colonel Muammar Qadhafi is facing powerful domestic constraints on any formal handover. One of the suspects, Amin Khalifa Fahima, is distantly related to Colonel Qadhafi, through his tribal group, the Qadhafa, and the other suspect, Abd al-Basset Maghrahi, enjoys a similar distant link with Major Abdesslam Jallood, Colonel Qadhafi's second in command. It is therefore very difficult for either leader to sanction any kind of handover that could threaten their tribal status [*Middle East International,* 8/28/93].

Lebanon

The Lebanese government, headed by Prime Minister Rafiq al-Hariri, will continue to confront the almost total reconstruction of the country's political system, its economy and infrastructure, and its social fabric—all of which were severely devastated by the civil war. Since his assumption of power in late October 1992, Prime Minister al-Hariri has formulated a broad program designed to confront Lebanon's major problems. These problems were identified as (1) the liberation of south Lebanon from Israeli occupation; (2) settling the issue of internal refugees displaced during the civil war; (3) the extension of state authority to all parts of the country; (4) the establishment of a stable relationship with Syria; and (5) extensive economic, financial, and administrative reforms [*Middle East Insight,* Vol. IX, No. 2].

In late July 1993, **Israel launched its largest assault on Lebanon since the 1982 invasion.** The heavy shelling and air attacks by Israel ended after Hizbullah fighters and the Israeli government agreed on a cease-fire brokered by the United States. Prime Minister al-Hariri itemized the physical damage to his country after nearly seven days of heavy Israeli bombardment: 128 people killed, including eight Hizbullah fighters; 470 injured; 300,000 refugees; 10,000 houses in the south destroyed and 20,000 houses or apartments damaged [*The New York Times,* 8/1/93; *Financial Times,* 8/2/93]. During the Israeli offensive the **U.N. Security Council was kept out of the picture,** despite Lebanon's formal request for a meeting. Meanwhile, the Lebanese government **refused to disarm Hizbullah.** Mr. al-Hariri said Hizbullah was resisting Israel's occupation of south Lebanon; if Israel withdrew its forces, there would be no need for resistance against them [*Financial Times,* 8/2/93]. Mr. al-Hariri spoke of Security Council Resolution 425 to legitimize Lebanese armed resistance to Israeli occupation. Adopted on March 19, 1978, it called on Israel, after a previous attack on Lebanon, to withdraw its forces from all Lebanese territory. Resolution 425 is likely to remain in limbo for some time until a new security border arrangement is reached with Israel.

On May 20, Israeli commandos flew deep into Lebanon and abducted **Mustafa Dirani,** the head of a pro-Iranian group, who Israel claims may have information on the whereabouts of Captain Ron Arad, an air force navigator who was shot down over southern Lebanon in 1986 and who is one of six servicemen missing in Lebanon for at least 12 years. Israel said it wanted to find out what Dirani knows about Arad's whereabouts. Fearing reprisals, Israel declared its diplomatic missions overseas and its soldiers along the northern border on alert [*The New York Times*, 5/23/94]. Lebanon lodged a strong protest with the U.N. Security Council and demanded the immediate release of Dirani. Prime Minister al-Hariri described his abduction as an "international act of piracy." The Secretary-General of Hizbullah threatened retaliation, warning that Israel has opted to widen the area of confrontation [*Al-Hayat*, 5/25/94].

The Arab-Israeli Conflict and the Occupied Territories

The signing of the **Declaration of Principles on Interim Self-Government Arrangements** by Israel and the Palestine Liberation Organization (PLO) at a dramatic ceremony at the White House on September 13, 1993, marked a major breakthrough in efforts to achieve a just, lasting, and comprehensive settlement in the Middle East. Worked out in months of secret talks mediated by Norway, the aim of the Declaration was to "establish a Palestinian Interim Self-Government Authority for the Palestinian people in the West Bank and the Gaza Strip, for a transitional period not exceeding five years, leading to a permanent settlement based on Security Council Resolutions 242 and 338" [Declaration of Principles, pp. 26–27].

Arab-Israeli peace talks came to a sudden halt following the Hebron massacre. On February 25, 1994, more than 30 Palestinians were gunned down by an Israeli extremist settler as they bowed in prayer in the Mosque of Ibrahim. After a three-week delay, the Security Council adopted Resolution 904 on March 18, strongly condemning the massacre and calling for measures to afford guarantees for the safety of Palestinian civilians in the occupied territory, including a temporary international presence *not under U.N. auspices.* The arrangement was described as being part of the peace process. The resolution was adopted without a vote following a paragraph-by-paragraph vote at U.S. insistence. **The United States abstained on two preambular paragraphs,** which were supported by all the other Council members. U.S. Ambassador Madeleine Albright said the United States could not support the description of the territories occupied during the 1967 as "occupied Palestine territory." It also opposed specific reference to Jerusalem, whose status was to be addressed at a later stage. Ambassador Albright said that the United States would have vetoed the resolution had those references been in the operative paragraphs [SC/5808]. This move by the United States marked a change in America's traditional policy on Jerusalem and occupied territory. During the 48th Session of the General Assembly, the United States lobbied hard to defer many resolutions on Middle East affairs. Israel also tried unsuccessfully to cancel resolutions condemning its record on human rights [*The New York Times*, 9/16/93].

Except for the active role of the **U.N. Relief and Works Agency (UNRWA)** for Palestine Refugees in the Near East, the role of the United Nations in the peace process has been marginal at best. However, UNRWA will continue to provide educational, medical, relief, and social services to the Palestine refugees. Ilter Turkmen, Commissioner-General of UNRWA, said the financing of UNRWA's activities would be a great help to the Palestine refugees, the local Palestinian economy, and the process of setting up Palestinian structures that would eventually take over the Agency's programs in the West Bank and Gaza. It is equally important, he said, to offer assistance to the 1.7 million Palestine refugees in Jordan, Lebanon, and Syria. For 1994, UNRWA has presented to the General Assembly budget proposals totaling some $294 million for the Agency's General Fund [U.N. press release GA/8611, PAL/1808]. During the **visit of PLO Chairman Yasser Arafat to the United Nations** on September 15, 1993, Secretary-General Boutros-Ghali assured him that the U.N. system was ready to coordinate assistance from its agencies and programs [SG/SM/5088, PAL/1804], and said a special coordinator would be appointed to liaise with the parties concerned. The General Assembly welcomed the PLO-Israeli agreement in several resolutions during the 48th Session, the last of which was Resolution 48/213 of December 1993.

Talks between Israel and the PLO, which were interrupted by the Hebron massacre and by attacks by the fundamentalist movement Hamas on Israeli citizens, were resumed in Cairo on April 10 as a result of intense efforts by the United States and Russia, co-sponsors of the peace talks. However, there was great doubt that agreement could be reached in time for the April 13 deadline stipulated in the Declaration of Principles. After laborious negotiations, **Israel and the PLO embarked on May 4 on a new phase of their historic peace process.** PLO Chairman Arafat and Israeli Prime Minister Yitzhak Rabin signed a final agreement in Cairo to inaugurate an era of limited self-government for close to 900,000 Palestinians living in the Gaza Strip and the West Bank town of Jericho [*The New York Times*, 5/5/94].

Under the terms of the agreement signed in Washington last fall, implementation of the accord triggers a five-year interim period of Palestinian self-rule. Even if no further steps are taken to broaden Palestinian autonomy to the rest of the occupied territory, the clock is ticking. Israel and the PLO are committed to begin negotiating on the permanent status of the territories within two years at the latest. They are also required by the terms of the Declaration to end the interim period in favor of permanent Palestinian status within five years. In fact, the countdown mechanism is perhaps the single most important aspect of the signing ceremony in Cairo. Voices have already been raised on both sides in favor of cutting short the five-year interim term and moving more swiftly toward permanent-status talks. However, this trend must also be **viewed in the context of the broader peace process.** In this framework there was a special significance to U.S. Secretary of State Warren Christopher's quick shuttle between Syria and Israel in the days preceding the signing of the Cairo agreement. Mr. Christopher proclaimed "a new, substantive phase" in the Israeli-Syrian negotiating track following his lengthy talks with Syrian President Hafez Assad and Prime Minister Rabin. As Israel and the Palestinians prepared to sign the Cairo agreement, the **World Bank** announced a program to spend $1.2 billion in emergency economic assistance for the new autonomous region. The money is to be distributed over a three-year period, expected to begin soon, and is designed to improve living standards in the occupied territories of the West Bank and the Gaza Strip.

Two weeks after the signing of the Cairo Accords, Secretary Christopher returned to the Middle East on a mini-shuttle between Jerusalem and Damascus that failed to achieve the breakthrough he had hoped for and declared that Syria and Israel were not ready to resume face-to-face talks. Mr. Christopher became the first senior U.S. official to visit the newly autonomous Palestinian area of Jericho, which was surrendered by the Israelis on May 13, ending its 27-year occupation. Israeli troops finished withdrawing from the Gaza Strip five days later. The PLO civilian administration will begin to take shape as soon as Arafat completes his appointments to the Palestinian Authority, the 24-member governing council. There is also a great need of immediate cash. Promises and pledges of funding from abroad have yet to materialize. In order to win the confidence of the prospective donors, the PLO announced that it had chosen Morgan Stanley Asset Management to monitor more than $2 billion in international aid committed to the West Bank and Gaza over the next five years [*Financial Times,* 5/25/94].

PLO Chairman Arafat, visiting autonomous Gaza and Jericho, July 1–5, after a 27-year exile, was greeted by exuberant crowds of Palestinians. In his first official act as the chief executive of the Palestinian administration, Mr. Arafat swore in 12 of his aides, referred to by PLO officials as the new "Palestinian Cabinet." The visit spurred protests by the Israeli right wing, culminating in massive demonstrations in Jerusalem [*The New York Times,* 7/2/94; 7/5/94]. Scheduled for October 15 are the first elections for an interim self-rule authority.

A few days after the Gaza-Jericho visit, Arafat and Israeli Prime Minister Rabin, meeting in Paris, moved into a new phase of peace talks and began to map the next stage of Palestinian self-rule. Messrs. Arafat and

Rabin and Israeli Foreign Minister Shimon Perez were in Paris to receive a UNESCO award for their peace accord of September 1993 [ibid., 7/7/94].

Yemen

The fragile four-year-old union between North and South Yemen collapsed when civil war broke out on May 4 following a year of differences between **President Ali Abdullah Salih** and his southern rival, Vice President **Ali Salim al-Baid.** Mr. al-Baid, Secretary-General of the Socialist party, claimed that southerners were politically marginalized following Yemen's first multiparty elections. Differences over power-sharing prevented the integration of the armed forces. The crisis intensified in August 1993, when Mr. al-Baid left the seat of government in Sana and returned to his political base in Aden, capital of the former South Yemen [*Financial Times*, 5/6/94; *Middle East Internatinal*, 5/13/94]. After weeks of fighting and military pressure from northern forces, southern Yemeni leaders formally abandoned their union with the North and **declared their independence on May 21** under the presidency of Mr. al-Baid. This infuriated the northern leader, Mr. Salih, who described the decision as illegal and threatened to capture Aden.

As the offensive against Aden intensified, the **Security Council met on June 1** and unanimously adopted **Resolution 924,** which called for an **immediate cease-fire** and requested the dispatch of a **fact-finding mission** to the area to assess prospects for a renewed dialogue among all those concerned. The Council also urged an immediate cessation of the supply of arms. The Council convened at the request of six countries: Bahrain, Egypt, Kuwait, Oman, Saudi Arabia, and the United Arab Emirates. The representative of Yemen informed the Council that his government considers the involvement of the United Nations as **interference in the internal affairs of Yemen,** contrary to Article 2, paragraph 7, of the U.N. Charter, concerning noninterference in the domestic affairs of member states. However, Resolution 924 considered the continuance of the situation in Yemen as a danger to peace and security in the region [Security Council press release SC/5854].

Four weeks after the adoption of Resolution 924, U.N. Secretary-General Boutros-Ghali reported to the Council his concern that the fighting had not stopped and called attention to the deteriorating humanitarian situation [S/1994/764]. He was unable to report any progress in the efforts of his Special Envoy, Lakhdar Brahimi, to start a political dialogue between the two sides. The Council met on June 29 and, based on the Secretary-General's report, issued Resolution 931, which called again for a cease-fire and for the continuation of talks by Mr. Brahimi with the parties to the conflict. It called too for the creation of a monitoring mechanism involving countries of the region. Northern forces were by now closing in on the southern stronghold of Aden, which remained desperately short of water [Reuters, 7/5/94] and was headed toward a humanitarian crisis of "catastrophic dimensions," in the words of the International Red Cross. Even as the fall of Aden seemed imminent, the Security Council's permanent five continued to maintain that the Yemeni crisis must be solved through political dialogue, as called for in Resolutions 924 and 931.

6. Central America and the Caribbean
By Edmund T. Piasecki

The United Nations met with mixed results in its efforts to establish and consolidate peace throughout the Central American and Caribbean regions in 1994. It guided El Salvador through that country's first peacetime presidential election in 64 years, but it has been unable to facilitate the implementation of other key provisions of the 1992 Peace Accords. It renewed its call for increased international assistance to Nicaragua [A/Res/48/161, 10/22/93], noting that the country still faces "exceptional circumstances" in its attempts to foster stability and development in the aftermath of war and numerous natural disasters. It worked out a framework agreement for the resumption of peace talks in Guatemala on January 10 [A/49/61-S/1994/13, 1/19/94], but bringing a formal end to Central America's longest civil war by year's end as scheduled will require unprecedented cooperation. (Government and rebel leaders signed three further agreements on March 29, including a request for a U.N. verification mission [U.N. press release SG/SM/5252-CA/88, 3/29/94].) And it watched with dismay as its 1991 initiative to return deposed Haitian President Jean-Bertrand Aristide to power stalled after achieving an initial settlement. The General Assembly will receive reports from the Secretary-General on all these matters at its 49th Session and is expected to reprise its annual resolutions on "the situation in Central America," "international assistance to Nicaragua," and "the situation of democracy and human rights in Haiti."

El Salvador

The Secretary-General was able to report that the Salvadoran peace process had "advanced significantly" and was "on course" in May 1993, five months after the signing of the Peace Accords in Mexico City and the formal end of hostilities between government and guerrilla forces [S/25812, 5/21/93]. Respect for a prolonged cease-fire by both sides and the conversion of the rebel **Frente Farabundo Martí para la Liberación Nacional (FMLN)** to a mainstream political party moved Boutros-Ghali to initiate preparations for what he called the "culminating point of the entire peace process," the general elections scheduled for March 1994. In its Resolution 832 of May 27, the Security Council agreed with the Secretary-General's proposals to establish an Election Division within the **U.N. Operation in El Salvador (ONUSAL)** to monitor and verify the results of the voting and to extend the mandate of the operation through November 30.

The peace process was soon to suffer a major disruption, however, when the May 23 explosion of an automobile repair shop in Managua, Nicaragua, led to the discovery of weapons hidden there by a faction of the FMLN. A clear violation of the Accords, the failure of the former rebels to disclose and destroy all their arms and equipment under U.N. supervision raised demands for the cancellation or suspension of the FMLN's status as a political party and questioned the effectiveness of U.N. verification overall. With the cooperation of the FMLN, ONUSAL located and destroyed 128 arms caches throughout El Salvador, Nicaragua, and Honduras—some 3,000 weapons, including 38 missiles [S/26790, 11/23/93]—by August 18. The Secretary-General reported on August 30 that the FMLN was in full compliance with the provisions of the Peace Accords calling for the dismantling of its military structure and the demobilization and reintegration into civil and political life of its combatants ["United Nations Observer Mission in El Salvador," PS/DPI/Rev. 4, 11/93].

While wrestling with the problem of the arms caches, the Secretary-General had to begin resolving the serious disagreements between **Salvadoran President Alfredo Cristiani** and the leaders of the FMLN that had left other key provisions of the Accords partly or completely unimplemented. These disagreements had delayed the deployment of the National Civil Police force, designed to replace the army-dominated National Police; the transfer of land to former combatants from both sides, the main component of the reintegration programs; and the implementation of all 40 recommendations of the **Commission on the Truth,** appointed to investigate human rights violations during the civil war.

Implementing the Peace Agreement

The considerable controversy that surrounded the report of the Truth Commission, released in March, focused on the recommended dismissal by the government of military officers, civil servants, and judges named as human rights abusers and the disqualification of those individuals, along with FMLN members similarly implicated, from holding public office. Both the government and the FMLN argued that disqualifications were unconstitutional under Salvadoran law, a view shared by the United Nations in its own legal analysis. The sides differed sharply on dismissals, however, with Cristiani strongly opposed, again on constitutional grounds, and the rebels strongly in favor [S/26581, 10/14/93, par. 5].

Although the government and the FMLN had accepted the Commission's recommendations as binding, the Secretary-General indicated that specific measures could be dropped with the concurrence of both sides [ibid., par. 13], and indeed the Secretary-General made no mention of disqualifications as an outstanding issue in a November report to the Security Council [S/26790, 11/23/93, par. 46]. But the FMLN continued to insist that dismissals, at least of eight implicated officers still holding their positions, go forward. (Boutros-Ghali had already certified on July 7 that the government was in compliance with the related recommendations of the Ad Hoc Commission on the Purification of the Armed Forces, mandated to remove human rights abusers from the army.)

In addition to the three recommendations of the Truth Commission on dismissal and disqualification, four others dealing with decentralizing the powers of the Supreme Court and two more concerning guarantees of due process and adherence to international standards of human rights remained outstanding. Cristiani refused to take any action with respect to the Court, claiming that the matter required constitutional amendment, a process involving the Legislative Assembly exclusively and one that the government was not empowered even to initiate. The Ministry of Justice did, however, submit six draft laws to the Assembly in October aimed at strengthening due process protections, including a proposed "modification" to the constitution. The Secretary-General termed the proposal "an important precedent" and "a very positive step" toward full implementation of the Commission's recommendations [ibid., par. 47].

Progress was less encouraging on phasing out the discredited National Police and phasing in the National Civil Police by the agreed-upon deadline of September 1, 1994. The government delayed for eight months before initiating demobilizations in October 1993 and did not intend to complete the process before October 1994, a month past the deadline. Moreover, the demobilization plan covered some 10,400 personnel, confirming U.N. suspicions that the government had significantly expanded the National Police in violation of an explicit provision of the Peace Accords. The government also intended to continue training National Police recruits through December 1993, two months after beginning the demobilization process. The Secretary-General reported in November that ONUSAL was pressing for accelerated reductions in line with the deployment schedule of the National Civil Police [ibid., par. 38–40].

The phasing-in process has had its own problems, including those surrounding the establishment and functioning of the National Public Security Academy, mandated to train the new police force. From its opening in September 1992 through November 1993, the Academy graduated only 2,300 recruits, well short of the nearly 6,000 required by July 1994—and the more than 10,000 foreseen by mid-1999. Applications from ineligible candidates remained a problem, as the admission of FMLN and National Police members was strictly limited to 40 percent of the total number of entrants during the "transition period." ONUSAL was to verify that former combatants did not attempt to circumvent the quotas by gaining admission as civilians. Former members of the Treasury Police, National Guard, and the immediate reaction army battalions, implicated in human rights atrocities, were to be denied admission altogether, though the government failed to supply ONUSAL with sufficient information to verify that none were admitted [ibid., par. 21–25].

The National Civil Police force itself continued to be troubled by direct and unregulated transfers of personnel from existing law enforcement entities, especially the Criminal Investigation Commission and the Special Antinarcotics Unit. The Peace Accords specified that government and FMLN members of COPAZ (the National Commission for the Consolidation of the Peace), under ONUSAL verification, had to determine that civil police authorities observed established hiring practices before such transfers could take place. The Secretary-General charged that the government bypassed both COPAZ and ONUSAL on the matter. The Secretary-General also criticized the government for a $20 million budgetary shortfall in financial support for the new force, which he said also suffered from poor working conditions in the field, inadequate communications capacity, and a shortage of vehicles [ibid., par. 29–37].

The land transfer program, proposed by the United Nations in October 1992, has turned out to be the least successful of the postwar peacebuilding exercises in El Salvador. By November 1993 only 10 percent of the 47,500 potential beneficiaries had received land titles, but the Secretary-General hoped that an agreement reached between the government and the FMLN on the number of noncombatants to be included in the program—rebel sympathizers who had occupied land during the war and continued to hold it—would permit the distribution of 12,000 more titles by year's end. Resolving the remaining holdups in awarding titles was crucial to the completion of the reintegration process, the Secretary-General said, in that only title holders could obtain credit to finance agricultural production and housing [ibid., par. 48–54].

In recommending an extension of ONUSAL's mandate through May 1994, Boutros-Ghali expressed "considerable concern" that such key elements of the Peace Accords as land transfers, the new police force, and the Truth Commission recommendations remained only partly implemented as elections were set to open. Nevertheless, he concluded that the implementation process had "on the whole progressed well" and emphasized that six of the seven presidential candidates had publicly committed themselves on November 5 to the implementation of the Peace Accords in their entirety. The Security Council agreed to the mandate extension and requested a formal report by May 1, 1994 [S/Res/888, 11/30/93].

The Council used the opportunity of reviewing ONUSAL's activities to condemn yet another threat to the successful conclusion of the peace process: the **reemergence of a pattern of politically motivated violations of human rights,** including assassinations of public figures, believed to be perpetuated by paramilitary organizations. In response to the killings of two FMLN leaders in late October, the Secretary-General directed ONUSAL to assist the government in conducting an immediate and thorough investigation of "illegal armed groups," one of the outstanding recommendations of the Commission on the Truth [S/26689, 11/3/93].

After extensive consultations between representatives of the Secretary-General and "all concerned parties," agreement was reached on the terms of reference of the investigatory body, called the **Joint Group** [S/26865, 12/11/93]. Established on December 8, the Group consists of two representatives of the government, the National Counsel for the Defense of Human Rights (an office created under the Peace Accords), and the Director of the Division of Human Rights of ONUSAL. Operating under a six-month mandate, the Joint Group is to make a public report, including recommendations for remedial action, to the Salvadoran president and the Secretary-General. The Security Council welcomed the establishment of the Group, especially its "independent, impartial, and nonpolitical character" [S/26866, 12/11/93].

The Elections

By promoting action to stem political violence, the United Nations cleared the last hurdle to an orderly election campaign, which had officially opened three weeks previously. Twelve parties were competing for the presidency, 84 seats in the National Assembly, 262 mayoral slots, and 20 seats in the Central American Parliament. The majority **National Republican Alliance (ARENA)** party and the FMLN, participating in organized elections for the first time, were heavy favorites.

Problems had plagued the voter registration process since the summer, and by October, some 27 percent of those eligible to vote were still not registered. The Secretary-General ascribed the poor results to voter "lethargy," but the complexity of the process (citizens had to first make a formal request, wait at least a month for their birth certificates to be forwarded to their local registries, and then pick up their electoral cards in person) seemed to guarantee slowness and frequent cases of lost or missing records. The Secretary-General also reported that the **Supreme Electoral Tribunal,** set up to oversee registration and voting, lacked sufficient information to delete the names of the deceased from the electoral rolls, prevent double registrations, or resolve discrepancies between names on the rolls and those on the electoral cards [S/26606, 10/20/93].

In response to an appeal from the Security Council on November 5, 1993, ONUSAL's Electoral Division became more directly involved in facilitating voter registration, developing and implementing plans in all 262 towns for locating birth certificates while its 36 observers continued to monitor the electoral process overall. Some 788,000 requests for new registrations, or for renewals or changes in existing ones, had been received by the November 19 deadline. When the electoral rolls were closed on January 19, 1994, 80 percent of the voting age public had been issued electoral cards. Taking into account the estimated 400,000 registrations covering voters who had died, left the country, or failed to convert temporary cards to permanent ones, ONUSAL projected that 2.3 million Salvadorans, 85 percent of those eligible to vote, would be registered by election day [S/1994/179, 2/16/94].

The campaign itself was marred by political violence in October and November, including the murders of 15 ARENA and FMLN members, but the level of violence had declined by January 1994. The Secretary-General noted that assassinations as well as intimidation and threats against public figures had little effect on "the relatively normal climate in which the electoral process [was] unfolding" [ibid.]. ONUSAL observers attended more than 800 campaign events up to election day and reported that most had taken place in an "orderly, well-organized manner." The Electoral Division had received some 300 complaints of electoral irregularities, however. Most dealt with "arbitrary or illegitmate action by public authorities," including the government's use of public resources in its own campaign advertising. Just before election day the Secretary-General declared that "conditions for the holding of free and fair elections are generally adequate" [S/1994/304, 3/16/94].

The more than 900 election monitors deployed by ONUSAL at the 355 polling centers around the country on March 20 observed "no serious incidents involving law and order . . . and no ballot-rigging," the Secretary-General reported. Voter turnout was low at 1.5 million, or 55 percent of all those registered, due in part to the significant distances voters were expected to travel and the lack of public transportation. Difficulties in transporting tally sheets to the counting center and the Supreme Electoral Tribunal's inability to rapidly collect and disseminate information on the results led to an "information vacuum" lasting several days and initial questions as to the fairness of the vote.

By official figures, ARENA had received 49.03 percent of all ballots cast, while the FMLN, running in a coalition with the Democratic Convergence (CD) and the Revolutionary National Movement (MNR) parties, garnered 24.9 percent. As no party could claim an absolute majority in the presidential election, ARENA and the FMLN coalition, as the top two finishers, would face each other in a runoff election on April 24. ARENA won a majority 39 seats in the National Assembly, however, against 21 for the FMLN, and outpolled the former rebels 206 to 16 in the mayoral contests [S/1994/486, 4/21/94].

Although the FMLN challenged the results of more than 40 local elections, the Secretary-General emphasized that these objections were likely to be resolved quickly. Indeed, 37 challenges were dismissed within a month, though perhaps prematurely in ONUSAL's view [ibid.]. All parties accepted the results of the presidential and most of the legislative voting, the Secretary-General reported, and ONUSAL had received only eight reports of serious voting irregularities, none of which had a "significant effect on the results." In a March 21 statement, ONUSAL concluded that "in general the elections . . . took place under appropriate conditions in terms of freedom, competitiveness, and security [and] can be considered acceptable" [S/1994/375, 3/31/94].

Nevertheless, ONUSAL recommended that the Supreme Electoral Tribunal take remedial action before the runoff election regarding observed delays in opening voting tables at polling stations, overcrowded conditions in polling centers, the slow pace of voting, and the absence of at least 25,000 names of valid electoral cardholders from the voting register [U.N. press release CA/86, 3/26/94]. In an April 7 statement, the Security Council congratulated the Salvadoran people on the success of the elections, noted ONUSAL's assessment, and called for correction of the enumerated shortcomings [S/PRST/1994/15, 4/7/94].

With the first round of voting completed, the Secretary-General informed the Security Council that little progress had been made since November 1993 in implementing the key agreements on public security, reintegration, and human rights. He referred to "disquieting signs of reluctance" to fully deploy the National Civil Police and eliminate the National Police; reported that land transfers, scheduled to reach 12,000 by December, were still below 11,000; and urgently requested the National Assembly to approve constitutional amendments on judicial reform at its current session, lest their entry into force be postponed to 1997 at the earliest. Boutros-Ghali called on the Council to support his efforts aimed at winning agreement from President Cristiani on an updated timetable for implementing these provisions [S/1994/361, 3/30/94]. The Council said it "share[d] his concerns" and "urge[d] all concerned to make every effort to ensure that further delays . . . are avoided" [S/PRST/1994/15, 4/7/94].

Earliest indications in the second round of presidential balloting on April 24 gave **ARENA candidate Armando Calderon Sol** some 70 percent of the vote against **Ruben Zamora of the FMLN-supported coalition.** Voter turnout was reported light. A lawyer and protégé of ARENA founder Roberto D'Aubuisson, the 45-year-old Calderon Sol previously served in the National Assembly and as mayor of San Salvador [*The Washington Post*, 4/25/94].

Haiti

The United Nations was confident in the summer of 1993 that it had finally succeeded in brokering a durable accord between **deposed Presi-**

dent Jean-Bertrand Aristide of Haiti and the Commander-in-Chief of the army that ousted him. The **Governor's Island Agreement** [A/47/975-A/26063, 7/12/93], signed by Aristide and **Lieutenant-General Raoul Cédras** on July 7, represented the first diplomatic breakthrough of the 20-month effort by the United Nations and the Organization of American States (OAS) to reverse the September 1991 coup that drove the duly elected president from power. Engineered by **Dante Caputo**, U.N. and OAS Special Envoy to Haiti, the agreement called for the restoration of Aristide to office on October 30 and permitted Cédras "to avail himself of his right to early retirement." The crisis in Haiti appeared close to resolution.

In its other provisions, the July 7 accord mandated the appointment of a new prime minister, the establishment of a civilian police force, amnesty for the coup plotters, and suspension of the international sanctions voted by the United Nations and the OAS. The United Nations, for its part, was to deploy personnel to assist in "modernizing" the armed forces and organizing the new police force. With the OAS, the United Nations was also to verify the overall implementation of the agreement. Finally, Aristide and Cédras agreed to the opening of "political dialogue" between supporters and opponents of the deposed President in the Haitian parliament.

The political dialogue, held at U.N. Headquarters, produced a follow-up agreement on July 16. Signatories to the **New York Pact** [A/47/1000-S/26297, 8/13/93] declared a six-month "political truce" during which they pledged to refrain from taking a vote of "no confidence" in the new government or any action that could lead to violence. They called for an end to human rights abuses and agreed to promote fundamental freedoms and judicial reform while securing the immediate release of all political detainees. The signatories also stated their willingness to confirm "without delay" the President's nominee for prime minister.

The New York Pact bound the parliamentarians to adopt through emergency legislation a series of laws establishing the new police force and a compensation fund for victims of the coup as well as granting amnesty, abolishing paramilitary forces, and reforming prison administration. The agreement also recognized Aristide's authority to review the constitutionality of all executive decisions taken during his absence. Similarly, all legislators elected after the coup were to "voluntarily" step down, and a "Conciliation Commission," established by parliament, was to resolve the problem of their disputed status.

Following the Secretary-General's notification to the Security Council that both chambers of the Haitian parliament had confirmed Robert Malval as Aristide's choice for prime minister [S/26361, 8/26/93], the Council "suspended" the oil and arms embargo and the financial restrictions it had imposed on Haiti in June under Resolution 841. In adopting Resolution 861 on August 27, the Council warned that it would "terminate immediately the suspension" should the parties to the Governor's Island Agreement "or any other authorities in Haiti" fail to abide by their obligations "in good faith." Sanctions would be lifted "definitively," the Council said, once the Secretary-General could confirm that the agreement had been "fully implemented."

Having fulfilled its pledge to remove the embargoes on Haiti, the United Nations began preparations for carrying out its monitoring and verification tasks under the Governor's Island Agreement. At the request of President Aristide [S/26180, 7/28/93], the Secretary-General agreed to expand the U.N.'s policing function to include monitoring the activities of the existing security forces in the short term as well as assisting in the establishment of a civilian police force later on. To fulfill this requirement, the Secretary-General recommended the deployment of approximately **567 police monitors** as part of a **U.N. Mission in Haiti (UNMIH).** They would be joined by 60 trainers and a 500-strong military construction unit to assist in the modernization of the armed forces and to provide "on-the-job training" to the military in various public works projects, such as renovating medical facilities and repairing roads. UNMIH was to coordinate its activities with the 200 human rights monitors deployed in Haiti since February 1993 as members of the **U.N.-OAS International Civilian Mission (MICIVIH)** [S/26352, 8/25/93].

Concerned in general about the cost and scope of new peacekeeping operations, the Security Council delayed establishing UNMIH but approved the dispatch of a 30-member advance team to Haiti on August 31 [S/Res/862, 8/31/93]. The team reported that "deep mistrust and suspicion," violence, and "widespread" abuses of human rights continued to plague the country despite the conclusion of the Governor's Island Agreement. To help establish conditions more conducive to the implementation of the accord—and provide concrete evidence of the international community's "commitment . . . to the solution to the Haitian crisis"—the team recommended that UNMIH be enlarged and formally established without further delay.

The Secretary-General increased the size of the military contingent to 700 in light of this information and raised his estimate of the cost of fielding the entire operation, including the police monitors and 270 civilian staff, from $37 million to $49.9 million for the initial six-month period [S/26480 and Add. 1, 9/22/93, 9/23/93]. The Security Council authorized the establishment of UNMIH on September 23 and requested the Secretary-General to dispatch it "on an urgent basis" [S/Res/867, 9/22/93].

Breakdown of the Agreement

The spirit of the July accords that the peacekeepers were supposed to reinforce was already on the wane, however. On September 17 the Council had met to "deplore" the "assassination" of some dozen Aristide supporters, including prominent businessman Antoine Izmery, gunned down on September 11 during services at a Port-au-Prince church. It called on Malval's government to take control of all security forces, disarm the "organized armed civilian groups" perpetrating the violence, and remove those officials directing such groups. The Council also promised to hold the military and security authorities "personally responsible" for the safety of all U.N. personnel deployed in Haiti [S/26460]. In authorizing UNMIH, the Security Council likewise appealed to the government to ensure the safety of the mission and the freedom of movement and communication of its members. It requested the Secretary-General to report if such conditions did not exist and called on all factions to "explicitly and publicly" renounce violence [S/Res/867].

The Council's fears that UNMIH personnel would be subjected to threats and harassment were realized on October 11, when the **USS *Harlan County*** with 193 U.S. and 25 Canadian peacekeepers aboard was blocked from docking in Port-au-Prince by a group of about 100 armed civilians or "attachés," supported by police. The Secretary-General called the incident "the culmination of a situation which had been deteriorating in Haiti in recent weeks." He cited the Haitian military's "observed lack of will" in facilitating UNMIH's deployment and the complicity on the part of the police, documented by MICIVIH, in numerous acts of violence perpetrated by armed civilian gangs, including the assassination of Izmery, an October 5 attack on the offices of the prime minister, and a "general strike" in Port-au-Prince on October 7 "against UNMIH." The armed forces and the police had refused to obey "most of the instructions" from the civilian government, he added. Concluding that Cédras and **Lieutenant-Colonel Michel François, chief of police and commander of the Port-au-Prince metropolitan area,** had failed to fulfill their obligations under the Governor's Island Agreement, Boutros-Ghali recommended the reimposition of sanctions on August 27 [S/26573, 10/13/93].

In statements to the press, Cedras condemned the violence but claimed that the peacekeepers—engineers in the military construction unit—had been armed with assault rifles and were perceived by the protesters as threats to Haitian sovereignty. He went on to reject as insufficient the presidential pardon he and other members of the high command had received from Aristide in July for their participation in the coup and renewed an earlier demand that parliament complete action on a blanket amnesty before he would agree to step down. As pro-military legislators continued to deny the parliament a functioning quorum, the General's demand would effectively "scuttle" the Governor's Island Agreement, according to unnamed diplomatic sources quoted by the media. Cédras's position was further strengthened by the U.S. decision to withdraw the *Harlan County* on October 12 without first resolving the status of

UNMIH or informing the United Nations or the civilian government [*The Washington Post*, 10/14/93].

On October 13 the Security Council terminated the suspension of the sanctions, effective midnight on October 18, with the hope that agreement could be reached in the interim on deploying the mission. The Council also attempted to ease the effects of the sanctions on the constitutional government by permitting either Aristide or Malval to access Haitian funds otherwise frozen and to request that exceptions be made to the oil embargo in specific instances [S/Res/873, 10/13/93]. At the urging of the United States, the Council would consider imposing unspecified "additional measures" should the activities of UNMIH continue to be "impeded."

Aristide requested a strengthening of the sanctions following the assassination of the newly named Minister of Justice, François-Guy Malary, on October 14 [S/26587, 10/15/93], and the Council responded by authorizing member states to stop ships bound for Haiti "as necessary" and inspect their cargoes for prohibited goods [S/Res/875, 10/16/93]. Aristide's further request, in his address to the General Assembly on October 28 [A/48/PV.41, 11/17/93], for a "total blockade" of the country, enforced by sea and air and including food and medicine, was considered premature. At the United Nations, Aristide repeated his standing offer to convene the parliament and approve an amnesty only after his return and the departure of Cédras, François, the High Command, and the Military Staff.

On October 30, the date for Aristide's return to power under the Governor's Island Agreement, the Security Council issued a statement demanding "unconditional compliance" with the agreement, which it called the "only framework for the solution to the Haitian crisis." But the accord had apparently already unraveled following the departure of the USS *Harlan County*. The United Nations and the OAS had "relocated" 180 monitors of the International Civilian Mission to the Dominican Republic by October 16 [A/48/532/Add.2, 11/30/93], and withdrew UNMIH police monitors soon after. A November 5 meeting of the Haitian parties convened by Caputo to focus on "roadblocks" to the implementation of the July accord was boycotted by Cédras and adjourned after 45 minutes [S/26724, 11/11/93]. Efforts toward a negotiated settlement collapsed.

In its annual resolution on "the situation of democracy and human rights in Haiti" [A/Res/48/27, 12/6/93], the General Assembly reiterated its condemnation of attempts to replace Aristide through violence and "military coercion." It also condemned attempts to "delay or prevent" his immediate reinstatement, and again declared "unacceptable any entity arising from this unlawful situation." The Assembly "energetically" supported the Special Envoy's mission and agreed with the Security Council that the Governor's Island Agreement "continues to be the only valid framework for resolving the crisis in Haiti." The resolution also called for the return of the International Civilian Mission and the deployment of UNMIH, and asserted that the Haitian military authorities were "fully responsible" for the current suffering.

Steps Toward a Total Embargo

Efforts to resume talks aimed at implementing the Governor's Island Agreement stumbled repeatedly on Aristide's fear of being pressured into a power-sharing arrangement with the military. The deposed President refused to support attempts by his Prime Minister to convene a "reconciliation conference" of the various social and political factions in December that could have led to the formation of a broad governing coalition [*The Washington Post*, 12/17/93], and he continued to insist that such consultations could commence only subsequent to his return to power. Malval officially resigned his post but agreed to stay on as "acting prime minister."

Pressure increased on Aristide to accept immediate talks once the governments comprising the "Friends of the Secretary-General for Haiti"—Canada, France, the United States, and Venezuela—backed the reconciliation conference and agreed to work toward the global trade embargo advocated by the deposed President, should Cédras fail to abide by his previous commitments by January 15, 1994 [ibid., 12/23/93]. Aristide countered by holding his own conference in Miami, focusing on coalition building among pro-democracy forces; neither Caputo, Malval, nor any representatives of the business community or the military attended [ibid., 1/18/94]. The United States and others allowed the January 15 deadline to pass without formal action, exerting further pressure on the deposed President to accept reconciliation talks or forgo the embargo.

Despite its pro-Aristide tilt, the Miami International Conference recommended that Aristide take a fresh approach to solving the Haitian crisis by naming a new prime minister to represent him in Port-au-Prince and to form a "government of national concord." The conference further recommended that Aristide seek the lifting of the sanctions (not their strengthening) once Cédras had retired, the prime minister and the government were installed, and security and respect for human rights had returned. It was also proposed that the President hold a national reconciliation conference following his return. Provisions in the Governor's Island Agreement specifying the date of Aristide's return, the establishment of a civilian police force, and the deployment of U.N. peacekeepers were apparently dropped.

More significant than the "mini-plan" itself was its endorsement by a delegation of Haitian parliamentarians, both supporters and opponents of Aristide, on February 19. The bipartisan delegation also stated its willingness to adopt an amnesty and establish "a police force," though perhaps not under civilian leadership. The Secretary-General concluded that "agreement has been reached between the elected supporters and opponents of President Aristide on a plan . . . [to] break the present impasse and resume progress in implementing the Governor's Island Agreement" [A/48/879, 2/23/94]. While conceding that the plan contained no specific timetable, Caputo emphasized that it did not "replace" the July accord but instead signified the building of a "political center" that would create the conditions necessary for its successful implementation. For example, the recommendations did not require the parliament to ratify the prime minister immediately as before but called for the development of broad parliamentary support for Aristide's nominee in advance of such a vote [Press Briefing by Special Envoy on Haiti, 2/22/94].

Although Caputo and the Friends of the Secretary-General believed the mini-plan held the best hope of passing an amnesty that might persuade the military to step down, Aristide rejected the proposal and substituted a three-phase timetable. It called for the resignation of the military leadership and the imposition of a global trade embargo; the adoption of the amnesty and the establishment of the civilian police followed by the redeployment of UNMIH; and the nomination of the new prime minister, the return of the duly elected president within 10 days, and the lifting of the embargo [*The Washington Post*, 2/24/94]. Aristide was no happier with a U.S. offer to revise the mini-plan to stipulate that Cédras's retirement, the naming of the prime minister, and adoption of the amnesty should occur simultaneously [ibid., 3/29/94].

The deposed President finally gained the upper hand in his dealings with the United States in April, as reports of increased political repression in Haiti and widespread evasion of the fuel embargo heightened demands from Congress and human rights groups for a radical shift in Clinton administration policy. The administration announced plans on April 22 to seek a global embargo and reportedly forced the resignation of **Lawrence A. Pezzullo,** U.S. Special Envoy to Haiti, who had vocally advocated power-sharing between Aristide and the military. The Security Council voted the embargo on May 6, 1994 [S/Res/917], excluding only medicine, food, and cooking fuels, and banning private plane flights, which the military had used to resupply itself. The Council also barred foreign travel for some 600 military and police officers and their families, but could only "urge" member states to freeze foreign assets of coup supporters, due to legal considerations. Cédras, François, and Cédras's deputy, General Philippe Biamby, were given 15 days to step down before the sanctions were to take effect. On May 8, Clinton announced plans to abandon the controversial policy of summary repatriation of Haitian refugees and to allow those interdicted to make their claims for political asylum aboard ship or in third countries. A day later the President named **former Congressman William H. Gray III** his new special envoy to Haiti.

Not only did the Haitian military not comply with the demands of the Security Council, the Secretary-General reported, Cédras went so far as to name his own president, Chief Judge Emile Jonassaint of the Haitian Supreme Court, on May 11 [S/1994/593, 5/19/94]. The global embargo took effect as scheduled on May 21, but growing concern about a lucrative trade in contraband gasoline across Haiti's 240-mile border with the Dominican Republic moved the United Nations to dispatch a three-man expert team to the area on May 23 to formulate measures for plugging that major leak in the embargo [*Financial Times*, 5/24/94]. Ambassador Gray won assurances from Dominican President Joaquin Balaguer on May 25 that the border would be sealed [*The Washington Post*, 5/27/94], but increased daytime patrolling simply shifted the illegal traffic to nighttime hours [ibid., 6/19/94].

The United Nations also became involved in the processing of Haitian applicants for asylum in the United States. After almost a month of difficult negotiations, the **U.N. High Commissioner for Refugees (UNHCR)** and the United States signed an agreement on June 15, allowing the refugee agency to monitor shipboard interviews with Haitian expatriates in the harbor of Kingston, Jamaica, and at a processing facility in the Grand Turks and Caicos islands, a British dependency [ibid., 6/16/94]. While abandoning summary repatriations eased domestic and international criticism on Washington, it also dramatically increased the outflow of asylum seekers and forced President Clinton to reopen the processing facility at the U.S. Naval Base at Guantanamo Bay in Cuba, closed since 1992 [ibid., 6/29/94].

The United States continued to adopt unilateral measures targeting coup leaders and their wealthy supporters. On June 11, President Clinton announced an immediate cutoff of all financial transactions with Haiti, including those routed through third countries, and a halt to commercial air traffic between Haiti and the United States, effective June 25. The transaction ban was widened on June 23 to include a freeze on all assets in the United States belonging to Haitians living in Haiti, not just the 600 military leaders and their supporters whose bank accounts were frozen in May [ibid., 6/11,23/94].

7. Cambodia
By Frederick Z. Brown

On May 26, 1993, the long Cambodia peace process reached its crescendo when **fair, free, and open national elections**—the first ever in Cambodia's history—were held. The elections were a culmination of an international effort, spearheaded by the United Nations, which had placed 22,000 U.N. military and civilian peacekeepers in Cambodia. Key to this effort were the **Agreements on a Comprehensive Political Settlement of** the Cambodia Conflict, signed in Paris on October 23, 1991, by 19 nations and the four contending Cambodian factions [U.N. Department of Public Information, DP/1180-920077, 1/92]. The Agreements established the U.N. Transitional Authority in Cambodia (UNTAC), which was mandated to maintain a cease-fire; to canton, disarm, and demobilize the armed forces of the Cambodian factions; to create a neutral political environment; and to prepare for and oversee the national elections, which would in turn provide the basis for a new Cambodian government representing the political sentiments of the Cambodian people.

Election Results and Aftermath

Although many elements of the Agreements' mandate were not fulfilled, the election itself was nonetheless carried out meticulously [Statement by Special Representative of the Secretary-General for Cambodia, S/25879, 6/2/93]. The Party of Democratic Kampuchea (PDK, the Khmer Rouge) exhibited considerable confusion of attitude, threatening in March and April to attack polling places and to disrupt the election by all means possible, yet in May apparently deciding not to harass voters. In some localities, the PDK did not interfere with villagers under their control from voting; in others, the PDK lobbed mortar rounds at polling stations. There were even reports that the PDK had told voters to vote for FUNCINPEC (the acronym in French for "National United Front for an Independent, Neutral, Peaceful, and Cooperative Cambodia), the party of Prince Norodom Ranariddh. In any event, on advice of UNTAC, the U.N. Secretary-General certified the election as free and fair, and the results binding [*Report of the Secretary-General on the Conduct and Results of the Elections in Cambodia, S/25913, 6/10/93*]. A total of 4,267,192 voters, representing 89.56 percent of the registered voters, went to the polls. In what most observers considered to be a major upset, FUNCINPEC won 1,824,188 votes (45.47 percent), while the Cambodian People's Party (CPP), led by former Prime Minister of the State of Cambodia, Hun Sen, won 1,533,471 votes (38.23 percent). The Buddhist Liberal Democratic Party (BDLP), led by Son Sann, won 152,764 votes (3.81 percent). Seventeen other registered parties garnered the remainder.

Given the proportional representation system by province established by the Paris Agreements, this translated into a 120-person constituent assembly made up of 58 FUNCINPEC and 51 CPP members, 10 from the BDLP, plus 1 from a FUNCINPEC splinter party that immediately pledged support to Ranariddh, giving FUNCINPEC a total of 59 votes.

The CPP's initial reaction was to angrily demand new elections in certain key provinces (Kompong Cham, Kompong Chhnang, Prey Veng, Battambang, Phnom Penh City) where the CPP had expected to do well but lost. The CPP charged that "irregularities" and "UNTAC prejudice" had slanted the elections toward FUNCINPEC. **U.N. Special Representative Yasushi Akashi** rejected these charges, and UNTAC negotiations with the CPP during the first week of June led to their acceptance of the results. The problems caused by FUNCINPEC's upset victory, however, were by no means at an end. On June 3, Prince Norodom Sihanouk announced his intention to form an interim coalition government with himself as prime minister and head of the armed forces, with his son Ranariddh and Hun Sen as deputy prime ministers. Sihanouk's move reflected the harsh political reality that the State of Cambodia (SOC) seemed unwilling to relinquish power and that FUNCINPEC was apparently ill-equipped to assume it. Yet it went directly counter to the Paris Agreements' insistence on a democratic electoral process reflecting the will of the Cambodian people, and it denied Ranariddh the primacy he had earned through that process. At about the same time, Prince Norodom Chakrapong, another of Sihanouk's sons with political pretensions (he had been a deputy prime minister of the SOC), announced **formation of a secessionist government** comprised of Cambodia's seven easternmost provinces along the Vietnamese border [*Far Eastern Economic Review, 6/24/93*].

Interim Government and New Constitution

It was unclear whether this was a genuine (and grossly ill-advised) power-grab attempt by Chakrapong or a Sihanouk gambit to strengthen the CPP's hand against UNTAC. It took strong pressure from the governments of the Security Council Perm Five and UNTAC itself to thwart the rogue effort, which threatened to return Cambodia to a state of civil war. When the secession collapsed, an **Interim Joint Administration** (or Provisional National Government) was formed in which the CPP and FUNCINPEC shared power over the summer of 1993 while the constitution was being written. This coalition arrangement would carry over into Cambodia's first formal government under the new constitution in September. **Prince Ranariddh and Hun Sen** were named co-chairs of the Administration. Also a preview of the constitution, **Prince Sihanouk was named head of state** as a "stabilizing mechanism in the Cambodian polity" [*Report of the Secretary-General Pursuant to Paragraph 7 of Resolution 840 (1993), S/26090, 7/13/93*]. At UNTAC's urging, the United Nations agreed to provide the Interim Joint Administration $20 million to pay the salaries of the civil service, police, and the military during the transition period [S/26095, 7/16/93].

The drafting committees of the **Constituent Assembly** began work on June 14, 1993. UNTAC made technical comments, mainly strengthening the human rights-related provisions in accordance with annex 5 of the Paris Agreements. By late August the committees had completed 120 articles, and in early September the constitution was submitted to Sihanouk. Two major sticking points were the status of the head of state and the powers of the post of prime minister, and these continued to be unresolved even as the constitution was submitted to the Assembly for ratification on September 15. Sihanouk vacillated on the question of becoming monarch but finally succumbed to the "will of the people." The **constitution was ratified** soon thereafter in a secret ballot with 113 in favor, 5 opposed, and 2 abstentions.

The constitution called for the king to appoint **two prime ministers,** one senior (Ranariddh) and the other junior (Hun Sen), both from parties represented in the National Assembly, thus ruling out any eventual appointment of a Khmer Rouge leader. UNTAC said that the United Nations supported the constitution, noting that "in general terms we are satisfied that it corresponds to the principles of the Paris Agreements." Other observers, however, were not satisfied that the constitution created sustainable institutions. In particular, it was tailored to conform to the personalities of Ranariddh and Hun Sen and the FUNCINPEC–CPP balance of power instead of promoting long-term stability [*Indochina Digest,* 9/24/93]. The nagging question of **royal succession** was finessed by stipulating that a five-member throne council drawn from the National Assembly would select a new king from either the Norodom or Sisowath lineage in the event of the monarch's death. Given Sihanouk's frail health, this provision was not insignficant.

Withdrawal of UNTAC

UNTAC's withdrawal in three phases began in July 1993. UNTAC's military battalions, which had provided such firm security and logistical support for the electoral process, were withdrawn throughout the summer, with the final unit—the French—departing in early November. The large election component of UNTAC's presence stood down soon after the election and was followed by other civilian components in rapid order; the last of the civilian police component departed by the end of September [*Further Report of the Secretary-General Pursuant to Paragraph 7 of Resolution 840 (1993), S/26360,* 8/26/93]. Security Council Resolution 860 (1993) confirmed that UNTAC's functions under the Paris Agreements should end upon the creation of a new government of Cambodia consistent with those Agreements [S/26529, 10/5/93]. Thus, with the **signing of the new Cambodian constitution by King Sihanouk** on September 24, 1993, the Kingdom of Cambodia was reborn and UNTAC ceased to exercise its formal authority. On September 26, Special Representative Akashi and the commander of UNTAC's military component, **Australian Lieutenant General John Sanderson,** departed Phnom Penh.

Although all UNTAC units had been scheduled to depart by mid-November, several exigencies made this impossible. **Twenty unarmed UNTAC military observers** were, at the new Cambodian government's request, retained in the field for six months following the end of the UNTAC mandate on November 15, 1993. Their assignment was to report on matters affecting security in the countryside, to build up the confidence of Cambodians living in insecure areas, and to perform military liaison with the Royal Cambodian Armed Forces [*Further Report of the Secretary-General Pursuant to Paragraph 7 of Resolution 840 (1993), S/26546, 10/7/93*]. Second, the presence of millions of land mines strewn about the Cambodian landscape continued to be a severe impediment to rural reconstruction. UNTAC requested, and U.N. Headquarters concurred, that the **Cambodian Mine Action Centre (CMAC)** remain in operation to train Cambodian demining teams and to keep its equipment in operation. The U.N. Trust Fund for Demining Programmes in Cambodia was, at the last moment, kept open and eventually replenished by contributions from donor countries in concert with reconstruction activities coordinated by the U.N. Development Programme [Letter, 10/28/93, Secretary-General to President of the Security Council, S/26675, 11/1/93].

Cambodia's Precarious Future

With the exception of the above activities, **UNTAC stood down formally on November 15, 1993.** All things considered, it had been the most successful U.N. peacekeeping operation in the Organization's history. Yet it had failed to achieve national reconciliation among the Cambodian factions, and this became evident soon after the installation of the new government in Phnom Penh.

During the summer, PDK forces had initiated several **attacks against ethnic Vietnamese** people; they attacked railways in Kampot and Kompong Chhnang provinces, killing dozens of passengers and looting trains. Numerous small skirmishes occurred, some involving attacks upon UNTAC units. At the same time, UNTAC reported that the number of defectors from the Khmer Rouge had reached about 3,000, perhaps responding to the government's propaganda campaign made in tandem with offers to negotiate a modus vivendi with the PDK (and King Sihanouk's renewed overtures in this direction). But it was by no means clear how profoundly the armed potential of the Khmer Rouge had been diminished or, more important, what strategy they would employ in the wake of a national referendum that had unambiguously demonstrated the Cambodian people's preference for a peaceful political solution to Cambodia's problems via the ballot box.

Hostilities escalated toward year end, mainly in the northwestern areas of Siem Reap and Preah Vihear provinces along the border with Thailand and Laos. The ability of the Khmer Rouge, when pressed militarily, to retreat across the Thai border with the reported tacit cooperation of the Thai Army became a major diplomatic issue between Phnom

Penh and Bangkok. In December, Thai police announced they had raided an arms cache just inside Thailand and seized 1,500 tons of weapons guarded by a Thai Army officer and 22 Khmer Rouge cadres. **Thai Prime Minister Chuan Leekpai's visit to Phnom Penh** in January 1994 and a treaty of cooperation, including border security measures, did little to quell the subsequent uproar. Any hope of reconciliation with the PDK through negotiation was dashed in February 1994 when government forces captured the Khmer Rouge base at Anlong Veng. After trumpeting the victory as an indication of the Khmer Rouge on the run, the government was embarrassed three weeks later when Khmer Rouge forces retook the Anlong Veng base. The same pattern was repeated in March when 7,000 government troops assaulted the military base and important gem-mining town of Pailin, a few miles from the Thai border. Pailin was captured, creating 25,000 refugees and occasioning yet another round of bitter criticism against the Thai military, who reportedly facilitated the escape of Khmer Rouge leader Pol Pot from his headquarters into Thai territory. To make matters worse, on April 19 the **Khmer Rouge successfully counterattacked Pailin,** recapturing it one month to the day after it had been seized by the government [*Indochina Digest* and *Far Eastern Economic Review*, 12/93–4/94].

Internal security in Cambodia became more precarious following the withdrawal of UNTAC's military component [*Mid-Term Report of the Secretary-General on the United Nations Military Liaison Team in Cambodia*, S/1994/169, 2/14/94]. The **depressed state of the economy** continued, and the prolonged nonpayment of salaries to civil servants and soldiers and the widespread availability of weapons aggravated the situation. Many illegal checkpoints were set up throughout the country by soldiers who extorted money from travelers. **Banditry** was, and remains today, widespread; **kidnapping** of foreigners for ransom has become the latest trend; and **killings** of ethnic Vietnamese civilians have continued. Although the Khmer Rouge are the suspected perpetrators, these killings are symptomatic of an **extraordinary lawlessness in the Cambodian countryside,** which the new government has not been able to stem.

International Reconstruction Assistance

The second meeting of the **International Committee on the Reconstruction of Cambodia (ICORC)** was held in Tokyo, March 10–11, 1994. The meeting brought together representatives of 31 countries, the European Union, and 12 international organizations. They agreed that the situation had improved markedly as a result of the May 1993 elections and the creation of a coalition government. The economy was being liberalized according to free market principles, and the government had drawn up a broad plan of medium-term development in cooperation with the U.N.

Development System (UNDS), the umbrella coordinator for the international agencies at work in Cambodia. The U.N. Centre for Human Rights was in place in Phnom Penh.

These positive factors recognized, the **macroeconomic picture** and the condition of the country's **physical infrastructure** remained grim. The report of the U.N. Resident Representative in Cambodia highlighted the impoverished state of Cambodia's rural population. Some 35 percent of all families are headed by single mothers. Only 12 percent of the rural population have access to a safe water supply; village-level health services are nonexistent; one child in five does not reach his fifth birthday, while less than a third have been vaccinated against the six basic childhood diseases. The school system is grossly inadequate qualitatively and quantitatively; hundreds of thousands of school-age children are added each year with no increase in facilities. Agricultural productivity is extremely low and hampered by millions of mines, which cause hundreds of casualties each month. Access to markets is almost universally hampered by roads that are difficult in dry weather and impassable when wet [Joint Statement of U.N. Resident Representative in Cambodia, UNDP, 3/3/94].

The ICORC meeting noted that an **infusion of international financial and technical assistance** over a period of years was imperative to rebuild Cambodia's devastated economy and social institutions. ICORC members pledged $773 million in new aid—$486 million in 1994 and $271 million in 1995, plus $15.8 million for mine clearance. The leading donors for 1994 were Japan ($87.7 million), the World Bank ($75 million), the Asian Development Bank ($50 million), the International Monetary Fund ($40 million), France ($40 million), and the United States ($33 million, plus $40 million for 1995). It was thus well recognized that UNTAC's political accomplishments would be meaningless unless the current relative stability can be secured through economic development.

Economic development can have meaningful effect only if the fundamental conflict between the Khmer Rouge and the elected government is diminished and eventually brought to an end, either by force or by compromise. At this point compromise and reconciliation seem unlikely. In King Sihanouk's words of April 22, while calling for a new round of peace talks: "The fratricidal war continues to destroy the country. If this continues our country will die." As of mid-May 1994, heavy fighting was taking place in several western Cambodian provinces, and the Khmer Rouge were embarking on a fresh campaign of terrorism elsewhere in the country, including the kidnapping of foreign business people and aid workers. In late May, two days of roundtable peace talks in Pyongyang, North Korea, where King Sihanouk was in residence, failed to achieve an agreement for a cease-fire. Upon his return to Phnom Penh, First Prime Minister Norodom Ranariddh stated bluntly that the Khmer Rouge had shown that the only way to resolve the country's problems was "through war, through fighting" [*Indochina Digest*, 6/3/94]. Further talks were scheduled for later in June in Phnom Penh, but few observers were optimistic that the Khmer Rouge would accept the government's conditions or that the government would (or could afford to) modify its conditions adequately to satisfy the Khmer Rouge. The international donor community will have to take this uncertain situation into account as it plans and attempts to execute its future assistance programs in Cambodia.

8. Cyprus
By Edmund T. Piasecki

The United Nations took a new approach to the situation in Cyprus in 1993, revising the financing arrangements for its cash-strapped peace-keeping operation while directly addressing for the first time the atmosphere of deep distrust between the rival governments of that Mediterranean island nation. The Security Council and the Secretary-General hope that the decision to meet shortfalls in voluntary contributions to the **U.N. Force in Cyprus (UNFICYP)** through mandatory assessments [S/Res/831, 5/23/93], and the opening of negotiations on a set of U.N.-proposed "confidence-building measures," will allow the world body to maintain a viable peacekeeping presence on the divided island and encourage the conclusion of an overall framework agreement for peace.

The new approach has already moved the **internationally recognized Republic of Cyprus** and its patron, Greece, to increase their annual voluntary contributions to UNFICYP to $25 million, more than half of the operation's total yearly cost [S/25912, 6/9/93]. Turkey, the other external actor, has embraced confidence-building in principle and has encouraged its ally, the self-styled "Turkish Republic of Northern Cyprus," to do the same.

U.N. Secretary-General Boutros-Ghali had first proposed a confidence-building strategy in November 1992, after failing to win final approval from all sides for the **"Set of Ideas,"** a comprehensive draft agreement under discussion since 1990. The Secretary-General's **Deputy Special Representative,** Gustave Feissel, broadened and refined the eight original proposals to 14 specific steps in preparatory talks with the leaders of the two Cypriot "communities" held in April and May 1993 in Nicosia. The negotiators reached full agreement on 12 rather modest measures, including intercommunal cooperation at the expert level on problems relating to water supply, education, health and the environment, and electricity generation. More significant, both sides supported an expansion of the 1989 "unmanning agreement" to cover all areas of the U.N.-patrolled buffer zone where Greek and Turkish Cypriot forces are in close proximity. An expanded agreement would lead to more voluntarily withdrawals by the respective forces from forward positions along the zone and further decrease the likelihood of renewed hostilities.

Of greatest importance to the effort to build confidence and reach an overall peace agreement were the proposals calling for resettlement of the town of Varosha and the reopening of the Nicosia International Airport. Part of the town and all of the airport have been closed to traffic from either side after a resurgence of intercommunal violence in 1974.

At joint meetings in New York, chaired by the Secretary-General and his **Special Representative** Joe Clark, the Greek and Turkish Cypriot leaders worked out detailed provisions for U.N. administration of both a "free trade zone" in Varosha and a refurbished airport accessible to both communities. But in mid-June 1993, **Turkish Cypriot leader Rauf Denktash** (President of Northern Cyprus) balked at giving his final approval to the proposals, demanding that part of Varosha remain under the exclusive control of his government and that the United Nations lift embargoes on air and sea ports in northern Cyprus. Despite this setback, the Secretary-General remained "hopeful" that agreement was still within reach and declared that implementation of the Varosha/airport "package" "would, without doubt, constitute the most important forward step in Cyprus in almost two decades" [S/26026, 7/1/93].

After the failure of Clark and Feissel to advance the proposals through visits to Cyprus, Greece, and Turkey in the summer of 1993, the **Security Council publicly criticized Turkish Cypriot intransigence** in September and called on that side to "give its active support to the effort." The Council also approved the Secretary-General's further proposal to dispatch a technical mission in Cyprus to analyze (and publicize) the benefits of the package to both communities. Assembled with the assistance of the U.N. Development Programme (UNDP) and the International Civil Aviation Organization (ICAO), two expert teams—six international economists and four authorities on civil aviation—conducted field work in Cyprus during October and November and submitted their findings to the Secretary-General in mid-December. In his November 22 report to the Security Council, Boutros-Ghali underscored the support the Varosha/airport proposals enjoyed "at the highest level" of the Turkish government and Ankara's belief that "there should be speedy developments in the search for a solution to the Cyprus problem" [S/26777, 11/22/93, par. 49].

In the same report, the Secretary-General addressed the possibility of converting UNFICYP from a peacekeeping force to a smaller, unarmed, and less costly observer mission. Boutros-Ghali argued for retention of the current arrangements, noting that troop strength had already been reduced from 2,078 to 1,203 since November 1992. In support of his argument, the Secretary-General cited the absence of formal agreements in Cyprus delineating the cease-fire lines and defining permissible activities under the cessation of hostilities. He also emphasized that the opposing forces were only meters from each other in some areas. These conditions led to frequent "incidents" along the buffer zone, requiring the rapid dispatch of armed troops to physically occupy the ground between the sides and prevent a large-scale renewal of hostilities. Boutros-Ghali also rejected a second proposal—to reduce troop strength and increase the number of unarmed observers—on the grounds that many of UNFICYP's troops already perform observer duty and participate in, rather than merely request, armed patrols in response to cease-fire violations [ibid., par. 97–99].

Also in the November 22 report, the Secretary-General responded to the charge that after nearly 30 years in the field, UNFICYP had become part of the problem in Cyprus, not part of the solution. He suggested that the Security Council consider several factors in determining how long it should maintain the U.N. presence on the island, including: Greek Cypriot concerns about the large numbers of Turkish army troops and Turkish civilians in the north; the certainty of renewed hostilities should UNFICYP be withdrawn under the current circumstances; and the indispensability of continued "tranquility" to the negotiation of a political settlement [ibid., par. 100].

These observations formed the basis of the Security Council's "comprehensive reassessment" of UNFICYP—the second since 1990—called for in Resolution 831 of May 27, 1993. The Council supported the Secretary-General's conclusions in its Resolution 889 of December 15, deciding against a further restructuring of UNFICYP and for an extension of the operation's mandate through June 15, 1994. But the Council also planned another thorough review of the situation—"including the future role of the United Nations"—and promised to "consider alternative ways" to reach an overall settlement should disagreements persist on implementing the package of confidence-building measures.

Following the adoption of Resolution 889, the Secretary-General released the reports of his technical mission to Cyprus. Focusing on the advantages of the confidence-building measures to the depressed Turkish Cypriot economy, the experts estimated that the northern part of the island could realize some $53 million a year by reopening Varosha and another $63 million from a reactivated Nicosia Airport through increases in tourism alone [UNDP Update, 1/94]. The General Assembly, for its part, authorized continued financial support for UNFICYP on December 23 and concluded that, in light of the increased voluntary contributions and the $8.8 million already assessed on member states [A/Res/47/236, 9/14/93], no additional assessments on member states were required [A/Res/48/474].

Renewed negotiations on the confidence-building measures showed some promise in early 1994. On January 28, President Denktash finally confirmed that the Turkish Cypriot side would join the Greek Cypriots in accepting the Varosha/airport package "in principle." By February 15, both Denktash and **Greek Cypriot President Glafcos Clerides** had signed off on a seven-point agenda for further talks aimed at reaching agreement on the precise means for implementing the package as well as the other 12 measures.

In proximity talks opened on February 17, the leaders discussed the definition and timing of U.N. "administration" over Varosha and the airport; the establishment and functioning of the free trade zone of Varosha; guarantees of traffic rights, safe operation, and free access at the airport; and the immediate implemention of the other 12 measures following agreement on the Varosha/airport package. In his report to the Security Council of March 4, Boutros-Ghali announced that talks could conclude "within a few weeks" [S/1994/262]. Welcoming the acceptance in principle of the confidence-building measures by both sides, the Council "stresse[d] the need to conclude . . . an agreement without delay" and requested the Secretary-General to report again by the end of March [S/Res/902, 3/11/94].

Negotiations stalled again, however, on March 21, when President Denktash charged that the Secretary-General's representatives had revised a consolidated text of ideas in favor of the other side. President Clerides, while unhappy with some of the revisions, would have supported the text, according to the Secretary-General, had Denktash done the same. Both Joe Clark and Gustave Feissel confirmed publicly at the end of March that objections from the Turkish Cypriot side alone were blocking a final agreement [S/1994/380, 4/4/94]. The Security Council expressed its "concern" that the talks had not concluded successfully or within the expected time frame and "underlin[d] the need" to reach an agreement "before the end of April" [S/1994/414, 4/11/94].

After a further series of meetings in Nicosia, Washington, and Ankara involving the Secretary-General's representatives and those of both Cypriot communities, Denktash announced on April 28 that the talks had "collapsed." In a final but unsuccessful attempt to break the deadlock, Feissel and U.S. diplomats met with the Turkish and Turkish Cypriot sides alone on May 11–12 in Vienna. The Secretary-General informed the Security Council on May 30 that "the absence of an agreement [was] due essentially to a lack of political will on the Turkish Cypriot side" [S/1994/629].

Boutros-Ghali argued vociferously in his report that the draft ideas of March 21 were completely "faithful" to the original confidence-building measures, despite continued Turkish Cypriot claims that "significant" changes had been introduced, tipping the balance of benefits toward the Greek Cypriot side. To reestablish "parity," Denktash had proposed several additional changes. The surrender of the fenced area of Varosha to immediate U.N. administration would be delayed until Nicosia Airport became operational in 12 months' time. Landing rights for Cyprus Airlines, the Greek Cypriot carrier, would not be automatic but subject to negotiation by U.N. administrators. The Turkish Cypriot side, not the United Nations, would collect customs duties at the airport and in Varosha. Access to the fenced area at Varosha would be "protected" by Turkish Cypriot civilian police and only "observed" by UNFICYP. And the actual size of the area that would come under U.N. control would be significantly reduced.

The Secretary-General doubted that his representatives could further revise the draft ideas to take these proposals into account without losing the support of the Greek Cypriot side. He presented the Security Council with five options: "redirect" U.N. resources to other regional disputes more amenable to resolution; resort to "coercive measures" to compel compliance with previous U.N. resolutions; resume negotiations toward an overall framework agreement on the basis of the "set of ideas"; request the Secretary-General to consult with all concerned parties on a fundamentally new approach; or renew the effort at confidence-building. Boutros-Ghali suggested that the Council consider several preparatory measures before choosing among the options—holding an international conference, dispatching an ad hoc committee of Council members to the island, or returning the Special Representative with a new mandate.

After 30 years the Secretary-General's good offices mission in Cyprus as currently constituted appears to be at an end. Sanctions seem an unlikely alternative as does continuation of the confidence-building approach. Return to comprehensive negotiations may also be unworkable in the absence of the trust that confidence-building was intended to provide. But as long as troop contributors are willing to maintain their forces on the island, the United Nations will doubtless continue some effort at peacemaking. Although he did not say so, Boutros-Ghali seems inclined toward taking a pause for reflection that could produce informal consultations and the fundamentally new approach so long overdue.

II
Arms Control and Disarmament
By Ivo H. Daalder and Howard A. Moyes

The past year witnessed a consolidation of the arms control agenda. After much cajoling on the part of the United States, Ukraine agreed to ratify the START I Treaty in early 1994 and immediately to commence the arduous task of implementing that agreement. The way to further reductions in U.S. and Russian strategic forces, as provided for under START II, was therefore finally open. However, the difficulties of securing the ratification of the START treaties left little room for new bilateral negotiations to reduce strategic forces still further, although some progress on changing nuclear operating procedures was achieved during the **Clinton-Yeltsin Moscow summit in January 1994.**

On the multilateral front, formal negotiations on a comprehensive nuclear test ban treaty were begun under the auspices of the U.N. Conference on Disarmament. While initial progress proved promising, it remained uncertain whether an initial agreement would be completed by early 1995, when the states parties to the nuclear Non-Proliferation Treaty (NPT) will convene to decide on that treaty's extension. And although progress on a test ban increased the chances for garnering a large majority in favor of a long-term or indefinite extension of the NPT, North Korea's continuing defiance of the international community and outright violation of the treaty cast some doubt on the continuing viability of the nuclear nonproliferation regime. On the other hand, developments in Latin America and Africa provided new hope that the threat of regional nuclear proliferation could be stemmed at least in these areas, though the failure of similar progress in the Middle East and the Indian subcontinent underscored how difficult it is to negotiate meaningful restrictions on nuclear and other weapons of mass destruction on a regional basis.

In the chemical weapons area, progress toward the entry into force of the **1993 Chemical Weapons Convention** some time in early to mid-1995 proceeded apace. Though only eight countries had ratified the convention by mid-1994, some 157 nations had signed and many were expected to ratify the convention before the end of the year. There were also welcome efforts to strengthen the **Biological and Toxin Weapons Convention,** notably by strengthening the means to secure compliance with the convention. A group of governmental experts concluded in early 1994 that a variety of transparency measures, including mandatory data exchanges and periodic on-site visits, could enhance confidence in compliance and deter violations of the agreement. A special conference of states parties was to convene in September 1994 to discuss ways of adopting these measures in a legally binding manner. The past year was also the first in which the **U.N. Register on Conventional Arms** became fully operational. Over 80 countries submitted data on arms exports and imports completed the preceding year, setting the stage for the registry's enlargement in 1995.

Many of these developments are sure to be welcomed by the 49th Session of the General Assembly. As during the 48th Session, the coming General Assembly will likely continue to call for the consolidation of arms control and disarmament efforts, particularly in the area of nuclear testing and nonproliferation, while searching for ways in which the progress achieved over the past few years can be extended to new and more challenging areas.

1. Nuclear Arms Control

Contrary to previous years, in 1993–94 there was no major new agreement reducing U.S. and Russian nuclear weapons. Instead, the focus of intensive efforts was on securing the promise of past agreements, notably by implementing the unilateral but reciprocated elimination of thousands of nonstrategic nuclear weapons and ensuring **Ukraine's acquiescence in START I,** which would enable the United States and Russia to fulfill their commitment under **START II** to reduce their strategic forces to 3,000–3,500 weapons by the end of the decade [see *A Global Agenda: Issues/47,* pp. 119–23; *A Global Agenda: Issues/48,* pp. 130–31].

The dismantling of U.S. and Russian nonstrategic nuclear forces proceeded smoothly throughout 1993, with between 1,500 and 2,000 weapons destroyed on each side. Moreover, despite awaiting the formal entry into force of the START I Treaty, the **United States** and, to a lesser extent, **Russia** continued to reduce their forces as called for by the treaty. In fact, by the end of 1994 the United States will have removed all warheads from weapons slated for elimination under START I, while a quarter of the warheads will have been removed from Russian forces [DOD *Annual Report to the President and Congress, 1994,* p. 60]. However, Washington has indicated that it will not proceed with the implementation of the START II Treaty until Moscow is fully committed to the same path [*The New York Times,* 5/13/94]. And Russia has made clear that its commitment to START II depends largely on whether Ukraine fully implements its obligations under START I, including the complete elimination of nuclear weapons on its territory.

Throughout 1993 the critical nuclear arms control cards were therefore held by Kiev. Under the terms of the 1992 **Lisbon protocol to START I** and accompanying statements, Ukraine had agreed to eliminate all 1,804 warheads for missiles and air-launched cruise missiles on its territory within the seven-year reduction period of the START agreement and to accede to the nuclear **Non-Proliferation Treaty (NPT)** in the "shortest possible time." However, having made that commitment, Kiev sought new security, political, and financial concessions from the United States and Russia before agreeing to its ratification [*Issues/48*, pp. 131–33]. Washington's and Moscow's reluctance to agree to these terms led to the conditional ratification of START I by the Ukrainian Rada, or parliament, on November 18, 1993 [CD/1229]. In its resolution of ratification, the Rada included 13 conditions, inter alia stipulating that it would agree to the elimination of only 36 percent of the missiles and 42 percent of the warheads on its territory and that it did not consider the clause committing Ukraine to the NPT as a non-nuclear weapon state to be binding.

The partial ratification of Ukraine's commitment elicited a strong Russian reaction, including an explicit threat to take the matter to the U.N. Security Council [CD/1230]. To prevent a further breakdown in Russian-Ukrainian relations (which were already on edge as a result of disagreements over the Black Sea fleet), the United States intensified efforts to reach a solution acceptable to all sides. These efforts met with success in early January 1994, just as President Clinton was to arrive for a long-scheduled summit meeting with President Yeltsin.

Under a **trilateral agreement** made public by the presidents of Russia, Ukraine, and the United States in Moscow on January 14, 1994, Ukraine finally and openly agreed to full implementation of its obligations, including the rapid elimination of nuclear weapons from its territory and early accession to the NPT [CD/1243]. In return, the United States promised Kiev at least $175 million in financial assistance for the dismantlement and transport of weapons on its territory; Russia agreed to compensate Ukraine, Kazakhstan, and Belarus for the value of highly enriched uranium contained in the nuclear weapons stationed on their territory (in the case of Ukraine, this compensation would take the form of fuel assemblies for nuclear power stations); and the United States, Russia, and Britain announced that once Ukraine had acceded to the NPT it would enjoy a full range of security assurances. What clinched the deal, however, was agreement to begin immediate implementation of its main elements. Thus, Kiev agreed to transfer at least 200 warheads and completely deactivate all 46 SS-24 missiles on its territory within ten months; Moscow agreed to ship 100 tons of low-enriched uranium fuel assemblies within the same time frame; and Washington would provide Russia with an advance payment of $60 million for the fuel assemblies, which would be deducted from later payments to Moscow for the 500 tons of highly enriched uranium Russia had agreed to sell to the United States over the next 20 years.

The trilateral agreement appeared to have resolved the Ukrainian problem, at least for the moment. The Ukrainian Rada voted to endorse the statement on February 3, 1994, and also to remove its earlier reservation with regard to the NPT [CD/1244]. Approximately 60 warheads a month are being transferred from Ukraine to Russia, which, if continued at this pace, will allow the transfer of all warheads to be completed within three to four years [*RFE/RL Daily Report*, 5/17/94]. Despite temporary difficulties and disagreements, it would appear that the issue has finally been resolved, thus allowing for the full implementation of not just the first but also the second START agreement by the end of the decade. This result is sure to be welcomed by the 49th Session of the General Assembly, which is likely to urge the rapid implementation of the START treaties while calling on all nuclear weapons states to embark on new efforts to reduce their nuclear forces still further.

2. The Return of the ABM Treaty

In late 1993 another arms control issue, hotly debated in the 1980s, returned to the forefront, namely, the question of the **Anti-Ballistic Missile (ABM) Treaty,** which bars the deployment of strategically significant missile defense systems by the United States and the former Soviet Union. Few had expected that the ABM issue would return under a Democratic president, and in July 1993 the Clinton administration had indeed announced that the United States would fully abide by the traditional interpretation of the treaty's provisions, thus abandoning its predecessors' efforts to change the terms of the treaty by fiat [*The New York Times*, 7/15/93] However, the growing threat of missile proliferation and the increased attention given to **anti-tactical ballistic missile (ATBM)** defenses as a possible response to this threat once again raised the question of U.S. compliance with the **ABM Treaty.** Although the treaty does not prohibit the testing or deployment of systems capable of intercepting tactical ballistic missiles, it does ban systems that can defend against strategic missiles; and the question of where to draw the line between systems capable of the former but not the latter is not spelled out in the treaty. Since the ABM Treaty's signing, the United States has informally adhered to guidelines that considered ABM systems to be those that were tested against targets with an entry speed in excess of 2 kilometers per second and flying at an altitude above 40 kilometers, which would be sufficient against tactical missiles of about 1,000-kilometer range.

In the future, tactical missiles with ranges greatly in excess of 1,000 kilometers may well be deployed, raising the question whether more capable ATBM systems are needed. For example, a new system—the **Theater High Altitude Area Defense (THAAD) system**—would be capable of intercepting missiles with a range of 3,500 kilometers. In order to enable the development of the THAAD system without calling U.S. compliance with the ABM Treaty into question, the Clinton administration proposed in November 1993 that the demarcation between prohibited and nonprohibited anti-missile systems be clarified. Specifically, the administration proposed that an ATBM system be regarded as ABM-capable if it possessed a "demonstrated" capability (i.e., were tested) against targets entering with speeds in excess of 5 kilometers per second [*The New York Times*, 12/3/93; *Inside the Pentagon*, 12/9/93]. Since strategic ballistic missile warheads reenter at a speed of some 7 kilometers per second, the proposed demarcation implies that ATBMs deployed under these guidelines may have some, or even a "nontrivial," capability against strategic ballistic missiles, a capability that the ABM Treaty is supposed to prohibit. The Clinton administration's proposal has therefore been particularly controversial in the arms control community [*Arms Control Today*, 24, no. 3 (4/94), pp. 3–8]. Moreover, since the administration seeks to settle the matter through a clarification rather than an amendment, some U.S. senators have expressed unease about an executive reinterpretation of an arms control treaty that did not require the Senate's advice and consent.

In contrast to the U.S. arms control community and some U.S. senators, **Russia** has greeted the proposal with considerably more sympathy, reflecting in part a recognition that missile proliferation may pose as great, if not a greater, threat to Russian security. Rather than rejecting the U.S. proposal, Russia has therefore sought to define the demarcation line between prohibited and nonprohibited activities and systems in a way that, though more restrictive than the U.S. proposal, would still allow the deployment of highly capable ATBM systems. Specifically, while accepting the 5-kilometer-per-second target speed, Russia has proposed adding two additional restrictions: (1) that tests be conducted against missiles with ranges of 3,500 kilometers or less; and (2) that the interceptor speed not exceed 3 kilometers per second. Particularly the latter provision would limit the development of more advanced U.S. antimissile systems, though not of THAAD. While Washington has accepted the principle of interceptor limitations, it has not accepted the specific limits proposed by Moscow [ibid., no. 2 (3/94) *The Washington Post*, 7/2/94].

Although this issue is highly technical and therefore not likely to be a dominant one during the 49th Session of the General Assembly, it will be of interest to some members. For example, France has explicitly linked its endorsement of a nuclear test ban to the continuation of a number of arms control agreements, including the ABM Treaty [CD/PV.657, p. 16]. If the deployment of more capable antimissile systems were to be allowed under the proposed clarification, Paris may come to believe that the viability of the French nuclear deterrent, which relies to a large extent on missiles with ranges shorter than those deployed by Russia or the United States, is being called into question. Its continuing willingness to endorse further arms control measures, including in particular a test ban treaty, may therefore become doubtful. But whether this question will become a major issue of contention during the 49th Session remains to be seen.

3. Nuclear Testing

Of all the arms control issues in 1993, the negotiations on a **comprehensive nuclear test ban treaty (CTBT)** received the most attention during the 48th Session, and for good reason. Following the announcement by President Clinton on July 3, 1993, that the United States would join Russia and France in a testing moratorium and would push for the early conclusion of a CTBT (thus reversing a policy of previous U.S. administrations), the way to formal negotiations was opened. In late July and early August the United States, Russia, France, Britain, and finally, China all endorsed formal negotiations, and a mandate to this effect was concluded within the **Conference on Disarmament** on August 10, 1993 [CD/1209]. The new climate was also reflected in deliberations within the **General Assembly's First Committee** and, subsequently, in the 48th Session of the General Assembly, which for the first time passed a resolution in support of a CTBT by consensus [A/Res/48/70].

The negotiations have been influenced by two factors. First, they exposed differences among the major states on a number of key issues, notably with respect to the scope of obligations, verification, and entry into force. Second, and of more immediate concern, was the effect of China's refusal to abide by the informal testing moratorium on the positions of the other nuclear powers, notably France and Britain.

On October 5, 1993, China tested a large nuclear device, thus breaking an informal testing moratorium that had been in effect since China last tested a weapon 12 months earlier. The test was a direct defiance of the moratorium and was conducted despite public and private U.S. appeals not to do so [*The New York Times*, 9/18/93; and Speech of President Clinton to the U.N. General Assembly, 9/27/93]. In explaining its decision, Beijing issued a statement declaring that "History has shown that a conditional 'moratorium' designed to maintain [Western] nuclear superiority while refusing to renounce deterrence and commit oneself to complete prohibition and thorough destruction of nuclear weapons is of extremely limited significance" [*The Washington Post*, 10/6/93]. Since the U.S. decision of July 1993 not to test was predicated on no other country testing first, the Chinese test raised questions about whether the United States (and, by implication, others) would continue to adhere to the moratorium. Although a U.S. statement following the test indicated that the President had directed "actions as are needed to put the U.S. in a position to be able to conduct nuclear tests" in 1994 [*The New York Times*, 10/6/93], Washington did not follow Beijing and, in fact, announced in March 1994 that it would extend its testing moratorium until September 1995 [ACDA Official Text, 3/15/94]. This position was not changed even after China tested another device in June 1994.

Contrary to the restraint shown by Washington and Moscow, the Chinese test presented the occasion to reopen a **bitter debate in France** about the wisdom of continuing to abide by the moratorium. An ambiguous statement issued after the 1993 test, in which Paris stated that it would "examine the consequences" in consultation with the United States, Britain, and Russia, reflected the fact that President François Mitterrand favors the moratorium and a **CTBT** while the center-right government opposes both. Thus, President Mitterrand stated that France would only resume testing if other countries besides China did so, while the government, including a parliamentary commission, argued that France requires some 20 additional tests before it could agree to a CTBT [JPRS-TND-93-033, 10/14/93, p. 9; *Le Monde*, 12/17/93, p. 20]. The issue is unlikely to be resolved until after the French presidential elections in May 1995, but in the meantime the dispute has influenced France's negotiating position in Geneva.

On January 25, 1994, the Conference on Disarmament (CD) formally adopted a mandate directing "the Ad Hoc Committee to negotiate intensively a universal and multilaterally and effectively verifiable comprehensive nuclear test ban treaty" [CD/1238], echoing the language of the General Assembly resolution passed weeks before during its 48th Session. Two working groups were established—one dealing with verification and one with legal and institutional issues. The negotiations were significantly helped by the submission of **Swedish and Australian draft treaty texts** in December 1993 and March 1994 respectively. The negotiators addressed many issues, but critical disagreements that were central to a rapid conclusion revolved around four issues: the scope of obligations, the mechanisms for entry into force, verification, and linkage (if any) of the CTBT to the NPT.

A key issue in the negotiations concerns the scope of obligations, i.e., what actions are to be prohibited. Most countries favor a broad and traditional definition of what the treaty would ban, using, for example, the definition of a nuclear test as employed in the **Limited Test Ban Treaty:** "nuclear weapon explosion or other nuclear explosion." A ban on this activity would, therefore, include a ban on **peaceful nuclear explosions (PNEs),** both because many doubt the economic rationale for such uses of nuclear energy and because allowing PNEs would open a major loophole in the treaty. However, China does not share this view; it has proposed a definition of prohibited activity that would allow the conduct of PNEs [*Arms Control Today*, 24, no. 4 (5/94), p. 17].

Another issue of scope is whether to ban "preparations" for conducting nuclear tests, which is included in the Swedish but not the Australian draft treaty text. Many major powers believe that since this activity is often indistinguishable from nonprohibited actions, verification would be difficult and raise the cost significantly. Finally, some states, like Indonesia, would like to include computer simulations in the prohibition in order to prevent actions necessary to maintain the reliability of existing weapon stockpiles [CD/PV.670]. Again, the difficulty of verification, combined with the belief on the part of some that the CTBT should not be seen as a nuclear disarmament agreement, has raised opposition to this suggestion.

Related to the issue of scope is the question of whether the CTBT would ban testing for all time. France and Britain have suggested that a CTBT should not degrade the effectiveness of their nuclear arsenals (even if they have implicitly accepted that a test ban may prevent significant modernization). Therefore, both have proposed that the treaty allow periodic "safety tests" under full monitoring [ibid., p. 23]. So far, no other state has supported this position, and few are likely to do so, especially since a CTBT would be acceptable only if its provisions applied equally to all signatories.

While the specific details of the verification regime remain to be worked out, there appears to be agreement that verification should encompass seismic means, nonseismic means like atmospheric sampling, and on-site inspections. Moreover, in addition to reliance on national technical means, there is agreement that responsibility for verification should be vested in an international organization. The Swedish draft proposed that the **International Atomic Energy Agency (IAEA)** be assigned that responsibility, but following a briefing by IAEA officials to the negotiators, many delegations appeared to share Australia's view that the agency lacked the technical expertise for this task. Australia's proposal to set up a new organization modeled on the **Organization for the Prohibition of Chemical Weapons (OPCW)** would be a better way to go.

Another contentious issue concerns the number and types of countries that should ratify the CTBT before it enters into force. Both France and Russia have argued that all countries with a nuclear capability (defined by Russia as all countries that possess nuclear power stations and research reactors) should ratify the treaty before its entry into force. Britain has suggested that all CD members should ratify before entry into force, and it has noted that the current CD membership of 38 countries may soon expand to include 23 additional countries, among which would be Israel, Iraq, and North Korea. The United States favors ratification by all nuclear powers before entry into force, but it has expressed doubt "about making EIF contingent on ratification by a specific group of States, beyond the nuclear-weapons States. Hence we believe that the considerations that led to the rather conservative entry-into-force provisions of the CWC should not apply to the CTBT" [CD/PV.699, p. 13].

Finally, there is the issue of **linkage between the CTBT and the NPT's extension.** Many non-nuclear weapons states have long called for the conclusion of a CTBT as a *precondition* for the long-term or indefinite extension of the NPT, noting that Article VI of the NPT explicitly calls on the nuclear powers to negotiate such a treaty. Russia and the United States have explicitly rejected this linkage, although both are committed to completing negotiations in the shortest possible time and Russia has expressed the hope that a CTBT might be ready for signature in the spring of 1995, before the NPT extension conference opens [CD/PV.668, p. 9]. In contrast to Washington's and Moscow's implicit recognition (though explicit rejection) of the linkage between the CTBT and the NPT extension, Britain and France have openly linked the two treaties—but in a manner *opposite* to that intended by the adherents of linkage. Both countries have argued that if the CTBT is to contribute to nuclear nonproliferation, then endorsement of the treaty must be conditioned on securing the indefinite extension of the NPT. As the British delegate to the CD declared, "the prospect of indefinite extension of the NPT will be an important factor in convincing us that we can confidently move towards the conclusion of a CTBT" [CD/PV.666, p. 24].

With negotiations toward a CTBT gathering speed in the second half of 1994 and the NPT extension conference fast approaching in early 1995, the issue of implicit or explicit linkage between the two treaties will be a major point of discussion during the 49th Session of the General Assemby. Although the precise details of this and all other negotiating questions will properly be handled in Geneva, the debate on the CTBT during the 49th Session should prove to be a lively one.

4. Nuclear Proliferation and the NPT

The 49th Session of the General Assembly will be the last session before the states parties to the **NPT** convene to decide on its extension. The NPT, which currently has 163 parties and may reach the 170-mark by the time of the extension conference, will be a major topic of debate, particular if a draft resolution supporting indefinite extension were to be put forward by the many states that have openly declared this as their goal. Progress in the CTBT negotiations will also be an important factor in determining the nature of debate at the General Assembly, as will discussion of such issues as a production cutoff of fissile material for weapons purposes and the question of security assurances by the nuclear powers to nonnuclear states—the conclusion of both having been endorsed during the 48th Session [A/Res/48/75L; A/Res/48/73]. However, a key issue during the 49th Session, as during the 48th, is likely to be **North Korea,** which continued to defy the international community in refusing to accept inspections by the **International Atomic Energy Agency (IAEA)** mandated by the NPT and the safeguards agreement it had signed with the agency in 1992.

Article X of the NPT states that "Twenty-five years after the entry into force of the Treaty, a conference shall be convened to decide whether the Treaty shall continue indefinitely, or shall be continued for an additional fixed period or periods." Since the NPT entered into force on March 5, 1970, a conference must be convened in early 1995 to decide the treaty's extension. The decision will be made by the majority of the parties to the NPT, not by a majority of those attending the conference, and that decision will be immediately binding on all parties, not just those attending or those voting in favor. Moreover, by the terms of this provision, the treaty can only be extended, it cannot be terminated. However, anything less than indefinite extension will mean that after the period or periods of extension have lapsed, the treaty will expire unless it has been amended, which would require ratification by all the parties to the treaty. Finally, there can be no conditions attached to the extension of the NPT, since that would constitute an amendment to the treaty. In view of these factors, the decision to be made in early 1995 will determine the future of the NPT and, by extension, the nuclear nonproliferation regime for decades hence. That explains the importance many have attached to securing the treaty's indefinite extension.

One issue that will determine whether this outcome is feasible will be the effect of **North Korea's** defiance of established nonproliferation norms. Continued flaunting of this norm by Pyongyang will inevitably weaken the NPT regime and strengthen arguments for less than indefinite extension of the treaty. On the other hand, if the international community in general and the United States in particular are successful in forcing (diplomatically or otherwise) North Korean compliance with its obligations, this would strengthen both the NPT and arguments in favor of its indefinite extension.

Throughout the past year the United States has played an active role in securing Pyongyang's adherence to the NPT and acceptance of the inspections to which the North agreed when it signed the IAEA safeguards agreement in 1992. The United States held two high-level meetings with the North Koreans in the summer of 1993. These discussions produced a number of commitments by Pyongyang: (1) to suspend its withdrawal from the NPT, which it had announced in March 1993; (2) to commence discussions with the IAEA regarding the continuity of safeguards through routine inspections of declared nuclear facilities; and (3) to resume discussions with South Korea on the implementation of their 1991 declaration on a denuclearized Korean Peninsula. The United States made clear that the continuation of the high-level dialogue was predicated on (1) the North remaining a full party to the NPT; (2) the IAEA being in a position to declare the continuity of safeguards; (3) an exchange of envoys between North and South Korea as a first step toward implementation of the denuclearization declaration; and (4) the North not engaging in any activity to reprocess spent fuel to extract plutonium.

Having thus agreed to a number of steps, the North stalled on key demands throughout 1993. Although Pyongyang did not formally withdraw from the NPT, it repeatedly stated that its suspension of the withdrawal process meant that it enjoyed a "special status" under the treaty. In addition, no envoys were exchanged between the North and the South, discussions with the IAEA were unsatisfactory, and there was no resumption of inspections—routine or otherwise. By November 1993 the IAEA reported to the General Assembly that the continuity of safeguards was "damaged," though not yet "broken," which would have triggered Security Council action. The 48th Session of the General Assembly responded to this report by commending the agency for its impartiality in dealing with the North Korean situation (the supposed lack of which was a key criticism by Pyongyang), and urged the North "to cooperate immediately with the Agency in the full implementation of the safeguards agreement" [A/Res/48/14]. The resolution was passed with only North Korea in opposition and nine abstentions (including China).

To induce Pyongyang's compliance, the United States offered the North three new inducements: It would agree to suspend the U.S.-South Korean "Team Spirit" military exercise for 1994; spell out in detail the political and economic benefits of normalized relations that would follow the resolution of the nuclear issue; and defer discussions of the IAEA special inspections of two suspected nuclear waste sites that had led to the crisis in early 1993. In return the North had to accept routine IAEA inspections and exchange envoys with the South [*The Washington Post*, 11/17/93; *The New York Times*, 11/22/93]. Following another few months of North Korean brinkmanship, Pyongyang finally allowed IAEA inspectors to enter its facilities in early March 1994, having received assurances by the United States that a third high-level round of talks would be scheduled and the Team Spirit exercise would be suspended.

With inspectors in North Korea, the crisis appeared to have abated, only to flare up again when the North refused to allow the inspectors the access required to ensure that no materials had been diverted to illicit purposes. As a result, the inspection was terminated and on March 21, 1994, the IAEA Board of Governors voted to pass the matter on to the U.N. Security Council [*Arms Control Today*, 24, no. 3 (4/94), p. 19]. In the Security Council the United States failed to receive Chinese support for a tough resolution demanding that North Korea allow IAEA inspections or else face sanctions. Instead, a milder Security Council statement was issued setting an implicit deadline of mid-May 1994 for the North to allow the inspections [*The New York Times,* 4/1/94]. As usual, just as the deadline approached, Pyongyang announced a new agreement with the IAEA to allow for the continuation of inspections that had been abruptly terminated in March [ibid., 5/13/94]. This followed an earlier announcement by Seoul that it no longer insisted on an exchange of envoys before a third round of U.S.-North Korean talks could be held [*The Washington Post,* 4/16/94]. However, as IAEA inspectors were preparing to depart for the Yongbyon nuclear complex to continue their inspection, North Korea announced that it had commenced withdrawing spent fuel from its main reactor, a process that must be subject to IAEA inspection to ensure that no diversion of the fuel, which contains three to five weapons' worth of plutonium, occurs [ibid., 5/15/94].

The illegal defueling of the North's research reactor made it nearly impossible for the IAEA to reconstruct Pyongyang's past activities, including to determine how much plutonium it might have reprocessed when fuel had been withdrawn from the reactor in 1989. Faced with this new fait accompli, Washington announced its intention to impose sanctions on Pyongyang and initiated efforts to gain Japanese, South Korean, Russian, and Chinese support for this step. The movement toward sanctions was temporarily suspended, however, when former President Jimmy Carter, on a "private" visit to North Korea, secured Kim Il-Sung's agreement to freeze the North's nuclear program, including most importantly an agreement not to commence reprocessing of the spent fuel. In response, Washington shifted course, agreeing to a third round of high-level talks with Pyongyang.

Historic talks between the North and South, which were to commence July 25, were indefinitely postponed on July 11—two days after it was announced that Kim Il-Sung had died from a heart attack at the age of 82. Also postponed were the ongoing negotiations in Geneva with the United States. In that instance, the North Korean negotiator told his U.S. counterpart that the two sides could meet again after President Kim's funeral, scheduled for July 17, to discuss resuming the talks [*The New York Times,* 7/11/94]. President Clinton viewed the announcement of a postponement of talks, rather than a cancellation, as a positive sign, and expressed his hope that they would be resumed at an appropriate time [National Public Radio, 7/11/94].

While it appeared that power was being transferred to Kim's son, the 52-year-old Kim Jong Il, there was no way to follow the succession process closely within North Korea's closed society. Indeed, the government went so far as to announce that no foreign delegations would be permitted to attend Kim Il-Sung's funeral.

5. Nuclear Weapons-Free Zones

During the 48th Session significant progress was made toward making both **Africa and Latin America** nuclear weapons-free zones (NWFZ). The problems associated with **South Africa's clandestine nuclear weapons program** have largely been resolved to the satisfaction of the IAEA and regional states. In Latin America, Argentina, Brazil, and Chile have all acceded to the **Treaty of Tlatelolco,** thereby paving the way for a consolidation of that region's prohibition on nuclear weapons. The prospects for similar prohibitions in the Middle East and South Asia, however, have not improved greatly during the past year. Some progress has been made, though, in implementing additional confidence-building measures in these two regions.

The 48th Session of the General Assembly called upon the Secretary-General and the Organization of African Unity (OAU) to begin the process of drafting a nuclear weapons-free zone treaty for Africa during 1994 [A/Res/48/86]. This represented a dramatic change from just two years ago, when South Africa's secret nuclear weapons activities first came to light and questions were raised about the accuracy of Pretoria's accounting records submitted to the IAEA upon its accession to the NPT. Over the past year, however, the Secretary-General reported that the IAEA had conducted 22 inspections of South Africa's nuclear facilities and found no evidence that the inventory of nuclear material was incomplete. In addition, the report stated that it did not know of any undeclared nuclear facilities in South Africa and that the country's test shafts had been rendered useless. Finally, the report concluded that the remaining components of South Africa's nuclear weapons program had been converted either to commercial nonnuclear applications or to peaceful nuclear uses [A/48/339]. As a result, the main political obstacle to achieving an African NWFZ has now been removed, and it is expected that a treaty will be concluded and ready for signature in early 1995. The 49th Session is sure to welcome this progress and urge the rapid conclusion of negotiations.

The progress made toward an African NWFZ was mirrored by efforts in 1993 to bring into full force the Treaty of Tlatelolco in Latin America, which was first opened for signature in 1967. Having jointly submitted four amendments to the treaty that changed some verification and reporting requirements, Argentina, Brazil, and Chile moved to ratify the treaty in early 1994 [*Arms Control Reporter*, 1/94, p. 452.A.1]. Cuba is now the only major country in the region that has not signed or ratified the NWFZ treaty, although it has said that it would do so once it had been ratified by the other parties. The 49th Session is sure to welcome this development, thereby completing the NWFZ for the entire region of Latin America and the Caribbean.

Despite the progress made in Africa and Latin America, prospects for the establishment of nuclear weapons-free zones in the Middle East and South Asia have not changed much in the past year. In the **Middle East,** the long-standing and unresolved differences between Israel and its Arab neighbors continue to stymie progress on the issue. The Israeli-PLO interim peace accords have helped to ease tensions in the region, however. In order to help spur movement toward a NWFZ, several workshops and meetings were held in the past year to help promote confidence in the region. Among the issues discussed were ways to expand confidence-building measures between regional states and possible NWFZ verification options and safeguards approaches [ibid., 6/93, p. 453.B.157; A/48/399]. Israel has accepted the idea of a NWFZ in the Middle East, but only as the last step in the peace process. As in past years, the 49th Session is likely to take up the issue again by passing resolutions on the establishment of a nuclear weapons-free zone in the Middle East and on Israeli nuclear armaments [A/Res/48/78; A/Res/48/71].

The 49th Session is also likely to reiterate the 48th Session's call for the establishment of a nuclear weapons-free zone in **South Asia** [A/Res/48/72]. The creation of a NWFZ in South Asia faces many obstacles. The most prominent is the fact that India has long opposed regional disarmament measures relating to nuclear weapons, favoring instead accords that focus on global approaches. In addition, there is the persistent level of tension and distrust between India and Pakistan over their respective nuclear activities and the dispute over Kashmir. Some positive measures have been pursued in the past year, however, that have helped to build confidence in the region and improve the prospects for a NWFZ some time in the future. India has concluded several bilateral agreements with both China and Pakistan that are designed to reduce tensions and increase transparency in South Asia [*The Washington Post*, 4/11/94; *Arms Control Reporter*, 1/94, pp. 454.A.1-2].

More recently, the United States has increased its pressure on both India and Pakistan to cap their nuclear arsenals and accede to IAEA safeguards on all their nuclear facilities. The U.S. strategy has consisted of two parts: offering inducements to enlist cooperation and proposing multilateral forums to discuss the region's nuclear activities. As an incentive, the United States has offered to supply Pakistan with 38 F-16s that are currently being withheld, if Islamabad agrees to end the production of fissile materials and place its production facilities under IAEA safeguards. Washington has offered India increased strategic and technical cooperation, as well as security assurances, if it takes similar action to cap its nuclear weapons activities [*The Washington Post*, 4/9/94]. The United States has also proposed convening a nine-power forum—consisting of the five permanent members of the Security Council, plus India, Pakistan, Japan, and Germany—to discuss the nuclear issue in the region more generally. Pakistan has reiterated its willingness to attend such a forum, but India has thus far refused to reciprocate, arguing that any discussion addressing its nuclear activities must also include North and South Korea, Iran, Iraq, and Israel [*The New York Times*, 3/26/94]. This will be an issue the 49th Session will surely return to.

6. Chemical and Biological Weapons

After nearly a quarter-century of negotiations, the **Convention on the Prohibition of the Development, Production, Stockpiling and Use of Chemical Weapons and on Their Destruction** (also known as the **Chemical Weapons Convention, or CWC**) is in the process of being ratified by the signatory states. The CWC completes international negotiations on the elimination of chemical and biological weapons, the latter having been banned since 1975 under the **Biological and Toxin Weapons Convention (BWC)**. Some significant developments also occurred during the 48th Session regarding ways to implement and strengthen verification procedures for the BWC.

Since the CWC was opened for signature in January 1993, 157 countries have signed the accord and eight have deposited their instruments of ratification. Signers include the United States and Russia and most of the world's developing states believed to have pursued chemical weapons programs: China, India, Iran, Israel, and Pakistan. Other notable signatories include Argentina, Brazil, Cambodia, Chile, Cuba, South Korea, and Vietnam [CD/2455; A/48/666]. Thus far Australia, Sweden, and Norway have ratified the convention and the United States is expected to complete its ratification process by August 1994. Before entry into force, 65 countries must ratify the accord, which is expected to take place some time in 1995.

One of the major provisions of the CWC was the requirement to establish an organization from scratch to oversee the implementation of and compliance with the treaty. The CWC established a **Prepatory Commission** in 1993, which met five times during the year to initiate an oversight body for the convention. This new structure—the **Organization for the Prohibition of Chemical Weapons (OPCW)**—will have a permanent staff of 225, with an additional 163 people in the inspectorate division. The OPCW is now in the process of recruiting and training its staff and designing a set of rules and procedures to be followed once the CWC enters into force. Some of the first issues that the OPCW will likely address are implementation procedures for countries that have ratified the convention and resolving the dispute between developing countries and the West over the continuation of export controls on chemical technologies and products for parties to the convention.

There were important developments in the biological weapons area as well. Although the BWC treaty has been in force since 1975, there are no verification provisions to ensure that parties are abiding by the convention's provisions [see *Issues/48*, pp. 139–40]. Following the 1991 BWC Review Conference, an Ad Hoc Group of Governmental Experts (VEREX) was set up to identify, examine, and evaluate possible verification measures that could strengthen the regime's effectiveness [*Arms Control Reporter*, 1/94, p. 701.A.1]. This group evaluated 21 compliance measures, including data exchanges and on-site inspections, and concluded that several could be feasibly implemented if agreed to by parties to the convention. With a majority of states parties concurring, a special review conference will be held in September 1994 to explore the proposals put forth by the VEREX commission and negotiate legally binding measures to enhance confidence in and compliance with the convention's terms [A/Res/48/65].

The 49th Session is likely to address chemical and biological disarmament efforts by welcoming the many ratifications of the Chemical Weapons Convention. At the same time, the General Assembly will probably call upon those who have not signed or ratified the convention to do so promptly. The issue of how to verify compliance with the Biological and Toxin Weapons Convention will also likely be addressed during the 49th Session in reference to the work under way in the special review conference.

7. Transparency in Armaments

The 48th Session welcomed the widespread reporting of data to the **Register of Conventional Arms** in its first year of use [A/Res/48/62]. The Secretary-General's report in October 1993 noted that 83 countries supplied data on their imports and exports of armaments for the calendar year 1992, which covered approximately 90 percent of all interstate arms transfers [CD/1247; CD/Tia/Wp/21]. Among the countries supplying data to the Register were the six major arms exporters—the United States, Russia, the United Kingdom, France, China, and Germany—and all the parties to the Conference on Security and Cooperation in Europe (CSCE). Some notable countries that did not report information on their imports and exports were Israel and Saudi Arabia. Despite the fact that adherence to the Register by member states is done on a purely voluntary basis, the level of support for the venture in its first year marked a significant improvement over other U.N. data-collection exercises in the past [*Survival*, vol. 35, no. 4 (Winter 1993), pp. 113–29].

The General Assembly approved the Register of Conventional Arms in 1991 as a means of increasing openness and transparency in the military capabilities of member states [A/Res/46/36L]. In essence, the Register was designed as a confidence-building measure that could be used to create a framework for future arms control discussions, both in the conventional and unconventional fields. The ultimate goal of the Register and similar transparency measures is to strengthen international peace and security by increasing predictability about countries' military policies [A/Res/48/62]. The CSCE parties have found transparency in armaments so beneficial that they have gone beyond the requirements of the Register and are now exchanging information annually on military budgets and other sensitive issues.

Based on the success achieved in the CSCE, the 49th Session will likely address ways that the Register can be improved and expanded for all member states in the years ahead [A/Res/48/75]. The General Assembly has requested the Secretary-General to convene a group of governmental experts in 1994 to analyze the current operation of the Register and submit proposals for its further development [A/Res/48/62]. Indeed, modification and expansion of the Register is required under its founding charter. Some of the issues that are sure to be addressed by this committee include improving the Register's system of standardized reporting to limit discrepancies in data submitted; finding ways to broaden participation in the Register; adding additional equipment categories; and requiring the inclusion of information on military holdings and procurement through national production. Other confidence-building measures that the ad hoc group may discuss include exchanging information on closures or conversions of military production facilities and means of addressing transfers of anti-personnel land mines and small arms [CD/Tia/Wp/21; A/48/678K].

The continued success of the arms registry will depend to a large extent on how many members submit the requested information in the years ahead. Thus far, at least 47 countries have submitted data to the United Nations on their transfers in 1993. Major countries that have reported their imports and exports include the United States, the United Kingdom, France, Germany, Japan, India, Greece, and Turkey. Another encouraging sign is that nearly 60 percent of the countries reporting data for 1993 thus far have provided background information on their military holdings, compared to 40 percent in last year's Register [BASIC Reports, no. 38, 5/16/94].

Although many countries accept the fact that the Register represents a beneficial means of enhancing peace and stability, some developing countries are still uneasy about releasing sensitive information on their militaries. In fact, Mexico, Cuba, and Egypt have recently stated that they would like to see the Register discontinued after this year [ibid.]. Due to the support of the five permanent members and other major arms importers and exporters, however, it is likely that the Register will continue to operate for some time, albeit with some modifications. The 49th Session is sure to return to this issue.

III
Economics and Development
By George H. Mitchell Jr.

At midyear 1994 a number of major actors in, and students of, the world economy were beginning to breathe easier. The long international nightmare of seemingly endless stagnation appeared to be ending. Concrete evidence was hard to find, however, and much of that was not unambiguous. The principal locomotive of recovery was the U.S. economy, which, along with the economies of the United Kingdom, Canada, and especially East Asia, was apparently finally gathering steam. It was not clear, however, whether the U.S. economy was expanding at an inflationary or non-inflationary pace. What did seem clear was that the United States could not lead the recovery without the support of economic expansion in continental Europe and Japan.

Still, the international mood was noticeably sunnier than it had been a year earlier. Contributing mightily were political developments, such as all-race elections in South Africa and an agreement between the Israelis and Palestinians concerning self-rule in Gaza and Jericho. But there were important positive economic developments as well. The recession in Western Europe seemed to be ending. Several East Asian countries, including especially China, were booming. Several countries in East and Central Europe were recording positive growth. In South Asia, India's bold economic reforms were beginning to bear fruit. The developing-country debt crisis was declared "over." Resource flows to developing countries increased sharply—led, surprisingly, by private capital. There was historic progress at the multilateral level of the international trading system and important new cooperation at the plurilateral, or regional, level. And flows of foreign direct investment to the developing countries increased noticeably.

The world, it seemed, was no longer holding (and no longer needed to hold) its breath. Economic recovery was finally in sight.

1.   The World Economy: Retrospect and Prospect

1993: Another Letdown

As described in *A Global Agenda: Issues Before the 48th General Assembly of the United Nations,* various events forced the major producers of international economic forecasts to (a) repeatedly lower their estimates of 1992 growth and (b) adopt a cautious approach and conservative posture with respect to 1993. In 1993, they said, world output would increase by at least 2 percent, and perhaps more. Events proved them not to have been cautious or conservative enough, however: World output grew only between 1.0 and 1.7 percent. What happened? Or, more to the point, what didn't happen?

What did not happen was a bottoming out of recessionary conditions in Western Europe (except for the United Kingdom) and, most important, in Japan. These unexpectedly disappointing results in such major economies dampened the effects of stronger performance by the U.S. economy and impressive performance by a number of countries in South and East Asia, including especially China. The depressed conditions in Western Europe and Japan resulted in relatively high unemployment levels in both. And their slack demand for imports adversely affected world trade in general and the U.S. net export position in particular [ECOSOC, "The World Economy at the End of 1993," E/1994/INF/1; International Monetary Fund, *World Economic Outlook,* 10/93 (hereafter *WEO*)].

1994: Qualified Optimism, Again

Economic forecasters (convinced, and not unreasonably so, that one of these years the recovery from global recession must begin in earnest) have, as in 1993, offered cautiously optimistic projections of economic growth in 1994. As of May 1994, the International Monetary Fund (IMF) was expecting global growth of 3.0 percent in 1994, down from its 3.2 percent estimate of October 1993. The U.N.'s Economic and Social Council (ECOSOC), with its forecast of 2.5 percent growth in 1994, is even more cautious than the IMF. These projections are based largely on the expectation of continued U.S. growth of about 3 percent per year, continued rapid growth by several of the economies of South and East Asia, and nascent, if anemic, recovery in continental Western Europe and Japan.

The Group of Seven: Bottoming Out, If Not Taking Off

Together, the members of the so-called Group of Seven (G-7; the Seven)—the United States, Japan, Germany, the United Kingdom, France, Italy, and Canada—virtually determine conditions in the world economy. Since

Table III-1
World Output, 1991–94

	1991	1992	1993	1994*
Output (percentage of annual change)				
World	0.6	1.7	2.3	3.0
Industrial countries	0.5	1.7	1.2	2.4
United States	−0.7	2.6	3.0	3.9
European Community/European Union	0.8	1.1	−0.3	1.3
Japan	4.0	1.3	0.1	0.7
Germany	1.7	1.9	−1.2	0.9
United Kingdom	−2.2	−0.5	1.9	2.5
France	0.7	1.4	−0.7	1.2
Italy	1.3	0.9	−0.7	1.1
Canada	−1.7	0.7	2.4	3.5
Developing countries	4.5	5.8	6.1	5.5
Asia	6.1	7.8	8.4	7.5
Western Hemisphere	3.3	2.5	3.4	2.8
Middle East	2.4	7.8	4.7	3.0
Africa	1.6	0.4	1.1	3.4
Countries in transition	−12.0	−15.4	−8.8	−6.1
Central Europe	−12.6	−9.1	−1.4	1.8
Former Soviet Union	−11.8	−17.8	−11.9	−9.8

Source: IMF, *World Economic Outlook*, 10/93; *Financial Times*, 4/21/94.
*Estimate.

about 1990, the relatively poor economic performance of the G-7 countries has dampened global economic conditions significantly, offsetting
feverish growth in parts of South and East Asia. The poor performance,
with its related comparatively high rates of unemployment, has also had
domestic political consequences in the G-7 countries. It was to consider
ways of increasing employment levels that the Seven held a **"Jobs Summit"** in Detroit, Michigan, in mid-March 1994. In addition to the expected calls for more expansive macroeconomic policies in Germany and
Japan, participants and advisors recommended labor market reform and
greater investment in human capital.

It appears in mid-1994 that, as a group, the Seven are on the verge of
resuming respectable rates of output. According to the IMF, the Seven
will, after recording growth of only 1.4 percent in 1993, average 2.5 percent per year in both 1994 and 1995. The situation in each of the G-7
countries is discussed below.

United States

By the spring of 1994 the U.S. economy had moved into full recovery.
For example, in April, the unemployment rate dropped to 6.4 percent as

the economy created some 267,000 new jobs. Indeed, U.S. economic growth seemed to be so robust that a number of observers predicted not only a continuation of the Federal Reserve Board's efforts, begun in February 1994, to nip inflationary expectations in the bud, but also that the Clinton administration would (if reluctantly) acquiesce in the Federal Reserve's anti-inflationary-expectations strategy. The administration would, in other words, concede that the American central bank was correct in worrying more about the medium-to-long-term course of the recovery than about its near-term fits and starts. Steady, if moderate, growth through 1995 and especially 1996 would, of course, almost certainly enhance President Clinton's reelection prospects, no minor concern to the administration.

Several factors have been identified as contributing substantially to the U.S. recovery. One of the most important was the Clinton administration's Budget Reconciliation Act of 1993. The Act combined federal spending cuts with tax increases to generate a reduction in the federal deficit. That prospect, in turn, tended to reassure U.S. financial markets, with the result that interest rates on the federal—and much other public and private—debt stabilized at relatively low levels. With a reduced debt service burden and lower costs of borrowing, consumer and business confidence rose, and with them consumption spending and business investment. The external sector continued to act as a drag on overall growth as relatively rapid U.S. growth stimulated imports and relatively slow European and Japanese growth dampened exports, despite a gradually depreciating U.S. dollar.

Notwithstanding a noticeably tighter monetary stance by the Federal Reserve during the first half of 1994, U.S. growth is expected to remain steady at about 3 percent in 1994 (in May the IMF revised its forecast sharply upward from 2.6 percent to 3.8 percent) and 1995. As the OECD *Economic Outlook* observed: "The [fiscal and monetary] forces shaping the [U.S.] economic expansion over the next few years . . . appear to be relatively finely balanced" [12/93, p. 51]. As long as they remain balanced, the United States may enjoy, during the next few years, steady, if moderate, relatively noninflationary growth.

Japan

Japan's long-anticipated but long-delayed recovery from the downturn that began in late 1991 apparently may be delayed still further. In April 1994 the IMF lowered its forecast of Japanese economic growth in 1994 to 0.7 percent, down substantially from the IMF's October 1993 prediction of 2.0 percent [*Financial Times*, 4/21/94]. The revision was widely perceived as justified, notwithstanding the strenuous objections of some Japanese economic policy-makers [ibid., 4/22/94]. On the one hand, the yen has continued its steep rise against the dollar, even as Japanese consumer spending has remained weak. On the other hand, Japanese political turmoil has made it virtually impossible for the government to adopt and implement an effective anti-recession program. Reformist Prime Minister Yoshio Hosokawa resigned amid charges of corruption in mid-April 1994. Choosing a successor, former Foreign Minister Tsutomu Hata, proved difficult; and by the end of June, Japan had yet another Prime Minister, the Socialist Tomiichi Murayama, and a cabinet whose most important positions were in the hands of the conservative Liberal Democratic party.

The Japanese recession, the country's worst in at least 20 years, has its origins in a speculative bubble that, when it burst, simultaneously halted business investment and launched a period of corporate restructuring. These developments, in turn, had predictably negative consequences for consumer confidence and consumption. Despite the government's adoption of several fiscal packages, neither business nor consumer confidence has yet been restored. And the government's efforts in this regard have been stymied on the one hand by politics and on the other hand by the appreciating yen, which has led Japanese exporters to narrow profit margins to try to maintain market share abroad.

The Japanese economy grew 4.3 percent in 1991, 1.1 percent in 1992, and −0.1 percent in 1993, the last representing its worst performance since 1974. It is forecast to grow 0.7 percent in 1994 and by as much as 2.3 percent in 1995—an improvement, but a far cry from the 6.2 percent registered in 1988 [*Financial Times*, 4/21/94; WEO, 10/93].

Analysts at the Organization for Economic Cooperation and Development (OECD) and the IMF tend to agree that structural problems within the Japanese economy must be addressed if Japan is to resume relatively strong growth over the medium term. The OECD recommended "the implementation and accentuation of the process of economic deregulation" [OECD, *Economic Outlook*, 12/93]. The IMF, similarly, recommended deregulation and opening of the home market [*Financial Times*, 4/21/94].

Germany

Analysts generally agree that, even though various recessionary forces continue to operate, the German downturn that began in the first half of 1992 will become a recovery some time in 1994. Setting the stage for a recovery are moderating wage and price pressures and the gradual but ongoing easing of monetary conditions by the ever-cautious Bundesbank [OECD, *Economic Outlook*, 10/93].

The roots of the German recession lie in a wage-price spiral and, related to the unification process with the former German Democratic Republic, a ballooning federal budget deficit and a controversial monetary restructuring program. The Bundesbank reacted to all three by tightening German monetary aggregates, with the unsurprising result that interest rates soared, dampening consumer demand and business investment and causing the mark to appreciate, which further disadvantaged the already-vulnerable export sector. German monetary policy also created serious political problems for the leaders of other members of the European exchange rate mechanism (ERM). Modification of the ERM in August 1993 (see section 5, "International Monetary Relations," below) alleviated the pressure on Germany as well as on its economic and political partners in Western Europe.

The German economy grew 1.7 percent in 1991 and 1.9 percent in 1992. It contracted by 1.2 percent in 1993 but is forecast to expand by about 1 percent in 1994 and as much as 2 percent in 1995, still below the country's 1985–90 average of 3 percent per year [*WEO*, 10/93; *Financial Times*, 4/21/94].

Other G-7 Economies

The economy of the **United Kingdom** of Great Britain and Northern Ireland continued on the path of sustained, moderate noninflationary growth on which it embarked in mid-1992. Real gross domestic product expanded by about 2 percent in 1993 and is forecast to increase by 2.5 percent in 1994 and nearly 3 percent in 1995 [*Financial Times*, 4/21/94]. Analysts trace the recovery to the country's September 1992 decision to quit the ERM, which permitted an easing of monetary policy and a lowering of interest rates, admittedly at a risk of reigniting inflation. To date, however, there has been no resurgence of inflation in general or a wage-price spiral in particular. Indeed, labor market conditions remain weak: Unemployment still hovers well above 10 percent. Some observers would like to see a smaller public sector and larger private sector contribution to growth but seem satisfied with the government's assurances that, as the recovery consolidates, the government will pull back.

The United Kingdom, along with the United States and Canada, is an economic bright spot among an otherwise rather gray group of developed countries.

France's economy contracted by nearly 1 percent in 1993, due to a combination of depressing monetary, fiscal, and external factors. First, participation in the ERM required, at least until August 1993, relatively high interest rates to preserve the relationship of the deutsche mark and French franc. Second, a conservative government replaced France's socialist government early in 1993. As a result, French fiscal policy, especially with respect to government spending, tightened. And third, virtually the whole of Western Europe and Japan simultaneously descended into economic recession, with short-term negative consequences for French exports and export-related employment.

The widening of the ERM bands in August 1993 has permitted a gradual easing of French monetary policy. Fiscal policy remains relatively tight, however, although the government has undertaken tax reforms that will ease the tax burden on a substantial portion of the country's taxpayers—without, it is expected, worsening the budget deficit. Analysts maintain that a French recovery will depend on a resurgence of domestic investment and consumer confidence. Precisely when these will occur remains unclear. Still, the French economy is projected to grow by as much as 2.5 percent in 1995, in line with a number of other developed countries [OECD, *Economic Outlook*, 12/93; *Financial Times*, 4/21/94].

Italy's experience shares some elements with that of Britain and France. On the one hand, Italy, like Britain, dropped out of the ERM in mid-to-late 1992 and took the opportunity to ease monetary policy and depreciate the lira. On the other hand, Italy, like France, experienced a sharp drop in domestic demand, as industrial restructuring commenced, and negative growth of nearly 1 percent in 1993. Italy will experience an export-led mini-recovery in 1994 (about 1 percent growth) before joining most of the other developed economies at the approximately 2.5 percent level in 1995 as domestic demand picks up.

Canada shares the growth spotlight with the United States and the United Kingdom. The Canadian economy grew 2.4 percent in 1993, is projected to expand by 3.5 percent in 1994, and may well stand alone at the head of the developed-country pack with 4 percent growth in 1995 [*The Wall Street Journal*, 4/21/94]. While some of Canada's growth may be attributed to pent-up consumer demand associated with a recession that started sooner, dipped deeper, and lasted longer than that in the United States, observers tend to focus instead on the very high level of business confidence or optimism in Canada today [OECD, *Economic Outlook*, 12/93]. The latter may relate to the successful completion of the North American Free Trade Agreement and the Uruguay Round of multilateral trade negotiations (see section 3, "Trade and the Trading System," below). In any case, Canada has benefited from the U.S. recovery, a relaxation of monetary policy, and overall improved competitiveness.

Newly Industrializing Economies of East Asia: Moving Right Along

Among the 15 upper- and high-income nations that comprise the East Asian region, four are generally considered to be newly industrializing: **Taiwan, South Korea, Singapore,** and **Hong Kong.** The four recorded growth of 8.4 percent per year between 1975 and 1984, 8 percent between 1985 and 1992, and 6 percent in 1993. They are expected to grow by 6.2

percent in 1994 [all material in this subsection is drawn from the World Bank, *Global Economic Prospects and the Developing Countries, 1994,* or *WEO,* 10/93, unless otherwise noted]. A fifth economy, **China**'s, has emerged as one of the world's largest, although it lags behind substantially on a per capita gross domestic product (GDP) basis. Chinese growth averaged 7.2 percent between 1975 and 1984, 8.7 percent between 1985 and 1991, 13 percent in 1992, an estimated 11–13 percent in 1993, and 10–12 percent in 1994 [*The New York Times,* 1/3/94]. **Malaysia, Thailand,** and **Indonesia** are also turning in impressive performances.

There is no reason, especially considering the spectacular results above, why East Asia should not remain the fastest-growing developing region well into the next century. However, countries in the region are almost certain to encounter, if they have not yet encountered, significant infrastructural and environmental constraints. China, for example, has already had to address the inflation question. On the other hand, the region will probably benefit from expanding intraregional trade and the successful completion of the Uruguay Round negotiations.

The Transitioning Economies of Eastern Europe and the Former Soviet Union: Uncertainty Despite Effort

The conversion of the old command economies of East and Central Europe and the former Soviet Union is proceeding rapidly in some states and glacially in others [ibid.]. All, however, seem to have realized (intellectually if not practically) that there probably is no going back to the old system or any serious alternative to the Western approach to economic organization. And it appears that in the countries in which this realization occurred, and was acted upon sooner rather than later, economic conditions are much better than in the laggard states.

To date, the most successful of the 23 countries in this category (including Mongolia) has been Poland, which grew by 4 percent in 1993. Albania, the Czech Republic, and Turkmenistan also saw their economies expand last year, while the rate of contraction slowed dramatically in Romania, Estonia, Georgia, Latvia, and Lithuania.

Most worrisome was the largest economic actor in this group, Russia. Despite apparent progress in addressing deep-seated political conflicts, and despite the combined efforts of the Russian Prime Minister, the head of the Russian central bank, the Group of Seven, and the IMF, the Russian economy was said to be "in deep crisis" as of early May 1994, with industrial production 25 percent lower in the first quarter of 1994 than it was in the first quarter of 1993. The Russian Ministry of the Economy was reportedly fearing a "social explosion," due in large measure to high unemployment [*Financial Times,* 5/9/94]. Some sense of perspective may be found, however, in the fact that the Russian political economy has resembled nothing if not a roller coaster for a number of years, so far without causing either a social or an economic unraveling. Still, it probably would be a mistake to underestimate the seriousness of the multiple challenges Russia faces.

Other Developing Regions

Among the countries of **South Asia,** growth averaged 5.6 percent per year during the 1980s [ibid.]. India, which adopted an economic reform program in the aftermath of the collapse of its largest trading partner, the Soviet Union, enjoyed a significantly improved rate of output. Pakistan has reduced its fiscal deficit and improved its external accounts. The economic performance of Bangladesh has improved modestly. In Sri Lanka the private sector has become the main engine of growth, although prospects are clouded by continuing threats to domestic peace and unity.

Aggressive, often successful, attempts at economic reform have contributed to a very positive outlook for the economies of **Latin America.** Mexico, now a partner in the North American free trade area with the United States and Canada, looks forward to steady, if moderate, growth in coming years, provided domestic political problems remain contained. Chile, anticipating a separate free trade agreement with the United States, seems almost certain to sustain robust growth in the 5–6 percent range. Colombia and Costa Rica are also expected to enjoy robust growth. Joining Mexico in the modest growth range most likely will be Argentina and Peru. The greatest uncertainty surrounds Brazil and Venezuela, although Brazil is again beginning to attract intense foreign interest, especially from the United States. Venezuela must grapple with domestic political concerns as well as with economic ones.

Prospects for the countries of the **Middle East and North Africa** remain highly uncertain, although the peace agreement between Israel and the Palestine Liberation Organization, which may well be followed by agreements between Israel and Jordan, Israel and Lebanon, and Israel and Syria, may ease investors' fears and facilitate the inflow of official as well as private capital. The oil-exporting countries of the region have been grappling since the mid-1980s with the effects of relatively low oil prices, one rather destructive consequence of which was the Gulf War of 1990–91. For these countries, much depends on the situation in the world oil market, discussed in section 3, "Trade and the Trading System," below. Also important for their economic prospects is the oil exporters' openness to foreign direct investment. Non-oil-exporting countries in the region have also had a difficult time during the past decade, but most have undertaken structural adjustment programs by now and may benefit from foreign direct investment, regional economic arrangements, and an improved world trade climate.

The outlook for sub-Saharan Africa is not a bright one overall, although there is potential for growth in some states and some sectors. The region suffered noticeably during the 1980s under a range of pressures—from high oil prices to global recession, debt, the sharp and sustained decline in commodity prices, AIDS, donor fatigue, war, famine, and diversion of global interest, among others—and 28 of the region's 46 countries suffered declines in real per capita GDP during that decade. Most had structural adjustment programs in place. The number of poor is expected to grow not only in absolute numbers but as a proportion of the population. The good news, such as it is, is that in April and May 1994 the Republic of South Africa made a peaceful transition from minority to majority rule, raising the possibility of accelerated foreign investment and other forms of economic activity in that country and perhaps in neighboring states as well.

The External Debt Crisis: It's Over!

With the completion of a long-awaited agreement between Brazil and its largest commercial bank creditors in mid-April 1994, various unofficial observers declared to be "over" the developing-country external debt crisis that began with Mexico's near-default in 1982. The "proof" that the crisis is over is that, as indicated in the World Bank's *World Debt Tables, 1992–93,* developing-country debt no longer poses a threat to the international banking structure. However, as noted in *World Debt Tables, 1993–94,* most low-income countries continue to rely heavily on official concessional financing. In addition, the Bank said, there is a continuing need to address the debt burden of two dozen severely indebted low-income countries, mostly in sub-Saharan Africa.

2. Economic Development

Resource Flows to Developing Countries

Measured in 1991 dollars and exchange rates, total net resource flows to developing countries increased by 21 percent, or $28 billion, to $159 billion in 1992 [material in this section is drawn from the OECD Development Assistance Committee's (DAC) *Development Co-operation, 1993 Report,* unless otherwise noted]. This was the first significant expansion since 1989, when some of the donor countries began slipping into recession. Surprisingly, private, not public/official, flows were responsible for much of the increase.

There have been at least two important developments concerning private capital flows to developing countries. One is a resumption of commercial bank lending, which rose from $11 billion to $38 billion in 1992. This resumption is, in large part, a product of the resolution of the debt crisis. It also reflects the confidence generated by major economic reforms and restructuring in a number of developing countries, some of them, like Mexico, quite large in economic size. A second development has been a dramatic intensification of interest of developed-country portfolio-investment managers in developing-country or "emerging-market" securities. Foreign portfolio investment exceeded $10 billion in 1992, compared to only $3.1 billion in 1989. At the same time, official development finance (ODF) fell by $2.5 billion in 1992, led by a $2 billion decline in disbursements of official development assistance (ODA). The largest donors were the United States and Japan, at about $11 billion each, followed principally by France and Germany. Four countries—Norway, Sweden, Denmark, and the Netherlands—were at or above the U.N.'s target of 0.7 percent of gross national product (GNP). Nine countries, led by France, were at or above the OECD/DAC average of 0.33 percent. The United States, at 0.20 percent, was one of eight countries, including Japan and the United Kingdom, whose ratio was below the DAC average.

The New Context: Massive Change in Geopolitics

The past five years have witnessed a massive change in the geopolitical environment in which development assistance and development cooperation occur. The end of the Cold War between East and West, as important as it was, is now taken for granted. In part, that is because of at least two other geopolitical turnabouts. One is the settlement between Israel and the Palestine Liberation Organization concerning parts of the occupied territories of the West Bank and Gaza Strip. That agreement will probably facilitate several more agreements between Israel and its Arab neighbors. The other is the so-far peaceful transition to majority, democratic rule in the Republic of South Africa. In both cases the international community will almost certainly want to demonstrate concrete support for the historic "progress" by providing economic assistance. Without a larger "pie," however, some current recipients will almost certainly end up receiving less than they do now.

Also important have been somewhat more subtle, but no less revolutionary, changes. For example, the list of countries undertaking economic liberalization with respect to domestic markets and international transactions is an amazingly long and growing one. And foreign economies have responded to those changes with increased direct and portfolio foreign investment and commercial loans.

Not to be overlooked, of course, is the international macroeconomic environment in which development assistance and development cooperation also occur. Obviously, that environment has not been a very happy one for either donors or recipients since about 1990. It appears, however, that 1994 will witness a resumption of steady economic growth among

Table III-2
Selected Overseas Development Assistance Indicators

Sources of Overseas Development Assistance, 1992

Country	U.S.$ Amount (billions)*	Percent of GNP
United States	11.71	0.20
Japan	11.15	0.30
France	8.27	0.63
Germany	7.57	0.39
Italy	4.12	0.34
United Kingdom	3.22	0.31
Netherlands	2.75	0.86
Canada	2.52	0.46
Sweden	2.46	1.03
Spain	1.52	0.26
Denmark	1.39	1.02
Norway	1.27	1.16
Switzerland	1.14	0.46

Geographical Distribution of Overseas Development Assistance in 1991 & 1992 (percentage of total**)

	Sub-Saharan Africa	South Asia	Other Asia	Middle East	Latin America & Caribbean
1991 ($60.7bn)	28.5	13.0	11.0	8.1	9.0
1992 ($60.9bn)	31.1	11.3	14.7	6.5	9.1

Source: OECD, Development Assistance Committee (DAC), *Development Co-operation, 1993,* Chart V-1.

*Including forgiveness of non-ODA debt.

**Percentages will not total 100 because of omission of North Africa and developing Europe.

the developed countries, and a renewed commitment to development assistance could follow. The Development Assistance Committee, among others, certainly hopes it will. With the end of the Cold War, the DAC has said, we have an opportunity to address at long last the very serious economic and social problems around the world.

Challenges, Old and New

Those who devote their professional lives to economic development face many challenges, new and old. Among the older ones are rapid population growth, poverty, urbanization, and low agricultural productivity. Today, one cannot participate in economic development efforts without considering as well such relatively new concerns as AIDS, environmental protection, illicit drugs, ethnic conflict, and citizen participation in economic decision-making. In addition, there is an international consensus that donor-country assistance programs must be reformed. Several donor countries, including the United States, have already announced a restructuring of their foreign assistance agencies and policies.

Focus on Health

In its *World Development Report, 1993,* the World Bank examined the interplay between health, health policy, and economic development. Despite significant advances in health, the report notes, developing countries continue to suffer the burden of a high incidence of disease. And the developing countries, like so many other countries, face sharply rising health care costs.

The report, subtitled "Investing in Health" and prepared in partnership with the World Health Organization, makes three broad recommendations. First, governments need to provide an economic environment that permits households to adopt healthier practices. Second, government spending on health should be redirected to programs that do more for the poor. And, finally, governments should promote competition in the financing and delivery of health services.

UNCTAD's Research Program

In November 1993 the U.N. Conference on Trade and Development (UNCTAD) announced the publication of Volume III in its series of research papers called *International Monetary and Financial Issues for the 1990s* [UNCTAD/GID/G24/1,2,3]. The Introduction notes that the Group of 24 (G-24) was established in November 1971 to increase the negotiating strength of the developing countries in International Monetary Fund discussions about reforming the international monetary system. The 24 decided to meet regularly, as the developed countries' Group of Ten had been doing for some time, and, perceiving the need for technical support, soon launched a research program. The present series continues that program.

While the ultimate concern of the G-24 has been the international monetary system, much of its research, judging from the three volumes concerning the 1990s, has focused on more general issues of economic development. Among the offerings here are articles about debt, structural adjustment, private market financing, foreign direct investment, environment and development, financial openness, and adjustment strategies.

The Secretary-General's Agenda for Development

On May 25, 1994, U.N. Secretary-General Boutros Boutros-Ghali launched "An Agenda for Development," intended to complement his

June 1992 "An Agenda for Peace." The development-oriented report distributed at the launching was spearheaded by the General Assembly's request for "an analysis and recommendations on ways of enhancing the role of the United Nations and the relationship between the United Nations and the Bretton Woods institutions in the promotion of international cooperation for development" [A/Res/47/181]. The resolution asked the Secretary-General to include a comprehensive annotated list of substantive themes and areas to be addressed, as well as the Secretary-General's view of the priorities among them.

Boutros-Ghali said he hoped that "An Agenda for Development" would "correct a distorted perception of the United Nations." It simply is not true, he stated, that the United Nations only, or even mainly, deals with peacekeeping. In fact, the Secretary-General asserted, the main activity of the Organization is development, which is a prerequisite for peace. To that end, the U.N.'s annual expenditures on development—about $3.5 billion—exceed by far the Organization's annual expenditures for "peace"—some $2 billion [U.N. press release DH/1652, 5/25/94].

The "Agenda" calls for a "universal, human-centered 'culture of development,' built on . . . peace, economic growth, environmental protection, social justice and democracy" [ibid.]. The most urgent task for development, the Secretary-General said, is to attack the causes and symptoms of poverty, hunger, disease, and illiteracy. So-called "World Hearings on Development," hosted by the President of the General Assembly, were scheduled for June 6–10, 1994. It was expected that the Economic and Social Council would consider the "Agenda" at the conclusion of the hearings and that the Secretary-General would present his final conclusions during the 49th General Assembly.

3. Trade and the Trading System

International Trade 1993

According to preliminary estimates by the General Agreement on Tariffs and Trade (GATT), the volume of world merchandise exports increased by only 2.5 percent in 1993, down from a more respectable 4.5 percent in 1992 [*The Wall Street Journal*, 4/6/94]. Still, the rate of growth of world exports exceeded that of overall world output (about 1 percent) for the tenth consecutive year. The most important loci of export growth were North America (3.8 percent) among the developed market economies (1.6 percent), and South and East Asia (16.6 percent) among the developing countries (10.6 percent). The most important loci of slack demand for imports were recession-bound continental Western Europe and Japan. World export volume is expected to rise in 1994 by nearly 6 percent, the sharpest increase since 1989. Recoveries in Western Europe and Japan, along with continued strong export growth among the developing countries, are expected to account for much of the rebound, although the completion of the Uruguay Round of multilateral trade negotiations (see below) is expected to contribute substantially to world trade growth in coming years [material in this section is drawn from ECOSOC, "The World Economy at the End of 1993," E/1994/INF/1, unless otherwise noted].

Measured in terms of value, world merchandise exports declined by 2 percent in 1993, to $3.6 trillion. The United States was the largest exporter by this measure, accounting for $465 billion, or 12.6 percent of the total. Germany was second, with exports valued at $362 billion, and Japan a very close third, with exports valued at $361 billion. France, the United Kingdom, Italy, and Canada trailed behind. On a per capita basis, the world's largest merchandise exporters in 1993 were Singapore ($26,000), Hong Kong ($23,300), Belgium-Luxembourg ($11,000), Switzerland ($9,200), and the Netherlands ($8,800) [*The Economist*, 4/16/94, p. 115].

It was reported separately that in 1992 world exports of non-merchandise commercial services (including, but not limited to, transportation, travel and tourism, banking and insurance) were valued at $1 trillion, up 12 percent over 1991. The United States, at $162 billion, was the world's largest exporter of services and the second largest importer of services after Japan. In 1992 the United States had both the largest surplus on trade in services and the largest deficit on trade in merchandise [ibid., 1/29/94, p. 113].

Sectoral Developments and Issues

Perhaps the most interesting sectoral developments have revolved around **oil.** In late 1993 and early 1994, depressed world demand and oversupply pushed oil prices to their lowest levels in at least five years. Prices were about 10 percent lower in 1993 than in 1992, but the expectation of still lower prices in 1994 was called into question by several factors, including, principally, the rapid pace of the U.S. recovery.

Prices of **non-fuel commodities** declined about 4 percent in dollar terms in 1993, a rather modest drop compared to recent years. Prices of manufactured exports declined by 2 percent both in year-over-year terms and relative to manufactured exports.

Weak fuel and non-fuel commodity prices have worked mainly to the benefit of the developed countries, although some developing countries that must import oil and other commodities have also been aided. The 10 percent drop in oil prices resulted in a transfer of some $20 billion in real income from oil-exporting to oil-importing countries. The World Bank, in its *Global Economic Prospects and the Developing Countries, 1994,* focused on the depressed state of real commodity prices. It concluded that,

Table III-3
World Trade, 1989–93

	1989	1990	1991	1992	1993*
(Annual percentage change in export volumes)					
World	7.8	5.3	4.4	5.2 [4.5]	3.4 [2.5]
Developed market economies	7.1	5.0	3.7	3.9	1.6
North America	8.7	7.0	6.3	7.4	3.8
Western Europe	7.2	3.9	2.1	3.4	0.7
Japan	3.8	5.5	3.0	−0.5	−0.6
Developing countries	12.2	8.6	9.7	8.0	10.6
Latin America	7.7	3.6	6.3	4.6	8.1
Africa	4.5	14.4	7.0	0.2	8.4
Asia	14.6	8.5	12.0	10.8	11.7
Economies in transition	−0.9	−9.8	−29.7	−8.0	n/a

Source: ECOSOC, "The World Economy at the End of 1993" [E/1994/INF/1]. Bracketed figures are estimates by the General Agreement on Tariffs and Trade (GATT).
*Estimate.

over the long term, there seems to be little reason for pessimism about the commodity producers as such, although the extreme volatility of commodity prices creates serious challenges for commodity producers.

The International Trading System

The six-month period from November 1993 to the end of May 1994 was nothing less than momentous—or epochal, in the words of "The World Economy at the End of 1993"—for the international trading system.

On November 1, 1993, the Maastricht Treaty concerning **Economic and Monetary Union (EMU)** entered into force and the European Community (E.C.) became the European Union (E.U.).

On November 17, 1993, the U.S. Congress approved, by a larger margin than expected, the **North American Free Trade Agreement (NAFTA).** Highly controversial in the United States, especially in the eyes of environmentalists and organized labor, passage was by no means assured. However, President Bill Clinton, his aides, and congressional and business supporters waged an intense political and public relations campaign in support of the agreement. That agreement provides for a phasing out of barriers to trade and investment between the United States, Canada, and Mexico over a period of five to ten years.

Table III-4
Indices of Prices of Primary Commodities Exported by Developing Countries

	1989	1990	1991	1992	1993*
	(1985 = 100)				
Food	161	151	141	138	137
Tropical beverages	70	62	57	49	47
Vegetable oil-seeds & oil	85	74	80	86	84
Agricultural raw materials	129	137	129	125	123
Minerals and metals	164	149	135	131	115
Crude petroleum	59	75	62	63	57

Source: ECOSOC, "The World Economy at the End of 1993" [E/1994/INF/1].
*January–September 1993.

The following weekend, the leaders of some 14 Asian and North American nations met in Seattle, Washington, in the first-ever summit of the **Asia-Pacific Economic Cooperation forum (APEC)**. President Clinton, host of the meeting, said that U.S. economic and commercial interests in Asia were about to overtake such U.S. interests in Europe.

On December 15, 1993, in Geneva, the more than 100 nations participating in the Uruguay Round agreed in principle (after eight years of negotiations and missed deadlines three years in a row) on the overall text of a new world trade agreement. In what the *Financial Times* called "a victory for multilateral rules" [12/15/93], the more than 100 Contracting Parties of the General Agreement on Tariffs and Trade either reached agreement or agreed to disagree on a wide range of topics, including trade in agriculture, intellectual property rights, trade in services, national anti-dumping rules, dispute settlement, and a new World Trade Organization (WTO) to succeed GATT on January 1, 1995.

On January 1, 1994, 17 nations joined together formally as the **European Economic Area, or EEA**—the world's largest free trade zone. The membership of the EEA is comprised of the countries of the E.U. and those of the former European Free Trade Association (EFTA).

On April 15, 1994, in Marrakesh, Morocco, the Contracting Parties of GATT ushered in a "New Age of Trade" [*The New York Times*, 4/15/94] by giving final approval to the text of the **Uruguay Round agreement**. U.S. Vice President Al Gore, who signed on behalf of the United States, praised the agreement as a spur to global economic recovery.

And on May 4, 1994, the European Parliament approved the admission to full **membership in the European Union of Austria, Finland, Norway, and Sweden.** This becomes effective January 1995 and is subject to referendums in those countries.

The World Trade Organization

Many governments and scholars thought a WTO-type institution neces-sary because of certain fundamental weaknesses of GATT, which in any event was conceived as an interim arrangement. (The international com-munity "fell back" on GATT in the late 1940s when the proposal for an International Trade Organization failed to win the approval of the U.S. Congress.) According to *Focus: The GATT Newsletter* [May 1994], the WTO will "facilitate the implementation and operation of all [multilateral trade agreements], administer the Understanding on rules and Procedures gov-erning the Settlement of Disputes and the Trade Policy Review Mecha-nism, [and] cooperate with the International Monetary Fund and [World Bank] with a view to achieving greater coherence in global economic pol-icy-making."

Perhaps the most important provisions of the WTO agreement con-cern the dispute-settlement system, which, according to GATT, "repre-sents the new teeth [i.e., enforcement powers] of the World Trade Organi-zation," something that GATT conspicuously lacked. In addition, the WTO will have a legal personality, which GATT did not, and will be on the same legal, institutional, and political footing as the IMF and the World Bank. The new body will be headed by a Director-General ap-pointed by the ministerial conference.

By midsummer 1994 regional and interregional jockeying for the post was quite intense. Separately, the WTO had come under attack in the U.S. Congress as having considerable potential for infringing on U.S. sovereignty. On June 10, **U.S. Trade Representative Mickey Kantor** told the House Ways and Means Committee that the Clinton administration had concluded that the WTO would not restrict U.S. sovereignty, and probably would enhance it. A month later the Congress had yet to indi-cate when it would act on the Uruguay Round results, including the WTO.

4. International Monetary Relations

The Bretton Woods Commission

In late spring 1994, students of international economic relations began anticipating the expected summertime release of a report by the privately organized and financed Bretton Woods Commission concerning the con-dition and future of the international monetary system. The Commission is headed by Paul Volcker, a former Chairman of the U.S. Federal Reserve Board. According to unidentified sources cited in *The Wall Street Journal,* the report will propose a restoration of some of the discipline that was required under the old Bretton Woods system, which effectively ceased operation in August 1971 [5/9/94]. This proposal was anticipated by, among other commentaries, Volume II of UNCTAD's *International Monetary and Financial Issues for the 1990s* [12/92], in which contributor C. David Finch maintained that "the time will come when the major countries once again come to recognize their need for an IMF-type [fixed-exchange rate] mechanism" ["IMF Surveillance and the G-24," p. 109].

However, as *The Wall Street Journal* noted in its article on the prospective Bretton Woods Commission report, domestic political objections in the G-7 countries will almost certainly prevent their leaders from embracing any plan that would take even a small step back toward relatively fixed exchange rates. Moreover, for some time the management of international monetary relations has been more in the hands of the Group of Seven than in those of the International Monetary Fund; and the G-7 shows little readiness to return that authority to the Fund [*The Guardian* (London), 4/25/94].

Volcker and his cohorts on the Commission, including former Bundesbank Chairman Karl-Otto Pöhl, reportedly believe that the post-Bretton Woods system's volatility and currency misalignments have exacted a heavy toll. Loss of exchange rate discipline, they are said to have concluded, has contributed to the observed reduction in long-term growth in the major industrial countries since the early 1970s [*The Wall Street Journal*, 5/19/94; *The Guardian* (London), 12/31/93]. The prospects for the Volcker group's proposals were not at all enhanced by the 1992–93 crisis of the European Community's European monetary system and exchange rate mechanism, discussed below.

Exchange Market Tensions in Europe

The summer of 1993 saw the second European exchange market crisis in 12 months. In July, the Danish krone and French and Belgian francs came under intense downward market pressure as the German mark and Dutch guilder were pushed upward [all material in this subsection is drawn from *WEO*, 10/93]. European governments responded with massive official intervention, increases in overnight interest rates for the currencies under downward pressure, and decreases in interest rates for the currencies under upward pressure. Despite these measures, however, the three currencies under downward pressure were pushed below their exchange rate mechanism (ERM) floors. European Community finance ministers, central bank governors, and other officials met over the weekend of July 31–August 1 to consider their options. They finally decided to widen the bands around ERM parities from plus or minus 2.5 percent to plus or minus 15 percent, effective August 2. However, they simultaneously reaffirmed the existing central parities and declared their intention to return to a system with narrower bands as soon as possible.

Behind the crisis were two principal factors, quite apart from any that might be inherent in a relatively fixed exchange rate system. On the one hand, current account deterioration in several countries pointed to a need for either macroeconomic or exchange rate adjustment. When the market did not observe the former, it began to anticipate the latter. On the other hand, the market perceived, correctly, a serious inconsistency between the expansionary domestic monetary requirements of a number of countries whose economies were not performing well and the contractionary monetary requirements of Germany, which was experiencing a substantial macroeconomic expansionary impulse due to unification.

The long-run consequences for European Economic and Monetary Union (EMU) are not yet known. In the near term, however, returning to narrower bands seems unlikely. And the prospects for a single European currency have faded dramatically into the distant future, despite the establishment (at Frankfurt, Germany) of the **European Monetary Institute**—the likely precursor to a European central bank.

5. Transnational Corporations and the Global Economy

Integrating International Production

According to UNCTAD, about a third of the world's private sector productive assets are under the control of multinational or transnational corporations (MNCs or TNCs), and the universe of TNCs is "large, diverse and expanding" [material in this section is drawn from UNCTAD's *World Investment Report, 1993*]. Whether these developments are a source of pleasure or dismay depends on one's beliefs about the benefits, costs, or risks of allowing TNCs to operate in, or from, a particular country. Still, for better or for worse, the number and reach of TNCs are expanding rapidly in a world in which private enterprise is now widely and sometimes wildly celebrated. What TNCs do, or supposedly do, that other economic actors are less able or willing to do is to maximize efficiency in production by drawing on relatively low-cost factors of production worldwide. This, presumably, they have always done. Now, however, says UNCTAD, TNCs are moving beyond "simple integration" strategies to "complex integration" strategies, in which *all* activities across the entire "value chain" are viewed as candidates for execution by affiliates. Certainly, complex integration has been facilitated by technological advances in communication and transportation, but its usefulness would be limited in the absence of policy changes in a number of countries in which affiliates might be located.

Trends in Foreign Direct Investment

Worldwide outflows of foreign direct investment, $230 billion in 1990, declined in recession-colored 1991 to $180 billion—the first such drop since the 1981–82 recession. The decrease was mostly attributable to sig-nificantly reduced outflows from Japan and Western Europe. Outflows from the developing countries also declined after several years of strong growth.

Inflows into developed countries declined in 1991 to $108 billion (from $172 billion in 1990) and are estimated to have further declined in 1992, to $86 billion. Inflows into developing countries, in contrast, in-creased to $39 billion in 1991 (from $31 billion in 1990) and apparently increased again in 1992, to $40 billion.

Developing countries accounted for over 25 percent of total inflows in 1991. While strong growth of inflows to East, South, and Southeast Asia persisted, most other parts of the developing world, including Latin America, the Caribbean, and Africa, also benefited. However, the ten largest developing-country host states continue to receive two-thirds of all inflows into developing countries.

Sectoral Developments and Issues

In recent years the sectoral composition of foreign direct investment has changed significantly. Once concentrated in the primary sector and re-source-based manufacturing, foreign direct investment is today mainly in services and technology-intensive manufacturing. **Services** accounted for about 50 percent of the world stock of foreign direct investment by the early 1990s. Just the same, foreign investment in **manufacturing,** espe-cially in developing countries, remains strong. And, surprisingly, foreign investment in the primary sector is strongest in the developed countries.

Table III-5
Inflows and Outflows of Foreign Direct Investment, 1991–92

Countries	1991	1992	1991	1992	1991	1992
	(Billions of U.S.$)		*Share in Total (Percentage)*		*Growth Rate (Percentage)*	
Developed countries						
Inflows	108	86	74	68	−37	−20
Outflows	177	145	97	97	−21	−18
Developing countries						
Inflows	39	40	26	32	21	3
Outflows	5	5	3	3	−39	0
All countries						
Inflows	149	126	100	100	−27	−15
Outflows	183	150	100	100	−22	−18

Source: UNCTAD, *World Investment Report, 1993: Transnational Corporations and Integrated International Production* [ST/CTC/156].

One important contemporary development is the opening up of capital-intensive service industries to foreign investors. Chief among the new areas for foreign direct investment are air transportation and telecommunications.

Multilateral and Regional Arrangements and Agreements Relating to Transnational Corporations

Worldwide, the policy environment has become more supportive of foreign direct investment during the past decade or so. Important developments have occurred at the multilateral and regional levels, as well as at the bilateral and unilateral levels.

One of the most significant indicators of a new consensus between developed and developing countries was the adoption by the World Bank in the fall of 1992 of the **"Guidelines on the Treatment of Foreign Direct Investment,"** a set of recommendations to be implemented on a voluntary basis. The Guidelines address such topics as the admission of foreign direct investment, transfer of capital and revenues, expropriation and compensation, and the settlement of investment disputes. They do not deal with standards of corporate conduct, however, largely because that subject was being addressed by the U.N. Commission on Transnational Corporations. Other international agreements set minimum standards for the supervision of banks and address environmental issues relating to foreign direct investment.

There were interesting and important developments at the regional level as well. In Western Europe, the **"Europe 1992"** program, which took effect on January 1, 1993, had implications for intracommunity investment as the now-designated European Union sought to establish a Single Market, providing for the free flow of goods, services, capital, and people. Perhaps the most advanced provisions regarding foreign investment were to be found in the **North American Free Trade Agreement,** which entered into force on January 1, 1994. NAFTA's investment provisions address such topics as portfolio investment, direct investment, national treatment, most-favored-nation treatment, performance requirements, local content, domestic purchasing, and trade balancing. NAFTA also deals with transfers of funds and expropriation. According to UNCTAD, the adoption of this North American agreement "is likely to give impetus to further integration and liberalization efforts throughout the world."

IV
Global Resource Management

1. Environment and Sustainable Development
By Gail V. Karlsson

One of the primary challenges facing the United Nations, and the international community, is to generate agreement on the concept of "sustainable development" and cooperation in achieving it. At the U.N. Conference on Environment and Development (UNCED, or the Earth Summit), held in Rio de Janeiro in 1992, the more than 178 governments represented agreed to a comprehensive program of action—**Agenda 21**—aimed at achieving environmentally and socially sustainable economic development. They, along with U.N. bodies, nongovernmental organizations, and private sector groups, are to be the agents of this program of action extending into the 21st century. Its premise is that global environmental protection and issues of economic and social equity are directly linked. In the words of Agenda 21 itself:

> Humanity stands at a defining moment in history. We are confronted with a perpetuation of disparities between and within nations, a worsening of poverty, hunger, ill health and illiteracy, and the continuing deterioration of the ecosystems on which we depend for our well-being. However, integration of environment and development concerns and greater attention to them will lead to the fulfillment of basic needs, improved living standards for all, better protected and managed ecosystems and a safer, more prosperous future. No nation can achieve this on its own; but together we can—in a global partnership for sustainable development. [Agenda 21, Preamble, par. 1.1]

Agenda 21, for all its lofty language, lacks the force of law. Its implementation depends on a sense of moral obligation, which may be difficult to sustain, especially when it requires substantial new financial commitments, considerable restructuring of existing institutions and economic policies, and an increase in multilateral cooperation, not to mention the adoption of life-styles that are more in harmony with the Earth's carrying capacity. Nevertheless, extensive efforts are currently under way to inte-

153

grate the concept of sustainable development into the operations of the U.N. system, related international financial institutions, the World Trade Organization soon to be established under GATT, national governments, and private enterprises.

The Earth Summit was only the first of a series of conferences organized by the United Nations to define a new people-centered mission for the Organization in the post-Cold War era. Principle 1 of the **Rio Declaration on Environment and Development,** also adopted at the Earth Summit, proclaims that "Human beings are at the centre of concern for sustainable development. They are entitled to a healthy and productive life in harmony with nature." The notion of development as a universal and inalienable human right was reaffirmed by the **World Conference on Human Rights,** held in Vienna a year after UNCED. Vienna's Declaration, echoing Agenda 21, states that the right to development should be fulfilled so as to meet equitably the developmental and environmental needs of present and future generations [Vienna Declaration, par. 11]. The **International Conference on Population and Development in Cairo,** scheduled for September 1994, will emphasize the critical relationship between sustainable development and women's access to health care, education, family planning services, political rights, and economic opportunities. The **World Summit on Social Development** (Copenhagen, March 1995) will address worldwide poverty, unemployment, and social marginalization. And the **Fourth World Conference on Women** (Beijing, September 1995) will confirm the vital role women play in environmental management and reaffirm the need for full participation by women in the development process.

In addition to establishing this series of conferences, the General Assembly called upon Secretary-General Boutros Boutros-Ghali to prepare an "agenda for development" aimed at enhancing the role of the United Nations in global economic and social decision-making and at increasing the effectiveness of U.N. development bodies. Boutros-Ghali's earlier "An Agenda for Peace," prepared for the Security Council, described the promotion of equitable social and economic conditions as an essential element of global peacekeeping efforts.

The Secretary-General's draft **"Agenda for Development,"** released in May 1994, calls development a fundamental human right and the "most secure basis for peace." And it identifies five essential and linked dimensions of the development process: peace, economic growth, environmental sustainability, social justice, and democracy. Citing the unique role of the United Nations in the area of global development, the new "Agenda" calls for increased coordination with the World Bank and the International Monetary Fund, greater consultation with NGOs, an effective division of labor among the many actors involved in development, and a commitment to work toward common goals. Regarding the link between environment and development, the Secretary-General states that "preserving and protecting the ecological equilibrium of our environment is a vital component not only of human development, but also of human survival" [A/48/935, par. 77].

Commission on Sustainable Development

The principal U.N. vehicle for promoting the implementation of Agenda 21 and monitoring UNCED follow-up is the new 53-member **Commission on Sustainable Development (CSD),** which comes under the authority of the Economic and Social Council (ECOSOC). Addressing CSD's first substantive meeting in June 1993, one year after the Earth Summit, U.S. Vice President Al Gore described the Commission's work as "primarily catalytic":

> It can focus attention on issues of common interest. It can serve as a forum for raising ideas and plans. . . . It can monitor progress. It can help shift the multilateral financial institutions and bilateral assistance efforts towards a sustainable development agenda. It can help revitalize the United Nations system to ensure that sustainable development is a central theme in each organization. . . . But it can do none of these things unless each country makes a strong commitment to change. This Commission will simply be a meeting about meetings if the members fail to bring to the table a strong sense of national responsibility. [Press release USUN#97-(93), 6/14/93]

In organizing its plan of work, the CSD agreed to divide Agenda 21's 40 chapters into program clusters. Certain cross-sectoral issues, such as financial resources, transfer of environmentally sound technologies, cooperation, and capacity-building, will be considered at each annual meeting. Other, more specific, program areas were grouped together for review in phases over a three-year period: in 1994, health, human settlements and fresh water, and toxic chemicals and hazardous waste; in 1995, land management, desertification, forests, and biodiversity; and in 1996, the atmosphere, oceans, and seas. The 1997 session will feature an overall review and appraisal of the implementation of Agenda 21 in preparation for a special session of the General Assembly that year [Report of the CSD on Its First Session, E/1993/25/Add.1].

To monitor progress in implementing Agenda 21 the CSD will review reports submitted by national governments, U.N. bodies, international financial institutions, intergovernmental organizations outside the U.N. system, and NGOs. Recognizing the limitations of a once-a-year meeting, the Commission established two ad hoc intersessional working groups to focus on specific ways of promoting environmentally sound technologies and mobilizing the financial resources for sustainable development.

The Rio Declaration states—and all the industrialized countries acknowledged in adopting it—that developed countries have a special responsibility for supporting sustainable development because of the pressure they place on the global environment and the technologies and financial resources they command. Agenda 21 itself calls upon governments to provide $125 billion more per year in financial assistance to developing countries between 1993 and 2000, and in the same document the industrialized countries pledge to attain overseas development assistance levels of 0.7 percent of GNP. To date, however, funding has fallen "significantly short of expectations and requirements" [E/CN.17/1993/L.5/Rev.1]. The Group of 77 (G-77) developing countries warned that "temporary recessionary conditions in the industrialized world should not be used as a justification for diminishing the flow of such resources" [statement by Ambassador Luis Fernando Jaramillo of Colombia, Chairman of the G-77, at the 1993 CSD session]. Nevertheless, reluctance on the part of would-be donor countries to provide new or additional funding for implementing recent and upcoming environmental treaties and sustainable development programs led to substantial North-South conflict throughout the year.

At the February 1994 meeting of the **CSD intersessional working group on financial resources,** some government representatives argued that external debt relief and the removal of trade restrictions would provide substantially more in the way of financial resources than would any increase in foreign aid. Other delegates explored innovative financial mechanisms, such as international environmental taxes; coordinated, international reductions in environmentally damaging subsidies that encourage overuse of fossil fuels, pesticides, and water; tradeable emission permits; venture capital for environmental projects; and transferable development rights designed to protect habitats important to maintaining biodiversity [E/CN.17/ISWG.II/1994/2].

The other CSD intersessional **working group, on technology transfer and cooperation,** considered proposals for improving information on and access to environmentally sound technologies [E/CN.17/ISEG.I/1994/2]. Environmentally sound technologies are defined as those that protect the environment and pollute less, consume fewer resources, and recycle more and dispose of wastes better than do technologies in current use. The objective of technology-sharing and cooperation is to allow developing countries to achieve economic growth without following environmentally destructive and clearly unsustainable models of industrial production; and Chapter 34 of Agenda 21 affirms the need for favorable terms of access to and transfer of such technologies, especially in the case of developing countries.

Developed countries, responding to domestic demand for cleaner and less-wasteful manufacturing processes and consumer goods, have been developing new technologies that aid those goals in the industrialized world. Although many developing countries employ environmentally sensitive, traditional methods of resource management, few have the financial, scientific, and technical resources to conduct the sort of research that will support their own *long-term* environment goals. The financing of technology transfer and the protection of intellectual property rights are among the issues that are a continuing source of North-South frictions.

Nor was there much progress on financing and technology-transfer issues at the May 1994 meeting of the CSD. To increase the effectiveness of the intersessional working group on finance, the Commission recommended involving experts from the private sector and from NGOs, preparing pilot projects and case studies, and cooperating with the Organization for Economic Cooperation and Development (OECD) on monitoring financial flows. Regarding technology, the Commission concluded that, since foreign direct investment is a major source of technology transfer, U.N. agencies should assist governments in providing appropriate policy and regulatory environments. And it saw the need for a U.N. focal point for technology assessment and for improved computer-based information networks.

Deciding to discontinue the working group on technology transfer, the CSD established a new intersessional ad hoc working group to consider the sectoral issues scheduled for consideration in 1995: land management, desertification, forests, and biodiversity. Cooperation in the technology field and financing mechanisms will be raised in these and other intersessional discussions.

Recognizing the importance of the new World Trade Organization, the CSD agreed to an annual review of developments affecting trade and the environment. The aim is to promote cooperation and coordination in integrating environment and development goals with the process of trade liberalization. The Commission also recommended measures to change consumption and production patterns, with an emphasis on developed countries. Its suggestions include public-awareness campaigns and economic mechanisms that encourage energy conservation, use of renewable energy resources, the minimizing of waste, reducing the packaging of goods, water conservation, and environmentally sound purchasing, processing, and pricing decisions.

The CSD went on to recommend that governments and international organizations work with business and NGOs to develop the non-legally binding agreements that could serve as a first step toward international regulation of particular environmental problems. Governments were specifically urged to begin work on an international convention on the safety of radioactive waste management. At the high-level segment of the CSD meeting, participants supported the idea of giving legally binding status to the prior-informed consent procedures relating to the export of domestically banned chemicals as well as the subsequent ban on the export by OECD countries of all prohibited chemicals.

With fewer than 40 national progress reports submitted to the CSD (and most of these just prior to the May session) there was little opportunity to review and share the information from these (sometimes lengthy) documents. The participants recognized the need for a simplified reporting and monitoring framework—to begin with an elaboration of realistic sustainable development indicators for measuring national progress.

The U.N. System and Sustainable Development

One of the principal criticisms of U.N. operations in the economic and social field has been the lack of coordination and cooperation among its plethora of agencies, commissions, councils, and committees. It is unclear whether the CSD, with no administrative or budgetary authority over other U.N. bodies or programs, will be able to coordinate a system-wide sustainable development campaign. It is also unclear exactly how its coordinating functions relate to the responsibilities of ECOSOC itself.

In December 1993, after much discussion about the need for reform of ECOSOC to eliminate duplication of work, the **General Assembly** disbanded the functional committees of ECOSOC and affirmed its own primacy as the forum in which governments are to pursue the development dialogue [A/Res/48/162]. **ECOSOC** will serve principally as a cross-sectoral coordinating body when it comes to implementing policies formulated by the Assembly that involve international cooperation in development. In another measure to consolidate supervisory authority over U.N. development funds and programs, ECOSOC will assume most of the functions of the governing bodies of the U.N. Development Programme, the U.N. Population Fund, UNICEF, and the World Food Programme, all of which are to be replaced by executive boards supervised by ECOSOC.

Within the **Secretariat,** Boutros-Ghali has also sought ways to increase efficiency and strengthen policy work in the economic and social field. The new Department for Policy Coordination and Sustainable Development (DPCSD) is charged with coordinating the policy-making functions of all U.N. bodies that have a role in sustainable development. It oversees not only the CSD but other newly established organs as well, among them the Commission on Science and Technology, the Committee on Natural Resources (focusing on minerals and water), and the Committee on New and Renewable Sources of Energy for Development.

In 1993, pursuant to Chapter 38 of Agenda 21 on new international institutional arrangements, the Secretary-General established an **Inter-Agency Committee on Sustainable Development** to coordinate a system-wide response to implementing the Rio action program. He also appointed a **High-level Advisory Board on Sustainable Development** composed of persons eminent in the fields of environment and development. At its first meeting in September 1993, the 20-person board agreed to create three panels to focus on linkages between economic, social, and political development; new approaches to finance and technology; and new partnerships between the United Nations and other organizations active in the field of sustainable development [A/48/442].

The Advisory Board met again in March 1994 and prepared a report for presentation at the CSD meeting in May [E/CN.17/1994/13]. Here the board suggested that a questionnaire be circulated to NGOs and representatives of national and local governments soliciting ideas on measures for promoting those new partnerships. The Secretary-General asked the board's assistance in changing the public perception of the United Nations as a mainly peacekeeping body, and the board's report recommended making better use of U.N. public relations materials to promote the Organization's role in sustainable development and forming partnerships with commercial sponsors and NGOs with the aim of publicizing and projecting a more integrated image of the United Nations. The Advisory Board will meet again in October 1994.

Citing the need for better system-wide coordination to fulfill the Organization's wide-ranging development responsibilities, the Secretary-General announced that the April 1994 meeting in Geneva of the Secretariat's Administrative Committee for Coordination—composed of executive heads of all U.N. programs and specialized agencies—would be devoted to assessing the U.N. system's progress in responding to Agenda 21, mobilizing resources for the various upcoming international development conferences, and reviewing linkages between human rights and development issues [*Development Update*, 3–4/94]. The 48th General Assembly's Resolution 162, noting the potential of Secretariat reform for strengthening the U.N. role in coordinating research and analysis of global development trends, requested the Secretary-General to consider setting up a system of integrated reports on economic and social issues.

The **U.N. Development Programme (UNDP)** itself has been struggling to redefine its mission despite (and because of) funding and staffing shortages. According to its new Administrator, James Gustave Speth, "without a compelling new vision, the case for channeling resources to UNDP will weaken [letter to colleagues and friends, 1/21/94]. An external advisory panel of experts recommended that UNDP work much more closely with NGOs and women's groups and rely more on local expertise and talent, with the effect of promoting wider participation in the development process [*UNDP Update*, 1/31/94]. Addressing a February meeting of the newly established Executive Board, Speth outlined an "Agenda for Change" through which UNDP would build its capacity for helping the United Nations to become a more powerful and unified force for sustainable development [*International Documents Review*, 2/14–18/94].

UNDP, with offices in 124 countries, has played a central role in funding and facilitating technology cooperation and assistance. In 1993 it launched a "Capacity 21" fund to assist countries in formulating sustainable development strategies, and it has been an important participant in the operations of the Global Environment Facility. Through its annual Human Development Reports UNDP analyzes the effectiveness of current development-assistance models.

The 1994 UNDP Human Development Report elaborates a new development paradigm that puts people at the center, regards economic growth as a means rather than an end, protects life opportunities of present and future generations, and respects the natural systems on which all life depends [p. 4]. Emphasizing the essential linkage between environmental sustainability and economic equity, the report warns that a new global ethic is required in a world in which a quarter of humanity is unable to meet its basic needs and in which the rich nations consume four-fifths of humanity's natural capital without being obliged to pay for it [p. 21].

The **U.N. Environment Programme (UNEP)** is also wrestling with the challenges of implementing the sustainable development agenda despite its small staff, limited funding, and relative isolation from other U.N. bodies at its headquarters in Nairobi. Chapter 38 of Agenda 21 calls for an enhanced role for UNEP with regard to policy guidance and coordination in the field of the environment, but much of the political leadership on the environment has shifted to the CSD. Still, UNEP plays a key role in its three priority areas: providing expert advice to countries regarding the development of environmental institutions and policies; coordinating scientific research and environmental monitoring; and initiating new instruments of international environmental law. UNEP has been active in preparations for the implementation of the biodiversity treaty and is expected to have an enhanced role in the newly restructured Global Environment Facility (GEF). The GEF will be used as an interim funding mechanism to assist developing countries in implementing the biodiversity treaty and the climate change convention.

At the May 1994 meeting of the Commission on Sustainable Development, the UNDP Administrator and the Executive Director of UNEP, Elizabeth Dowdeswell, issued a joint statement proposing that the two organizations combine their relative strengths in support of Agenda 21, particularly in three areas: the creation of national frameworks for sustainable development that integrate environmental protection with national economic plans and structural-adjustment agreements; assistance to governments in servicing and implementing the new international environmental conventions; and the dissemination of environmental information through UNDP's country offices. They hope eventually to create joint programs in support of sustainable development in a wide range of areas, including trade and environment, environmental economics, energy conservation, and forestry.

Biological Diversity

UNEP first called on governments to consider an international legal instrument to protect biological diversity in 1987. Formal negotiations began in 1991 and concluded just before the Earth Summit. The **Convention on Biological Diversity** was signed in Rio by more than 150 countries and ratified by a sufficient number to enter into force on December 29, 1993. The first meeting of the parties to the convention is scheduled for November 1994.

Article 1 of the Convention on Biological Diversity states its objectives as the conservation of biological diversity, the sustainable use of the components of such diversity, and the fair and equitable sharing of the benefits of genetic resources through appropriate access and technology transfer. There is general agreement that plant and animal species are being lost at an alarming rate because of human destruction of natural habitats through rural development, urban sprawl, overharvesting, overfishing, air and water pollution, unsustainable mining and timber operations, and conversion of tropical rain forests to agricultural use. Coral reefs and tropical rain forests, particularly rich in natural variety, are among the fragile ecosystems easily destroyed by the pressures of growing human populations. Some 40 million–44 million acres of tropical forests are believed to disappear annually [*UNDP Choices*, 12/93]. Many life forms being lost within those ecosystems were not even identified: Scientists have named only about 1.4 million species in the world out of an estimated 10 million–100 million [ibid.].

Countries that are parties to the convention commit themselves to develop national strategies for the conservation and sustainable use of biological diversity, to establish a system of protected areas for natural habitats, to facilitate access to genetic resources for environmentally sound uses by those in other countries, and to share the benefits of commercial use of genetic resources with the countries providing those resources. Since most of the world's genetic diversity is found in developing countries but most pharmaceutical and biotechnology companies seeking to commercialize medical, agricultural, and industrial uses for genetic materials are based in industrialized countries, negotiations concerning international cooperation have been highly contentious.

Developing countries have been concerned that foreign corporations will raid their storehouses of biological resources and traditional knowledge and obtain patent protections for any commercially lucrative products, curtailing the rights of traditional users without providing any financial or technological benefits to the communities that discovered, preserved, or cultivated the exploited life forms. But countries like the United States with growing biotechnology industries argue that patent protections are essential to firms undertaking expensive research and development projects to identify new medicines, disease-resistant crops, and other useful innovations.

At Rio, U.S. President George Bush refused to sign the convention because of concerns about the adequacy of patent protections and about provisions that seem to make compulsory the sharing of biotechnology. On Earth Day 1993 his successor, President Bill Clinton, did sign the convention, but the administration has not presented it to the U.S. Senate for ratification while it completes an interpretive statement designed to emphasize the importance of patent protections and the voluntary nature of any biotechnology sharing. Related issues arise from provisions of the new GATT agreement that requires the parties to meet minimum standards in providing legal protections for intellectual property rights. Under the agreement, rights to plant varieties must be legally secured, whether through patents or through an alternative system.

Financing and technology transfer are critical elements of the biodiversity convention. All parties agree to provide access to and transfer of technologies, including biotechnology, that are relevant to conservation and sustainable use of biological diversity [Article 16, par. 1]. Recognizing the concentration of biological diversity in the developing countries and the fact that economic and social development and eradication of poverty are the overriding priorities of developing countries, the developed countries agree to provide new and additional financial resources to assist developing countries in implementing their biodiversity conservation plans [Article 20].

In May 1993, preparing for the implementation of the convention, UNEP's Governing Council established an **Intergovernmental Committee on the Convention on Biological Diversity (ICCBD),** which held its first meeting in Geneva in October 1993. Here, much of the discussion centered on the convention's Article 21, which calls for a financing mechanism to provide grants to developing countries, with program priorities and eligibility criteria to be determined by the conference of the parties. The GEF was designated the interim financing institution for the period between the convention's entry into force and the first meeting of the conference of the parties—provided it was restructured in such way as to become more democratic and transparent [Article 39]. Although at the October ICCBD meeting the industrialized donor countries expressed confidence that the GEF would be suitably restructured [Non-governmental Liaison Service, E&D File, 12/93], agreement on the new form of governance was not easily attained.

GEF Restructured and Replenished

The Global Environmental Facility was established in 1990 on an experimental basis to provide funds to developing countries for projects aimed at addressing global (rather than national) environmental problems, including global warming, destruction of biological diversity, pollution of international waters, and depletion of the ozone layer. Although implemented jointly by the World Bank, UNEP, and UNDP, it was primarily administered by the World Bank, which is dominated by the donor countries. During its three-year pilot phase, critics charged that the GEF grants were often attached to environmentally destructive World Bank projects and that the Facility lacked openness and accountability.

A meeting in Cartagena, Colombia, in December 1993 was expected to finalize the restructuring and financial replenishment of the GEF, but the 70 participating governments were unable to reach agreement about the distribution of seats on the GEF's new governing council or the means of designating its chair. They did agree, however, on making its secretariat more independent of the World Bank, reporting to the GEF governing council rather than to the Bank's board of directors, with an independent chief executive officer (CEO) selected by all the implementing agencies. They also agreed that all fund projects will be subject to a permanent, independent monitoring-and-evaluation process, with greater participation by NGOs and affected communities.

The debate over the composition of the GEF governing council reflected concerns about who should control the funds and choose the projects under the new system. Developing countries, as the intended recipients of the fund's resources, sought a greater voice in the decision-making process. At Cartagena, the donor countries proposed a 30-member governing council chaired by the CEO of the secretariat, with 14 seats for industrialized countries, 14 for developing countries, and 2 for countries whose economies are in transition. The Group of 77, representing the developing countries, sought a majority of the seats on the council and a chair elected from the council membership. Various options were considered and a compromise appeared to be in sight until France was perceived as withdrawing its support for it. The donor countries emphasized the need for efficiency and operational decision-making, concerned that, with an elected chair, the GEF council might become another forum for political speeches; the developing countries objected that the CEO of the secretariat could become too powerful if also serving as the chair of the governing council and insufficiently responsive to the participating governments.

When the GEF participants met again in March 1994, they agreed on a 32-member governing council, with 16 seats for the developing countries, 14 for the donor countries, and 2 for the countries with economies in transition. The plan also provides that, if the council cannot reach consensus on a substantive matter, its decisions must be approved by two separate voting methods, each requiring a minimum of 60 percent of the votes. The first method is based on money, with votes allocated according to donor contribution levels. The second is based on membership, with the developing countries controlling more votes than do the donors. Thus, in a power-sharing compromise, either group will be able to block a decision of the governing council. Whether this arrangement will lead to greater cooperation on project priorities between donors and recipients or inhibit the GEF from operating effectively remains to be seen. The restructuring plan is expected to be in place by the end of 1994.

Participants in the March meeting reached another complicated compromise on control over governing council meetings. According to the restructuring plan, the governing council will meet every six months to discuss funding projects. For each meeting a chair will be elected by members of the council, alternating between a representative of the developing countries and a representative of the donor countries or of the countries with economies in transition. Council meetings will be chaired jointly by the CEO of the secretariat and the elected chair. The CEO, responsible for running the GEF on a daily basis, will take the chair only when matters relating to program administration and implementation of GEF activities are being discussed. The elected chair will preside over other discussions at that meeting but will have no responsibilities between sessions. The governing council itself will not be directly involved in administering fund projects but will have the power to block projects it determines to be inconsistent with GEF policies and priorities.

Responsibility for implementing GEF activities will continue to be shared by UNDP, UNEP, and the World Bank. Through its country offices, UNDP will help to identify projects, provide technical assistance, and administer the Small Grants Program for community groups. UNEP will manage the Scientific and Technical Advisory Board, which provides analytic environmental guidance to the GEF. The World Bank is trustee of the fund and responsible for investment projects.

At the March 1994 GEF replenishment meeting, donor countries pledged an additional $2 billion in funding for the next three to five years, beginning in July 1994—the expiration date for the pilot phase of the GEF. Upon adoption of the restructuring plan by UNEP, UNDP, and the World Bank, the GEF will become a permanent international institution. The secretariat will be located in and given administrative support by the World Bank but is intended to function independently. Specific provisions for greater transparency and participation by NGOs and affected communities have yet to be established and will have to be taken up by the governing council and the implementing agencies. The terms of the restructuring await review and acceptance by the parties to the international conventions on biological diversity and climate change.

Ozone Depletion, Climate Change, and Other Natural Disasters

The **Copenhagen Amendment to the Montreal Protocol on Substances That Deplete the Ozone Layer** entered into force on June 14, 1994, after ratification by 20 parties. The original Montreal Protocol, signed in 1987 and ratified by 132 countries to date, identified certain ozone-depleting substances and set schedules for phasing out their use. In 1992, however, after a report of the Scientific Assessment Panel revealed that ozone depletion was even more severe than projected, parties to the protocol adopted adjustments to the schedules for phasing out chlorofluorocarbons (CFCs), carbon tetrachloride, and methyl chloroform. The new amendment adds hydrochlorofluorocarbons, hydrobromofluorocarbons, and methyl bromide to the list of substances controlled under the protocol.

The Montreal Protocol was one of the first international agreements to incorporate the principle of economic fairness in dealing with a global environmental problem. After scientists began presenting evidence that the Earth's ozone layer, which filters out harmful ultraviolet radiation, was rapidly being depleted by chemical reactions in the atmosphere involving certain manmade chemicals, particularly the CFCs used in refrigerators and air conditioners, most of the CFC-producing countries agreed to phase out production and consumption of CFCs and related chemicals. Although developing countries were reluctant to sign on to the protocol and deny themselves the economic and social benefits of using these refrigerants, many were encouraged to join it by the establishment of a Multilateral Fund to help them purchase CFC substitutes and by provisions promising that they would be able to obtain environmentally safe substitutes and technologies on a fair and favorable basis. In the three years between the protocol's entry into force and December 1993, the Multilateral Fund raised $165 million to assist the 90 developing countries that ratified the protocol with plans and projects to phase out ozone-depleting substances [U.N. press release HE/849, 3/22/94].

Agenda 21 does not propose any new programs for dealing with ozone depletion, but it does encourage states to pay their contributions to the Multilateral Fund promptly (promised payments have been slow to materialize) and to expedite the development of CFC substitutes and their transfer to developing countries.

The **Framework Convention on Climate Change,** opened for signature in Rio during the Earth Summit, entered into force on March 21, 1994, three months after ratification by 50 countries. The first meeting of the contracting parties is scheduled for March 1995 in Berlin. The objective of the convention is to stabilize greenhouse gas concentrations in the atmosphere at levels that will prevent dangerous interference with the climate system resulting from human activities [Article 2]. These greenhouse gases—among them carbon dioxide, methane, and nitrogen oxides—trap heat in the Earth's atmosphere. Although uncertainty surrounds the degree and consequences of the expected global warming, potential effects include the melting of polar ice caps and a consequent rise in ocean levels, posing a threat to low-lying islands and coastal areas; increased drought and desertification; more frequent and intense storms; and destruction of coral reefs.

A substantial proportion of carbon dioxide increases in the atmosphere results from the burning of fossil fuels in industrialized countries to meet transportation, heating, and energy needs. The preamble to the convention notes "that the largest share of historical and current global emissions of greenhouse gases has originated in developed countries, that the per capita emissions in developing countries are still relatively low, and that the share of global emissions originating in developing countries will grow to meet their social and development needs." Developing countries have been concerned that they will be expected to limit their own efforts at industrialization and economic development to avert global disaster. Recognizing that environmental protection cannot be dealt with separately from issues of economic survival, the convention calls for financial and technical assistance and transfers of alternative technologies to developing countries to encourage their participation in the international effort to address climate change. As in the biodiversity convention, the GEF is designated as the interim funding mechanism for financial assistance, contingent on the satisfactory outcome of its restructuring efforts.

Acknowledging the differentiated responsibilities and capabilities of developed and developing countries, Article 4 of the climate change convention calls on the developed countries to take the lead in mitigating climate change by adopting measures "with the aim of" returning their greenhouse gas emissions (jointly or individually) to 1990 levels by the year 2000. This commitment is phrased in a vague way because of the U.S. refusal to agree to mandatory targets or timetables for reducing emissions. Instead, the parties are to meet regularly to review the adequacy of national policies and the progress being made toward stabilizing emissions in light of the best scientific information available. The developed countries are required to submit detailed reports on national greenhouse gas inventories and emissions-control policies by September 21, 1994, six months after the convention's entry into force.

There is already concern that the current aims for emissions reductions are insufficient to prevent dangerous climate changes. A number of developed countries, including the United States and members of the European Union, have called for additional measures to limit greenhouse gas emissions [*NGLS Go Between,* 2/94]. The **Intergovernmental Panel on Climate Change,** set up by UNEP and the World Meteorological Organization in 1988 to investigate the potential severity and impact of global climate change and suggest policy responses, will be preparing a special report in 1994 to assess the situation. As a "framework" convention, the climate change treaty was intended to outline general principles and obligations; specific targets for emission reductions can be added as protocols.

In related action to mitigate the effects of global climate conditions, a program for reducing the impacts of hurricanes, floods, droughts, earthquakes, and other natural disasters was prepared for adoption at the May 1994 World Conference on Natural Disaster Reduction in Yokohama, Japan. Developing countries sustained losses from natural disasters of $62 billion in 1992—more than the total they received in development aid [*Development Update*, 3–4/94]. The plan gives importance to early-warning systems to track storms and predict drought, disaster preparedness and rapid assistance programs, disaster-resistant construction techniques, and improved site-planning land-management measures.

Small Islands and Sustainable Development

Concern about the effects of climate change and natural disasters was also at the forefront of preparations for the **Global Conference on the Sustainable Development of Small Island Developing States,** held in Barbados in April 1994. Responding to pressure by the Alliance of Small Island States (AOSIS) at the Earth Summit, Chapter 17 of Agenda 21 called for a global conference to address the special sustainable development problems of small islands—the result of ecological fragility, limited resources, geographic isolation, and rich diversity of cultures and natural resources [par. 17.124–17.127]. Of particular concern, especially to the Pacific islands, is their vulnerability to the increased storm activity and sea-level rise that would accompany global warming. In fact, small islands represent a sort of global laboratory for sustainable development practices, since one finds concentrated in a limited land area all the environmental problems of coastal-zone management.

Within the U.N. system, the Barbados Conference was viewed as a test of post-UNCED acceptance of global responsibility for sustainable development. Many of the environmental problems of small islands are caused by industrialization in other parts of the world, and AOSIS members sought new and additional assistance from industrialized countries in responding to those problems. During preparations for the conference, however, some donor countries asserted that redirection of existing financial aid resources would be sufficient.

Although members of the preparatory committee were able to agree on a detailed program of action for sustainable development of small islands—including measures to address the impacts of climate change and natural disasters; waste management strategies; and initiatives to improve the management of coastal, marine, land, energy, and freshwater resources—they left unresolved issues relating to financing and implementing the action plan. In the end, the financing section of the action plan did call for new and additional financial resources (although none were specifically identified) and for better application of existing development assistance, use of the GEF, and increased market access for the exports of small island states. In general, financing for the action plan will come from these countries' own public and private sectors. Implementation plans emphasized the need for regional and subregional cooperation among island states as well as national efforts and international assistance.

The Barbados Conference failed to attract much publicity or international attention. Few developed countries sent high-level representatives. U.N. Secretary-General Boutros Boutros-Ghali did attend, despite a pending crisis in the former Yugoslavia, to show his commitment to small island states and their development. He acknowledged donor fatigue but recommended more active diplomatic efforts to convince the donor countries of the importance of development [U.N. press release note No. B/3, 4/27/94]. He noted that follow-up cooperation by member states is more important than attendance at a conference. The conference participants have requested that the CSD monitor implementation of the program of action for sustainable development in small island states, that the Secretary-General prepare analytic reports in time for CSD reviews in 1996 and 1999, and that a special small islands unit be established within the Department of Policy Coordination and Sustainable Development.

Desertification and Drought

According to Agenda 21 "desertification affects about one-sixth of the world's population, 70 percent of all drylands, and one-quarter of the total land area of the world." Among its most obvious impacts, in addition to widespread poverty, are a decline in soil fertility and the degradation of rangeland and cropland [par. 12.2]. Drought is a recurring phenomenon throughout much of the developing world, especially Africa, where an estimated 3 million people died of its effects in the mid-1980s [par. 12.45].

Following the Earth Summit in 1992, the 47th General Assembly adopted Resolution 188 establishing an intergovernmental negotiating committee for the **Elaboration of an International Convention to Combat Desertification** in countries experiencing serious drought and/ or desertification, particularly in Africa. Five negotiating sessions were scheduled for this intergovernmental negotiating committee on desertification (INCD), and it was directed to produce an agreement by June 1994. An extra session of the INCD was later scheduled for January 1995, after adoption of the convention, to review implementation programs adapted to the specific needs of each region.

At the first working session of the INCD in May 1993, regional differences emerged, notably on the proposal to give priority to Africa. In later sessions the committee agreed to attach separate annexes to the convention elaborating separate implementation programs for each of three regions: Africa, Asia, and Latin America and the Caribbean. Although emphasizing national programs to promote the alleviation of poverty, food security, sustainable agricultural practices, and efficient energy sources, the convention encourages complementary subregional and regional action programs. It notes that desertification is caused by the complex interaction of physical, political, and socioeconomic factors, including trade and other aspects of international economic relations, and it seeks international cooperation in the form of technology transfer, scientific research, information collection, and financial resources.

Financing was a controversial topic in these negotiations as well. At the third session of the INCD, in January 1994, traditional donor countries objected to proposals for a new anti-desertification fund, citing the need for better use of existing programs, and they maintained that financial assistance ought to come from a wider group, including some developing countries in a position to help. Rabah Hadid of Algeria, representing the G-77 and China, complained that developed countries were trying to shirk their responsibility to provide funds and technology assistance because desertification affects them hardly at all, most deserts and drylands being located in the least-developed countries, and he expressed concern over the direction the negotiations had taken—toward a "convention of the poor," with responsibilities shifted toward South-South cooperation [U.N. press release ENV/DEV/240, 1/24/94].

Although not officially acknowledged, some resistance to the convention may have resulted from recent suggestions that there is little scientific basis for claims of expanding desertification, at least in the Sahara [*The New York Times*, 1/18/94]. W. Franklin G. Cardy, Director of UNEP's desertification-control program, recommended that the term "desertification" be jettisoned, explaining that it serves mainly as a political tool, a way to call attention to a regional manifestation of the global land-erosion problem and attract financial assistance [ibid.]. African countries reportedly were promised a desertification treaty at the Earth Summit in exchange for their support on other issues [ibid.]. Some affected countries complained that negotiations on the desertification convention seemed to be taking a back seat to other, more clearly global, environmental issues addressed at the Earth Summit, such as climate change and biodiversity.

Forests and Timber

The Earth Summit did not produce an international convention on sustainable forest management, as some had hoped, only a non-legally binding **statement of general principles on forestry.** The forest principles encourage sustainable use but recognize too the "sovereign and inalienable right" of states to manage their forests in accordance with development needs, including conversion to other uses. Closely linked with issues of habitat loss, species extinction, global warming, and desertification, rapid deforestation has become an issue of global environmental concern. But developing countries view efforts to halt the destruction of tropical rain forests as an unfair restriction on their economic development and self-determination, especially when industrialized countries have not been willing to apply the same standards to their own remaining forests. Tropical timber sales are estimated at $7.5 billion a year in an $85 billion per year global industry.

Negotiations on a new **International Tropical Timber Agreement (ITTA)**, conducted under the auspices of the U.N. Conference on Trade and Development (UNCTAD), offered another disappointment for those who sought to strengthen existing provisions on conservation and sustainable management and extend them to all forests. The 1983 ITTA, which expired on March 31, 1994, concentrated primarily on improving conditions of international trade in timber products among producer and consumer nations, with little emphasis on environmental protection. The new ITTA, agreed to on January 26, 1994, in Geneva, was described by UNCTAD's Deputy Secretary-General Carlos Fortin as "designed to increase trade in tropical timber without favoring either ecological or commercial interests" [*International Environment Reporter, 2/9/94*]. The 1983 ITTA was extended until the new agreement becomes effective, in early 1995. It will be operative for an initial period of four years.

Although the new agreement calls on the parties to encourage sustainable development through national policies, financial assistance, and technology transfers, it is short on substantive conservation plans or commitments. Consumer countries agreed to set up a fund—named the Bali Partnership Fund—to provide "appropriate resources" to assist producer countries in establishing forest conservation programs but failed to agree on a funding level. This fund will commemorate the commitment made in Bali, Indonesia, in May 1990 by all ITTA members "to achieve exports of tropical timber from sustainable managed sources by the year 2000" [draft agreement, TD/TIMBER 2/L.9].

Developing countries, despite cries of "double standard," were not able to expand coverage of the agreement to timber production in northern forests, obtaining only a non-legally binding pledge by consumer countries to respect conservation guidelines. They did, however, manage to obtain a nondiscrimination provision to the effect that nothing in the agreement is to be construed as authorizing the use of trade bans or restrictions on tropical timber imports to discourage unsustainable timber consumption or forest management practices [U.N. press release TAD/1722, 2/2/94].

Trade in Hazardous Waste

In a successful effort to impose trade-related environmental-protection restrictions, parties to the **1989 Basel Convention on the Control of Transboundary Movements of Hazardous Wastes and Their Disposal,** meeting in Geneva in March 1994, unanimously agreed to an immediate ban on shipments of hazardous industrial wastes for disposal in non-OECD countries. Such shipments were previously allowed under the convention if advance consent was obtained from the recipient country.

Exports of wastes to non-OECD countries for "recycling or recovery" (about 90 percent of the trade in hazardous waste) will not be banned until December 1997, however. Environmentalists seeking an immediate ban on all shipments of hazardous wastes, including those allegedly earmarked for "recycling," have charged that industrial wastes often end up in developing countries lacking the environmental regulations, facilities, and safeguards for handling wastes, which are often contaminated by toxic chemicals and heavy metals. Many developing countries have already banned imports of hazardous wastes, including those destined for recycling, through such regional agreements as the Bamako Convention in Africa. But industry representatives at the Geneva meeting warned that the ban could have a negative effect on the environment and development of some countries by denying them the option of obtaining certain materials through the recycling of waste imports [U.N. press release HE/851, 3/31/94].

In June 1993 the World Conference on Human Rights singled out the illicit dumping of toxic wastes as a serious threat to the human right to life and health. The Vienna Declaration calls on all states to adopt and vigorously implement existing conventions related to the dumping of toxic wastes and to cooperate in preventing illicit dumping [Vienna Declaration, par. 11].

Prohibitions on waste dumping at sea under the 1972 London **Convention on the Prevention of Marine Pollution by Dumping Wastes and other Matter** were strengthened at the November 1993 meeting of the 72 contracting parties. The parties agreed to ban disposal of all radioactive wastes at sea, including low-level radioactive wastes, and to prohibit the incineration of industrial waste at sea, effective February 21, 1994. A general prohibition on disposing of industrial waste at sea will take effect at the end of 1995. On February 18, 1994, the Russian Federation lodged a formal reservation to the ban on disposing of radioactive waste at sea. In October 1993, it had dumped low-level radioactive wastes in the Sea of Japan, claiming that the country lacked financial resources for developing alternative disposal methods [*International Environment Reporter*, 3/9/94].

Trade and Environment

On April 15, 1994, ministers from the 117 countries that are parties to **GATT** met in Marrakesh to sign the agreement negotiated during the seven-year-long **Uruguay Round of global trade talks.** The new multi-lateral trade accord will generally lower tariffs and trade barriers; expand trading rules to cover agriculture, textiles, and services; and establish a **World Trade Organization** to supervise international trade. Despite pressures from environmentalists for "greener" trade policies, environmental issues were not central to the Uruguay Round negotiations.

Reflecting the importance of global trade liberalization to economic growth in developing countries, Chapter 2 of Agenda 21 urged successful completion of the Uruguay Round. It states that the ability of developing countries to benefit from international trade and mobilize the resources necessary to finance sustainable development has been impaired by low commodity prices and by protectionist measures limiting their access to export markets [par. 2.7]. It further argues that an open multilateral trading system allows for a more efficient allocation and use of resources, contributes to an increase in production and incomes and a decrease in demands on the environment, and provides additional resources for economic growth and improved environmental protection [par. 2.19].

Environmentalists, however, are generally less optimistic about the ecological benefits of increased trade: They argue that the new agreement will encourage challenges to national environmental laws and standards based on the claim that such measures constitute unfair barriers to international trade, and they also argue that it will undermine the effectiveness of international treaties in allowing the use of trade sanctions as an enforcement mechanism. Developing countries, for their part, fear that the application of environmental standards to products or manufacturing processes will simply become one more barrier to trade—a sort of "green" protectionism.

The new GATT accord does call for the creation of a **Committee on Trade and Environment** to integrate trade and sustainable development objectives and to indicate whether modifications of the multilateral trading system are necessary. The committee will provide policy analysis, research, and information on environmental issues to trade negotiators and GATT dispute-resolution panels. (Discussions about the relationship between international trade and environmental measures will clearly continue during the establishment of the World Trade Organization in 1995, and in the next round of multilateral trade talks now getting under way.) In June 1994, Peter Sutherland, Director-General of GATT, hosted an unprecedented public symposium in Geneva to examine and debate the role of trade policies in environmental protection and sustainable development.

Within the U.N. system, **UNCTAD** is the primary forum for considering the linkages between trade liberalization and economic development in nonindustrialized countries. Its effectiveness has been called into question, however, because it has no real decision-making powers and can only recommend policy options to GATT. Nevertheless, UNCTAD has been working on a number of technical projects that address such topics as environmental labeling and standards, environmental effects of commodity production and processing, and incorporation of environmental costs into the pricing of products.

In cooperation with UNEP, the secretariat of UNCTAD is considering a special certification scheme for "environmentally friendly" goods produced by developing countries. Citing the need for equivalent rather than universal production standards, Kenneth Dadzie, Secretary-General of UNCTAD, explained that environmental policies and standards of industrialized countries are perceived as potential barriers to trade with developing countries because they do not take into account the characteristics of products or the production processes of developing countries. Further, information and certification requirements may be too onerous for small-scale production units [U.N. press release TAD/1726, 2/17/94]. Dadzie also noted that "excessive use of environmental resources" [ibid.] is not due to trade per se but to pricing policies—and that development of a multilaterally accepted method of pricing that incorporates the item's cost to the environment would be a way to begin building the peace between trade and the environment.

With respect to development financing, UNCTAD is promoting an international scheme for tradeable carbon permits. If developing countries were allocated permits that could be sold to industrialized countries, they could generate substantial financial resources and reduce development assistance requirements [*Development Issues in the Aftermath of UNCTAD VIII*, UNCTAD/NGLS/45, 11/93, p. 20].

Debt and Development

A meeting in Cartagena in February 1992 strengthened the UNCTAD secretariat's mandate to work at reducing the burden of debt that is draining financial resources from the economies of developing countries. Agenda 21, adopted later that year, described the debt crisis as an impediment to sustainable development:

> Many developing countries have experienced a decade-long situation of negative net transfer of financial resources, during which their financial receipts were exceeded by payments they had to make, in particular for debt-servicing. As a result, domestically mobilized resources had to be transferred abroad instead of being invested locally in order to promote sustainable economic development. [par. 2.23]

Despite progress in restructuring and reducing indebtedness to commercial banks, many poorer countries, especially in Africa, continue to struggle with overwhelming multilateral and bilateral debt obligations. In June

1993, the World Conference on Human Rights called upon the international community to alleviate the debt burden of developing countries to advance the realization of the economic, social, and cultural rights by their people [Vienna Declaration, par. 12].

Many indebted countries have undertaken the economic structural adjustment programs required by the World Bank and the International Monetary Fund in connection with debt rescheduling or new loans— sometimes with adverse social and environmental effects, as when cuts are made in health care, education, and environmental protection. The adverse effects of structural readjustment were recited by participants at the first session of the preparatory committee for the **World Summit for Social Development** in early February 1994. The Secretary-General's report on the core issues to be addressed by the Summit states that there is a growing acceptance of the need to address the social costs of adjustment at the beginning of policy formulation rather than after its effects on income and jobs have become apparent [A/Conf.166/PC/6, par. 50]. The report also points out the need for debt relief combined with additional assistance to allow low-income countries to pursue a policy of growth and social development [par. 56].

With the pressure for debt relief and for revised structural adjustment programs comes criticism of the funding policies of the World Bank. As the primary funding institutions for development assistance, the World Bank and its affiliates are central to any new agenda for people-centered sustainable development. Over the last 20 years the United States and other major donors have contributed four times more to these institutions than to the rest of the U.N. system. In 1993 the World Bank and its affiliates extended over $23 billion in loans and assistance to the developing world; the rest of the U.N. system provided less than $3 billion.

In response to criticisms of the World Bank's record on environmental issues, the office of vice president for environmentally sustainable development was created to oversee coordination of the Bank's economic development and environmental protection policies. According to Ismail Serageldin, the Bank's appointee to the new position, sound stewardship of the Earth's resources requires the integration of social and ecological viewpoints with those of economists [*World Bank News*, 10/7/93]. In September 1993 the Bank initiated an annual conference on environmentally sustainable development in conjunction with its annual meeting. It also increased substantially the number of environmental specialists on its staff; it has agreed to provide greater public access to project information, including environmental impact assessments; and it will conduct an annual performance review of its entire $400 billion portfolio of loans for development projects, to include an examination of project impacts on poverty and environmental protection. Mohamed El-Ashry, director of the World Bank's environment department, acknowledged that the institution's record on the environment is not a good one but claimed that there has been a change in culture and attitude [*International Environment Reporter*, 7/28/93, p. 543].

Public Involvement in Sustainable Development

Reflecting the U.N.'s growing emphasis on the needs and rights of individuals, not just governments, representatives of nongovernmental organizations played an unprecedentedly important role at the Earth Summit and at the Vienna Human Rights Conference, and NGOs continue to press for greater participation in upcoming U.N. meetings and conferences. They are also seeking input into the operations of U.N. agencies and international financial institutions.

Agenda 21 specifically encourages the broadest possible public participation in decision-making and the active involvement of nongovernmental groups in attaining sustainable development goals. In fact, much of Agenda 21 is devoted to outlining the needs and roles of various sectors of civil society, and it calls on the United Nations to review its formal procedures for NGO involvement in policy-making, decision-making, and implementation with an eye to strengthening the role of NGOs [par. 27.6].

Despite repeated proclamations about a new partnership, however, NGO involvement in official U.N. proceedings is still not welcomed by some delegations, and government representatives alone take part in the decision-making process. In July 1993, ECOSOC called for an open-ended review of relations between the United Nations and NGOs [E/1993/80]. The resolution governing this relationship [ECOSOC resolution 1296], which has not been revised since May 1968, established criteria for granting consultative status to certain groups. At a time when more and more local and national organizations are seeking greater access to and input into U.N. proceedings, this process is viewed as inadequate. The U.N. management, for its part, worries about accommodating and coordinating the participation of so many new groups. To complicate the issue further, conferences organized by the General Assembly are not bound by the ECOSOC rules for NGO participation, and some ECOSOC bodies (such as the CSD) have made their own arrangements for accreditation. All the NGOs accredited at the Earth Summit were given the opportunity to register for participation at the CSD meetings, but there was considerable confusion about the procedures NGOs had to follow if they wished to participate in the numerous meetings on environment and sustainable development-related issues held at the United Nations over the past year.

The Open-ended Working Group on the Review of Arrangements for Consultations with Non-governmental Organizations held its first organizational meeting in New York in February 1994. This group is considering ways of improving arrangements for NGO involvement and will make recommendations to ECOSOC about updating its current rules. At the opening session of the Working Group, Nitin Desai, Under-Secretary-General for Policy Coordination and Sustainable Development, stated that the NGO situation had undergone not only a quantitative but also a qualitative transformation. He hailed the emergence of a "civil society" in which local, national, and regional organizations and networks engage in dialogue and cooperation with governments, and he emphasized the importance of these group in realizing the U.N.'s objectives. Nevertheless, some NGOs are concerned that they will continue to be denied access to U.N. proceedings.

In fact, pragmatism dictates that NGOs be given a role in U.N. forums when it comes to critical issues of global interdependence. In the area of sustainable development in particular, the setting of goals and the implementation of action plans cannot be left to governments and international institutions alone. Through NGOs, citizens and groups are informed about the international consequences of decisions they make in their daily lives and are encouraged to join in the quest for solutions to global environmental-development problems as well as local ones. Without such a concerted effort to mobilize public support and involvement, U.N. efforts to build a global partnership for sustainable development will pass largely unnoticed.

2. Food and Agriculture
By Martin M. McLaughlin

At first glance the global food situation seems promising. Even with a slight decline in grain production in 1993, harvests remain adequate on a per capita basis. Prices continue to be relatively low, and yields have generally increased. The *World Economic Survey 1993* [E/1993/60 ST/ESA/237] says that "with distribution of the available food supplies strictly according to need, at the global level and even within the developing countries themselves as a group, there would, theoretically, have been enough food to go around to prevent chronic undernourishment." Yet a seventh of the world's people—nearly 800 million—mainly in the developing countries of the South, lack access to a diet adequate for a normal human life [U.N. Food and Agriculture Organization, *Agriculture Toward 2010*, C 93/94, 11/93].

Four U.N. agencies deal with food and agriculture: The **Food and Agriculture Organization (FAO)**, which monitors the world food situation and provides technical assistance to agriculture; the **World Food Programme (WFP)**, created in 1963 as a joint program of the United Nations and the FAO, which combats hunger and promotes social development in poor countries; the **International Fund for Agricultural Development**

(IFAD), a product of the 1974 World Food Conference, which targets its programs toward small farmers and other low-income rural people; and the **World Food Council (WFC),** the central policy body created by the 1974 World Food Conference, which coordinated U.N. food policy for at least a decade. The Council has not met since the summer of 1992; and the functions of its secretariat have been absorbed into the **U.N. Department of Policy Coordination and Sustainable Development,** in New York [UNGA 47/212 B, 5/6/93], whose mandate is to implement the follow-up to the 1992 U.N. Conference on Environment and Development (UNCED). The headquarters of the first three agencies are in Rome.

During the 18-year tenure of Director-General Edouard Saouma, which ended in 1993, the FAO became the leading U.N. agency in presenting an overview of the world food situation and in providing technical assistance to improve food production in the developing countries. Mr. Saouma was succeeded by M. Jacques Diouf of Senegal, who took office January 4, 1994 [FAO/3587].

In recent years, especially 1993, the WFP has been forced by the sharp increase in natural and manmade disasters to concentrate more of its resources in the provision of food aid for relief, especially in drought and conflict-stricken areas of sub-Saharan Africa; its target for 1995–96 is $1.5 billion in voluntary contributions [WFP/CFA: 35/18; document E/1993/91]. Two-thirds of this represents 13 million tons per year of commodities pledged by donor nations—a total that falls short of both basic consumption requirements and nutritional need.

During its nearly two decades of leadership on food policy, the WFC, though compelled to respond to the more visible food emergencies that captured public attention and stimulated public sympathy, nevertheless attempted to maintain the focus of policy on the less visible chronic hunger, which systematically and continually afflicts far more people than the dramatic situations represented by periodic famines. In its report on its most recent annual meeting (the 18th), in Nairobi, the Council reminded ECOSOC that "As we approach the third millennium, the challenges posed by hunger, poverty, population growth, and environmental decline are greater than ever" and that "The largest increases in the numbers of hungry people have been in Africa" [Suppl. No. 19: A/47/19].

Convergent with these views, IFAD has differed with the conventional wisdom that general economic growth benefits the poor and that a social-safety-net approach would take care of any victims, as well as with the common portrayal of the poor as "a net burden on the growth process" [*The State of Rural Poverty*, A/C.2/47/SR.32, p. 3]. IFAD's message is unambiguous: "The perspective is not that growth achieved by the better-off will pull the poor out of poverty, but that the mobilization of the poor themselves can uphold their dignity and free them from the shackles of misery, while at the same time making a vital contribution to overall sustainable growth" [ibid., p. 14].

The U.N.'s current schedule for focusing on global problems includes the **Conference on Population and Development** (Cairo, September 1994), which marks the 20th anniversary of the Bucharest Conference on population; the **World Summit on Social Development** (Copenhagen, March 1995); and the **World Conference on Women** (Beijing, September 1995). There is no plan, it should be noted, for an anniversary of the 1974 World Food Conference; the United Nations considers that its December 1992 World Conference on Nutrition (Rome, FAO) paid sufficient attention to that problem.

Nevertheless, hunger clearly appears to have reemerged on the international development agenda. In November 1993, FAO's *Agriculture Toward 2010* (see above) became the major agenda item for the biennial FAO Conference. The document assessed "prospects for world food and agriculture to the year 2010, with special focus on the developing countries" [ibid., 1.1]. Neither the diagnosis nor the prognosis was encouraging: The document estimated the number of hungry people at 786 million and said that "progress would be very slow for many countries and population groups . . . chronic undernutrition would persist and its incidence would continue to be significant. . . . Pressures on agricultural resources and the environment would continue to build up . . ." [ibid.].

On December 1, 1993, the **World Bank,** in cooperation with several nongovernmental organizations, conducted a conference on Overcoming Global Hunger, in which World Bank President Lewis Preston, former U.S. President Jimmy Carter, U.N. Secretary-General Boutros Boutros-Ghali, and IFAD President Fawzi al-Sultan, among others, participated. The conference was a direct result of the 22-day fast undertaken by U.S. Representative Tony Hall (D–Ohio), former chairman of the House Select Committee on Hunger, which was abolished, along with several other select committees, at the start of the 103rd Congress. Hall undertook the fast to call attention to the fact that the problem of hunger persisted beyond the death of his committee; he called it off when the World Bank decided to convene the conference, in which he, too, then took a prominent part.

In order to broaden both the sponsorship of the conference and participation in it, the Bank approached several of the nongovernmental organizations (NGOs) that serve on its standing Bank/NGO Committee. A steering committee including NGO representatives met more than a dozen times to prepare for the event and has continued to work with the Bank on follow-up, although their differing assessments of the conference continue to lead them in varying directions. In particular, the NGOs fault the World Bank for not making adequate efforts to make sure that poor people participate in decisions about sustainable agriculture, and about development in general.

In his prepared remarks at this conference, the Secretary-General, while acknowledging the incidence of famine brought on by weather and war, placed his major emphasis on systemic causes. "The world now produces enough food to feed its population," he said. "The problem is not simply technical. It is a political and social problem. It is a problem of access to food supplies, of distribution and of entitlement. Above all, it is a problem of political will." "Hunger," he continued, "is often the result of development models that tended to favour the urban economy and lifestyle at the expense of the countryside and agricultural production."

World Bank President Preston echoed these sentiments, asserting that "Fundamentally, hunger is caused by poverty," the elimination of which, he said, is the central goal of the institution he heads. World Bank Vice President for Environmentally Sustainable Development Ismail Serageldin, the point man for the conference, treated these themes at somewhat greater length and held out the hope that the situation of the poorest groups in society could be improved in our lifetime.

Former President Carter, speaking "not as a former President but as the leader of an NGO," the Carter Center in Atlanta, emphasized the need for "peace, freedom, democracy, and human rights" as inseparable from a solution to the problem of hunger. While many of his comments described practical examples, he also emphasized the lack of coordination of remedial activities, the decline in public attention to the problem, and the reluctance of donors to deal with what he called "generic" problems. Though not lacking in hope, his remarks were tinged with skepticism about the practical value of conferences.

From March 29 to 31, 1994, the **International Food Policy Research Institute (IFPRI),** one of the institutes known collectively as the **Consultative Group on International Agricultural Research (CGIAR),** held a Symposium on Ending Malnutrition, which focused on nutrition policies and programs that had met with some success in developing countries. The conference and its documentation followed the theme of the *Second Report on the World Nutrition Situation* [ACC/SCN, 10/92], prepared for the World Conference on Nutrition (Rome, December 1992).

While fairly technical, the reports described actions taken in particular countries (India, Indonesia, Tanzania, and Thailand) and highlighted some of the context: "protein-energy and micronutrient malnutrition continue to affect large numbers of people. An estimated 20 percent of the population [of developing countries] has inadequate food consumption. . . . Nutritional trends have generally deteriorated or remained static in Sub-Saharan Africa during the 1980s . . ." [*Second Report*, p. 1].

These reports and events were mainly informative and analytical; except for the World Bank's conference, they did not attempt to offer broad solutions or policies. In most cases, updating the analysis was almost directive enough. The FAO estimates that even with a projected drop in cereal production of 3 percent, those supplies will be adequate for global food security [*Food Outlook*, 10/93]; the U.S. Department of Agriculture agrees that exportable supplies remain abundant, especially for wheat [*Food Aid Needs Assessment*/GFA-4, USDA, ERS, 11/93]; and the Feinstein World Hunger Program at Brown University believes that there is more than enough food to provide a minimum requirement of 2,350 calories per day for everyone [*The Hunger Report 1993*].

Clearly there is no lack of consensus on the single central fact: Chronic hunger persists for a seventh of the human race despite the availability of enough food to feed everyone. The question, acknowledged by almost all observers, is access: i.e., a seventh of the world's population cannot obtain the food they need, because they lack the income to produce it or purchase it.

Every conference, every report, every study, every analysis, at least since the 1974 U.N. World Food Conference, has acknowledged that poverty is the cause of hunger. But few have gone the next step—to recognize that poverty stems from the lack of the power to choose otherwise. Poor people are as wise as others; if they can, they will choose not to be poor. But to move in this direction is to relinquish the temptation to opt for the technological solution—the supply-side miracle that will obviate the necessity of looking more deeply into the demand-side social, political, and economic arrangements that prevent poor people from having a choice and thus taking steps to relieve the poverty that keeps them hungry.

The Issues Paper prepared by the World Bank for its December conference proposed three kinds of action to relieve hunger: for the short term, elimination of famine; for the medium term, food and agriculture programs targeted on the poor and hungry; and for the long term, measures that will "sustain and increase growth that uses the capacities of the poor" [Issues Paper, 11/19/93]. In his own report on the conference, Vice President Serageldin agreed "that the task of reducing hunger is an integral part of the broader task of poverty reduction" [letter to NGO steering committee, 1/13/94].

This thinking clearly acknowledges the hunger-poverty nexus; but along with the World Bank's documentation and other follow-up materials, it also continues the tendency to see the solution of the hunger problem as behavioral rather than systemic. The stress is on "interventions," i.e., new policies and projects, rather than on altered structures and new basic arrangements.

Many observers, including NGOs, are very doubtful about the effectiveness of what is essentially a remedial approach. They concede that symptoms of underdevelopment, like hunger, have to be dealt with. But they also continue to call for measures that, under the banner of popular participation, would enable the poor and hungry to take part in the decisions that affect the quality of their lives. In other words, they see both the hunger issue and the poverty issue as questions of development; and they have a fundamental disagreement with the conventional development model, which emphasizes economic growth, modified by some environmental considerations and supplemented by a "social safety net" for those who do not share in the benefits of that growth.

Nevertheless, the conceptual framework and the practical problems appear to be moving the world inexorably toward focusing on the central problem, which is development. The dramatic geopolitical changes of the past decade have provided motivation for this movement. With the Cold War waning as the major security consideration, it has been replaced by boundary disputes, civil wars, and ethnic and religious conflicts. These clashes, though often more violent and cruel than Cold War posturing, seem less threatening on the global level. Thus the attention of the world community has shifted to quality-of-life issues, i.e., development, protection of the environment, etc.—what might be called "geo-economics."

For this reason perhaps, and along with continued attention to personnel, organizational, and budgetary issues, the United Nations has begun to inject the concept of sustainable development into the agendas of its functional agencies as an overriding concern. Thus there are conferences on environment and development (UNCED) and population and development (Cairo), as well as the "summit" on social development. But having included development in the title, the United Nations seems unable to persuade the national delegations from the North, which tend to dominate such conferences, to focus on that aspect of the agenda.

The environment has become a concern to the rich countries of the North, but they are tempted to lecture the poor countries of the South about reducing their pressure on the natural resource base. Similarly, the impact of population growth on the environment has become a concern to the rich countries of the North, which are then inclined to lecture the poor countries of the South on the necessity of limiting their populations. Both of these attitudes ignore the enormously greater stress inflicted on the environment by the voracious consumerism of the North (and its minority of emulators elsewhere) than by the grinding poverty of most of the South, which is to some extent a product of the North's insatiable craving for the assets of the latter.

Notable examples of this consumerism can be found in many commodity areas in which the North greatly outconsumes the South. The Union of Concerned Scientists (UCS), in a February 1994 *Briefing Paper*, which focused its six-page critique mainly on the United States, nevertheless pointed out that most North Americans, Japanese, Europeans, etc., "consume enormous quantities of all sorts of things: energy, metals, minerals, forest products, and fresh water, as well as fish, grains, and meat. . . . [A] typical citizen of an industrial country uses 3 times as much fresh water, 10 times as much energy, and 19 times as much aluminum as a typical citizen of a developing country." Moreover, the favored modes of transport in the North, "cars, trucks, and jet aircraft . . . are among the least energy-efficient forms of transportation. . . ."

But it is the food and agriculture system that provides one of the clearest and most compelling examples of differential consumption. Although, as the UCS paper points out, caloric intake in the North is only about 35 percent higher than in the South, consumers increasingly appear to prefer frozen foods, packaged and processed foods, drinks in disposable cans and bottles, and meat. In addition to dietary problems of consumption, meat production uses large amounts of cropland to grow grain to feed to cattle (40 percent of the nearly 2 billion tons of grain grown last year), which in turn increases the use of fertilizers, pesticides, and water. Irrigation and transportation to market, as well as food packaging and freezing, require large amounts of energy; and livestock generate "millions of tons of animal wastes each year, which often end up untreated in lakes, streams, and groundwater."

The world food problem seems as clear today as it did at the time of the 1974 World Food Conference: Hundreds of millions of people get too little to eat because about a fifth of the world's population consumes too much and because the global economic system is skewed against the hungry. The solution to this problem is also clear: More food has to be produced where the hungry people are. Other implications of this solution are also becoming clearer: Most people in the North consume too much food and produce it in an inefficient and wasteful fashion; they also consume products that are higher on the food chain, limiting the availability and quality of the diet of the South and not necessarily improving the health of Northern consumers; and they perpetuate a food system that is driven mainly by agribusiness profit rather than by human need.

One can preserve the hope that food production will rise and that its distribution will improve. Yet that rise cannot be expected to match the production gains of the past four decades, during which yield almost tripled [Lester Brown, *State of the World 1994*, p. 181; see also *World Food Trends and Future Food Security*, IFPRI, 3/94]. As Brown puts it, "where cropland area is not expanding, grain yield per hectare has to rise as fast as population growth merely to maintain the existing inadequate supply of food" [ibid., p. 193]. When the North's overconsumption is added to the expected global population growth of nearly 100 million per year (96 percent of it in the South), the increased yield requirements become far more problematic.

The driving force behind food production since World War II has been trade, not need; yet only about a tenth of the grain harvest is traded [*Food Aid Needs Assessment*/GFA-4, USDA, ERS, 11/93, Table 2]. The industrialized countries are net exporters; and while prices have generally declined over the past two decades [*The World Food Outlook,* Donald O. Mitchell and Merlinda D. Ingco, International Economic Department of the World Bank], it is expected that the recently signed GATT agreement will bring about a gradual reversal of that trend—a result that may place poor people at greater risk.

The future seems grim for the poor and hungry, however hopeful some individual program results might have been. But some major players on the world agricultural scene are beginning to agree with the views of, among others, **U.N. Development Programme Administrator James Gustave Speth,** who pointed out in October 1993 that "whatever the causes of particular instances of violation or social disintegration, development is surely the major ingredient of the *cure*" [CGIAR, 10/25/93]. One of the central objectives of such development, Speth emphasized, is "sustainable food security," which requires mainly a new political will. Helping the developing countries achieve that security, Speth said, is a priority for the UNDP.

Unfortunately, the deteriorating food situation in several countries, confirmed once again by the *Second Report on the World Nutrition Situation* [Vol. 1, ACC/SCN, 10/92], coincides with the continued fall-off in development assistance to agriculture by donor institutions and governments. Most observers concur that this decline must be reversed and sustainable development policies pursued vigorously, if hunger in the developing countries is to abate. Although perhaps inclined to quibble with a figure here and there, they also generally agree on the extent of the problem and degree of urgency for a solution.

There is no lack of prescriptions for such a solution. IFPRI's list is representative: (1) economic growth and economic policies that will sustain in developing countries; (2) population growth must be contained and the growth in urbanization arrested; (3) the rural infrastructure must be created or improved, and access must be had to alternative agricultural production technology and modern inputs; and (4) natural resources must be managed in a fashion that distributes their benefits equitably and prevents general deterioration of the environment [IFPRI, op. cit., pp. 10–16 passim].

But in the end all of these proposals rely on that elusive factor identified by President John F. Kennedy at the World Food Conference in Washington, D.C., in the fall of 1963: "We have the technology to eliminate hunger from the face of the world in our lifetime . . . we need only the will."

3. Population
By Craig Lasher

The outcome of the deliberations of four major international conferences—the U.N. Conference on Environment and Development (1992), the International Conference on Population and Development (1994), the Fourth World Conference on Women (1995), and the World Summit for Social Development (1995)—will have an important impact on the U.N. response to global population problems in the future and on the question of whether the international community will be mobilized to find the necessary political will and financial resources to stabilize world population.

World population currently stands at 5.7 billion. Actions taken during the remainder of the decade will determine the size and pace of population growth into the next century. The **population projections** of U.N. demographers for the year 2050 range from a low of 7.8 billion people to a high of 12.5 billion [*The New York Times*, 4/3/94]. But if fertility remained constant at today's levels, world population would increase to 21 billion by 2050 [*The Washington Times*, 4/6/94]. Under any of these scenarios, demographic factors pose serious environmental and development challenges to the international community.

The magnitude of these challenges was highlighted in a joint statement of 58 national academies of science from developed and developing countries issued at the conclusion of a summit on population held in New Delhi in October 1993. "Humanity is approaching a crisis point with respect to the interlocking issues of population, environment and development," the statement declared. The summit noted the recent decline in food production relative to population growth and threats to the global environment linked to population and resource use [*ICPD 94*, 11–12/93].

UNCED and Population

The U.N. Conference on Environment and Development (UNCED) of June 1992 established principles (an Earth Charter) and an action plan (Agenda 21) that give greater recognition to the interrelationship of widespread poverty and environmental degradation. Unfortunately, governments disagreed throughout the preparatory process on the importance of the population issue. Many of the developing nations believed, for example, that too little weight was given to the development side of the UNCED agenda and that the effect of focusing attention on population problems would be to shift the blame for environmental degradation unfairly away from consumption patterns in the North. A number of developing countries maintained that the international population conference in 1994 was a more appropriate forum for discussing population issues [*E Magazine*, 5–6/92]. In the end, most references to population as an important factor in environmental degradation were deleted [*The Washington Post*, 4/12/92].

The final version of Agenda 21, adopted in June 1992, also made no specific mention of "family planning" or "contraception." The exclusion of the terms was a result of vigorous **lobbying by the Holy See** with the support of Argentina, the Philippines, and a few other governments [*Dallas Morning News,* 6/5/92]. Nor does the document offer any concrete recommendations for programs to stabilize global population or for providing the necessary financial resources to accomplish the goal.

The Search for Consensus at the Cairo Population Conference

Preparations for the decennial **International Conference on Population and Development (ICPD),** which will be held in Cairo, September 5–13, 1994, have been in full swing for some while. The conference itself will have been concluded by the start of the 49th General Assembly. The overall aim is to increase awareness of population issues, encourage governments to adopt effective and updated population policies, and secure the commitments and resources needed for both international and national efforts to address global population and related development problems [A/48/430]. The U.N. Secretary-General appointed **Dr. Nafis Sadik,** Executive Director of the United Nations Population Fund (UNFPA), as Secretary-General of the conference, and **Dr. Shunichi Inoue,** director of the Population Division of the U.N. Secretariat, as her deputy.

The 1994 meeting will be the fifth in a series of population conference convened by the United Nations at ten-year intervals. The first two were purely technical meetings, while the two subsequent meetings in 1974 at Bucharest and 1984 at Mexico City set goals and made recommendations for governments on population issues. The 1994 conference will review progress on the **World Population Plan of Action** revised in 1984 and will prepare a new plan of action for the coming decade.

The preparatory process for the 1994 conference has included expert group meetings convened around the world on six topics: population policies and programs; population and women; population and environment; family planning, health, and family well-being; demographic structure; and international migration. Also held were five regional conferences for Asia and the Pacific, the Arab states, Latin America and the Caribbean, Africa, and Europe and North America, organized by the United Nations jointly with various regional institutions [A/CONF. 171/PC/2]. Reports indicate that the preparatory meetings were well organized and involved broad representation of policy-makers, program managers, academics, and multilateral and nongovernmental organizations. Among the recommendations, the need for improvements in the status of women and the quality of family planning services have been prominent and are themes that will be emphasized at the conference itself.

The recommendations prepared by the expert group and regional meetings provide the basis for the final action to be presented in Cairo. Each national delegation has also prepared a report on its own country's situation. Although governments are the primary participants at the conference, the United Nations is encouraging the involvement of NGOs and helping to organize a separate NGO meeting to coincide with the official conference. During debate in the Second Committee of the General Assembly in November 1993, a resolution was adopted making the Preparatory Committee of the ICPD a subsidiary body of the General Assembly, elevating the conference's status within the U.N. system [A/Res/48/186].

PrepCom II

The second Preparatory Committee meeting (PrepCom II) for the ICPD was held in New York during May 1993. At that time country delegations began the process of formulating actionable recommendations to be agreed to at the ICPD. Official delegations from more than 100 countries participated in the PrepCom, joined by a massive NGO presence. Over 420 organizations were reportedly represented.

One highlight of PrepCom II was the announcement of dramatic **changes in U.S. population assistance policy,** which received a wildly enthusiastic reception from the other official delegations and from the gallery filled with NGO observers. The official head of the U.S. delegation, State Department Counselor Tim Wirth, stated that "President Clinton is deeply committed to moving population to the forefront of America's international priorities." In a complete reversal of recent policy, he announced that the U.S. position is "to support reproductive choice, including access to safe abortion," and noted that the "abortion issue should be addressed directly with tolerance and compassion, rather than officially ignored while women, especially poor women, and their families suffer" [*The New York Times,* 5/12/93].

The Clinton administration indicated that it would take a broader approach to reproductive health and will strive to advance women's rights and educational and economic empowerment as part of its population strategy. However, the statement also noted that the United States would work to develop international consensus around "priority, long-term and quantitative goals for stabilizing world population."

A major subject of controversy at PrepCom II was the extent to which the conceptual framework for the conference action agenda should be modified to address broad development and health issues. Some Southern and feminist NGOs lobbied to shift the emphasis away from demographic realities to the negative impacts of structural adjustment and gender inequality. Alternative language circulated by some NGOs actually sought to eliminate references to population stabilization and family planning. These efforts to dilute the focus on concrete actions necessary for the achievement of population stabilization led to objections from several official delegations and family planning activists, including representatives from India, Bangladesh, and Indonesia. In commenting on the annotated outline prepared by the ICPD Secretariat following PrepCom II, the General Assembly reaffirmed the "need to maintain the centrality of population issues in the final document of the Conference" [A/CONF. 171/PC/2].

The issue of abortion proved to be controversial with some country delegations (particularly those nations where the procedure remains illegal) and some official observers (most notably the Holy See). Nevertheless, several speakers, including the leader of the Indian delegation, made powerful official statements on the crucial importance of access to safe abortion services.

The Vatican, supported by delegates from at least two countries, argued that the desired outcome of the Cairo conference should be to turn the clock back to the agreement reached by the international community at the first population conference in 1974 at Bucharest, which declared that "development is the best contraceptive." In response to the Vatican's intervention by Archbishop Renato Martino condemning abortion and artificial contraception, the chairman of the PrepCom, Dr. Fred T. Sai of Ghana, thanked him for introducing the moral and ethical dimensions of the issues but questioned his call for sharing the benefits of modern medicine while declaring certain contraceptive methods illicit [*The Earth Times*, 5/18/93].

PrepCom III

The third preparatory committee meeting (PrepCom III) took place at U.N. Headquarters in New York, April 4–22. Delegations from over 180 countries participated in negotiations to finalize the exact wording of the **Programme of Action of the Conference** to be adopted in Cairo. Following agreement on a conceptual framework at PrepCom II, the ICPD Secretariat prepared a draft document, which it circulated to member states, international organizations, and NGOs [A/CONF. 171/PC/5].

As at the previous preparatory committee meeting, a broad range of NGOs and women's groups participated and were highly influential overall [*Earth Negotiations Bulletin*, 4/25/94]. More than 500 organizations were in attendance, and NGOs were well represented on several country delegations, including those of Bangladesh, Pakistan, the Philippines, and the United States. Despite this virtually unprecedented degree of involvement by NGOs, PrepCom III was an official U.N. meeting in which only country delegations could participate in the formal negotiating sessions.

The text of the 83-page document was painstakingly negotiated in plenary meetings, two working groups that met concurrently throughout much of PrepCom III, and in informal negotiating sessions. Progress was often excruciatingly slow, especially on chapters and paragraphs dealing with controversial issues. At the end of the third week, a plenary session was reconvened for a final reading of the document in a largely unsuccessful attempt to reach consensus on key outstanding issues.

The main drama at PrepCom III was provided by the Vatican's efforts to weaken the conference document. At the initial plenary session, the representative of the Holy See, Monsignor Diarmuid Martin, sharply criticized the Draft Programme of Action as lacking a "clear ethical vision" [Associated Press, 4/5/94]. The Holy See has permanent observer status at the United Nations, which gives it the right to participate in all negotiations although it cannot vote. The PrepCom process, which sought consensus through negotiation, enabled the Vatican to exercise considerable influence even though its views were usually in the minority. As the document was negotiated, the Vatican objected to specific language and demanded that all references to "safe abortion," "family planning," "sexual and reproductive health," "fertility regulation," "contraceptives," "condom," and even "safe motherhood" be placed in brackets, indicating that final agreement had not been reached [The New York Times, 4/24/94].

The Vatican denounced the document's promotion of the concept of reproductive rights as a veiled attempt to secure the international community's acceptance of a basic right to abortion. The Vatican was also especially troubled by references to expanding access to contraceptive services to "couples and individuals," some of whom would undoubtedly be minors or unmarried. At one point, to the dismay of other delegations and NGO observers, the Vatican even attempted to substitute its own language for the introductory section to Chapter VII on Reproductive Rights, Reproductive Health, and Family Planning.

Prior to the start of PrepCom III, the Vatican pursued an aggressive public relations and diplomatic strategy. **Pope John Paul II** met with Dr. Sadik, Executive Director of UNFPA and Secretary-General of the ICPD, and lectured her on the evils of sterilization, abortion, and contraception [Reuters, 3/18/94]. The Pope then summoned all ambassadors accredited to the Holy See to an unprecedented meeting in an attempt to influence the conference [ibid., 3/25/94]. The Pope also wrote to all heads of state criticizing the draft Programme of Action, and devoted several of his weekly sermons in St. Peter's Square to attacking the U.N. conference for what the Pope believes is its promotion of a right to abortion and the threat it poses to the traditional family unit [ibid., 4/18/94].

Despite Vatican pressure on national leaders, including President Clinton, to instruct their delegations to support weaker language, only a few countries, including Argentina, Benin, Ecuador, Guatemala, Honduras, Malta, Nicaragua, and Venezuela, supported the Vatican line [The New York Times, 4/24/94]. The Holy See's efforts to lobby other predominantly Catholic countries, such as the Philippines, proved unsuccessful. The Vatican was also reported to be working closely with Islamic states, such as

Algeria and Morocco, which opposed the draft document's emphasis on equal rights for women.

Despite efforts to weaken it, the document breaks new ground in a number of areas [*The Earth Times*, 4/22/94]. It stresses the interrelationships among population, sustained economic growth, and sustainable development, while maintaining a focus on population issues. It emphasizes the mutual responsibilities of developed and developing countries on issues relating to population and environment, calling for efforts to slow population growth in the South to be balanced by efforts to address consumption and life-styles in industrialized countries.

The document also takes a broad approach to population policy, championing the empowerment of women. It frames family planning within the context of reproductive health and individual rights, emphasizing that women's needs and freedom of choice must be extended in all family planning programs. Quantitative goals in the document relate to the education of girls and the reduction of infant, child, and maternal mortality, as well as the provision of universal access to family planning and reproductive health services. The document also has strong language on the importance of the role of NGOs, and the urgent need to serve youth and adolescents and to prevent unsafe abortion and eliminate harmful traditional practices like female genital mutilation. It also calls for greater male responsibility for contraception [*Earth Negotiations Bulletin*, 4/25/94].

Although most countries agreed that unsafe abortion is a major public health concern, no issue proved more controversial than access to safe abortion. Many delegations called for the need to respect national sovereignty and differences in each country's laws and religious and cultural values. Several governments, however, emphasized the need for safe abortion services. The U.S. delegation called for abortion to be "safe, legal, and rare." India also spoke to the importance of safe abortion.

The other major issue that remained unresolved concerned estimates of future resource requirements to address global population problems and the failure to secure funding commitments from both donors and developing countries [Reuters, 4/25/94]. Initial opposition from some European countries apparently reflected a perception that the large increase in funding proposed for family planning in the draft Programme of Action, combined with only a small amount recommended for women's reproductive health, undermined the broad approach to population policy outlined in the document. But even after the ICPD Secretariat significantly increased the cost estimates for reproductive health initiatives, final agreement was not achieved. As a result, the entire section on "Resource Mobilization and Allocation" in the chapter on "National Action" was bracketed by the European Union and remains unresolved. The European countries also resisted a specific target for donor assistance to population activities and bracketed language calling for 4 percent of official development assistance to be spent on population activities.

Outstanding unresolved issues were left to be settled in Cairo. There had been continuing speculation that the ICPD might be moved from Cairo on account of security concerns resulting from recent terrorist attacks on foreigners in Egypt. But no such announcement was made by the ICPD Secretariat, which appeared to proceed on the assumption that the conference would take place as planned. Alternative sites reportedly under consideration were Tunis, New York, and Geneva [The InterDependent, Fall 1993, p. 3].

China, UNFPA, and U.S. Policy

After a 12-year absence of U.S. leadership in international family planning, the inauguration of Bill Clinton signaled a dramatic improvement in the political climate for international population assistance in Washington and set the stage for the reversal of Reagan-Bush policies [Sharon L. Camp, "Population: The Critical Decade," Foreign Policy, No. 90, p. 135]. One of the policies most damaging to global population stabilization efforts was the U.S. withdrawal of its contribution to UNFPA.

The Clinton administration did eventually restore U.S. support to UNFPA, although the release of a $14.2 million contribution was delayed until August 1993 because of congressional action in response to reports of a renewed family planning crackdown in China. Population assistance supporters had been concerned about administration attempts to re-fund UNFPA since April 1993, when the Chinese government released data from a demographic survey suggesting a dramatic decline in fertility, accompanied by anecdotal reports of human rights abuses by overzealous local officials [The New York Times, 4/25/93]. A draft eugenics law, proposed in late 1993, mandating marriage bans and compulsory sterilization and abortion to "improve the quality of the Chinese population" may be the next political land mine waiting to explode, threatening future U.S. funding [Time, 5/2/94].

From 1985 to 1993 the **U.S. Agency for International Development (AID)** withheld the U.S. contribution to UNFPA, normally budgeted at $25 to $30 million, because of the presence of a UNFPA program in China. AID claimed that UNFPA was co-managing China's population program and that the Chinese program relied on coercive abortion and involuntary sterilization to implement its "one child per couple" policy. AID officials during the Reagan and Bush administrations cited as the basis for the decision to withhold funding the so-called Kemp-Kasten amendment, part of a 1985 supplemental foreign aid appropriations bill prohibiting U.S. funding of any organization that "supports or participates in the management of a program of coercive abortion or involuntary sterilization." UNFPA has repeatedly pointed out that it does not support abortion in China or anywhere else in the world, and denies the charge that it "manages" China's program.

Critics of Washington's policy have long maintained that the U.S. government has never produced evidence of UNFPA complicity. Rather than conditioning the restoration of a contribution to UNFPA on its withdrawal from China, say such critics, the United States should take more appropriate steps to end family planning abuses in the Chinese program by placing these concerns on the Sino-American bilateral agenda, along with other important human rights issues, and linking them to trade and other negotiations, such as the annual renewal of most-favored-nation trading status.

Defenders of UNFPA believe that the Fund plays a positive role by strengthening voluntarism in the Chinese population program. The Fund's program in China, undertaken in collaboration with other U.N. agencies, such as UNICEF and WHO, includes support for production of high-quality, modern contraceptives, especially IUDs; training for family planning workers in better interpersonal and counseling skills; and public education programs to raise public awareness of China's population problems and the benefits of family planning. All of these elements were designed to enhance client satisfaction and to reduce reliance on abortion or compulsion. The program was designed to accommodate the critics of UNFPA's presence in China by eliminating the types of activities in the previous five-year program that had provoked objections.

Despite the change in administrations, the U.S. government continues to regard the birth control policies of China as coercive and does not allow U.S. funds to be used by UNFPA in China [*The Washington Times*, 2/23/94]. Using the accounting system maintained by UNFPA that designates each project by funding source, U.S. funds are placed in a segregated account easily monitored by independent auditors to ensure that they are used exclusively to finance non-China projects.

In congressional testimony at the time PrepCom II was taking place in New York, **Secretary of State Warren Christopher** indicated that the United States would favor UNFPA's withdrawal from China in order to "simplify" U.S. re-funding. As politically expedient as this course of action might seem, UNFPA has never withdrawn from a recipient country and such a step would require the approval of its Governing Council. Since few, if any, of the other members of the UNFPA Governing Council favor withdrawal, and because decisions of the Governing Council are made by consensus, withdrawal from China is not a viable solution. In addition, the Chinese government has given no indication that it would unilaterally request the termination of UNFPA assistance.

At the UNFPA Governing Council meeting in June 1993, the U.S. delegate reiterated the Clinton administration's intention to contribute to

UNFPA and delivered a strongly worded statement condemning coercion in the Chinese population program and questioning whether the efforts of UNFPA have significantly improved voluntarism in China. While the American expression of concern was joined by the Netherlands and Australia, no nation advocated a UNFPA pullout. In response to the U.S. intervention, UNFPA Executive Director Sadik stated that "coercion has no part in population and family planning, it is morally wrong and ultimately it will not be effective" and made a compelling case justifying UNFPA's continued presence in China [Statement of Dr. Nafis Sadik to the 40th Session of the Governing Council, 6/2/93].

Some members of Congress took Christopher's remarks as an invitation to further condition the timing and the level of the U.S. contribution to UNFPA. These conditions were added to the list of restrictions on UNFPA's use of U.S. funds that population supporters in Congress have crafted over the last several years as a compromise with critics of human rights abuses in China. An amendment attached to the fiscal year 1994 foreign aid appropriations bill would reduce the funds contributed to UNFPA if it spends more than the $10 million remaining to be spent in UNFPA's five-year program of assistance. The amendment also restricted the release of U.S. funds to UNFPA until March 1994.

Further complicating the release of the $40 million approved for UNFPA for fiscal year 1994 was a lawsuit filed in Federal District Court in November 1993. The lawsuit, brought on behalf of Congressman Chris Smith (R–N.J.), a strong abortion opponent, and two Chinese nationals seeking political asylum in the United States, argued that a U.S. contribution to UNFPA is illegal because it would allegedly assist the Chinese government in the enforcement of a policy of involuntary abortion and sterilization [*The Washington Times*, 11/20/93]. In March 1994 the judge dismissed the case, ruling that the Chinese plaintiffs had no legal standing and that the charges made by Congressman Smith were moot. Although the case was dismissed, the State Department had not released the 1994 funds to UNFPA as of May. The Clinton administration has requested $60 million for fiscal year 1995, and, if approved, such a contribution would again make the United States the largest donor to UNFPA.

U.N. Population Awards

The winners of the U.N. Population Award for 1994 are President Mohamed Hosni Mubarek of Egypt and the Family Health and Planning Foundation of Turkey [U.N. press release POP/516, 2/24/94]. President Mubarek was selected for his national and international leadership on population issues and no doubt in recognition of his country's offer to host the ICPD. At the national level, he has recently established a Ministry for Population and Family Affairs and has ensured the inclusion of family planning and population issues in the country's five-year plans. As president of the Organization of African Unity (OAU), President Mubarek has highlighted the need to stabilize population growth in the OAU's deliberations.

The Family Health and Planning Foundation of Turkey was honored for its work in raising public awareness of population problems and extending information and services to rural areas, factories, and underserved populations, particularly migrants. Founded in 1985, the Foundation is engaged in national media and education campaigns, training of local and national officials and business leaders, and the provision of family planning and other health services.

4. Law of the Sea, Ocean Affairs, and Antarctica
By Lee A. Kimball

The **U.N. Convention on the Law of the Sea** will **enter into force on November 16, 1994**—almost a dozen years after it was signed in Jamaica and exactly one year from the day on which the 60th country to ratify it deposited documents to this effect at the United Nations. The 1982 treaty establishes national rights and obligations for all ocean uses and for protecting the marine environment. An Agreement modifying the plans for implementing the Convention's controversial deep-seabed mining provisions [Part XI] is expected to be adopted by the U.N. General Assembly during a resumed session, scheduled for July 27–29, and will be opened for signature immediately thereafter. That Agreement has been the subject of informal, but intensive, consultations and negotiations convened by the U.N. Secretary-General beginning in July 1990 and attended by states that are already parties to the LOS and some (among them the United States and Germany) that are not. Completion of the Agreement should remove the final obstacles to widespread ratification of that treaty—a milestone in the progressive development and codification of international ocean law, and a triumph for the Secretary-General's consultation process. In late June 1994 the U.S. Secretary of State announced that the United States would sign the treaty as the first step toward ratification.

By treaty provision, the **Assembly of the International Seabed Authority (ISA)** is to meet on the day of the Convention's entry into force and elect a 36-member Council. Because the U.N. General Assembly will be in session in New York on that date, the first ISA Assembly will be a ceremonial event in Jamaica (the Authority's home base), November 16–18, with a full session to be convened in February 1995. Within six months of the LOS Convention's entry into force, the states parties are to elect the members of the **International Tribunal for the Law of the Sea,** which will be housed in Hamburg, Germany. (The final meeting of the Preparatory Commission for the ISA and the International Tribunal on the Law of the Sea will coincide with the first formal meeting of the ISA Assembly in 1995, and PrepCom will present the Assembly with a final report. PrepCom's report on the Tribunal will be presented at the meeting to elect Tribunal members.) And within 18 months of the Convention's entry into force, the parties are to elect members of the **Commission on the Limits of the Continental Shelf** [Annex II of the Convention].

One result of the Convention's entry into force is to place on the agenda of the 49th General Assembly the issue of **secretariat support** for implementing it. (The Convention and the new Agreement [see below] make provisions for a secretariat for the ISA, whose responsibility is limited to mineral resources in the seabed beyond national jurisdiction.) The broad scope of the LOS Convention—from coastal state offshore zones and rights to international navigation and overflight; from the conservation and development of all marine living resources and minerals to third-party dispute settlement; and from piracy and illegal drug trafficking to international cooperation in marine research and development—brings into play still other, related treaties and programs at both the global and regional levels. In view of this scope, and the explosion of international marine issues and programs since the Convention was adopted in 1982, there is a crucial need to monitor international and national developments, to establish a focal point when addressing such developments, and to begin creating an institutional memory to ensure that all national and international laws are consistent with the Convention. Although many states have already enacted national legislation to implement aspects of the LOS Convention, its entry into force will spur efforts to fill in the gaps [see A Global Agenda: Issues Before the 48th General Assembly of the United Nations, pp. 201–2].

The LOS Convention makes no explicit provision for a secretariat other than the one for deep-seabed mining. Prior to entry into force, the role of secretariat has been played by the **U.N. Division of Ocean Affairs and the Law of the Sea (OALOS)**, which reviews other international agreements and programs to ensure consistency; assists states in drafting national legislation; and responds to government requests for advice on managerial, scientific, and technical aspects of implementation, including dispute resolution. OALOS also prepares a comprehensive annual report for the General Assembly on developments related to the Convention—an invaluable overview of marine-related international programs, state practice, and decisions by international tribunals—and has convened expert workshops to develop handbooks and other guidelines for interpreting and applying the Convention. Responsibility for OALOS was transferred to the Under-Secretary-General for Legal Affairs in early 1992 [see discussion of the U.N. Environment Programme's land-based activities conference and of the Inter-Agency Committee on Sustainable Development below].

Among the significant international developments that illustrate the "framework" nature of the LOS Convention and its relation to other international treaties and programs are the following.

1. **The U.N. Conference on Straddling Fish Stocks and Highly Migratory Fish Stocks,** set in motion by Agenda 21, which scheduled substantive sessions for July 1993, March 1994, and August 1994. Whether a legally binding convention or a non-binding instrument will emerge from this process is very much at issue, but its broad purpose is to promote the implementation of the LOS Convention's provisions on fisheries. If the decision is made to pursue a legally binding convention, further negotiating sessions are probable. In a related initiative, the Food and Agriculture Organization's (FAO) General Conference adopted in February 1994 an **Agreement to Promote Compliance with International Conservation and Management Measures by Fishing Vessels on the High Seas.** This is the first element of an International Code of Conduct for Responsible Fishing, which is expected to be completed in 1995 [see A/ 48/479; A/Conf.164/13, Rev.1, the negotiating text before the Conference; and U.N. press release SEA/ 41424, 3/31/94, a report of the March session]. These documents are likely to influence both the elaboration of existing regional fisheries agreements and the possible conclusion of new agreements [see A/48/527]. The Antarctic fisheries agreement [see "Antarctica" below] has been cited during debates as a useful model.

2. The **U.N. Global Conference on the Sustainable Development of Small Island Developing States (SIDS),** held in Barbados, April 25– May 6, 1994. Another of the events set in motion by Agenda 21, the conference was preceded by regional technical meetings in May–June 1993 (Vanuatu) and June–July 1993 (Trinidad and Tobago); and by preparatory sessions at U.N. Headquarters in August–September 1993 and March 1994. The conference adopted a Programme of Action and the Barbados Declaration [see A/Res/48/193 and A/Conf.167/L.5].

3. The **intergovernmental meeting on the protection of the marine environment from land-based activities** (as called for by Agenda 21), to be convened in late 1995 under U.N. Environment Programme (UNEP) auspices and preceded by three preparatory meetings: November 1993, June 1994, and March 1995. This meeting is likely to stimulate new regional agreements on land-based activities affecting the marine environment as well as further elaboration of existing agreements. UNEP often serves as secretariat for these agreements and helps to fund their implementation. How UNEP's regional seas program ought to interact with OALOS and a LOS Convention secretariat warrants consideration.

4. The U.N. Commission on Sustainable Development's review, in 1996, of the **Agenda 21 chapter on oceans and coasts.** Among the institutions created as a follow-up to the 1992 U.N. Conference on Environment and Development (UNCED, or the Earth Summit) is the Inter-Agency Committee on Sustainable Development (IACSD), which gave

birth to an oceans subcommittee in September 1993. The subsidiary's purpose is to integrate and coordinate the activities of the many U.N.-system bodies involved in implementing Agenda 21's provisions on oceans. IACSD is staffed by the office of U.N. **Under-Secretary-General for Policy Coordination and Sustainable Development** Nitin Desai, while the secretariat for the oceans subcommittee is provided by **UNESCO's Intergovernmental Oceanographic Committee (IOC).** The subcommittee will designate individual U.N. agencies as task managers for the different issues addressed in Agenda 21, e.g., FAO, UNEP, IOC, International Maritime Organization (IMO). How this structure dealing with "sustainable development" issues will mesh with the broader LOS Convention mandate served by OALOS and with a LOS Convention secretariat remains to be determined.

5. The restructuring and replenishment of the **Global Environment Facility (GEF) in March 1994** [see "Environment and Sustainable Development"—section one of the present chapter], and, with it, strong international support for using the GEF to fund programs and projects that implement international marine agreements, in particular the regional seas agreements, the regional fisheries agreements, and protection of related habitats. This Facility—sponsored jointly by the World Bank, UNEP, and UNDP—has explicit and direct links to the conventions on biodiversity and climate but no such links to the comprehensive LOS Convention or to the many global and regional agreements consistent with Convention provisions. Under its "international waters" program, covering both marine and fresh water, the GEF could begin to address those links. (The GEF has also been cited as a possible funding mechanism for the SIDS Programme of Action.)

6. The **ongoing development by IMO of numerous legally binding and recommendatory instruments to govern safety at sea and the control of pollution from ships** [A/48/527], and the meetings under IMO auspices of the parties to the **1972 London (anti-dumping) Convention.** At the November 1993 meeting it was agreed to prohibit the ocean disposal of low-level radioactive wastes, and to prohibit by the end of 1995 the ocean dumping of industrial wastes and the ocean incineration of industrial wastes and sewage sludge. Harmonization of the **Basel Convention on the Control of Transboundary Movement of Hazardous Wastes and Their Disposal** with regional agreements on the same subject and with various IMO agreements and regional seas agreements is under consideration in several regional forums.

The annual **General Assembly** resolution on the LOS was adopted on December 9, 1993, by a vote of 144 to 1, with 11 abstentions. For the third year in a row, the United States merely abstained, and noted the progress made in the informal consultations "to remove the remaining obstacles to broad-based acceptance of the Convention before its entry into force" [Council on Ocean Law, *Oceans Policy News,* 12/93]. The U.N. Secretary-

General's annual report on the LOS was considered at this time [A/48/527 and Add.1].

The **Agreement Relating to the Implementation of Part XI of the U.N. Convention on the Law of the Sea of 1982 and the Annex** integral to it—the results of the Secretary-General's informal consultations—are intended to be interpreted and applied with the seabed mining provisions as a single instrument; where there are inconsistencies, the Agreement will prevail. The Agreement deals with the procedures for entry into force and provisional application; the Annex interprets and modifies specific Convention provisions on deep-seabed mining [A/48/950, Annex I].

Under the Agreement, each state may select one of four options to ensure that it is bound by the Agreement (cum Annex) and Convention. These options accommodate states that will have ratified the Convention prior to adoption of the Agreement and states that will ratify the two together. Forty countries are required to accept the Agreement before it enters into force, at least seven of which must be entitled to "pioneer investor" status (identified in Resolution I of the LOS Convention), and five of these must be developed states. Upon the LOS Convention's entry into force in November 1994, the Agreement will be applied provisionally until it too enters into force. If the "pioneer investor" condition has not been met by November 16, 1998, despite the fact that 40 states may have accepted the Agreement, the Agreement will be terminated.

The Annex takes up costs to states parties and institutional arrangements; the establishment of the Enterprise (the proposed mining arm of the ISA); decision-making in the ISA Assembly and Council; the proposed conference for reviewing the seabed mining provisions 15 years after commercial production begins; transfer of seabed mining technology; policies on the production of seabed minerals and on economic assistance for developing nations whose economy or export earnings are seriously affected by a reduction in the export volume or price of minerals that is attributable to deep-seabed mining; financial terms of deep-seabed mining contracts; and the establishment of a Finance Committee. In several instances these Annex provisions state that particular articles of the Convention will not apply.

To address the concerns of industrialized countries the Annex calls for cost-effective institutions that can evolve in response to need and in step with the activities of the ISA. The ISA will be funded through the U.N. budget until the Agreement has been in force for a year, after which it will be funded by the ISA members. Where the text of the 1982 Convention requires states parties to fund the Enterprise and to transfer technology, the Annex provides that initial operations will be conducted through joint ventures. The Annex also establishes a new four-chambered voting procedure for the ISA Council, which permits a majority in any of the four to block a decision. (One chamber would consist of four major minerals consumer/importer nations; another, four of the eight states with the largest investments in seabed mining; yet another, four major net exporters; and the last, a group of developing nations, whose number may vary.) And the Annex makes clearer than does the Convention the lines of authority between the ISA's 36-member Council and the plenary Assembly.

The review conference provision has been substantially altered too. It now permits a general review based on matters and principles specified in the article, but amendments will be binding only on states that explicitly accept the amendment. The Annex eliminates specific limits on the production of seabed minerals. It prohibits any country from subsidizing its operations or granting preferential market access to seabed minerals, subject to GATT rules and dispute settlement. And it eliminates the detailed rules for financial payments by mining contractors to the ISA. The Annex goes beyond the Convention in making provision for a fund to assist developing nations affected by a drop in mineral prices or export volume. At the same time, the Annex creates a Finance Committee and stipulates that, until the ISA can finance itself from seabed revenues, the five largest contributors to the ISA's administrative budget may sit on it.

In February 1994 the Republic of Korea applied to become a **registered pioneer investor.** This will be taken up at the August 1994 PrepCom session in New York, as will a request from France, Japan, and the Russian Federation for an adjustment of their pioneer investor obligations. One such adjustment would waive, or reduce, the fees paid by registered pioneers, given the distant date on which commercial seabed mining can be expected to get under way—this according to an assessment by experts that was presented at the February 1994 session. Other key items for the August PrepCom include the preparation of the provisional agenda for the first session of the Assembly and Council, recommendations for the ISA's first budget (and staff), and practical arrangements for establishment of the Tribunal, together with their cost. The Preparatory Commission's draft final report, consisting of the provisional final report approved in March 1993 and any further decisions, will be ready for adoption at that August session [LOS/PCN/L.114].

Antarctica

In 1993, U.N. General Assembly consideration of Antarctica followed the well-established pattern: A single resolution was adopted by a vote of 96 to 0, with 7 abstentions, and 66 nations (including the parties to the Antarctic Treaty) did not participate in the vote [A/Res/48/80]. One notable departure from the pattern was the absence of a paragraph calling on the parties to the treaty (ATCPs) to prevent South Africa from participating fully in their meetings—this in anticipation of universal, democratic elections in the Republic. Otherwise, the resolution renews its request that the Secretary-General receive an invitation to attend Antarctic Treaty Consultative Meetings (ATCMs) and that the 50-year ban on minerals activities be made permanent; welcomes the information on Antarctic developments now being provided to the United Nations; urges publication as official U.N. documents of extracts of the Antarctic environmental data received and the convening of an annual seminar/symposium on environmental issues; supports effective implementation of the 1991 Madrid Protocol on Environmental Protection; and renews its request that any effort to establish Antarctica as a nature reserve/world park be negotiated with the full participation of the international community. The Secretary-General's annual report on the question of Antarctica was supplemented by a report on the Antarctic environment [A/48/482 and A/48/449, respectively], and mention was made in the debate of a new U.N. Department of Public Information publication, "Protecting the common heritage of Antarctica."

XVIII ATCM took place in Kyoto, Japan, April 11–22, 1994, and XIX ATCM is scheduled to convene in Seoul in May 1995. By the spring of 1994, nine of the 26 ATCPs had ratified the **1991 Protocol on Environmental Protection.** Despite consensus at XVII ATCM (1992) to establish a secretariat for the Antarctic Treaty and the Protocol's new **Committee for Environmental Protection (CEP),** failure to agree on its location prevented further action at XVIII ATCM. The 1994 meeting did agree to restructure the ATCMs even in advance of the Protocol's entry into force, however, effective with the ATCM in Seoul. A **transitional environmental working group** (to be replaced by the CEP, when the Protocol enters into force) will meet during the first week and report its advice and recommendations for Plenary decision during the second week. Informal groups of legal experts will discuss (i) the status, privileges, and immunities of the secretariat and (ii) liability issues, the latter building on two meetings of a working group to consider a possible liability annex to the 1991 Protocol.

The single recommendation of XVIII ATCM consolidates as practical guidance a series of Recommendations adopted under the Antarctic Treaty that affect visitors, tour groups, and other nongovernmental activities in Antarctica. There was considerable discussion of the means of improving Antarctic inspections, including inspection of protected areas, and the meeting agreed on terms of reference for a technical workshop on environmental monitoring and on principles and next steps for the development of an Antarctic data directory.

The 12th annual meeting of the **Commission of the Convention for Conservation of Antarctic Marine Living Resources (CCAMLR)** took place at headquarters in Hobart, Australia, October 25–November 5, 1993. In addition to its regular review of fisheries activities and the status of stocks, the Commission adopted procedures for monitoring new fisheries, developing an information base to inform decisions and avoid over-exploitation. Specific measures were articulated for the **first of these experimental fisheries, in Antarctic crab.** Still other decisions and measures endorse a precautionary approach to catch levels; direct the 1994 Commission meeting to consider management under conditions of uncertainty; promote data collection and reporting on incidental mortality of seabirds and marine mammals in longline fisheries and in beach debris in the Convention area; and seek to reduce species' entanglement in marine debris. The parties to CCAMLR were also urged to accede to the IMO agreements on vessel-source marine debris. The Commission adopted a resolution urging those who fish for stocks within the treaty area and in adjacent areas both within and outside national jurisdiction to act responsibly and to respect CCAMLR conservation measures [Report of the XII Meeting of the Commission].

In May 1994 the International Whaling Commission established a sanctuary for whales in the southern ocean, which bans commercial whaling permanently (though subject to review every ten years) [interview with Greenpeace officials, 6/17/94].

V
Human Rights and Social Issues

1. Human Rights
By Erika H. Burk

The **World Conference on Human Rights,** held in Vienna, June 14–25, 1993, served both to highlight the importance of human rights and to spark debate worldwide about the whole gamut of issues that fall under the "human rights" rubric—in the process, exposing cracks in the consensus over the very nature of human rights issues. These fissures were evident during the regional preparatory meetings, where a number of Asian and Islamic nations, and Cuba, continued to argue that human rights can mean different things in different cultural contexts and that state sovereignty and economic development rate a higher priority than do civil and political rights. Many Western nations saw such assertions as a frontal attack on the whole notion of universal human rights.

After heated debate at the Vienna Conference, a compromise was struck: The Vienna Declaration and Programme of Action states that "All human rights are universal, indivisible and interdependent and interrelated . . . [w]hile the significance of national and regional particularities and various historical, cultural and religious backgrounds must be borne in mind" [I. (5)]. The same uneasy compromise is evident in the Declaration's reaffirmation of the "right to development, as established in the Declaration on the Right to Development, as universal and inalienable," followed by the assertion that "the lack of development may not be invoked to justify the abridgement of internationally recognized human rights" [I. (10)].

On the subject of ways to strengthen the observance of human rights throughout the world, the delegates discussed the creation of a High Commissioner for Human Rights—a mechanism for which such human rights advocates as Amnesty International had lobbied over many years. The delegates agreed that they would ask the next session of the General Assembly to give priority to "consideration of the question of the establishment of a High Commissioner" [II.A. (18)], which fell short of a call to action and disappointed many. The 48th General Assembly, after considerable debate, created the new post [A/Res/48/141] and, in February 1994, named José Ayala Lasso, Ecuador's Ambassador to the United Nations, to fill it.

Some human rights advocates are disappointed by the Commissioner's mandate, which allows him to engage in a "dialogue" with governments and carry out investigations at their request but not to initiate investigations. And although the Commissioner is charged with coordinating the U.N. system's wide range of activities that contribute to human rights protection and promotion, and with summoning a rapid, high-level response to gross violations of human rights anywhere in the world, he is not asked specifically to "integrate" human rights elements into the work of such departments as, for example, peacekeeping.

The Conference addressed a bewildering array of human rights issues, giving a good deal of attention to women's and children's rights and the rights of indigenous peoples, due in large part to the efforts of the NGOs that are organized around these issues. The Conference urged the universal ratification of the Convention on the Rights of the Child by 1995; the designation of an international decade of the world's indigenous people, to begin in 1994; and the completion of the draft declaration on the rights of indigenous people in time for the next meeting of the Sub-Commission on the Prevention of Discrimination and Protection of Minorities.

The Programme of Action urged the universal adoption of the Convention on the Elimination of All Forms of Discrimination against Women by the year 2000, the integration of women's concerns into every facet of U.N. activities, and the creation of a special rapporteur on violence against women. In the spring of 1994 the Commission on Human Rights did create the post of **Special Rapporteur on Violence against Women,** naming Sri Lankan jurist Radhika Coomaraswamy as the first occupant [HR/CN/561]. The Economic and Social Council was asked to approve the appointment at its summer 1994 session. General Assembly adoption of the **Declaration on the Elimination of Violence against Women** [A/Res/48/104] has further bolstered the cause of women's rights and placed a number of heretofore domestic (that is to say, private) issues on the international agenda.

The Vienna Conference elaborated 20 new tasks for the Human Rights Centre and called for universal ratification of all human rights conventions. With 678 states parties and seven treaty bodies to which they must report, the paperwork is tremendous, and the government delegates at Vienna asked the General Assembly to "increase substantially the resources for the human rights program" [II.A. (9)], but failed to suggest where such funds would come from, a timetable, or even a target sum. They left much of this task to the Human Rights Centre, which turned in a detailed report to the 48th General Assembly requesting $39.64 million over two years to cover the costs to the United Nations of carrying out its part of Conference-inspired activities. The Assembly allotted $1.14 million. One Western diplomat explained that the Western delegations had remained silent on the money question to avoid giving Third World delegations an excuse to reopen the debate over the High Commissioner, the establishment of which many of them resisted, fearing the results at home of a more coordinated and effective U.N. human rights program.

Financially strapped, the U.N. human rights programs must get as much mileage as they can out of the mechanisms established over the years to monitor and promote adherence to human rights treaties, to investigate global human rights problems and assess the situation in individual countries, and to take diplomatic action in the interest of preventing or halting abuse.

Human Rights Mechanisms

The General Assembly is supervisor of the U.N.'s human rights programs and final arbiter of the standards adopted, the issues addressed, and the administrative and budgetary resources allotted to U.N. human rights machinery. The General Assembly not only approves drafts and decisions taken in subsidiary human rights bodies but also instructs those bodies about which of the (often controversial) problems are to be addressed and establishes the working groups and special rapporteurs for dealing with them. Universality vs. cultural relativism; civil and political vs. social, economic, and cultural rights; and the human rights-development-aid linkage—all continue to be debated in the General Assembly.

The 53-member, intergovernmental **Commission on Human Rights** has established itself as the most important U.N. human rights body, despite the fact that it is only one of several commissions answerable to ECOSOC, through which it reports to the General Assembly. The Commission is charged with human rights standard-setting, monitoring, promotion, and protection. Its "working groups" have created draft declarations on disappearances and on the rights of members of minority groups and of human rights defenders. (The Declaration on the Protection of All Persons from Enforced or Involuntary Disappearances and the Declaration on the Rights of Persons Belonging to National or Ethnic, Religious, and Linguistic Minorities—adopted in 1992 at the 47th General Assembly—are recent results of the Commission's standard-setting efforts.) And the Commission examines gross violations of human rights under the so-called "1503" confidential procedure.

The **"1503" procedure** originates in a five-member working group of the **Sub-Commission on the Prevention of Discrimination and Protection of Minorities (the Sub-Commission),** a body of experts from 26 countries that examines cases submitted by individuals or groups claiming to be victims of human rights violations (as well as by those claiming direct knowledge of or reliable information about them), accumulating evidence of violations affecting a large number of people over a period of time. The Sub-Commission decides which cases to refer to the Commission, which will then determine whether a thorough study of the situation is required and whether it will share the findings of that study with ECOSOC via a report and recommendations. Under "1503," the study remains confidential and no report is sent to ECOSOC. The "1503" procedure is all-inclusive—that is, it can be applied to all states, it covers violations of all human rights and fundamental freedoms, and any person, group, or NGO may submit the complaint that triggers an investigation. It is also, to the dismay of many human rights observers, a nontransparent process: Even the author of the communication that has launched a "1503" investigation is not involved at any stage of the proceedings, nor is that party informed of any action taken by the United Nations, unless the Commission decides to "go public."

The 1994 Commission considered under the "1503" rubric Estonia, Germany, Kuwait, Somalia, Vietnam, Armenia, Azerbaijan, Chad, and Rwanda. It decided that no further study will be made of Estonia, Germany, Kuwait, and Vietnam; that Somalia will now come under public scrutiny; and that the remaining four will continue to be examined under the confidential procedure. (An "independent expert" will be helping to review the situation in Chad; and the Commission "accepted Rwanda's suggestion" that the Secretary-General's Special Representative prepare the report on the human rights situation in that country.)

Providing the legwork for the Commission's activities are the "special procedures"—theme and country mechanisms that go by the name **"working groups"** and **"special rapporteurs"** (and occasionally **"representatives"**)—that it establishes to investigate (and often "take effective action on"; read: bring to the attention of the General Assembly) particular abuses of human rights or the human rights situation in particular countries. Those selected to carry out these activities (the original mandate of one-to-three years' duration is usually renewed and renewed again) are experts, who serve in an individual capacity, not as government representatives. In 1993 the Human Rights Commission maintained a total of 23 such special procedures [A/C.3/48/SR.40]. The latest additions are the Special Rapporteur on Violence against Women, noted above; and the **Special Rapporteur on Independence of the Judiciary** [E/CN.4/1994/L.11/ Add.4].

On the agenda of the **50th Session of the Human Rights Commission,** held in Geneva, January 31–March 11, 1994, were reports by special rapporteurs (or representatives) on human rights violations in the Israeli-occupied territories, southern Africa, Iran, Equatorial Guinea, Afghanistan, Myanmar, Cuba, the former Yugoslavia, Haiti, Sudan, East Timor,

Bougainville (a province of Papua New Guinea now seeking indepen-dence), Zaire, Togo, Cyprus, and Sudan. It also examined reports by the Special Rapporteurs on Summary or Arbitrary Executions; on the Use of Mercenaries; and on Contemporary Forms of Racism, Racial Discrimina-tion, Xenophobia, and Related Intolerance (established the previous year). And the Commission reviewed the advisory services it is providing to governments needing help in a variety of areas.

Also under the Commission's wing is the Sub-Commission, de-scribed above, which may enlist the help of its own special rapporteurs and working groups in supplying the Commission with advice about the U.N.'s response to gross human rights violations.

The Sub-Commission's work has expanded considerably since its in-ception—due, among other factors, to the independence of its expert members, its general receptivity to NGO input, and its own efforts at stretching its mandate. The topics it covers range from **"traditional prac-tices" harmful to the health of women and children** (currently under the scrutiny of Special Rapporteur Halima Embarek Warzazi, who is charged not only with studying the issue but with formulating a plan of action for eliminating such practices) to **protecting the cultural and intellectual property of indigenous people** (Special Rapporteur Erica-Irene A. Daes has been asked to begin elaborating draft principles and guidelines for a preliminary report to the Sub-Commission at its 1994 session [HR/CN/549]).

During its four-week session in August 1993, the Sub-Commission reviewed reports about its ongoing study of the rights of indigenous peo-ples, current forms of slavery, compensation for the victims of gross viola-tions of human rights, discrimination against people with AIDS, and the human rights situations in Iran and East Timor, among other issues. It went on to adopt resolutions on human rights violations in Bosnia, My-anmar, Iraq, and the Occupied Territories to present to the Commission, which itself usually adopts the Sub-Commission's recommendations. And it decided that the first subject for its newly appointed Special Rap-porteur on Contemporary Forms of Racism would be the increase of xenophobic incidents in developed countries. The Rapporteur will also be asking U.S. authorities for information on a hunger strike carried on by a Texas group that was prevented from making "donations destined for religious institutions in Cuba" [HR/CN/482].

The "Charter-based" Commission and Sub-Commission—political organs with a broad mandate to promote awareness of and respond to violations of human rights—are joined in supporting human rights by a family of "treaty-based" organs. Each of the six principal U.N. human rights treaties has given birth to a body of independent experts who moni-tor compliance with specific treaty regimes by examining the reports sub-mitted by the state parties to the treaty. The six are:

- International Covenant on Civil and Political Rights: Human Rights Committee (18 members)
- International Covenant on Economic, Social and Cultural Rights: Committee on Economic, Social and Cultural Rights (18 members)
- International Convention on the Elimination of All Forms of Racial Discrimination: Committee on the Elimination of All Forms of Racial Discrimination (CERD—18 members)
- Convention against Torture and Other Cruel, Inhuman or Degrading Treatment or Punishment: Committee against Torture (CAT—10 members)
- Convention on the Rights of the Child: Committee on the Rights of the Child (CRC—10 members)
- Convention on the Elimination of All Forms of Discrimination against Women: Committee on the Elimination of All Forms of Discrimination against Women (CEDAW—23 members)

(A seventh treaty—the International Convention on the Protection of the Rights of All Migrant Workers and Members of Their Families—adopted by the 48th General Assembly [A/Res/48/148] and ratified by only two states by May 1994, has not yet entered into force.)

The **movement to clip the wings of the human rights special procedures** saw some success at the March 1993 session of the Commission, which passed an Iranian-sponsored resolution that placed additional conditions on the U.N.'s human rights fact-finders [Res. 1993/94]. According to one of its terms, reports will be no more than 32 pages, with the effect of limiting their detail and scope (the 1993 reports on torture, disappearances, and executions were more than three times that length). According to another provision of Resolution 94, reports must be circulated six weeks in advance of the date on which the General Assembly will consider the agenda item—leaving country-situation rapporteurs (whose mandates must be endorsed at the July session of ECOSOC in order to be funded by the Assembly in the fall) less than three months to visit the country involved, if the government concerned has granted permission, and write the report. The resolution also called for adjusting a putative geographic "imbalance" among the rapporteurs. All five of the U.N.'s regional groups are well represented, in fact, and the only imbalance is one of gender—not a single one of the special rapporteurs is a woman—but the resolution does not address this issue.

As ever, those who give testimony to the special rapporteur during his visit to the country may find themselves under government scrutiny, or worse. On September 24, 1993, relates the **Special Rapporteur for Sudan**, Gaspar Biro, the Sudanese police arrested four women who had just met with him at the U.N. office in Khartoum. And Biro goes on to note that government security officers followed him throughout his stay and even threatened visitors to the U.N. library in Khartoum [A/48/601]. The 1993 Commission asked the Secretary-General to draw up a list of all the cases of intimidation that are reported.

Human rights activists note that when fact-finders are limited to one quick visit a year, if that, it is difficult to set up and maintain a protection system, such as Biro's visitors might have benefited from. The establishment of a **human rights field office** in each of the countries under scrutiny would permit a more thorough investigation and reduce the need for special protection of visitors. But for a number of reasons, most prominently the issue of state sovereignty, action on this has been slow. At present there are only five human rights field offices, all within the former Yugoslavia.

The report of the **Committee on the Elimination of All Forms of Racial Discrimination (CERD)** to the 48th General Assembly [A/48/18] discussed changes in the pattern of abuse targeted by the Convention, which was adopted in 1965. During the 1960s, when the primary concern was discrimination by whites against blacks, racial discrimination was frequently described as the dissemination of doctrines of racial superiority by the institutions of colonial rule and the policies of racist regimes. But the centrifugal forces at work in the 1980s, weakening the authority of national political structures and dissolving broad regional alliances, and even whole states like the Soviet Union, have exposed ethnic minorities to a resurgence of nationalist sentiment and nationalist movements. Rapid population growth, the global economic downturn, and new technology, increasing the competition for jobs, have only heightened such tensions. The report of CERD notes that "racial or ethnic conflicts are appearing in areas previously characterized by tolerance," adding: "These forms of discrimination spring not from any belief in racial superiority but from a sense of difference. When a conflict becomes acute it is only with members of their own ethnic group that people feel secure" [A/48/18, p. 6].

The Committee decided to establish an open-ended working group to consider ways in which U.N. bodies can work to prevent and respond to violations of the Convention. Also on its agenda was a working group paper on early warning of ethnic conflict and procedures for acting on urgent situations, which the Committee went on to adopt as a guide. CERD continues its practice of using the work and documentation of country rapporteurs to aid its examination of the reports submitted by state parties. The Committee has been exchanging information with other human rights treaty bodies and with the Charter-based human rights organs, including the Commission on Human Rights and its Sub-Commission. The Committee Chair expressed the intention of having the same sort of cooperative relationship with the Commission's **Special Rapporteur on Contemporary Forms of Racism,** Racial Discrimination, Xenophobia, and Related Intolerance as soon as an individual was named to the post [E/CN.4/1994/L.11].

The Commission subsequently named Maurice Glele Ahanhanzou of Benin, who was given the mandate (expanded in March 1994) to examine "incidents of contemporary racism, racial discrimination, any form of discrimination **against blacks, Arabs and Muslims, negrophobia, anti-Semitism and related intolerance,** as well as governmental measures to overcome them." The Commission's decision to name anti-Semitism among the forms of discrimination to be condemned follows the successful three-year U.S.-led campaign to repeal the 1975 General Assembly resolution equating Zionism with racism ("negrophobia" was included at Nigeria's insistence) [*The New York Times,* 3/10/94].

States parties to the 1984 Convention against Torture and Other Cruel, Inhuman or Degrading Treatment or Punishment commit themselves to taking legislative and administrative measures to prevent torture and punish it under criminal law. The **Committee against Torture** was called for by the treaty itself and assigned the job of monitoring the progress states parties were making in enacting and enforcing these laws. As of May 11, 1994, 89 states were parties to the Convention.

The **U.N. Voluntary Fund for Victims of Torture** was created by the General Assembly in 1981 to channel financial assistance from governments, NGOs, and private individuals to programs that provide medical, psychological, social, and/or legal assistance to torture victims and their families anywhere in the world. Many of those needing help are lawyers, journalists, trade unionists, leaders of rural communities, and human rights activists. The U.N. Secretary-General reports annually to the Human Rights Commission and the General Assembly on the work of the Fund [A/48/520]. Management of the Fund is shared by the U.N. Secretariat and the Commission, with the assistance of a Board of Trustees whose members, appointed by the Secretary-General, serve in a personal capacity.

The Human Rights Commission itself has established a **Special Rapporteur on Torture** to report on the phenomenon, investigate, and respond to well-documented allegations of torture. Searching for information, sending urgent appeals to governments, transmitting information to governments with the intention of preventing the recurrence of abuse, and attempting to secure an invitation for a visit so as to obtain direct knowledge of the situation and identify ways to prevent such practices are among the activities outlined by Special Rapporteur Nigel S. Rodley in his most recent report to the Commission [E/CN.4/1994/31]. Rodley explained that, to preempt torture, he does not always wait for firm evidence of abuse or impending abuse before making an urgent appeal to a government, usually through its permanent representative to the United Nations, but will often act when there are grounds for believing that the risk of torture is great. At the same time, he noted, the limited resources that the Human Rights Centre can make available to the Special Rapporteur dictate a certain rigidity of procedure and limit the volume of correspondence he can carry on with governments. In the course of 1993 he sent 84 urgent appeals to 31 governments concerning approximately 400 individuals and 42 letters inquiring about 500 cases. During that same period not a single government took the initiative to invite the Special Rapporteur for a visit.

The Special Rapporteur asked the Commission whether his mandate applied to acts of torture committed by parties to an armed conflict, whether he should pursue such cases, and, if so, how he is to determine (1) that such a conflict exists and (2) what entities should be considered the parties to the conflict. Rodley concluded his report by noting that wherever torture persists and wherever those who torture do so with impunity, there is a "gap between the commitment to its eradication and the political will required to enforce the commitment" [E/CN.4/1994/31, p. 136].

An intersessional working group of the Human Rights Commission is currently at work on an **optional protocol to the Convention against Torture.** The protocol is intended to establish a system of visits by a committee of experts to places of detention that are under the jurisdiction of states parties to the Convention.

Reporting on its 1993 activities, the Commission's **Working Group on Arbitrary Detention** noted that it had transmitted 45 letters to 31 governments concerning 183 newly reported individual cases of alleged detention [E/CN.4/1994/27]. The Group may declare the detention to be "arbitrary" if it lacks legal grounds, if it has anything to do with the exercise of certain protected rights or freedoms, or if there has been a grave violation of the international guarantees concerning a fair trial.

The cases requiring "urgent action" in this period were more numerous and varied than ever before. In 1992 the Working Group addressed 12 emergency (or urgent action) appeals to governments, while in 1993 there were 17 in the first 10 months alone, each involving a different government. Most appeals are the results of information about the deteriorating health (or worse) of the individual in such detention.

The Working Group noted with concern that, in approximately half its cases, the governments did not answer the communication forwarded to them, and that a large number supplied incomplete information (and often only after the established time limit). The report also drew attention to the fact that, as of November 1993, a state of emergency was in effect in 29 countries, covering all or part of the territory under their jurisdiction. A state of emergency invariably sets aside many of the rules and procedures that help to guarantee the safety and freedom of the individual. The Working Group went on to note that, as in previous years, a large number of the cases before it involved persons who had been deprived of their freedom for some years. In many cases too, governments used such vague terms as "treason" or "collaboration with the enemy" to describe the offense that had resulted in detention.

The arbitrary detention group recommended that the Centre for Human Rights support the ongoing efforts of the Sub-Commission to draft **a declaration on habeas corpus,** with a view to providing **another protocol to the International Covenant on Civil and Political Rights.** And the Working Group's report notes that it will leave wartime detention cases to the Red Cross [E/CN.4/1994/27], which is given competence in this area by the Geneva Conventions of 1949 and Additional Protocols. Many observers continue to maintain that a truly viable system of protections for those detained in wartime will require the development of additional linkages between U.N. human rights mechanisms and U.N. peacekeeping and humanitarian relief operations at the conflict site.

Responding to the Commission's request [Res. 1993/48] that special rapporteurs and working groups pay particular attention to the consequences for human rights of acts of violence committed by armed groups (including drug traffickers) that spread terror among the population, the Working Group on Arbitrary Detention stated that it was unable to cooperate. Its mandate, the group noted, limits its investigations to a particular type of abuse and one particular sort of perpetrator, to wit: cases of "detention imposed arbitrarily or otherwise inconsistently with the relevant international standards set forth in the Universal Declaration of Human Rights or in the relevant international legal instruments accepted by the States concerned" [Res. 1991/42].

Another theme mechanism, the **Working Group on Enforced or Involuntary Disappearances,** acts as a "channel of communication between families of the missing persons and the Governments concerned, with a view to ensuring that sufficiently documented and clearly identified individual cases are investigated and the whereabouts of the missing persons clarified" [E/CN.4/1994/26]. To this end, the group reported to the 50th session of the Human Rights Commission, it continues to employ special "urgent" procedures when the case is one that is said to have occurred no more than three months before the group was informed about it. The Working Group has also promptly intervened with governments in cases in which relatives of missing persons (or other individuals or organizations, or their legal counsel) have been subject to intimidation, persecution, or reprisals.

The total number of **cases under active consideration and yet to be clarified stands at 33,843.** During 1993, the Working Group continued its processing of a backlog of 2,639 reports of disappearances submitted since 1991 and received 5,523 new cases of disappearances in 30 countries. Despite the impressive number of cases processed in 1993 (3,162), there remains a backlog of approximately 8,000, for which the Working Group blames the chronic lack of resources made available for its work. This backlog does not include the cases of disappearances in the former Yugoslavia reported to the Working Group in 1991: 11,000 back then and growing.

In its conclusions and recommendations, the Working Group stressed the need to enforce and supervise the **U.N. Declaration on the Protection of All Persons from Enforced Disappearance** [Res. 47/133], especially Article 4 concerning impunity. And the group reiterated its conviction that one of the most efficient means of putting an end to the practice of disappearances is to punish the perpetrators of such crimes, with no exceptions to the rule.

The report drew attention to the visit to the former Yugoslavia by a member of the Working Group on Enforced or Involuntary Disappearances [E/CN.4/1994/26/Add.1]—a trip made at the request of **the Commission's Special Rapporteur on the Situation of Human Rights in the Former Yugoslavia.** It noted that the Working Group had previously asserted that to take up cases arising out of an "international armed conflict" would be to overwhelm its resources—and, indeed, that the **International Committee of the Red Cross** has had more experience in, and proven methods for, tracing disappearances under such conditions. Now the group has reconsidered its position, arguing that it is difficult to distinguish a national armed conflict from an international one in the Yugoslav case, difficult to say on what date the conflict has assumed one or the other character, and difficult to ascertain whether various parts of the conflict might not be characterized in different ways at any given time. The Security Council itself avoids such distinctions by referring simply to "the armed conflict," the report points out, and when all is said and done it is not only impractical but nearly impossible to distinguish one sort of missing person from another. Similarly—and especially in a chaotic situation like that of Bosnia and Herzegovina, the Working Group goes on to say— it is difficult to establish whether there was government "acquiescence" in particular cases of disappearance. Drawing the lines wider to embrace the entire category of "missing persons," whether or not the government acquiesced in their disappearance, does not necessarily contradict the principles of the Declaration that the Working Group is helping to enforce.

Again, the Working Group, following traditional U.N. practice, "usually transmits cases to governments only," and usually through the permanent missions and ministries of foreign affairs, declining any assistance from NGOs, liberation movements, and others when seeking clarification of the status of such cases. But in the context of Yugoslavia (and arguably in many other situations in the post-Cold War world) this would accomplish little: Certain parts of the territory are not states; others proclaim statehood but are not recognized as states by the community of nations; and still other areas are under the protection of the United Nations. The Working Group's report recommends taking a pragmatic approach—that is, seeking information on pending cases wherever and from whomever the information can be obtained, including other U.N. agencies and NGOs (and sometimes from many sources simultaneously).

Admitting that the missing of Yugoslavia might fall under a somewhat expanded mandate of the Working Group but that special considerations—not least of them cost—precluded its taking them on, the report weighs the possibility of establishing a special rapporteur on disappearances for former Yugoslavia. This, it argues, would be to graft one mandate upon another, to the detriment of the important distinction between a thematic mechanism (the Working Group and others that investigate a single human rights phenomenon worldwide) and a country-specific mechanism. The Working Group recommends the creation of a special process under the Human Rights Commission in the form of a **joint venture between the Special Rapporteur on Former Yugoslavia and one member of the Working Group on Enforced or Involuntary Disappearances.** It was suggested that the two individuals report to the Commission's 51st session and to the 49th General Assembly.

Country Situations

Among the documents before the 50th Commission under the agenda item "Violation of Human Rights and Fundamental Freedoms in Any Part of the World" were reports on the situation of human rights in the former Yugoslavia, Cyprus, Sudan, Iran, Zaire, Cuba, Afghanistan, southern Lebanon, Equatorial Guinea, Myanmar, and Bougainville. The 48th General Assembly heard reports from and expressed support for the work of the **Special Rapporteurs** for Cuba [A/Res/48/142], Iraq [A/Res/48/144], Myanmar [A/Res/48/150], Haiti [A/Res/48/151], Afghanistan [A/Res/48/152], and the former Yugoslavia [A/Res/48/153]. It welcomed the establishment of a **Special Representative** to Cambodia [A/Res/48/154] and the continuation of the work of the Special Representatives to Iran [A/Res/48/145] and Sudan [A/Res/48/147], and the establishment of an independent human rights monitor in **Somalia once political stability and security were restored** [A/Res/48/146].

The General Assembly requested that the Human Rights Commission ask the **Special Rapporteur on Yugoslavia** to continue his investigations into the rape and abuse of women and children there [A/Res/48/143]. Specifically engaged in gathering evidence for an international tribunal, located in The Hague, that intends to prosecute war crimes in the former Yugoslavia is the **Commission of Experts** established by the Security Council. This body of experts approved at its December 1993 session a Plan of Action for an in-depth investigation of allegations of sexual assault, extrajudicial executions, torture and alleged violations of international humanitarian law in detention camps in connection with the hostilities in the former Yugoslavia [A/48/858]. In early June the experts turned over their findings to the tribunal [*The New York Times*, 6/3/94].

All these country situations will be reviewed by the 49th Session of the General Assembly.

In the **case of Sudan,** international scrutiny of its human rights record began at the Human Rights Commission's 47th session in 1991. That inaugural review took place behind closed doors—the "1503" procedure—but in March 1993 the Commission decided [Res. 1993/60] that the human rights situation in Sudan had deteriorated even more and should be examined public. It established the post of Special Rapporteur and named Gaspar Biro to fill it.

After Mr. Biro's visit to Sudan, he filed an interim report that drew attention to serious violations of the right to life, security, liberty, and dignity of the person in northern Sudan [A/48/601]—the area to which his movements had been restricted by the government. He expressed special concern over the fate of the indigenous Nuba community and smaller ethnic groups as the armed conflict continued to escalate in the area in which they make their home. And he noted the importance of a second mission to investigate the situation in southern Sudan, particularly with regard to violations committed in the context of civil war by government forces and factions of the Sudanese People's Liberation Army.

The Permanent Representative of Sudan to the United Nations responded with a 56-page letter [E/CN.4/1994/122]. It denigrated Special Rapporteur Biro's work and accused him of, among other things, ignorance of Sudan's Muslim laws, lacking the requisite expertise, reporting only the abuses committed by the government in a country engaged in civil war, and "wrong reporting" over all.

Iran's representative also accused the Commission's Special Rapporteur, Reynaldo Galindo Pohl, of deliberate fault-finding when he presented his report on the situation in that country [A/48/526; A/C.3/48/SR.49, par. 25]. The government of Iran had not authorized a rapporteur visit to the country since 1991—and then, only after the European Community, sponsor of past resolutions on Iran, had threatened to sponsor another at the 46th General Assembly. Mr. Pohl's most recent report listed a wide range of human rights violations. He emphasized that the principle of the universality of human rights had been upheld by all member states at the World Conference on Human Rights the previous summer, and that he had repeatedly raised the issue with Iranian authorities, pointing out that "national laws could dictate the mechanisms for enforcing human rights but never their content, which was defined in instruments of unquestioned validity, such as the Universal Declaration of Human Rights" [SR.40]. Iranian exiles across the political spectrum served as one source of the information contained in Mr. Pohl's report, and the assassination of such exiles was one of the subjects covered.

From the government in Baghdad came the claim that the Special Rapporteur investigating **Iraq,** Max van der Stoel, was a "blatant liar" who had exposed "his ignorance of the peoples and ethnic communities in the area" [A/C.3/48/SR.52, par. 119]. In the case of Iraq, it took war in the Gulf and its aftermath for the Human Rights Commission to begin its scrutiny of human rights violations; and in 1992 the General Assembly began to circulate Mr. van der Stoel's reports to members of the **Security Council**—a body likely to have a direct role in accomplishing any plan to send a human rights monitoring mission to Iraq. The Human Rights Commission, at the Rapporteur's insistence, did recommend sending human rights monitors into the country [Res. 1994/74], but there the effort has stalled. Failing to receive Iraq's authorization for his own visit, Mr. van der Stoel has asked the international community to put pressure on Iraq to accept the idea of an assessment of the situation by impartial international observers. In the Special Rapporteur's view, Iraq takes on priority status, given conditions that are "worse than any witnessed since the Second World War" [A/C.3/48/SR.40, par. 30].

The Realization of Economic, Social, and Cultural Rights

The Commission has also been studying the problems faced by developing countries in their efforts to fulfill the economic, social, and cultural rights of their citizens—a subject that generated a good deal of rhetoric, but little more, in the days of the polarizing Cold War. This was the time when the developing states talked about redistributing wealth in the interest of social justice, and many of them went on to assert that human rights were the luxury of those who had full bellies. Today, debate and dialogue are more likely to be concerned with the efforts of structural adjustment, free trade, economic reform, and deregulation of industry—regarding which GATT and the international financial institutions are more apt to be major players than are the agencies of the regular United Nations. Obviously, national and international economic policies have repercussions for the fulfillment of economic and social rights. And if few countries still argue outright that respect for civil and political rights must await a higher level of economic development, there is no denying that economic pressures are making it difficult for many governments to *prevent* the sort of social and political upheaval that erodes the domestic institutions now protecting human rights.

Unlike other treaties, the **International Covenant on Economic, Social and Cultural Rights** does not provide for the establishment of a monitoring committee and makes no provision for receiving complaints. Since 1987, however, the **Committee on Economic, Social and Cultural Rights**—a body of independent experts created at the request of member governments of ECOSOC—has been meeting to receive reports from states parties on the progress they have made in implementing the Covenant. The task is a difficult one, given the problem of quantifying "the enjoyment of economic, social, and cultural rights."

The 49th and 50th sessions of the Commission reviewed reports of a U.N.-sponsored seminar on appropriate indicators to measure the progressive realization of economic, social, and cultural rights; reports by the Secretary-General on the repercussions of the debt crisis and adjustment programs for human rights, for those who live in extreme poverty, and for the practice of forced evictions; and an updated report of the independent expert, Luis Valencia Rodríguez, on the right to own property [E/CN.4/1994/19/Add.1].

At its 49th session, February 1–March 12, 1993, the Human Rights Commission created a **working group** of 15 experts [Res. 1993/22] **to identify obstacles to the realization of the Declaration on the Right to Development,** adopted by the General Assembly in 1986. The Declaration establishes the right to development as "an inalienable human right," whose specific standards are "to be read in conjunction with many other human rights endorsements," prominently, the Universal Declaration of Human Rights [United Nations, *The Realization of the Right to Development*, Geneva, 1991]. In the Working Group's first report [E/CN.4/1994/21], it placed the obstacles to development in four categories: (1) threats to international peace and security; (2) the heavy demands placed on (and cooperation required from) all concerned—individuals and national, regional, and international authorities; (3) the shortage of resources available to realize an ambitious agenda; and (4) the unsatisfactory functioning of both the national and multilateral mechanisms for promoting development.

The Group identified five means of strengthening cooperation between governments and other international bodies in the interest of promoting the right to development: educating the public and national and international officials about the Declaration; formulating clearer principles for defining and assessing progress toward implementing the right to development; enlisting cooperation between and among institutions, especially human rights and development NGOs; creating systems for effective reporting on the progress made in incorporating the right to development into development activities; and devising efficient machinery to facilitate the implementation of the right to development.

The Working Group was scheduled to hold two more sessions in 1994, in May and October. U.N. observers note the rich lode of materials the Group might consider mining for its own cause, prominently: (1) reports prepared for the preparatory meetings anticipating the March 1995 World Social Summit, which will focus on alleviating poverty and unemployment and creating jobs, and the social integration of marginalized people; (2) the relevant standards already enshrined in the Convention on the Rights of the Child, the Convention on the Elimination of All Forms of Discrimination against Women, and the International Convention on the Protection of the Rights of All Migrant Workers and Members of Their Families; and (3) the U.N. Development Programme's annual Human Development Report, including a review of the methods UNDP has explored in its attempts to establish development indicators and measuring tools.

Implications for U.N. Human Rights Instruments of the Post-Cold War World

For most of the past four decades, international human rights instruments have sought to protect the individual's freedom from abuse by government and to expose patterns of abuse by governments or government agents where they exist. This approach was based on two assumptions: (1) Violations are perpetrated by governments, which control the agents of abuse and thus have the means of preventing and/or punishing such abuses; and (2) governments can be shamed into respecting human rights.

The success of such an approach has been mixed. Despite the international pressure placed on such countries as Sudan, Iraq, and Myanmar over several recent years, the United Nations has achieved limited success in mitigating abuses there. What the present rules for operating the U.N.'s human rights mechanisms fail to take into account is the fact that the worst abusers today are apt to be **not recognized governments at all but fighting factions or mercenaries,** such as in Afghanistan, Bosnia, Somalia, and Haiti. An increasing proportion of the torture, disappearances, arbitrary detention, and other human rights violations reviewed by the Commission are the outgrowth (or even instruments) of **internal conflict,** and noncombatants are often the direct target—this in violation of the Geneva Conventions. In many such cases there is **no functioning central government** to hold accountable, much less an effective judiciary to punish offenders.

For **countries in transition** (or in the process of disintegration), the exposure of abuses is clearly insufficient for reconstructing civil/democratic societies based on the rule of law. Nor can the human rights machinery as presently constituted mount a rapid or effective response when the **targets of abuse are entire groups,** irrespective of individual beliefs, and the abuses are carried out in wholesale fashion. The rape and ethnic cleansing perpetrated in Bosnia, citizen-led discrimination against foreigners in Western Europe, and Iraqi poison gas attacks against the Kurds—these are increasingly typical of the challenges to which the international community has had a problem responding [see Iain Guest, "The New Agenda: Challenges That Await the U.N. High Commissioner for Human Rights," International Human Rights Law Group, 2/94].

Among the U.N.'s ad hoc attempts to address the human rights problems of the post-Cold War world is an increased emphasis on advisory and technical services. This is apparent from the range of applications suggested and number of times these services were mentioned in the Vienna Declaration (33 separate references) and in resolutions passed by the Commission (20 times at the 49th session alone).

Advisory services and technical assistance, administered by the Human Rights Centre, provide help for countries interested in drafting constitutional provisions, in holding democratic elections, and in training judges, magistrates, lawyers, prosecutors, police, prison, and military officials. There are also services to encourage ratification of human rights treaties, assist countries in meeting their reporting obligations under those treaties, and help in developing human rights curricula and in training teachers, and more. However, there are drawbacks in the present approach to delivering these services. For one thing, the Human Rights Centre provides support only to governments and only upon government request. Although this last has the advantage of ensuring government cooperation (or at least acquiescence) in the project, there may be key sectors within the country that resent the U.N. presence. Then, too, nongovernmental groups might have a better idea than the national bureaucracy of the kind of advice and services the country actually needs, especially in situations in which the agents of government itself are prime suspects in human rights abuse. And as noted by close observers of U.N. Human Rights Commission proceedings [*Issues Before the 45th General Assembly of the United Nations,* pp. 157–58], the government that is tapping the advisory services may not, in fact, be serious about carrying out the promised reforms, having requested U.N. advice and technical support for reasons that range from the cynical to the dilatory.

Advisory and Technical Assistance: Country Cases

Somalia. At the request of the 49th Human Rights Commission [Res. 1993/86], the U.N. Secretary-General appointed an **independent expert** to assist the Special Representative for Somalia **for one year.** The hope is to develop a long-term program of advisory services aimed at reestablishing the rule of law through the drafting of a democratic constitution and the holding of free and fair elections at defined intervals. The program of advisory services of the Human Rights Centre would work closely with the Special Representative, with U.N. peacekeeping operations in Somalia and such other bodies as the U.N.'s Electoral Assistance Unit, and with international relief organizations as well as other NGOs.

Reporting on the Somalia situation, independent expert Fanuel Jarirentundu Kozonguizi argued that "the development of any programme, long-term or short-term, must depend on the final resolution of the political disputes amongst the Somali factions, since any programme for human rights in Somalia must be acceptable and endorsed by those who are expected to implement it." Furthermore, "without a central administrative structure, it is not possible to lay down the foundations of a permanent programme of human rights for Somalia" [E/CN.4/1994/77/Add.1].

Somalia readily illustrates the difficulty of providing human rights advisory and technical services (not to mention peacekeeping services and humanitarian aid) when there is no central government to provide consent and no single, authoritative state structure to establish and enforce laws that protect human rights and fundamental freedoms. In this particular case, not only is the central authority lacking to accomplish such things, but the very peacekeeping troops that were sent to ensure the delivery of humanitarian aid may have perpetrated human rights violations of their own. According to Kozonguizi's report, several NGOs and U.N. bodies **allege that UNOSOM II forces have violated the human rights of Somalis,** thus violating the principles of humanitarian law enshrined in the Geneva Conventions of 1949 and the Additional Protocols of 1977. The expert welcomed the proposal that UNOSOM establish a team of international specialists to investigate, in cooperation with the Somali police, violations of the human rights of Somalis and of international assistance workers [E/CN.4/1994/77].

Cambodia. The 49th Human Rights Commission requested the Secretary-General [Res. 1993/6] to ensure a continued U.N. presence in Cambodia after the mandate of the **U.N. Transitional Authority in Cambodia (UNTAC)** expired through the establishment of an on-the-ground presence of the Commission and the appointment of a special representative. Both were approved by the General Assembly [A/Res/48/154], and on October 1, 1993, after a scramble for funds and the departure of UNTAC from Cambodia, the Commission established an office at Phnom Penh.

The **human rights mandate of UNTAC** itself is described by Special Representative Michael Kirby as "the most extensive in the history of U.N. peace-keeping" [E/CN.4/1994/73]. Under that mandate it was asked to conduct a program of human rights education, carry out general human rights monitoring during the transition period and through the conclusion of national elections, investigate human rights complaints, and where appropriate, take corrective action. These human rights efforts were linked to UNTAC's role in organizing and conducting free and fair elections and otherwise overseeing the transition to a democratic government. The success of UNTAC's human rights program in stemming human rights violations is debatable, not because of anything UNTAC personnel did or failed to do, but because a country with weak judicial and other institutions and a history of repressive practices and arbitrary authority is unlikely to make the transition to democracy in short order.

Among the most formidable obstacles to meeting the expectations for UNTAC's human rights mandate is the matter of funding. Although salaries and the operation of the office are to be financed by the U.N. regular budget, all activities carried out by the local human rights center will be financed from extrabudgetary resources—in short, from voluntary contributions [Res. 1993/6]. A second obstacle is the fact that the Phnom Penh center now operates in an advisory capacity only and Cambodians no longer accord it the status it had during the transition period, when UNTAC exercised joint authority with Cambodia's Supreme National Council. Third, and perhaps most formidable of all, is the actual process of institutionalizing democracy in a country with anything like Cambodia's history, however well the process of peace-brokering and constitution-drafting and electioneering has gone.

El Salvador. The United Nations has had a long history of monitoring and attempting improvements in El Salvador's human rights situation. From 1981 to 1992 the Human Rights Commission maintained a **Special Representative** to investigate reports about grave violations of human rights and recommend solutions. In 1992, the U.N. Secretary-General appointed an **Independent Expert** "to provide assistance in human rights matters to the Government of El Salvador" [A/Res/47/140]. Since then Pedro Nikken has been supplying information about the human rights situation in the country and about the effects of implementing the Peace Agreements on the citizens' enjoyment of human rights. He continues to investigate the manner in which the government *and* the forces of the Farabundo Martí National Liberation Front (FMLN) have applied the recommendations of the final report of the Special Representative, the recommendations of the **U.N. Observer Mission in El Salvador** (ONUSAL, whose mandate continues through November 30, 1994), and the recommendations of the **Truth Commission** during the peace negotiations between the government and the FMLN. The Independent Expert reports to the General Assembly and to the Commission on Human Rights.

In December 1993 the 48th General Assembly commended the government of El Salvador and the FMLN for fulfilling most of their commitments but noted persistent violations—primarily of "the right to life" and the "capacity of the judicial system to clarify and punish such violations" [A/Res/48/149]. The Assembly saw the need to "step-up" the land-transfer program, the program for reintegrating ex-combatants into the community, the deployment of the National Civil Police, and the "phasing out" of the old National Police, among other measures.

The Independent Expert's most recent report [E/CN.4/1994/11] noted the increased political violence of December and January 1994, during which time the government prevented him from visiting the country (though never issuing a direct refusal) and tried to place the responsibility for thwarting the visit on him and on the Centre for Human Rights. Nikken concluded that the pace of implementing the Peace Agreements had slowed in 1993. El Salvador illustrates that the success of any advisory or technical services program, alike with other human rights mechanisms, has a good deal to do with the political will of government.

The Problem of Coordination

The lack of effective coordination within the U.N. system has long been lamented, but since the Vienna Conference the problem has received-greater attention. Nearly every working group report since that summer of 1993 conference has noted the Declaration's recommendation for increased cooperation among and between U.N. human rights mechanisms, U.N. agencies and other international organizations, national and regional bodies, and NGOs. The effort got off to a rather inauspicious start when the U.N.'s specialized agencies were excluded from the committee that was drafting the Vienna Declaration, which considered such issues as labor rights, child abuse, education, and health—areas in which these agencies have acknowledged expertise. (The U.S. insistence on capping U.N. spending has only exacerbated the problem, because it increases the competition among agencies for funding and leads various divisions to assert the importance of their programs over all others, downplaying the worthiness of would-be partners.)

There have been mixed reviews for the attempts at cooperation between human rights and peacekeeping agencies. Late in 1993, for example, the Human Rights Centre was not informed of a meeting at U.N. Headquarters to review an outline of a human rights program for the former Yugoslavia. Learning about it only one day in advance, the Centre had to scramble to send an official [Iain Guest, "The New Agenda: Challenges that Await the U.N. High Commissioner for Human Rights," International Human Rights Law Group, 2/94]. On the other hand, Special Rapporteur for the **former Yugoslavia** Tadeusz Mazowiecki noted in his sixth periodic report [E/CN.4/1994/110] that UNPROFOR has been able to collect various types of evidence concerning human rights violations and violations of humanitarian law, that it has "considerably increased" its sharing of information with him, and that it has given full support to the establishment of two field offices of the Human Rights Centre. Mazowiecki, for his part, argued for expanding UNPROFOR's mandate to cover the entire territory of Bosnia and Herzegovina—not merely the U.N. "safe areas"—and to collect information on human rights abuses. At the same time, he noted, the forces' ability to cooperate is limited, since "UNPROFOR forces have not been effectively empowered to intervene to protect against human rights violations as they occur and have been forced to observe passively many serious breaches of international humanitarian law owing to the inadequacy of their mandate and resources" [ibid.].

Close **cooperation between the human rights and peacekeeping**

agencies of the United Nations is critical not only to ensuring a human rights component to peacekeeping but also to **protect U.N. personnel** engaged in humanitarian and peacekeeping efforts in crisis situations. The Sub-Commission, recognizing this need, recommended [Res. 1992/24] that the Human Rights Commission request the various human rights mechanisms to provide the Secretary-General with relevant parts of their own reports. He, in turn, would include this information in his report to the Commission and to the General Assembly on the **Detention of International Civil Servants and Their Families.** The Secretary-General's most recent report on the subject [E/CN.4/1994/30] notes an increase in the number of cases of abuse of U.N. staff, such as kidnapping and casualties (especially in the Middle East and Afghanistan), and asserts that the protection of U.N. staff has taken on a special urgency with the increase of peacekeeping operations mandated by the Security Council. This urgency, he stated, has much to do with the conditions under which some U.N. personnel now operate (extremely hazardous) and the level of risk considered acceptable (especially in areas where government is unable to exercise much authority or has none at all). Within the past year alone the number of staff killed has doubled—from an average of one death per month to one every two weeks [E/CN.4/1994/30, par. 59]. On December 9, 1993, the General Assembly established an **ad hoc committee to elaborate an international convention on "the safety and security of U.N. and associated personnel,** with particular reference to responsibility for attacks on them" [A/Res/48/37]. A convention signed by governments may be of only limited use, however, since many of these conflicts are civil in nature.

Human Rights NGOs

Under the U.N. Charter, NGOs may be granted consultative status with ECOSOC. NGOs often provide extensive, on-the-ground documentation of human rights violations that U.N. mechanisms may be unable to provide, given their need to obtain governmental approval for a visit, their overwhelming caseloads, and their limited budgets. The accreditation is currently awarded by a committee of 19 governmental representatives, which, until early 1993, made its decisions by consensus. So it was that a small but vocal group of member states was able to block the accreditation of such NGOs as the Lawyers Committee for Human Rights, Human Rights Watch, and the Minority Human Rights Group. However, in early 1993, when a majority vote was able to override minority objections for the first time, the committee granted consultative status to Human Rights Watch, and other groups have gained entry since.

NGOs face obstacles other than a committee vote in making their voices heard in U.N. human rights forums. When it comes to **NGOs from the developing world,** the first problem is to obtain the funds simply to travel to U.N. Headquarters in New York or the Human Rights Centre in Geneva. Some other NGOs, for their part, may not be making optimal use of their presence and resources because they focus on exposing abuses by a small group of governments (for example, China, Burma, and Iraq), providing little information that is new and tending to duplicate past efforts. Furthermore, a sophisticated enough government can manipulate the agenda to ensure that NGOs speak late on a Friday night, when media interest is minimal. Working the corridors to influence resolutions and help create new U.N. procedures is sometimes a more valuable use of an NGO's time. Quite a few NGOs did lobby extensively in the ultimately successful bid for 48th General Assembly approval of the establishment of a U.N. High Commissioner for Human Rights.

The Vienna Conference offered an opportunity for NGOs from all corners of the world to exchange information and pave the way to greater cooperation in the future. And the media attention to the event helped to publicize their cause. This was even more likely to be the case when NGOs got together and focused on a "headline" topic—for example, the women's groups that held a Global Tribunal on Violations of Women's Human Rights at which women from 25 countries offered testimony about such abuses as rape. At the same time, the event illustrated the challenges that NGOs in the human rights field face in attempting to be heard. The NGO forum, although lively, was held in the basement of the Conference building, and the NGO representatives had no official access to the official delegates or input into the Declaration drafting process. Contact was made only when some governments, such as the United States and Canada, chose to give a public press conference and briefed NGOs on the Vienna drafting proceedings or, as during the preparatory process, officials sought information from these groups. And over a dozen human rights NGOs, including Chinese, ethnic Kurdish, and Iranian groups, were barred from the Conference and the U.N.'s NGO forum under pressure from such countries as Indonesia and China in the General Assembly.

Also disturbing to many in the human rights community is the mention they are given in the final text of the Vienna Declaration. Although it "recognizes the important role of nongovernmental organizations in the promotion of all human rights and in humanitarian activities at the national, regional, and international levels" [I. (38)], the Declaration states that only those "genuinely involved in human rights" are entitled to "the protection of national law" [ibid.]. Without defining what makes for an "ungenuine human rights group," the statement permits governments to question the authenticity of their critics and places no pressure on governments to provide security for human rights defenders.

2. Refugees
By Kathryn C. Lawler

A number of developments in the refugee field over the past year are indicative of the directions in which refugee problems and policies are moving. First, the refugee population has increased by approximately 2 million persons [UNHCR, *State of the World's Refugees* (New York: Penguin Books, 1993), p. 3; *UNHCR at a Glance*, 5/12/94]. An extreme example of the sudden and large-scale refugee movements occurring today is that of the approximately 250,000 Rwandans who flooded into Tanzania during one 24-hour period in April 1994 [UNHCR update, 4/29/94]. Second, due largely to economic and political constraints, a number of traditional countries of asylum have begun to implement more restrictive policies toward asylum seekers. In February 1994 the United States became the only country to charge asylum seekers for filing an asylum application [*The New York Times*, 2/17/94]. Third, the resolution of conflict and the consolidation of peace in many countries allowed more than 3 million refugees to return home between January 1992 and October 1993 [EC/1993/SC.2/CRP.4/Add.1; EC/1993/SC.2/CRP.35]. Over the course of 1993–94, thousands of refugees returned to Mozambique from Malawi, South Africa, Zimbabwe, Swaziland, Tanzania, and Zambia.

The Changing Nature of U.N. Response to Refugee Issues

The burgeoning refugee population and the increasing complexity of the situations that cause population displacement have forced the United Nations to take a more comprehensive approach to refugee issues. The U.N. agency responsible for responding to refugee problems, the **U.N. High Commissioner for Refugees (UNHCR)**, was established in 1950 with a rather limited mandate: to provide refugees with international protection and to seek durable solutions to their plight through voluntary repatriation, local integration in countries of asylum, or third-country resettlement. These objectives reflected the notion that little could be done within the countries from which refugees originated to eliminate their need to leave.

As a result of the end of the Cold War, however, the international community has increased opportunities both to prevent and to resolve refugee problems within countries of origin. While the central focus of UNHCR's work continues to be the provision of assistance and protection to refugees after they have left their countries of origin, today the agency considers the **prevention of refugee flows** as one of its primary objectives. UNHCR has engaged in preventive activity in the former Yugoslavia by providing assistance and protection to civilians caught in the midst of conflict; in Sri Lanka by establishing Open Relief Centres, where shelter and relief are provided to returning refugees and internally displaced persons; and in Somalia by implementing "cross-border" operations through which food, seeds, agricultural equipment, and livestock are brought from Kenya with the aim of stabilizing potential refugee-producing areas and of creating conditions conducive to the voluntary repatriation of Somali refugees in neighboring countries.

Those whom UNHCR finds most in need of its attention today often fall outside the scope of the agency's official mandate. The **1951 Convention Relating to the Status of Refugees** defines a refugee as a person fleeing his or her country of origin because of a well-founded fear of persecution based on race, religion, nationality, membership in a particular social group, or political opinion. Now, out of a commitment to respond to the most pressing humanitarian problems confronting the international community, UNHCR is assisting and protecting groups of people in need, regardless of whether they are refugees. In Ethiopia, for example, UNHCR is implementing a "cross-mandate" approach under which it operates on a community-wide basis, providing assistance to refugees, returnees, internally displaced persons, demobilized soldiers, and civilians affected by war and drought.

Institutional Collaboration on Refugee Issues

Through extending its work to activities and beneficiaries beyond the official scope of its mandate, UNHCR has become more connected to and interdependent with other parts of the U.N. system. In conflict situations, most notably in the former Yugoslavia, UNHCR relies heavily on the military to protect its humanitarian operations. When involved in the repatriation of refugees to a country undergoing a transition from war to peace, it often works closely with peacekeeping forces assigned to that country, such as the U.N. Transitional Authority in Cambodia (UNTAC), the U.N. Observer Mission in El Salvador (ONUSAL), and the U.N. Operation in Mozambique (ONUMOZ). UNHCR is also working in close collaboration with the U.N. Development Programme (UNDP) and other development agencies to link the humanitarian relief that it provides to returnees to the longer-term development of the country of origin. In focusing on measures to foresee and prevent refugee flows where possible, UNHCR will need to work closely with human rights bodies of the United Nations to identify and address the human rights violations that could cause refugee movements. As the **U.N. High Commissioner for Refugees,** Sadako Ogata, reported to the General Assembly at its 1993 session, the success of her agency's program depends largely on "the ability of the United Nations to develop a comprehensive and integrated response, linking humanitarian action and protection of human rights with peace-making, peace-keeping, and peace-building, in the context of a strengthened partnership of all concerned actors: governmental, intergovernmental, and nongovernmental" [A/48/12].

Among UNHCR's most indispensable partners are the **nongovernmental organizations (NGOs)** that often serve as its operational arm, actually implementing the programs under its responsibility. In many of its operations, UNHCR hires international and indigenous NGOs to provide medical care or distribute food in refugee camps; to handle the logistics of transporting refugees back to their homelands; and to deliver relief and water supplies to populations caught in the middle of conflict. NGOs also play an important role in gathering information about potential refugee flows and identifying the local capacities that could be mobilized in response to refugee situations. In recognition of that important relationship with NGOs, UNHCR, in collaboration with the International Council of Voluntary Agencies (ICVA), recently sponsored a series of consultations, referred to as **Partnership in Action (PARINAC)**, to "facilitate closer practical collaboration and enhanced understanding between UNHCR and NGOs in order to produce improved operational results in the field" [UNHCR/ICVA Information Note on PARINAC]. PARINAC consisted of six regional meetings during 1993–94 and a global conference in June 1994 in Oslo, Norway.

Large-Scale Humanitarian Emergencies

In recent years the international community has been confronted by a number of humanitarian emergencies of massive proportions, most notably in the former Yugoslavia, Somalia, Burundi, and Rwanda. The causes of these crises have been a complex mix of ethnic tensions, civil conflict, human rights violations, and drought and famine.

Large-scale refugee movements present the tremendous logistical challenge of providing adequate food, sanitation, shelter, and medical attention to massive numbers of people under emergency circumstances. Other challenges relate to protection: how to protect civilians in the midst of conflict, how to preserve the civilian nature of refugee camps, how to protect internally displaced persons, and how to gain access to populations at risk. A central question the international community faces in becoming involved in humanitarian intervention in conflict situations is whether the benefits of its efforts are such as to warrant risking the lives of international personnel. In recognition of this dilemma, at its 1993 session the General Assembly expressed "deep concern at conditions in a number of countries and regions that seriously endanger the delivery of humanitarian assistance and the security of the staff of the High Commissioner and other relief workers," and it "deplore[d] the recent loss of lives among personnel involved in humanitarian operation" [A/Res/48/116].

The complexity of these crises and the magnitude of the humanitarian needs they create have forced the United Nations to call upon the full range of expertise available in its diverse humanitarian agencies. Central to the U.N.'s ability to coordinate humanitarian response in a way that avoids duplication or large gaps in coverage is the **U.N. Department of Humanitarian Affairs (DHA)**, established in early 1992 and operating under the leadership of the **Under-Secretary-General for Humanitarian Affairs** (a position created by a General Assembly resolution in December 1991). DHA's work includes serving as the focal point for identifying the early warnings of potential humanitarian emergencies, determining which humanitarian emergencies require U.N. action, raising funds for responding to humanitarian emergencies, and assigning responsibilities to the various U.N. agencies involved in humanitarian response.

The quintessential example of the expanding responsibilities of UNHCR, and its collaboration with other parts of the international system, is supplied by the former Yugoslavia. There, UNHCR is the lead U.N. agency with primary responsibility for logistics and transportation, food monitoring, health, and protection. The total population benefiting from UNHCR operations in the former Yugoslavia—which includes refugees, internally displaced persons, and people who have never left their place of origin—is approximately 4 million [UNHCR Update on Ex-Yugoslavia, 5/11/94]. UNHCR relies on the **World Food Programme** to mobilize, deliver, and distribute food; on the **World Health Organization** to provide health care; and on **UNICEF** to address the survival and development needs of women and children. NGOs are also making a major contribution to the humanitarian response in the former Yugoslavia.

Internally Displaced Persons

Internally displaced persons leave their homes for many of the same reasons that refugees flee their countries: human rights violations, ethnic tensions, and civil conflict. It is estimated that there are 24 million internally displaced persons in the world today [E/CN.4/1993/95]. There is no agency in the international system with a mandate to assist and protect internally displaced persons. Nor is there a body of law that defines the rights of internally displaced persons or the responsibilities of governments toward them. Unlike refugees who have reached the relative safety of a country of asylum, internally displaced persons often confront the very same problems that caused them to flee in the first place. Among the countries with the largest internally displaced populations are Sudan, South Africa, Mozambique, Somalia, and the Philippines.

The United Nations has made some progress toward creating a focal point on internally displaced persons. In 1992 **the U.N. Secretary-General appointed a Representative on internally displaced persons** to report on their situation and recommend ways in which the international community can assist and protect this population more effectively. The Representative submits annual reports on his activities to the Commission on Human Rights and the General Assembly. Among the issues that the Representative is mandated to examine are the existing rules and norms that apply to internally displaced persons, the root causes of internal displacement, prevention and long-term solutions, and institutional arrangements for addressing the problem. The mandate of the Secretary-General's Representative will be up for review by the U.N. Commission on Human Rights at its 1995 session.

The Representative's function is not an operational one, and other international actors are required to respond to the on-the-ground assistance and protection needs of the internally displaced. In a number of instances UNHCR has worked with the internally displaced either upon the request of the U.N. Secretary-General or because internally displaced persons were gathered in areas where UNHCR was implementing projects for returned refugees. In support of UNHCR's efforts to provide assistance and protection for internally displaced persons, the General Assembly at its 1993 session "welcomed the decision of the Executive Committee of UNHCR to extend, on a case-by-case basis and under specific circumstances, protection and assistance to the internally displaced" [A/Res/48/135].

The **Inter-agency Standing Committee,** chaired by the Department of Humanitarian Affairs and consisting of U.N. agencies and intergovernmental and nongovernmental organizations concerned with humanitarian issues, has formed a **Task Force on Internally Displaced Persons.** Among the items that the Task Force intends to provide are case studies of situations of internal displacement and recommendations on how the United Nations should respond to such situations.

Given that the internally displaced population is significantly larger than the refugee population, and that the U.N.'s institutional capacity for responding to the needs of the internally displaced is only a fraction of what it has available for refugees, this is clearly an issue that requires serious consideration by the United Nations in the years ahead.

International Refugee Protection

The 1951 Convention Relating to the Status of Refugees defines the fundamental rights of a refugee to seek asylum and not be forcibly returned to a country where he or she fears persecution. One of the clearest examples of the denial of these rights is the U.S. government's policy toward Haitian asylum seekers between May 1992 and April 1994, whereby asylum seekers were interdicted and forcibly returned, with no opportunity to present their claims for asylum. Under mounting pressure from the refugee advocacy community and with the continued failure of efforts to reach a political settlement in Haiti, the Clinton administration changed its policy in April 1994 to allow shipboard screening of asylum claims. By June 1994 it was working with a number of countries in the region to set up safe havens where Haitians could find protection on a temporary basis. In a 1993 resolution the General Assembly expressed concern that the protection of many refugees under the care of UNHCR "continues to be seriously jeopardized in many situations as a result of denial of admission, unlawful expulsion, refoulement, unjustified detention, other threats to their physical security, dignity, and well-being . . ." [A/Res/48/116].

A major chapter in the history of the U.N.'s response to asylum seekers from Southeast Asia is coming to a close as the **Comprehensive Plan of Action (CPA)** enters its final stage. Put into place in 1989 to find comprehensive solutions to large-scale migration from Vietnam, the CPA has enlisted the cooperation of countries of asylum, countries of resettlement, and Vietnam itself. Participating countries have worked together to afford protection to Vietnamese who qualified as refugees, and to assure the humane treatment of those who did not meet the international standard. A meeting of the Steering Committee of the International Conference on Indochinese Refugees decided in February 1994 that "as of February 14, 1994, Vietnamese arriving by boat would no longer be treated under a special programme but would be considered in the same way as asylum seekers from any other country . . ." [UNHCR press release, 2/14/94].

In October 1993 the Executive Committee on the High Commissioner's Programme, the body of 47 governments that oversees UNHCR's assistance budgets and advises on refugee protection, issued a **"Note on Certain Aspects of Sexual Violence Against Refugee Women,"** which examined the problem of sexual abuse of refugee women and girls—whether as a cause of their flight, during their flight, or in countries of asylum. The document notes that "rape and other forms of sexual violence against women and girls are being used as a form of persecution in systematic campaigns of terror and intimidation, which have forced members of particular ethnic, cultural, and religious groups to flee their homes and, often, to seek refuge in another country" [A/AC.96/822]. It emphasizes the need for legal measures to protect and defend the victims and to punish perpetrators of such crimes. It also calls for practical measures, such as those laid out in the **UNHCR Guidelines on the Protection of Refugee Women,** including increased security in camps, the participation of refugee women in decisions affecting security, support for law-enforcement activities, and employment of female staff in field protection, health, and social service positions.

Repatriation

The settlement of many regional conflicts has opened the way for the return of refugees to their homelands. UNHCR is in the midst of a three-year $203 million repatriation program for 1.5 million Mozambicans in Malawi, South Africa, Zimbabwe, Swaziland, Tanzania, and Zambia [UNHCR Update on Refugee Developments in Africa, 2/8/94]. In recent years UNHCR has facilitated the large-scale voluntary repatriation of refugees to Afghanistan, Cambodia, and El Salvador.

Repatriation presents many challenges to the international community. First is the question of when it is safe for refugees to return home. Many of the countries to which refugees are returning are affected by continued violence and unresolved political tensions. In some cases, the very land the refugees must cross to return home is laced with land mines. Second is the challenge of reintegrating refugees in the country of origin. Years of warfare usually limit the country's capacity to absorb returning refugees; infrastructures have been damaged; documentation has been lost or destroyed; and tensions over land tenure remain. While returning refugees no longer fall officially within the mandate of UNHCR once they cross the border into their home country, UNHCR increasingly is involved in efforts to facilitate their reintegration within the country of origin. In such places as Nicaragua, Cambodia, and Somalia, UNHCR has mounted **Quick Impact Projects (QIPs)**—that is, mini-development projects aimed at providing immediate, focused support to communities trying to absorb large numbers of returned refugees. Examples of QIPs are the building or reparation of bridges, schools, and clinics; rehabilitation of water supply; and investment in small livestock or other productive community enterprises. In its efforts to facilitate the reintegration of refugees, UNHCR works to forge links with development and indigenous organizations that can continue this work after the U.N. agency withdraws.

At its 48th Session the General Assembly took into consideration the "complexity and urgency of global refugees and the need for the international community to adopt a comprehensive approach for the coordination of action with regard to refugees, returnees, displaced persons, and migrants" [A/Res/48/113]. In this connection, the General Assembly invited governments and international, regional, and nongovernmental organizations to submit their recommendations regarding the appropriateness of convening a conference on these issues. The Secretary-General will submit a report of these recommendations to the General Assembly at its 49th Session.

3. Health
By Yvette P. Cuca

The **World Health Organization (WHO),** the specialized U.N. agency that coordinates global health activities, continues working toward

"Health for All by the Year 2000"—the overarching goal it set for itself more than a decade ago. The hope is to develop effective and affordable health care services, with an emphasis on primary care and considerable input from the community involved. Serving this goal are WHO programs aimed at improving infrastructures and health institutions, education, food supply and nutrition, safe water supply and sanitation, maternal and child health, family planning, immunization, disease-prevention, and the supply of essential drugs [WHO pamphlet, "Health for All: One Common Goal," n.d.].

Gathering in May 1994 for its **47th World Health Assembly (WHA),** WHO's governing body approved the ninth of its General Programmes of Work, this one covering the final years (1996–2001) of the "Health for All" effort. The emphasis is on tailoring health programs to meet specific regional and development concerns—and on the actual delivery of health services to all populations [resolution WHA47.4, 5/9/94].

Disease Control

One of WHO's great victories is the **eradication of smallpox;** the last death from this acutely contagious virus was reported in 1987. Since then, the virus has existed only in laboratories in Russia and at the Centers for Disease Control (CDC) in Atlanta, Georgia. WHO had called for destruction of the virus by New Year's Eve, 1994, but others argued that specimens should be preserved for future use [The New York Times, 8/30/93]. In June the virus got a year's "reprieve" [ibid., 6/7/94].

In the instance of **malaria,** the number of cases is increasing, especially in Sub-Saharan Africa, and the cause cited is growing resistance to the most widely used drug, chloroquine. One current estimate places the number of cases at 300 million–500 million per year around the world and the number of malaria-related deaths at 1.5 million–3 million [U.N. press release H/2839, 4/20/94]. There is hope that a vaccine developed by a Colombian doctor, Manuel Patarroyo, will prove effective in preventing new outbreaks of the disease. In 1993, Patarroyo gave "control of the vaccine" (SP f66) to international agencies, such as WHO and UNICEF, for further testing and possible distribution [UNICEF, First Call for Children, 7–9/93]. The return to health of those already infected rests with a drug derived from extracts of a Chinese herb, *ginghaosu*, "identified and analyzed" in a survey of traditional Chinese medicines 20 years ago. WHO has announced that two-year trials of the drug on the Thailand-Cambodia border "cut the death rate three-fold when compared with quinine" [U.N. press release H/2839, 4/20/94], although indicating one drawback: If treatment does not continue for seven days, despite the fact that the fever is down and a patient may think himself out of the woods, the parasites could return. Supporting the trials were WHO, the U.N. Development Programme's Programme for Research and Training in Tropical Diseases, and the World Bank.

Migration and civil conflict, with the inevitable disruption of health care and the destruction of sanitation systems, play a major role in spreading such diseases as **cholera,** a new strain of which has appeared in the past year in India and Bangladesh. Since 1991, 300,000 new cases of cholera and of dysentery—and 20,000 deaths from these causes—have been reported in Africa alone, and WHO and the CDC in Atlanta are concerned about a possible global epidemic. Current cholera vaccines and previous immunity offer no defense against the new strain, which is detected only through special test materials that WHO is now providing where needed. WHO calls for such preventive measures as improved drinking-water supplies and sanitation in the affected areas [press release WHO/98, 12/2/93].

UNICEF, the U.N. operation in Somalia (UNOSOM II), and a number of nongovernmental organizations joined in the fight against cholera in Somalia, where a water chlorination program and other preventive measures have finally succeeded in halting the spread of the disease. On March 31, 1994, WHO reported 1,500 cases of the disease in Mogadishu alone, nine times what it had been just one week earlier [UNICEF press release PR/94/07]; and by May 1 a total of 15,000 had been infected and 500 had died [UNOSOM II press release, 5/1/94].

In April 1993, WHO declared **tuberculosis** a global emergency—the leading cause of death from a single infectious agent—and has warned that the disease could kill more than 30 million people in the next decade [press release WHA/14, 5/14/93]. The rise in cases of TB has much to do with the spread of HIV infection, which allows the activation of dormant TB by weakening the immune system. By mid-1993, about 5.1 million people in the world were infected with both diseases [U.N. press release H/2824, 11/15/93]. Among the other causes for TB's spread are drug-resistant strains and, in Eastern and Central Europe and the former Soviet Union, drug shortages and the collapse of health care systems [press release WHA/14, 5/14/93]. Past neglect of governments and declining interest in infectious disease research in industrialized countries have also contributed to the situation. In the United States, notes WHO, a deterioration of access to health care services, worsening living conditions, and immigration are prominent causes of the spread of TB. The WHO Tuberculosis Programme hopes to cut TB deaths from the current figure of 3 million per year to a new low of 1.6 million per year within the next decade, and has recommended that aid agencies spend more than $100 million each year on treatment programs [U.N. press release H/2824, 11/15/93].

AIDS

AIDS continues its seemingly inexorable spread around the world, with 2.5 million cases reported by mid-1993 and another 14 million people infected by the HIV virus. According to one current estimate, the tally will reach as high as 30 million–40 million infected and 10 million dead from AIDS-related causes at the turn of the century [WHO, EB93/26, 12/6/93]. U.N. Secretary-General Boutros-Ghali has declared that "The world must mobilize against AIDS as it would against any common enemy. Our response must be united, determined, and universal" [U.N. press release SG/SM/ 5169, 12/1/93].

One new allied offensive begins with the agreement to create a truly **joint U.N. program on AIDS** (WHO's seven-year-old Global Programme on AIDS [GPA, formerly the Special Programme on AIDS] is concerned with the wide variety of WHO-based efforts) by coordinating the diverse AIDS-related programs of UNICEF, the U.N. Development Programme, the U.N. Population Fund, UNESCO, and the World Bank under the supervision of WHO [WHO, EB93.R5, 1/21/94]. Developing countries and donor organizations have complained about inconsistencies and lack of harmonization among the existing programs; and it is pointed out that, given the unlikelihood of a vaccine or cure in the near future, sharing the load will help to ensure that these organizations can stay the course. (WHO reports progress toward a vaccine but says that success is still years away [U.N. press release H/2821, 8/10/93].) Further, it is noted, when the agencies involved coordinate their programs, they are even more likely to avoid complacency, respond to the disproportionate and growing effects of AIDS on women and other vulnerable populations, address problems of discrimination against victims, and actually relieve some of the burdens on overloaded health care systems [WHO, EB93/27, 12/23/93]. A discussion of the specifics of the joint program will take place at the summer 1994 session of ECOSOC. (UNICEF has proposed a similar program to deal with AIDS-related issues affecting children [U.N. press release ICEF/1790, 4/25/94].)

WHO has said that effective prevention methods—promotion and distribution of condoms, treatment of other sexually transmitted diseases (STDs), AIDS education in schools and the mass media, a safe blood supply, and needle-exchange programs—could halve new infections of HIV at a predicted cost of $1.5 billion–$2.9 billion (in 1990 U.S. dollars). This investment in future world health, says Dr. Michael H. Merson, who heads WHO's GPA, "is a fraction of the cost of Operation Desert Storm and would hardly buy one can of Coke for every person in the world," not to mention saving the world up to $90 billion in AIDS-related costs by the year 2000 [WHO press release, IXth International Conference on AIDS, Berlin, June 7–11, 1993]. Cost will be a factor in the success of an eventual **vaccine,** since 80 percent of new infections occur in developing countries, where an expensive serum would be of little use [U.N. press release H/2821, 8/10/93].

The theme of **World AIDS Day** (December 1) 1993—an annual observance established by UNESCO—was "Time to Act," aimed at alerting educators to their role in AIDS prevention and in ending discrimination against AIDS victims [UNESCO News OPI/NYO/93-12A]. "Aids and the Family" is the theme of choice for World AIDS Day 1994, coinciding with the International Year of the Family [press release WHO/38, 4/28/94].

WHO **prevention strategy** targets several populations. In the case of **prisons,** where the rate of HIV infection is higher than in the general population, the suggested preventive measures are education and the availability of condoms and clean needles. To the objections that may be raised to such provisions, WHO responds: "Individuals have the right to health care, including preventive care, whether they are incarcerated or not" [WHO press release, IXth International Conference on AIDS, Berlin, June 7–11, 1993].

WHO estimates that in 1994 over a million more **women** will be infected with the HIV virus, for a total of 13 million by the year 2000, and that "about one-third of **babies** born to HIV-infected mothers are themselves infected" [press release WHO/69, 9/7/93]. Among the recommendations for reducing the rate of infection in women are treatment for STDs and raising AIDS awareness among those being treated, "abolishing" social traditions that increase the likelihood of infection, designing AIDS-prevention programs for both men and women, and giving top priority to the development of a vaginal virucide or microbicide active against HIV [ibid.]. WHO reports that some spermicides now used for birth control have killed the HIV virus in test tubes, that there is as yet no evidence they will prevent HIV transmission, but that there is some optimism about developing an effective microbicide within two or three years [press release WHO/90, 11/16/93].

While the number of children infected with HIV is growing, the number of otherwise healthy children orphaned by the AIDS pandemic is growing too. International aid organizations are encouraging donations of food, clothing, money, and other forms of support for these **"AIDS orphans,"** and some charities are providing rent money to enable the youngsters to stay in their own or in group homes [*The Christian Science Monitor,* 3/16/94].

Child and Family Health

UNICEF and WHO, concerned with the general **health and well-being of children,** are collaborating on attaining ten main goals by 1995. These include raising the percentage of infants and children immunized against childhood killer diseases (and wiping out one of them: polio); diminishing the incidence of neonatal tetanus; virtually eliminating vitamin A deficiency and guinea-worm disease; increasing the use of oral rehydration therapy in controlling diarrhea; encouraging breast-feeding and the universal iodization of salt; and overseeing the ratification of the Convention on the Rights of the Child in every country [press release WHO/10, 1/31/94].

Working with research and development institutes, pharmaceutical companies, and development agencies, the Children's Vaccine Initiative (1991), an arm of the joint **Expanded Programme of Immunization (EPI),** has kept its eye on the prize: providing every newborn child on earth with a single oral immunization that offers protection against all major childhood diseases [*World Health 46th Year,* 3–4/93]. These vaccine-preventable diseases—**measles, diphtheria, pertussis (whooping cough), tetanus, polio, and tuberculosis**—currently claim the lives of 2.1 million children a year. So far, about 80 percent of children have been immunized against the six diseases—reaching the target set for 1990—but such factors as growing demand and quality control are standing in the way of attaining even higher rates of immunization [ibid.].

EPI is also working at a reduction of **neonatal tetanus,** largely through the immunization of pregnant women, training in hygienic delivery practices, and investigation into all cases to determine their cause [WHO, EB/93/10, 12/8/93]. WHO reports that since 1980 the number of infant deaths from neonatal tetanus in the first three weeks of life has been reduced by a half, bringing the worldwide figure to about 500,000 annually, and that the deaths of about 30,000 women have been prevented each year. This is due largely to WHO's efforts at immunizing women against tetanus before or during pregnancy [U.N. press release H/2833, 1/25/94].

Thanks in good measure to immunization efforts in countries with large populations, such as China and India, and the large numbers of people reached on national immunization days, **polio** cases too were down in 1993. The 7,898 cases registered (86 percent of them in the former Soviet Union) were down 50 percent from 1992. And WHO reports that the number of countries with no incidence of polio rose to 141 in 1993—the highest ever [U.N. press release H/2838, 4/11/94].

With the finding that over 30 percent of children under the age of five are malnourished and underweight, WHO continues to encourage **breast-feeding** and to urge member states to adopt the International Code of Marketing of Breast-milk Substitutes [resolution WHA47.5, 5/9/94]. WHO and UNICEF also remained committed to their 1992 **Baby-Friendly Hospital Initiative,** which aims at producing an environment in which breast-feeding is the norm. A *Baby-Friendly Hospital Newsletter* is issued monthly.

WHO is focusing on still other malnutrition-related problems, including **vitamin A deficiency,** which causes blindness and death; **iodine deficiency,** which can cause brain damage in infants and young children; and **iron deficiency** (anemia) in pregnant women, which leads to low birth weight and iron deficiency in babies, slowing their cognitive development and sometimes causing death [press release WHO/2, 1/18/94].

When it comes to family health in general, arguably one of the most important developments is the decision of the Clinton administration to increase the U.S. contribution to the U.N. Population Fund after many lean years, and to resume U.S. donations to the International Planned Parenthood Federation after ten years (making it the IPPF's second largest donor after Japan) [*The Christian Science Monitor*, 11/24/93]. (See Chapter IV: Global Resource Management, Population.)

WHO recently approved the use of **monthly contraceptive injections,** two of which—Cyclofem and Mesigyna—were developed by the organization's Special Programme of Research and Development and are said to have almost 100 percent effectiveness [press release WHO/43, 6/4/93]. Further, in what is described as "a 14-nation study organized by the World Health Organization," the "abortion pill," **RU-486,** will be tested as a contraceptive. One of the trials reportedly will take place in San Francisco [*The New York Times*, 5/4/94].

WHO has come out once more against such **traditional practices** as female genital mutilation, early marriage, and early child bearing, calling these detrimental to the social and physical health of women and children. The 47th World Health Assembly has urged a social and medical assessment of the actual health effects of such practices as well as the establishment of national policies to abolish them, and it recommends working with NGOs on these issues [resolution WHA47.10, 5/10/94].

The 47th WHA, held at the midpoint of the U.N.'s Year of the Family, emphasized the importance of the family—and especially women and children—in promoting health for all. It went on to urge respect for human rights, equality of care, and community participation in all programs dealing with maternal and child health [resolution WHA47.9, 5/10/94].

Environment

The 47th WHA urged that development planners give far higher priority to health and environmental issues than they have in the past—and, indeed, that such issues be fully integrated into development plans [press release WHA/16, 5/12/94]. To this end, the World Health Assembly urges governments to commit themselves politically and otherwise to fulfilling the goals set forth in **Agenda 21,** the Programme of Action for Sustainable Development they agreed to at the UNCED Conference of 1992 [see *Report of the United Nations Conference on Environment and Development*, DPI/1344, 3/93].

The effects of the 1986 **Chernobyl** accident on environment and health continue to be felt eight years later. Among the health problems observed—and affecting children most acutely—are an increased incidence of thyroid cancer, changes in blood chemistry, and loss of memory and of energy [UNICEF, *First Call for Children*, 7–9/93]. A "Chernobyl Children's Forum" co-sponsored by UNESCO and held in Chambery, France, in April 1994, assessed the ongoing effects of the nuclear accident and will be presenting its recommendations to WHO [UNESCOPresse, 3/25/94]. The U.N. General Assembly continued its support of further studies of the environmental, socioeconomic, psychological, and health effects of Chernobyl and of action to minimize those effects [A/Res/48/206].

The good news on **World Health Day** (April 7) 1994, with its theme "Oral Health for a Healthy Life," was that people in the developed world have fewer cavities and are less likely to suffer from oral diseases than in the past. The situation is deteriorating, however, in many developing countries, said WHO Director-General Hiroshi Nakajima, who called for prevention programs emphasizing traditional methods of oral hygiene, such as the use of chewsticks. Various modern techniques were also suggested, among them the fluoridation of water and salt and the use of plastic sealants on back teeth, especially children's. The oral health needs of the elderly were noted as well [*World Health*, 47th Year, No. 1, 1–2/94].

4. Drug Abuse, Production, and Trafficking
By Lecia Renee Smith

Drug cultivation, trafficking, and sales are a $500-billion-a-year industry with global connections and global repercussions. Pitted against them at a global level are the **U.N. International Drug Control Programme (UNDCP)**, the umbrella agency for U.N. drug control activities, with a budget of $187 million for the biennium 1994–95 [nar/inf. lett./1994/1], and a **System-Wide Action Plan on Drug Abuse Control** adopted by the General Assembly in December 1992. This action plan is intended to streamline and intensify the cooperation between UNDCP and the **International Narcotics Control Board** (INCB, the body of experts that monitors the legal production of drugs and their movement from source to consumer) and the **Commission on Narcotics Drugs** (CND, the main policy-making organ for international drug control). As the **Decade against Drug Abuse, 1991–2000**, neared its midpoint, the 48th General Assembly urged these agencies to continue acting "collectively and simultaneously in the fight against all aspects of drug abuse and illicit trade" [A/Res/48/286].

In the end, member states are the ones responsible for translating policies into action. And when member states work together the results can be spectacular: A U.S./Colombia task force was responsible for tracking, and cornering, the head of Colombia's notorious Medellín cocaine cartel on December 2, 1993. The **death of Pablo Escobar Gaviria** brought to an end an "era of terror" by the organization that at one point supplied some 80 percent of the cocaine found in the United States [*The New York Times*, 12/17/93]. Yet, as one cartel slips from view, another may take its place—in Colombia's case, the Cali cartel. The U.S. Department of State's *International Narcotics Control Strategy Report* of April 1994 insists that "the hunt for Escobar demonstrates the value of international cooperation, persistence, and tenacity in destroying the myth of an invincible drug trade." At the same time, such missions take resources away from other important activities of the drug-enforcement agencies [*The New York Times*, 12/17/93].

One reason for the longevity of the drug trade is the Janus-like relationship between the drug cartels and their home countries. Although the cartels are responsible for an increase in violence, political unrest, and drug abuse, they often are also a source of employment, community services, and security. The once small town of Cali, Colombia, now boasts a building program as ambitious as the one in Colombia's capital of Bogatá. In Myanmar, with the world's largest harvest of opium, the "Pablo Escobar of Southeast Asia" transformed his jungle hideout into a bustling town with streetlights, schools, a modern hospital, hotels, discos, and public parks [*Far Eastern Economic Review*, 1/20/94].

During its **Special Session on Drugs in 1990,** the General Assembly initiated a **Global Programme of Action** that focused on promoting alternative development with the hope of reducing the economic reliance on the illicit cultivation and refinement of cannabis, opium, and coca. The 48th General Assembly's resolution on strengthening international cooperation against drug abuse, production, and trafficking reiterated the importance of **alternative development** in an anti-drug strategy [A/Res/48/12]. But to date, even the most promising development scheme has failed to come up with a lucrative enough substitute export commodity for the South American cocaine-producing countries and the opium-producing countries of the Golden Triangle [*The New York Times*, 11/21/93].

Failure to reduce the drug trade through such economic planning as well as through law-enforcement has led an increasing number of people to recommend **decriminalization of drugs** as a way of solving the global drug problem. Although the INCB continues to receive the support of member states for its "firm position against legalization of the non-medical use of drugs under international control" [Report of the International Narcotics Control Board for 1993, E/INCB/1993/1], such countries as Germany, the Netherlands, Great Britain, and Spain have decriminalized possession of small amounts of marijuana meant for personal consumption. In Colombia, President César Gaviria Trujillo firmly opposes any sign of tolerating drugs, while the leading left-wing candidate for the presidency, Antonio Navarro Wolff, as well as novelist Gabriel García Márquez and Prosecutor General Gustavo de Greiff, support decriminalization. The majority of Colombia's population appears to agree with President Gaviria that, in the words of the Secretary-General of Interpol, drug legalization would be a "desperate remedy" and very costly to society [U.N. press release SOC/NAR/661, 2/14/94].

(Giorgio Giacomelli, Executive Director of UNDCP, speaks of increasing difficulties in maintaining the distinction between licit and illicit drugs when tobacco and alcohol—both licit—"might represent greater threats to health than the abuse of some substances presently under international control" [U.N. press release SOC/NAR/660, 4/14/94]. Others go further, urging that tobacco and alcohol be included in demand-reduction programs.)

The 37th session of the CND, which met in Vienna in April 1994, decided to set up an ad hoc expert group to monitor the "strengths and weaknesses" of the present global drug control strategy as well as to inaugurate a "simplified draft questionnaire" to make it easier for nations to supply statistics on drug-related matters [U.N. press release SOC/NAR/666, 4/18/94]. The Commission also addressed such issues as the growing role and violence of criminal drug organizations, money laundering, and interdicting precursor and the other essential chemicals for producing narcotics.

Drug cartels and related organizations feed on political instability and disorganized or weak law-enforcement. To strengthen the latter and eventually root out these organizations, UNDCP provides technical advice through regional projects and scientific and technical assistance to national projects. It also provides laboratory equipment, conducts fact-finding missions, and sponsors numerous law-enforcement training and strategy programs around the world [A/48/329].

UNDCP has launched a prodigious number of **money laundering** seminars and lobbying efforts to raise national awareness of loopholes in banking regulations and has supplied legal assistance to over 50 countries that seek to close up such loopholes [ibid.]. Successfully tracking and preventing money laundering is essential to a drug-control strategy, since drug traffickers "seek out countries with weak central banks, restrictive bank secrecy practices and limited controls on foreign exchange" [INCB Report, E/INCB/1993/1]. Moreover, criminal drug organizations practice the most sophisticated forms of laundering and are therefore difficult to detect even in countries with tight banking regulations.

Countries suffering economic and political unrest are the "weakest link" in the international community's efforts to halt the drug trade, since the need for foreign capital often creates safe havens for money laundering and drug transit. The U.S. Department of State's *International Narcotics Control Strategy Report* of April 1994 highlights the importance of "national integrity expressed in political will" to resist corruption and defeat drug trafficking. The INCB's latest report advises member states to institutionalize and enforce administrative and regulatory mechanisms to combat the official corruption to which no society is immune [E/INCB/1993/1].

Another facet of the U.N.'s eighteen-month-old System-Wide Action Plan involves limiting the production and sales of **psychotropic substances,** such as methylenedioxymethamphetamine ("ecstasy") and phenylcycloherxylpiperidine (PCP), that are made from licit precursor chemicals. The Chemical Action Task Force, created in 1990 by the Group of Seven major industrialized countries and the Commission of the European Communities, was dismantled in 1993 and its duties assumed by the INCB and related U.N. bodies [ibid.]. These duties include assisting countries to develop laws that ensure the legitimate end use of these precursors and that provide for the interception of chemicals whose end use cannot be verified. The INCB was unable to assess the progress being made in this area in its last report, since only a few governments had provided the necessary data—one indication of the difficulty of monitoring these chemicals [ibid.].

The System-Wide Plan recognizes the interrelationship of drug demand and supply and the fact that it is more and more difficult to differentiate among drug-supplier, drug-consumer, and drug-trafficking countries. At the opening of the CND's 37th session, UNDCP Executive Director Giacomelli emphasized the need for a "balanced approach" to demand and supply reduction, which are "mutually reinforcing elements of a multidimensional strategy" [U.N. press release SOC/NAR/660, 2/14/94]. That approach entails considerable effort at **demand reduction** by governments and national NGOs, and the General Assembly urges member states to "place a higher priority on treatment, rehabilitation, information, and educational campaigns" [A/Res/48/12]. The **1994 World Forum on the Role of NGOs in Drug Demand Reduction,** to be held December 12–16 in Bangkok, will be the culmination of an effort to recognize the importance of—and incorporate NGOs into—this multidimensional strategy. UNDCP has sponsored regional conferences for NGOs to prepare for this event.

As of November 1993, 144 states were parties to the 1961 Single Convention on Narcotic Drugs, amended by the 1972 Protocol (12 more than in the previous year); 123 were parties to the 1971 Convention on Psychotropic Substances (up 18); and 89 to the 1988 Convention against Illicit Traffic in Narcotic Drugs and Psychotropic Substances (up 22). Africa, with 15 countries not yet party to any of these treaties, remains the weakest link in the international effort to halt drug abuse, production, and trafficking.

5. The Status of Women
By Clare M. Sievers

"The road to Beijing must be paved with vision and commitment," said Gertrude Mongella, Secretary-General of the **Fourth World Conference on Women,** addressing the 38th session of ECOSOC's **Commission on the Status of Women (CSW)** in March. As the September 1995 Beijing Women's Conference draws ever nearer, many U.N. bodies are doing the sort of roadwork Mongella called for. In the case of the CSW—the official preparatory body for the Conference—the work revolves around its responsibility for drafting the **"Platform for Action,"** the major document to be adopted at Beijing. The Platform, or plan, is intended to accelerate implementation of the **"Forward-Looking Strategies for the Advancement of Women to the Year 2000,"** adopted at the last U.N. conference on women, held in Nairobi in 1985. The 45-member CSW was founded in 1946 to monitor the status of women around the world and point out areas for immediate attention.

The CSW's 38th session considered the recommendations of an intersessional working group, which had convened in January 1994 to finalize the structure of the Platform. Its draft Platform flagged a number of "critical areas of concern" (access to power and decision-making; recognition of women's rights; poverty; economic participation; access to education, health, and employment; violence against women; and the effects of armed conflict), set strategic objectives in those areas, and recommended institutional arrangements to implement and monitor the Platform.

The CSW also reviewed a preliminary executive summary of the third **"World Survey on the Role of Women in Development,"** which looks at the gender dimension of poverty, productive employment, and participation in economic decision-making [E/CN.6/1994/13]. This "World Survey" will be presented in final form to the 49th General Assembly, and is intended as one of the principal references for the Beijing Conference. The CSW had before it too a report of the Secretary-General, **"Preparation for the Fourth World Conference:** Action for Equality, Development, and Peace," describing the preparatory activities of other U.N. bodies [E/CN.6/1994/9]. Another important official Conference document will be the **second edition of "The World's Women, 1970–1990: Trends and Statistics,"** which the Statistical Division of the Department for Economic and Social Information and Policy Analysis of the U.N. Secretariat is developing in collaboration with 14 U.N. agencies.

Supporting and assisting regional and national preparations for Beijing will be **UNDP,** which plans to devote the 1995 edition of its annual Human Development Report to the contributions of women to development; **UNIFEM,** the voluntary fund that "promotes the inclusion of women in the decision-making processes of mainstream development programs" [*Women: Challenges to the Year 2000*, DPI/1134, 12/91]; and the International Research and Training Institute for the Advancement of Women (**INSTRAW**).

Also on the CSW's agenda was the **monitoring of the implementation of the "Nairobi Forward-Looking Strategies."** Under this heading the CSW considered a variety of recommendations and a program of action to improve the situation of Palestinian women under Israeli occupation [U.N. press release WOM 734, 3/4/94], and it considered the implementation of an ECOSOC resolution urging that the concerns of women and children become a priority for those involved in South Africa's transition to a non-racist democracy. The same resolution had requested the development of specific programs to facilitate the participation of South African women in the transition [E/1993/13]. At the very end of its 11-day session, the CSW adopted a resolution declaring rape a heinous crime and encouraging the International Tribunal for the Prosecution of War Crimes in the former Yugoslavia to give priority consideration to such crimes [U.N. press release WOM/753, 3/22/94].

Once again, three **"priority themes"** served as the umbrella for the CSW's consideration of specific issues: **equality** (equal pay for work of equal value, based on a study conducted by the ILO, a leader on such issues), **development** (women in urban areas, with an emphasis on population, nutrition, and health factors), and **peace** (eradicating violence against women in society and in the family) [E/CN.6/1994/2, 3, 4]. The springboard for discussion on this last issue was a report by an expert group organized by the U.N. Division for the Advancement of Women in collaboration with the Center for Women's Global Leadership at Rutgers University [E/CN.6/1994/4]. The expert group took as its starting point the **Declaration on the Elimination of Violence against Women,** which the General Assembly adopted by consensus in December 1993 [A/Res/48/104], and went on to recommend specific actions to address the issue at the national and international levels.

In April 1994, in a vote conducted in the Economic and Social Council, the **United States lost the seat it has held on the CSW** for 46 years. When its current term expires at the end of 1994, the United States will be able to participate in CSW sessions only as an observer, lacking the right to vote or sponsor resolutions. According to the U.S. State Department, the United States will work to regain its seat in 1996 and, in the meantime, will take an active role in the Europe/North America preparatory meeting for the Beijing Conference as well as in the Conference itself [Interaction, *Monday Developments*, 4/9/94].

When the **Committee on the Elimination of Discrimination against Women (CEDAW)** met in New York in January 1994 for its 13th session, significant time was spent discussing ways to make its work more visible, including ways to provide critical input into such U.N. events as the International Conference on Population and Development (Cairo, September 1994), the World Summit for Social Development (Copenhagen, March 1995) the Beijing Conference, and the U.N.'s own 50th anniversary celebration (October 1995). CEDAW is composed of 23 experts (jurists, lawyers, teachers, diplomats, and experts on women's affairs), acting in their individual capacities rather than as representatives of governments, and serves as the monitoring body of the **Convention on the Elimination of Discrimination against Women (1979)**—"the single most authoritative legal instrument to have emerged from the U.N. Decade for Women (1976–85)" [U.N. press release WOM/733, 2/7/94]. Beijing Conference Secretary-General Mongella, appearing at the CEDAW session, recommended that a human rights unit be created within the U.N. Division for the Advancement of Women to link the work of the U.N. Centre for Human Rights and CEDAW [U.N. press release WOM/725, 2/1/94]. This, the experts agreed, would help to mainstream women's issues in the field of human rights [ibid.].

As the spring CSW session was about to consider the U.N. Secretary-General's progress report on efforts to improve the **status of women in the U.N. Secretariat** and curb sexual harassment there, *The New York Times* was reporting that a U.N.-appointed judge had "found in favor of" a U.N. staff member who accused her superior, a high-ranking official of the U.N. Development Programme, of sexual harassment [3/7/94, 3/8/94]. U.N. employees enjoy diplomatic immunity, and the U.N.'s internal justice system offers complainants the only recourse for staff grievances. That system does not require the Secretary-General to make public any aspect of the proceedings, and, in fact, Boutros Boutros-Ghali exercised that privilege in this case (the judge's report was eventually leaked to *The New York Times*).

Speakers at the U.N.'s celebration of **International Women's Day, March 8,** were the Secretary-General, President Mary Robinson of Ireland, U.S. Permanent Representative to the U.N. Madeleine Albright, and Gertrude Mongella, and their theme was "Women in Power." Ambassador Albright complimented the Secretary-General on his "goal of 50 percent representative in policy level jobs by the time of the U.N.'s 50th anniversary" (a goal he had articulated to the Fifth Committee of the General Assembly in 1992). She pointed out that to date, however, "only three women have headed one of the 31 top U.N. agencies, only 14 percent of upper level jobs within the U.N. Secretariat are held by women and only 31 percent of all professional jobs" [International Documents Review, 3/94].

6.   Other Social Issues

Children and Youth
By Jennifer E. Spiegel

The proliferation of civil conflicts in the post-Cold War era is challenging the U.N. family of humanitarian agencies as never before—and especially so when they must try to keep up with the needs of the Organization's most vulnerable constituents: mothers, infants, and children. This constituency's emergency *and* long-term interests are the concern of the U.N. Children's Fund, better known as UNICEF. The interests of older brothers and sisters—those in the 15–24 age bracket—are the concern of a tiny unit of ECOSOC's new Department of Policy Coordination and Sustainable Development. U.N. "youth" programs aim at generating understanding of those who are making the passage to adulthood, and at developing national responses to their problems.

UNICEF, headquartered in New York and supported by voluntary contributions, has traditionally sought, and aided in carrying out, permanent solutions to "silent emergencies": malnutrition, disease, and illiteracy. This it has done with campaigns and projects addressing not only the problem but also its causes: poverty, population expansion, and environmental degradation ("the PPE spiral," in a recent formulation). Cooperation with such agencies as WHO, FAO, and UNFPA is indispensable to this effort.

In the case of the myriad civil conflicts in which so many of UNICEF's young constituents are trapped today, temporary relief is all that any humanitarian agency can expect to supply; politics must supply the ultimate solutions. And daunting as it would be to carry out a dozen relief missions simultaneously under any conditions, the nature of today's civil conflicts adds to the difficulty of assisting civilian populations. UNICEF's hope to streamline the delivery of humanitarian aid by anticipating humanitarian emergencies rather than simply reacting to them led to the establishment of the **Office of Emergency Programmes** on January 1, 1993. A year later, the General Assembly agreed to a revamping of the structure of UNICEF, whose trimmed down (36-member) Executive Board will implement policy, determine the UNICEF agenda, monitor performance, and assign the use of emergency program funds [A/Res/48/162]. UNICEF's 1994 Annual Report provides evidence of new demands on its resources: In 1991 it spent $111 million in 50 countries; in 1992, $167 million in 54 countries; and in 1993, $223 million in 64 countries, of which $189 million was spent in ten countries with "the most serious emergencies": Afghanistan, Angola, Ethiopia, Iraq, Kenya, Liberia, Mozambique, Somalia, Sudan, and the former Yugoslavia.

Refugees and displaced persons—80 percent of whom are women and children [U.N. press release 1356-93550, 11/93]—now occupy a considerable portion of UNICEF's time and attention. Some of that time is used to publicize the effect of a particular crisis on the children—as, for example, the situation in and around the **former Yugoslavia,** where by January 1994 the refugee population had reached 4 million, 600,000 of them children, and where war had claimed the lives of about 15,000 infants and children [U.N. press release ICEF/1784, 1/31/94]. One such publicity/fund-raising effort is the publication of *I Dream of Peace: Images of War by Children of Former Yugoslavia,* containing the work of children from all of the localities affected. The book was offered in ten languages in the spring of 1994.

Among the other bodies active with young refugees in this region of Europe is the **U.N. High Commissioner for Refugees (UNHCR).** Its "Operation Reunite" (launched in cooperation with the International Committee of the Red Cross and Unaccompanied Children in Exile) will use CD-ROMs at ten computer stations in the former Yugoslavia and elsewhere in Europe to locate the parents of an estimated 40,000 to 60,000 "unaccompanied minors" scattered over 20 countries [U.N. press release REF/ 1068, 3/22/94].

UNICEF's Director of the Division of Public Affairs Richard Reid, appearing on the U.N.'s "World Chronicle" TV program, noted that UN-ICEF officials had spoken directly to members of the U.N. Security Council and the U.S. Congress about **the effect of sanctions on children.** Although acknowledging that political reasons sometimes "transcend our arguments," he stated: "We stand fast on the fact that sanctions are generally deadly for children. There isn't any way to fine tune them sufficiently to make sure that the undeserving of this punishment are not the ones mainly hit" [*World Chronicle,* No. 537, 1/14/94].

ECOSOC estimates that these "loud emergencies" that are making headlines now claim the lives of 500,000 children under the age of five each year [*The InterDependent,* Fall 1993]. The 48th General Assembly asked the U.N. Secretary-General to name an expert who, working in conjunction with UNICEF and the Centre for Human Rights (and enlisting the help of other U.N. bodies), will study the problem of promoting and protecting the rights of child "victims of especially difficult circumstances, including armed conflicts." It requested a report on the study by the 49th Session, and the Commission on Human Rights was "invited" to review the study at its next session [A/Res/48/157].

Yet the so-called silent emergencies generate far higher casualties over time, despite the dedicated efforts and well-documented successes of UN-ICEF and the U.N. bodies with which it cooperates. In sub-Saharan Africa, for example, there are 183 deaths per thousand live births (the corresponding figure for the whole industrialized world is 11 deaths per thousand live births). Nor are the grim statistics confined to the developing world: UNICEF's new annual *The Progress of Nations* also finds that one in five children in the United States lives in poverty. (Cooperative efforts in child and maternal health are described in the Health section of the present chapter.)

The **Convention on the Rights of the Child of 1989,** drafted under the auspices of the Commission on Human Rights and beginning as a consensus resolution of the General Assembly, sets minimum standards relevant to the survival, health, and education of children and offers protections against the exploitation and abuse of children. At the U.N.-sponsored **World Summit on Children in 1990,** heads of state and other high-ranking representatives agreed to upgrade the priority they give to children's needs and to meet certain goals by the year 2000—a Plan of Action, to be adapted to domestic circumstances, for implementing the rights affirmed in the Convention. These goals were, as phrased most recently in UNICEF's *The State of the World's Children 1994:* "a one-third reduction in under-five mortality rates, the halving of child malnutrition, the achievement of 90% immunization coverage, the control of major childhood diseases, the eradication of polio, the halving of maternal mortality rates, a primary school education for at least 80% of children, the provision of safe water and sanitation for all communities, and the making available of family planning information and services to all who need them."

As of early 1994, 92 National Plans of Action had been finalized (the U.S. "plan," released at the end of the Bush administration, provides a broad overview of U.S. activities on behalf of children [*A Culture of Caring: America's Commitment to Children and Families,* 1992])—up from 75 a year before [*A Global Agenda: Issues Before the 48th General Assembly of the United Nations,* p. 256]. As of March 31, 1994, 157 states (the United States the only industrialized country not among them) had ratified the **Convention on the Rights of the Child**—up from 136 the year before [ibid., p. 259]. Implementation of the Convention by ratifying states is monitored by the ten independent experts who make up the **Committee on the Rights of the Child,** as called for by the Convention. The monitoring is based on reports required of each nation beginning two years after ratifying the treaty. "We try to assess whether political will is evident, whether budgets reflect commitment to children's needs, whether statements from a government and its leaders give the Convention priority and whether administrative structures have been formed to benefit children," explains Committee member Thomas Hammarberg of Sweden [U.N. Centre for Human Rights and UNICEF, "The Convention at Work," n.d.]. The formal observations made by the Committee following its review of country reports are considered among its most valuable contributions to the cause of children [U.N. press release HR/3935, 2/1/94].

The reports considered in the spring of 1994 spurred Committee discussion of subjects ranging from currency devaluation in francophone Africa to adoption policies in Belarus, from the situation of girl children around the globe to child labor policies in both the industrialized and industrializing world. The Committee will be participating in the World Summit for Social Development in 1995 and in the Fourth World Conference on Women in the same year [ibid.]. Since 1990 the **Commission on Human Rights** itself has been examining the "Sale of Children, Child Prostitution, and Child Pornography" via a Special Rapporteur on the subject [E/CN.6/1994/84]. The holder of that post, Vitit Muntarbhorn, notes that the developed world often serves as the center of demand, providing customers to the poor nations [U.N. press release HR/CN/548, 3/4/94].

UNICEF has estimated that the needs of children in the areas of nutrition, clean water, basic health care, and primary education could be met by an expenditure of $25 billion annually until the year 2000. Speaking on "World Chronicle," Public Affairs Director Reid had called this the "$25 billion bargain"—no more than the sum "Americans spend on cigarette advertisements in a single year" or "what West Europeans spend on wine in half a year" [*World Chronicle*, No. 537, 1/14/94]. Like other voluntary agencies, UNICEF has financial woes; and even its private sector activities have suffered a downturn—notably in the United States, where the revenue from UNICEF greeting cards, at a $25.8 million high in 1974, had fallen to less than a third of that in 1992 [*The New York Times*, 10/31/93]. UNICEF funds its annual **Maurice Pate Award,** honoring the first Executive Director, from the monies it received as the winner of the Nobel Peace Prize in 1965. The 1994 recipient was the All-China Women's Federation—"the largest nongovernmental organization in the world," according to its leaders—which works to improve the status of women and children in the People's Republic [U.N. press release ICEF/1786, 2/25/94].

Linking up with the Organization for African Unity, UNICEF designated June 16 as the **Day of the African Child** in 1990, memorializing the children who died during the Soweto uprising of 1976. The U.S. Committee for UNICEF went on to establish an **Africa Fund** and has been receiving earmarked donations for Somalia and Angola [U.S. Committee for UNICEF Information Kit, "Day of the African Child," 1993]. Sweden's Committee, for its part, has taken on the cause of **Brazilian street children,** two of whom, it is said, are likely to be killed each day [UNICEF, *First Call for Children*, 10–12/93]. The U.N. Secretariat itself is working with the Children's Television Network to introduce the United Nations to the young viewers of "Sesame Street" in 110 countries [U.N. press release ANV/186, 4/21/94]. The United Nations Association of the USA is collaborating on the production of the segments intended for a U.S. audience.

Youth

International Youth Year (IYY) 1985 spurred the drafting of a "world programme of action for youth towards the year 2000 and beyond," which is intended to serve as a framework for U.N. activities affecting the 15–24 age group. The aim of the projected **tenth anniversary commemoration of IYY,** as with the IYY itself, is to bring the special problems of youth to the attention of governments and various U.N. organs. It is hoped that they, in turn, will integrate "youth policy" into other issue areas. Amr Ghaleb, one of the four members of the New York-based Youth Policies and Programmes Unit of the new Department of Policy Coordination and Sustainable Development, notes that youth sometimes suffer from a negative press and that the IYY and follow-up will help to overcome negative stereotypes of youth [interview with *A Global Agenda: Issues/49*, 4/

27/94]. The Youth Unit's activities include report-writing; networking with nongovernmental organizations (NGOs); and opening channels of communication between and among youth groups, NGOs, and governmental and intergovernmental bodies. These activities were formerly carried out by the Centre for Social Development and Humanitarian Affairs of the U.N. Office in Vienna, which has been abolished under a restructuring initiative of U.N. Secretary-General Boutros Boutros-Ghali.

The International Year of the Family 1994 and the Fourth World Conference on Women (1995) have sought to involve youth and youth organizations in their preparations and programs.

Aging
By Mariana Panova

In presenting the Secretariat's draft **"Global Targets on Ageing for the Year 2001,"** the U.N. Secretary-General drew the world community's attention to the fact that the world population is aging dramatically, with a steady stream of about a million people a month crossing the threshold of age 60. The total number of those 60 and above grew from 25 million in 1950 to 400 million in 1982 and is projected to reach 600 million in 2001 and 1.2 billion in 2025, over 70 percent of whom will be living in what are today's developing countries. The number of "old old"—those **80 and above—**has grown even more dramatically. This is, in fact, **the fastest-growing population group in the world.** If projections hold, the number of those in the over-80 group will have increased by a factor of ten between 1950 and 2025, while the number of those 60 and above will have increased by a factor of only six and the entire population by little more than a factor of three. Expressed another way, in 2025 the world population will be three times greater than it was in 1950, the 60 + population will be six times greater, and the 80 + group will be ten times greater [A/47/339].

A greatly enlarged population of active older persons will constitute a resource for society, although caring for and protecting growing numbers of the very old will present a challenge. At the same time, the radical changes in population structure now foreseen will set in motion other changes that inevitably affect both the life of the individual and the patterns of society. This is already evident in developed regions, but new issues will arise in the areas of infrastructure, health, housing, family, education, social welfare, employment, and income security, requiring changes in attitudes and policies to resolve them [A/47/369].

The **International Plan of Action on Ageing,** adopted by the **World Assembly on Ageing** in 1982, recommended that ECOSOC's Commission for Social Development review the implementation of the Plan of Action at the national and international levels every four years. The **third**

review and appraisal, in December 1992 (the tenth anniversary of the World Assembly), presented an opportunity to assess global, national, and community-level progress in (and obstacles to) the implementation of the Plan of Action since its adoption. This review supplied evidence that the demographic aspects of aging continue to receive considerable attention from the international community, government authorities, and nongovernmental organizations (NGOs) but that translating this growing awareness of aging population into action-oriented policies and programs is encountering difficulty. Developing countries especially have been daunted by the task of establishing the infrastructure to support the Plan of Action's specific objectives. A significant number of countries have set up national coordinating mechanisms on aging and report the existence of several NGOs concerned with the elderly within their borders. These governments have established a national day of the elderly and have promulgated either the **U.N. Principles for Older Persons** [A/Res/46/91] or other instruments on the rights of the elderly.

However, in at least a third of the reporting countries, there is no identifiable national coordinating body for programs on aging; only half of the countries have elaborated a national Plan of Action or established a national research or training center to deal with issues and problems related to the elderly; and national directories of organizations concerned with aging and the aged are almost nonexistent. In each case, and for quite obvious reasons, it is the less-developed countries that are apt to lag behind [E/CN.5/1993/7]. To streamline the implementation of the International Plan of Action in its second decade, the third review and appraisal offered a set of recommendations that took the form of global and national targets on aging.

The **World Summit for Social Development,** to be held in Copenhagen in March 1995, is the first occasion on which heads of state and government will examine questions of unemployment and social exclusion—both of particular concern to today's marginalized groups, the elderly among them. This "Social Summit" will also give members of the world community a chance to assess their social programs and strategies, exchange information on their successes, and identify reasons for their failures.

The Summit Preparatory Committee, noting that many countries are currently reexamining social policies in light of the principle that the elderly constitute a valuable resource for society, set as an immediate object for governments the development of national policies and mechanisms that will help such people lead healthy and productive lives, live independently in their own communities, and make good use of the skills and abilities they have acquired over a lifetime. Also required, the Committee has determined, is the development of appropriate health and social support systems for the elderly as well as policies encouraging multigenerational families [A/Conf.171/PC/L.6, 4/15/94].

In its Proclamation on Ageing of October 1992, the General Assembly designated **1999 the International Year of Older Persons** [A/Res/47/5] and, at its 48th Session, the Assembly requested the Secretary-General to outline a program for the Year and submit it to the Commission for Social Development for transmittal to the 50th Session in 1995 [A/Res/48/98]. (According to a recent restructuring initiative of Secretary-General Boutros-Ghali, responsibility for programs on aging, previously held by the Centre for Social Development and Humanitarian Affairs in Vienna, has been placed in the hands of the new New York-based Division for Social Policy and Development of the equally new Department for Policy Coordination and Sustainable Development. The economic and social aspects of development have thus been united, bureaucratically at least, at U.N. Headquarters on the East River.)

As the international community is acknowledging the value and vulnerabilities of an aging population and attempting to adjust national policies and programs to reflect that reality, the **U.N. Trust Fund for Ageing** is helping to supply some of the financial resources for accomplishing this. Among the several strategies to facilitate the setting of national targets on aging discussed at the Fifth Inter-Agency Meeting on Ageing, held in Vienna in February 1993, was the inclusion of a component on aging in the country programming exercises undertaken by UNDP and UNFPA.

Disabled Persons
By Richard J. Star

The 48th General Assembly's approval of the **"Standard Rules on the Equalization of Opportunities for Persons with Disabilities"** is a watershed in the international effort on behalf of disabled persons. These "rules," or principles, begin by defining the concept of disability and go on to list the many areas—from the cultural to the economic—in which legislative action must be taken to ensure that disabled persons enjoy an equal opportunity to participate in (and contribute to) society [A/Res/48/96].

This action came a year after the conclusion of the U.N. **Decade of Disabled Persons (1983–92),** whose objective was to further the aims of the **World Programme of Action Concerning Disabled Persons.** The U.N. Secretary-General is being asked to report to the General Assembly on the progress of governments and U.N. agencies in implementing the program, and in his report to the 48th Session he hailed the integration of disability-related issues into the global policy-making agenda. Among the examples cited were declarations and resolutions of the June 1993 World Conference on Human Rights, the "core issues" of the 1995 World Summit for Social Development, and the preparations for the 1995 World Conference on Women. The report of the Human Rights Conference, which called discrimination based on disability a violation of human rights, had an important influence on subsequent conferences, the Secretary-General noted. That report had also urged governments to ensure that "persons with disabilities [are] guaranteed equal opportunity through the elimination of all socially determined barriers, . . . which exclude or restrict full participation in society" [A/Conf.157/24 (Part I)].

The Secretary-General went on to call to the attention of the General Assembly some improvements in interagency collaboration on the World Programme of Action, the participation of high-level officials in the Working Group of Ministers Responsible for the Status of Persons with Disabilities, and the Asian and Pacific Decade of Disabled Persons (1993–2002). And he noted too that the **Clearinghouse Data Base on Disability-Related Information (CLEAR)** was now on-line and handling requests from governments and others.

For the U.N. staff closest to these issues, the greatest progress to date is not so much any particular program but the change in the "conception of disability, from a charity approach to a focus on accessibility and equality . . . to achieve a society for all" [Disabled Persons Unit, typescript copy for *U.N. Yearbook 1993*]. Prior to May 1993, the focal point for issues related to disabled persons was located in the Centre for Social Development and Humanitarian Affairs, based in Vienna. Today, these are the concerns of the Disabled Persons Unit of the New York-based Division for Social Policy and Development located within the Department of Policy Coordination and Sustainable Development. The move has held up progress in some areas, reveal sources close to the Department—among them further development of the CLEAR database and the translation of disability-related terms ("impairment," "disability," "handicap," "disabled person") into the five other official U.N. languages. But even while moving shop, the Unit managed to participate in several missions and workshops in developing countries and to act as consultant to the government of South Africa in developing new disability legislation and policy [ibid.].

The infant **U.N. Voluntary Fund on Disability,** introduced in February 1993, just after the Decade's close, has lent support to 12 training or consulting projects in five countries and to seven international projects [ibid.].

The second observance of the **International Day of Disabled Persons** took place on the third day of December 1993—the anniversary of the adoption of the World Programme of Action. The 48th General Assembly appealed to all members of the world community to observe the day and to consider ways of linking their observance to forthcoming U.N. events [A/Res/48/97].

Shelter and the Homeless
By Richard J. Star

Meeting for its 14th biannual session, the **U.N. Commission on Human Settlements** issued resolutions on assistance to Cuba and to victims of apartheid, housing requirements for the Palestinian people, and the human right to adequate housing, among other matters [A/48/8]. Also on the agenda for the delegates who had gathered in Nairobi in April 1993 for the ten-day session was the **U.N. Conference on Human Settlements (Habitat II)**, an event to be held in Istanbul in June 1996—the 20th anniversary of Habitat I.

The Commission—the intergovernmental body responsible for "coordinating, evaluating, and monitoring" [A/Res/43/181] the **Global Strategy for Shelter to the Year 2000 (GSS)**—agreed on two central themes to guide the work of the 1996 conference: sustainable human settlements in an urbanizing world and adequate shelter for all [ibid.]. Habitat II will review the progress made by governments and U.N. agencies in implementing GSS, develop a new plan of action for a new century, and review current trends in housing and human settlements [A/Res/47/180]. The shelter strategy links housing to employment opportunities and community services, and places these in the context of larger planning issues, such as environmental protection and sustainable development. The Commission meets next in 1995, and is considering a link up with a meeting of the Conference Preparatory Committee.

The **U.N. Centre for Human Settlements (UNCHS, or Habitat)**, which carries out the Commission's policies, has been the "institutional focus for human settlements activities within the United Nations system" [A/Res/32/162, A/Res/48/176]. For many years Habitat had an Executive Director who served the Centre exclusively and held the high rank of Under-Secretary-General. When Arcot Ramachandran retired from the post in February 1993, U.N. Secretary-General Boutros-Ghali placed Habitat in the charge of the Environment Programme's Executive Director, Under-Secretary-General Elizabeth Dowdeswell. Some months later, Boutros-Ghali announced the appointment of an Assistant Secretary-General to handle the Centre's day-to-day affairs, reporting through Dowdeswell. Fears, especially among the developing countries, that Habitat's importance was being downgraded by this new arrangement were dismissed by the U.N.'s chief executive, who spoke of filling the post of Habitat Executive Director sometime in the future [U.N. press release SG/SM/5196, 1/13/94]. At the spring 1993 meeting of the Commission on Human Settlements, which took place shortly after Ramachandran's retirement, the governmental delegates reconfirmed UNCHS as the U.N.'s lead agency in implementing policy on human settlements, and the 48th General Assembly went on to endorse this view [A/Res/48/176; see discussion in Chapter VII, Finance and Administration, on the level of the Habitat Executive Director post].

Addressing the first substantive session of the Preparatory Committee (PrepCom) for Habitat II, which was held in Geneva in April 1994, the Secretary-General directed attention to the Conference's focus on urban problems and its aim of mobilizing the resources for making "the world's cities . . . sustainable, safe, healthy, humane and affordable" [press release HAB/70, 4/11/94]. By the year 2000, some 50 percent of the world's population will live in urban areas. The Secretary-General has dubbed Habitat II the "City Summit."

One of the most controversial items on the PrepCom agenda was the **Urban Indicators Programme** initiated by Habitat and co-sponsored by the World Bank. The aim is to develop a set of indicators by which member states will measure the performance of the urban policies they have already put in place and assess the need for adjustments. These indicators, say the sponsors, are intended to aid states in the preparation of "country reports" and establish the foundation for urban programs in the future [A/Conf.165/PC.1/INF.3]. The program appears to have the support of the developed world, while a number of developing countries question the program's usefulness, and some point out that they have neither the money nor the technical ability to gather such data for the Conference.

The Conference secretariat agreed to establish a discussion group to review the program and pass on its recommendations. Two more Habitat II PrepComs have been scheduled: April 24–May 5, 1995 (Nairobi) and early 1996 [press release HAB/87, 4/19/94].

World Habitat Day 1993—held, by tradition, on the first Monday in October—sought to highlight the connection between "Home and Shelter Development." Under-Secretary-General Dowdeswell, in a statement prepared for the occasion, noted that shelter policies generally "have failed to take into account women's needs, . . . and it is high time [to begin]" [UNCHS, "Message of the Under-Secretary-General," n.d.]. Habitat's **Women in Human Settlements Development Programme** has sought to incorporate gender issues into human settlement programs and promote women's participation in GSS—through research projects, special training sessions, and support networks [UNCHS, "Why Focus on Women? . . . ," n.d.]. World Habitat Day 1994, in solidarity with the International Year of the Family 1994, will visit "Home and the Family."

Crime
By Lecia Renee Smith

At regional preparatory meetings early in 1994, U.N. member states reached a consensus on recommendations to place before the **Ninth U.N. Crime Congress on the Prevention of Crime and the Treatment of**

Offenders, to be held March 20–24, 1995, at a location still to be confirmed. The goals of this quinquennial congress are to "promote international cooperation in the crime control field" and to formulate "international instruments, guidelines, and standards on various crime prevention and criminal justice issues" [U.N. press release SOC/CP/92, 1/13/94]. The themes that these preparatory meetings decided the congress should stress are:

- strengthening international cooperation and technical assistance;
- taking action against organized crime, by criminalizing some of its activities, prominently those affecting the environment;
- managing and improving police and criminal justice systems; and
- preventing urban and juvenile crime and related violence [U.N. press release SOC/CP/96, 2/10/94].

The persistence of **organized crime**—whose annual profits are said to exceed $1 trillion, an estimated $1 billion of which is "washed" through the world's financial markets every day—was of major concern at the preparatory meetings [U.N. press release SOC/CP/100, 3/1/94]. Given the funds at their command, members of criminal organizations can readily afford the most modern computer and other technical means to escape detection. Delegates at the preparatory sessions recommended the establishment of an international forum for exchanging information on organized crime, and the U.N. Interregional Crime and Justice Research Institute (UNICRI) noted that it is currently working on a **"crime control information bank** accessible through electronic search and retrieval programs" [U.N. press release SOC/CP/104, 3/8/94].

For a program such as UNICRI's to serve its purpose, less-developed countries—often looked upon by organized crime as "safe havens" for money laundering—must obtain the skills and technology to access data and follow up with it effectively. Cuba's representative at the Latin America and Caribbean Regional Preparatory Meeting suggested that developed countries increase their contributions to the **U.N. Crime Prevention and Criminal Justice Trust Fund** and that the monies be used for technical training to combat money laundering [U.N. press release SOC/CP/107, 3/10/94].

The recognition that organized crime groups are frequently involved in the transportation of hazardous waste, and that many use waste disposal companies as "fronts" for money laundering, led to an exploration of the whole notion of **"environmental crimes."** Even after the Rio Earth Summit, the body of international environmental law is still relatively underdeveloped, and the regional meetings grappled with the best way to handle cross-border crimes against the environment [U.N. press release SOC/CP/96, 2/10/94].

On the subject of improving **police and criminal justice systems,** these meetings stressed the need to protect the rights of convicted criminals, urging the Congress to endorse more humane methods of incarceration, and to promote equality for children, minorities, and women in the eyes of the justice system [U.N. press release SOC/CP/109, 3/22/94].

NGOs that deal with women's issues presented a united front at these meetings in calling for a **U.N. convention on violence against women** as a follow-up to the Declaration on the Elimination of Violence against Women adopted by the 48th Session of the General Assembly. Such a convention would be the first step toward universal recognition that aggression directed primarily against women, such as domestic violence, sexual abuse, and forced prostitution, is a crime [U.N. press release SOC/CP/103, 3/4/94].

Under the rubric of **juvenile crime** the preparatory sessions noted a disturbing increase in the crimes committed *by* juveniles as well as in the crimes committed *against* juveniles. The growing number of cases of collaboration between children and adult criminals present a threat to safety throughout the world, it was noted, because children are apt to be more "impulsive," and therefore erratic, than adults [*The New York Times*, 5/16/94]. At the same time, the children of the world are being victimized by the traffic in body parts, by forced prostitution, and by the international trade in stolen babies [U.N. press release SOC/CP/103, 3/4/94].

Delegates at the regional preparatory meetings also discussed **the role of film and television in perpetuating violence** and some noted with regret the increase of violence on international networks like CNN. It was also noted that the media can play a role in preventing crime—for example, by disseminating information on international criminals [U.N. press release SOC/CP/112, 3/25/94].

The 48th General Assembly requested once again that the Secretary-General upgrade to Division status the U.N. Crime Prevention and Criminal Justice Branch of the Secretariat, the primary policy-making body in this field [A/Res/47/91, A/Res/48/103].

International Year of the Family 1994
By Jennifer E. Spiegel

A United Nations that has dedicated a year to women, to the child, and to youth could be expected to dedicate a year to the family itself at a time when such matters as domestic violence, incest, AIDS orphans, and single-parenting are finding their way onto the national agendas of U.N. member governments. At the General Assembly's launching of the International Year of the Family (IYF) on December 7, 1993, Secretary-General Boutros Boutros-Ghali alluded to one of the conceptual difficulties this particular year had presented: the fear that promoting the family would come at the expense of hard-won individual human rights. Other fears—that "the Year might impose a standard definition of the family and promote a specific family model; and that the Year, by stressing the rights of families, might neglect their important responsibilities" [A/48/293]—were overcome by a fluid **definition of family** ("**the natural and fundamental group unit of society**") and by adopting as its **theme** "**Family: Resources and Responsibilities in a Changing World.**" That definition could embrace, in the words of one account, "the nuclear family (whether tied biologically or socially or developed 'in vitro'), the extended family (whether linked by kinship, tribe, or a polygamous relationship), and the 'reorganized family' (taking into account remarriage, 'community living,' and 'same-gender' households)" [*The InterDependent*, Winter 1993–94].

The very fluidity of this definition continues to cause problems in some quarters. **Pope John Paul II,** for example, issuing a 102-page "Letter to Families" that welcomed the Year, had harsh words for what he labeled anti-family initiatives, particularly those aimed at giving "juridical approval to homosexual practices" [Holy See press release No. 15/94, 3/10/94].

The **goals of the Year** are less controversial: promoting awareness of family issues in all sectors of society, fostering national and international policies that are family-friendly, encouraging collaboration among organizations in a variety of fields, and using already-available instruments that address individual rights—as, for example, the rights of women, of children, and of aging or disabled persons ["1994 International Year of the Family" pamphlet, 1991]. The hope is to spur international action, national policies, and grass-roots programs.

Particular attention is being paid to the problems of refugee families, families impacted by war, impoverished families, single-parent families, and the victims of domestic violence and abuse [A/48/293]. The Year is also said to provide an opportunity to consider a "family-centered approach to development" and, in the case of the industrialized world, an opportunity to consider the successes and failures of welfare policies [ibid.].

There is a **Secretariat for the Year,** located in Vienna (under the aegis of the Department for Policy Coordination and Sustainable Development in New York), and a **Coordinator, Henryk Sokalski,** who has been coordinating the IYF-related activities of such bodies as the Commission for Social Development, the Commission on the Status of Women, and the Committee on the Elimination of Discrimination against Women. A **Voluntary Fund for the Year** had raised some $1.7 million as of January 1994 [Secretariat for the IYF, *United Nations System and the IYF,* 1/94].

There were four regional preparatory meetings in spring and summer 1993, and late in the year a **World NGO Forum on Launching the International Year of the Family.** This gathering, held in Malta and attended by over 1,000 representatives of national and international NGOs based in some 100 countries, highlighted the diversity of issues the Year brings to the fore. New York First Lady Matilda Cuomo, the keynote speaker, spoke of the costs of individualism and of a generation of middle-class children who come home to an empty house and essentially raise themselves [U.N. press release SOC/4275, 12/2/93]. Jordan's Princess Sarvath El Hassan urged the removal of the negative connotation now attached to the word "homemaker" and, at the same time, recommended the participation of women in their country's political life, "encouraging a process of nurtured evolution rather than an engineered revolution" [SOC/4274, 12/1/93]. One UNICEF official presented the case for community responsibility in child-rearing, "a practice long established in Africa" [SOC/4275, 12/2/93].

Among the formal assignments undertaken by U.N. member states in instituting the Year of the Family was preparation of a **national action plan.** The world organization has since published an inventory of the plans already available [IYF Secretariat, *Inventory of National Action*], updating it in March 1994. The collection is intended to signify the international commitment to the Year and serve as a reminder of efforts yet to be made. The plans themselves vary in extent and sophistication. The **United States,** where the Department of Health and Human Services is leading the IYF observance, lists ongoing domestic programs that benefit particular family members (Head Start, for example) and such international initiatives as the Agency for International Development's Family and Development Program, but foresees **a preponderance of grass-roots efforts.** To spur those efforts, Donna Shalala, Secretary of Health and Human Services, and Madeleine Albright, U.S. Representative to the United Nations, sent a joint letter to the mayors of the 100 largest U.S. cities and a select group of governmental associations and NGOs explaining the Year's objectives and urging local action [letter dated 2/4/94].

Since the launching of the Year by the General Assembly, the United Nations has held several interagency meetings to develop "a system-wide coordinated approach" to implementing IYF goals [*United Nations System and the IYF,* 1/94], and the IYF Secretariat has initiated an occasional paper series. Monies in the Voluntary Fund are already "providing substantive and organizational backstopping" to a variety of IYF-designated projects [ibid.].

In 1992, the General Assembly established **May 15** as the **International Day of Families,** stating that U.N. efforts concerning the Year are "expressions of the determination of the peoples of the United Nations to promote social progress and better standards of life in larger freedom" [A/Res/47/237]. **North Americans for the International Year of the Family,** which is spearheading grass-roots IYF activities throughout the United States and Canada, has noted that the international calendar offers no lack of "days" on which to contemplate the needs of family and take concerted action to meet them: International Women's Day (May 8), World Home Economics Day (March 30), World Day for Overcoming Extreme Poverty (October 17), and International Children's Day (November 20) [*The IYF Networker,* Winter 1994].

VI
Legal Issues
By José E. Alvarez

For every step toward implementing the rule of law among nations we seem to take one step backward. The proliferation of Council and Assembly resolutions on peace and security issues, for example, inspires hope—until one considers how little these resolutions have accomplished in such places as Bosnia and Herzegovina, Haiti, and Rwanda; how many countries defy these resolutions, sometimes quite openly; and the fact that the number of serious attacks on U.N. humanitarian workers and peacekeepers has led the United Nations to contemplate a new law simply to protect its beleaguered personnel. Again, one sees progress being made toward institutionalizing a war crimes tribunal for the former Yugoslavia and creating another tribunal for drug trafficking, hijacking, and other cross-border crimes—until one considers that not a single person has stood trial for war crimes in Bosnia and that large theoretical and practical problems continue to impede the establishment of effective international jurisdiction over other types of crime. Similarly, although the United Nations has created a High Commissioner for Human Rights and the General Assembly continues to promulgate norms to protect the most vulnerable among us (from disabled persons to battered women), these norms have not been given effect at the national level. Indeed, one of the first tasks given the High Commissioner was to investigate and attempt to halt the massacres that were becoming pandemic in Rwanda. And, finally, at the same time the U.N. Commission on International Trade Law (UNCITRAL) is promulgating legal standards that are intended to facilitate international trade, there is still disagreement over whether states have an actual "right to trade" or a "right to development"; and North and South continue to divide over whether a unilaterally imposed economic blockade on another U.N. member state is legal. More generally, those who believe they have little say in making the rules—the developing states especially—distrust the rules themselves and the organization that makes them.

1. The International Law Commission

The International Law Commission (ILC), established by the General Assembly to codify and develop international law, met in Geneva for its 45th session, May 3–July 23, 1993. The ILC's 34 members had an unusually productive session. They agreed to a draft statute for an international criminal court; considered draft provisions on state responsibility, on international liability for injurious consequences arising out of acts not prohibited by international law, and on international watercourses; and even decided to add two new topics to their agenda.

Responding quickly to the General Assembly's 1992 request for the elaboration of a **draft statute for an international criminal court** [A/Res/ 47/33; see also *A Global Agenda/Issues Before the 48th General Assembly of the United Nations*, pp. 273–76], an ILC Working Group produced for discussion at Geneva a detailed report containing the requested draft statute and commentary [see Report of the International Law Commission, A/48/10, Annex (henceforth "draft statute")]. The draft's 37 articles, to be discussed in the Sixth Committee and in the General Assembly, build on the pragmatic recommendations of the Working Group's prior reports to the ILC and attempt to resolve fundamental issues relating to the tribunal: establishment and composition, jurisdiction, applicable law, conduct of investigation, prosecution and trial, appeals, states' responsibility to cooperate and assist, and sentencing [see *Issues/ 48*, pp. 274–75]. The speed with which these articles were produced owes a great deal to the ILC's novel working method in this case: The draft statute is the product of three separate subgroups established by the Working Group to expedite its work rather than of a glacial process involving successive reports by special rapporteurs. What follows is a summary of some of the draft statute's more controversial provisions—those likely to provoke extensive debate during the 49th Session of the Assembly, and for some time to come.

The criminal court draft owes a great deal to the statute establishing an **ad hoc international war crimes tribunal in the former Yugoslavia** that was drafted by the Secretary-General and approved by the Security Council in 1993 [S/Res/808 (2/22/93); see *Issues/48*, pp. 284–85]. But the draft statute has its own lengthy history, from the criticisms directed at the Nuremberg and Tokyo trials after World War II to the ILC's ongoing discussions of a Draft Code of Crimes against the Peace and Security of Mankind [see *Issues/48*, p. 279, *Issues/47*, pp. 290–94]. There are significant differences between the Yugoslav Tribunal, which is now operating [see section on Peace and Security below], and the proposed criminal court.

The ILC's draft statute envisions a permanent body established by treaty rather than by the Security Council, with jurisdiction far beyond that given the Yugoslav tribunal, whose jurisdiction is limited to war crimes committed after 1991. While such crucial issues as the precise relationship with the United Nations and the site of the international tribunal remain to be resolved [see Articles 2 and 3], the draft statute envisions three organs: (1) an 18-member court [Article 5] trying cases in chambers of five judges, without a jury [37]; (2) a registrar, elected by the judges, as principal administrative officer [12]; and (3) a "Procuracy," composed of a Prosecutor, Deputy Prosecutor, and staff as required, elected by the states that become parties to the statute, charged with the conduct of investigations and with bringing cases to trial [13]. The judges would be elected to nonrenewable 12-year terms by the states parties to the statute [7] and, like the prosecutors, would not serve full time but only as required [4]. Like the judges of the Yugoslav tribunal, they would be responsible for the rules of procedure and evidence [19 and 20].

The articles on **jurisdiction** represent evident compromises between those who advocate compulsory jurisdiction for certain types of crimes and those who would require state consent, as in the case of the International Court of Justice. Three types of jurisdiction are proposed, in fact, each with novel features, but the whole is unlikely to satisfy either camp. Article 22 proposes that the tribunal have jurisdiction over crimes defined as *international crimes* in specific treaties now in force, such as the Genocide Convention, relevant Geneva Conventions concerning the law of war (including Protocol I additional to the Geneva Conventions of 1949), terrorism conventions, and the International Convention on the Suppression and Punishment of the Crime of Apartheid. (It would exclude, however, conventions not yet in force, such as the International Convention against the Recruitment, Use, Financing and Training of Mercenaries.) Article 23 offers various options for resolving the sensitive question of how states would cede jurisdiction to the court in such cases. Among these is a procedure similar to the one found in Article 36 of the Statute of the International Court of Justice (ICJ), permitting states to "opt in" for specific cases or for a general category of cases, even after the alleged crime occurs; another would require states to "opt out" by declaration, either at the time they accept the court's jurisdiction or afterwards. Article 24 provides that when a state has the jurisdiction to try a suspect in its own courts, as provided in a relevant treaty, or has jurisdiction under the Genocide Convention, it may confer jurisdiction on the international tribunal. If, however, the suspect is present "in the state of his/her nationality" or is present in the state where the act was committed, the consent of that state is also required. This cautious approach to jurisdiction, grounded in the consent of states, reflects the hope that, over time, states will gain confidence in the court and that its caseload will grow.

Article 26 confers a second, and more controversial, type of jurisdiction: jurisdiction by "special consent" to crimes under *"general international law"* and for crimes governed by conventions that suppress certain acts and make them *crimes under national law*. The statute does not enumerate the "general" crimes but says that they involve "a norm of international law accepted and recognized by the international community of States as a whole as being of such a fundamental character that its violation attracts the criminal responsibility of individuals." The commentary suggests that aggression, genocide, and crimes against humanity not encompassed by existing treaties are likely candidates for jurisdiction in this category. Article 26 also indicates that among the "suppression" conventions intended to be covered by the statute is the U.N. Convention against Illicit Traffic in Narcotic Drugs and Psychotropic Substances.

The third type of jurisdiction envisaged by the draft statute [Article 25] would permit the Security Council, on its own, to initiate cases with respect to the crimes encompassed by Article 22 or by Article 26's "crimes under general international law." In response to complaints that the Security Council should not be empowered to indict specific individuals, the Commentary indicates that the Council "would not normally . . . refer a 'case' in the sense of a complaint against named invididuals, but would more usually refer to the Tribunal a situation of aggression, leaving it to the Tribunal's own Prosecutor to investigate and indict named individuals." Article 27 goes on to stipulate that "a person may not be charged with a crime of or directly related to an act of aggression under Articles 25 or 26 . . . unless the Security Council has first determined that the State concerned has committed the act of aggression which is the subject of the charge" [Commenntary].

Regarding **trial procedures** [Article 44], the draft statute (like the Yugoslav tribunal) affirms the fundamental rights of the accused set forth in Article 14 of the U.N. Covenant on Civil and Political Rights, but it does not resolve whether anyone can be tried in absentia. The Working Group resolved merely to invite comments on the subject [A/48/10, p. 306]. Nor does the draft statute clarify the meaning of the guarantee against double jeopardy (*non bis in idem*) [Article 45], which replicates the one in Article 10 of the Yugoslav tribunal [S/25274]. As matters stand, the proposed criminal court would be able to retry individuals who had been tried in domestic courts for "ordinary crimes" or whose trials "were not impartial or independent or were designed to shield the accused from international criminal responsibility or [whose] case was not diligently prosecuted" [Article 45]. Going a step further than the Yugoslav tribunal, the proposed court is authorized to protect witnesses and others by conducting proceedings in camera, by allowing the presentation of evidence by electronic means, and by banning evidence obtained in violation of internationally protected human rights [46 and 48]. While the draft statute anticipates and authorizes appeals (to be heard by a chamber of seven judges), it leaves unresolved whether *both* the prosecution and the accused have the right of appeal [55 and 56]. States' duties to cooperate and to transfer accused persons would depend on whether they have accepted the court's jurisdiction with respect to the particular offense [see 58 to 63]. As with the Yugoslav tribunal, sentences are limited to a term in prison; there is no death penalty [53].

Reaction to the draft statute, both within the ILC and in the Sixth Committee, varied from enthusiasm for both the concept and its resolution [see, e.g., comments by Norway in the Sixth Committee, representing the views of the Nordic countries, A/C.6/48/SR.17; and Belgium, representing the views of the European Community, A/C.6/48/SR.18] to cautious optimism that many difficult issues could yet be resolved [see, e.g., comments by the United States, A/C.6/48/SR.18] to considerable skepticism [see, e.g., comments by China in the Sixth Committee, A/C.6/48/SR.19]. These views are much like those expressed in prior years and partly mirror these states' attitudes toward the Yugoslav Tribunal. Supporters of the draft statute in the ILC and the Sixth Committee argue that such a court would contribute to the development of international criminal law, increase the likelihood of enforcement, provide a more effective deterrent, and enhance the standing of the international rule of law in general [see, e.g., Virginia Morris and M.-Christiane Bourloyannis-Vrailas, "The Work of the Sixth Committee at the 48th Session of the U.N. General Assembly," 88 *American Journal of International Law*, 4.94, p. 351; *Issues/48*, pp. 275–76; *Issues/47*, pp. 293–94].

Some of those who continue to question the project believe that anything short of a standing, permanent court created as a permanent organ of the United Nations (as opposed to the ad hoc procedure contemplated) would fail to live up to the requirements for objectivity and for impartial, consistent application of the law [see, e.g., A/48/10, p. 31]. Others question whether the substantive law (particularly the vague category of crimes under "general" international law) is sufficiently developed to provide fair notice in accord with the principle *nullum crimen sine lege* (conduct does not constitute a crime unless it has already been declared so by the law). Still others would prefer to rely on national courts, and yet another group is concerned that the court would undermine existing bilateral and multilateral approaches to international cooperation on criminal matters, including extradition and mutual legal assistance treaties [see, e.g., Morris and Bourloyannis-Vrailas, p. 351; and comments by Cameroon in the Sixth Committee, A/C.6/48/SR.22].

There were also strong differences of opinion with respect to the right of the Security Council to initiate criminal proceedings in the course of determining the existence of "aggression." Some saw this as an unexceptional application of the Council's responsibilities under the Charter, others considered this inconsistent with the goal of establishing an independent, judicial, non-politicized body [ibid.], and others sought to accord the General Assembly a similar right to initiate trials, particularly with respect to crimes involving serious violations of human rights or in instances in which the Council was blocked by a veto from taking action [see, e.g., comments by Sierra Leone in the Sixth Committee, A/C.6/48/SR.17; Niger, A/C/6/48/SR.20; and Morocco, A/C.6/48/SR.21].

The last two views reflect concerns about the legitimacy of the post-

Cold War Security Council and its recent determinations on issues relating to peace and security. Some independent observers also ask whether the draft statute in fact sets up a mechanism whereby a judicial body can cast doubt upon the determinations of the Security Council in the course of resolving a case against a particular individual (see the World Court's ruling in response to Libya's challenge to certain Council actions [*Issues/47*, pp. 325–27]). Despite the doubts and questions, the General Assembly requested that states submit written comments on it by February 15, 1994 [A/Res/48/31]—a move that is likely to give a boost to the tribunal's supporters and put pressure on those who continue to resist the idea [for an in-depth survey of the draft statute, see James Crawford, "The ILC's Statute for an International Criminal Tribunal," 88 *American Journal of International Law*, 1/94, p. 140].

The ILC has resumed work on the topic of **state responsibility,** formally adopting compromise texts on a variety of issues. One new article would require states guilty of an "international wrongful act having a continuing character" to "cease that conduct, without prejudice to the responsibility it has already incurred" [A/48/10, Article 6, p. 130], and says that injured states are due "full reparation in the form of restitution in kind, compensation, satisfaction and assurances and guarantees on non-repetition" [ibid., Articles 6 bis–10 bis; for text of these articles, see A/48/303]. The ILC's scholarly commentaries to these new articles, replete with citations to arbitral and other precedents, indicate, among other things, that these provisions are without prejudice to the consequences of crimes committed by states (dealt with separately under Article 19); supply examples of the types of actions of a "continuing character" that give rise to the duty to cease those actions (e.g., nonenactment or nonabrogation of internal legislation, wrongful detention of a diplomat, unjustified occupation of territory or unlawful blockade); explain why the ILC has opted for a purely "restitutive" concept of compensation (that is, intended to reestablish the situation that existed before the wrongful act was committed); illustrate different types of restitution remedies; and explain the ILC's decision to distinguish pecuniary compensation for "material" damages from "satisfaction" designed to cover non-material damage such as "moral injury."

In view of the long-standing North-South controversy about the level of compensation due upon expropriation of alien properties, it is scarcely a surprise that the ILC's new Article 8 tackles the subject cautiously. This article provides that injured states are entitled to obtain compensation for any damage "not made good by restitution in kind," adding that the compensation covers "any economically assessable damage sustained by the injured States, and may include interest, and *where appropriate,* loss of profits" [A/48/10, p. 168 (emphasis added)]. As suggested by the ensuing debate in the Sixth Committee, this compromise language might not satisfy either North or South. China, for example, challenged the wording of Article 8 as "inconsistent" with practice since World War II [A/

C.6/48/SR.24], while the United States "disagreed strongly" with the "where appropriate" qualification, since, in its view, "[w]hen compensation for the injured party required the payment of interest, lost profit or both, it must be paid" [A/C.6/48/SR.27].

Four new articles on **countermeasures**—a subject that received considerable attention in 1992–93 [see Issues/48, pp. 276–78]—were sent from the drafting committee to the plenary but were not formally adopted because they still lacked the necessary commentaries. Draft Article 14 identifies prohibited countermeasures, that is, actions that states cannot take even in response to the wrongful actions of other states, here defined as (1) use of force contrary to the U.N. Charter; (2) "extreme economic or political coercion designed against the territorial integrity or political independence of a state"; (3) violation of the rights of diplomatic or other such persons; and (4) measures otherwise contrary to a peremptory norm of international law (*jus cogens*) [Robert Rosenstock, "The 45th Session of the International Law Commission," 88 *American Journal of International Law*, 1/94, p. 136].

Much of the discussion during the ILC's 45th session and in the Sixth Committee focused not on those prohibitions, however, but on the Special Rapporteur's elaborate proposals to resolve disputes concerning all issues of state responsibility. The Rapporteur had recommended that disputes be addressed first through negotiation and then by conciliation, arbitration, and/or judicial settlement, culminating in a possible appeal to the International Court of Justice (as when it is alleged that the arbitrators have exceeded their powers) [A/48/10, pp. 81–85; see also Fifth Report on State Responsibility, A/CN.4/453 and Add.1]. Since the Rapporteur was proposing what amounted to binding dispute settlement for the "whole of international law as any alleged breach gives rise to a claim of responsibility," many ILC members and member state representatives on the Sixth Committee criticized the proposal as unrealistic, impractical, and inconsistent with existing rules providing for the free choice of means by which to settle disputes [Rosenstock, *American Journal of International Law*, 1/94, pp. 136–37; A/48/10, pp. 85–113; and see, e.g., comments by France in the Sixth Committee, A/C.6/48/SR.23; compare, however, comments by Slovenia in the Sixth Committee praising these provisions as "realistic," A/C.6/48/SR.24, and the Special Rapporteur's strenuous defense of his proposal, A/48/10, pp. 84–85].

Also receiving some attention in the Sixth Committee was the ILC's Article 19 of its draft on state responsibility, which indicates that states, and not merely individuals, can commit international crimes. That provision has been controversial since it was first proposed in 1976, and the Sixth Committee's discussion was prompted by the Special Rapporteur's latest report on the subject, which addressed, among other things, the role of the Security Council in determining international delinquencies [A/48/10, pp. 113–28]. Among the continuing objections is the novelty of the idea, since there is a dearth of state practice on point. And there are those who deny that "criminal responsibility" should apply to an abstraction, that is, to a "state" [see, e.g., Rosenstock, p. 137].

With respect to the continually troubled third topic on its agenda—**international liability for injurious consequences arising out of acts not prohibited by international law**—the ILC adhered to its decision, taken in 1992, to focus initially on preventive measures in respect to activities carrying a substantial risk of transboundary harm and postponing its consideration of remedial measures once harm occurs [see *Issues/48*, pp. 278–79]. That decision remains controversial: Some states question whether these issues can be separated; others maintain that remedial measures demand equal attention [see, e.g., comments by the representatives of Sweden (on behalf of the Nordic countries) and Australia, A/C.6/48/SR.26]. Nonetheless, at its 45th session the ILC discussed the Special Rapporteur's ninth report, which dealt exclusively with preventive measures, and the drafting committee adopted the first five draft articles on this issue.

Discussion of these articles, which address the meanings of "risk," "prior authorization," "risk assessment," and "prior authorization," as well as discussion of an additional 11 articles proposed by the Rapporteur, led to more general, familiar debates that went to the viability of this topic as a subject for regulatory attention. Some member states continue to question the scope of the topic and its relationship to state responsibility [ibid.; see also, A/48/10, pp. 47–51], while some developing countries criticize as unduly onerous such proposed obligations as the requirement to undertake a transboundary impact assessment or to carry out consultations with potentially affected states [A/48/10, p. 56; see, e.g., comments by the representatives of Bahrain and China in the Sixth Committee, A/C.6/48/SR.25]. Moreover, even some developed countries, such as Japan, continue to question the need for "excessive" obligations as well as the overall coherency of the ILC's efforts on the topic to date. (They have suggested, for example, that state activities be distinguished by the magnitude of harm caused or the degree of risk posed [A/C.6/48/SR.25].) Some comments in the Sixth Committee were also directed at the generality and ambiguous nature of the proposed articles to date. China, for example, suggested that if preventive measures were to apply to "hazardous" activities, these needed to be clearly identified [ibid.]. The United States, for its part, urged the ILC to concentrate its efforts on "general" principles relating to actual harm incurred as a result of ultrahazardous activity, and argued against detailed regulation through a legally binding framework convention [A/C.6/48/SR.27].

The ILC has come much further along with respect to another long-standing agenda topic—**nonnavigational uses of international watercourses**—having nearly completed its second reading of Articles 1 to 10. These were not formally adopted, however, due to lack of revised commentaries, and there is still only tentative agreement on some of these articles. The ILC opened the topic with a discussion of whether the Commission ought to be aiming for a framework convention on the subject or merely model rules; and the Rapporteur did not express a preference for either option, simply noting that the utility of a convention would be measured by the extent of ratification while the acceptance of model rules would be evident if these were endorsed by the General Assembly [A/48/ 10, p. 218]. Both options garnered support, but most of the Commission members who commented indicated a preference for a framework convention, arguing that this had been the premise under which all work on the subject had been undertaken. Some indicated that the question was premature [ibid., pp. 219-20], and at least one member believed that the ILC should aim for a more general convention specifying the rights and duties of watercourse states [p. 220].

The question of whether to include dispute-settlement provisions within any eventual instrument was raised but not resolved [pp. 220-22]. Among the substantive issues also discussed but not resolved was the potential for conflict between Article 7 (which obliges watercourse states not to cause appreciable harm to other watercourse states) and the principle of "optimal utilization" (which affirms the right of each riparian state to reasonable and equitable use) [see Rosenstock, *American Journal of International Law*, 1/ 94, p. 139; A/48/10, pp. 234-36].

Turning to its future plan of work, the ILC decided that it would continue to address all topics on its current agenda, and specifically to (1) endeavor to complete a draft of a statute of an international criminal court in 1994; (2) complete, in 1994, the second reading of the draft articles on international watercourses; and (3) complete, by 1996, a second reading of the draft articles on the **Code of Crimes Against the Peace and Security of Mankind.**

Pursuant to a recommendation of a working group established to consider new topics, the ILC approved two of them for future work: **"state succession and its impact on the nationality of natural and legal persons"** and **"the law and practice relating to reservations to treaties"** [A/48/10, pp. 244-47]. It also endorsed a working group recommendation that the Special Rapporteur on international watercourses consider the possibility of extending that topic to include "confined underground waters" [ibid., p. 247]. The 48th General Assembly endorsed the ILC's program [A/ Res/48/31].

As of the 48th Session, the Assembly had yet to decide whether to convene an international conference to finalize a multilateral convention on **Jurisdictional Immunities of States and Their Property.** Draft articles for such a convention, adopted by the ILC in 1991, have been under study by a working group established by the General Assembly [see *Issues/ 48*, pp. 280-81]. During the 48th Assembly this Working Group focused primarily on long-pending issues, namely, the definitions of "state" and "state entities" that would be subject to jurisdictional immunities, the exceptions for "commercial transactions" and "contracts of employ-ment," and, finally, the question of immunity for measures of constraint in connection with proceedings before a court [ibid.]. There was no consen-sus with respect to proposed compromises on these subjects, and some members of the working group raised new questions, including whether the articles were to be given effect retroactively, whether provision should be made for aircraft and space objects, and whether the articles should be accompanied by a dispute-settlement mechanism [see Report of the Working Group, A/C.6/48/L.4].

Given these disagreements, some states maintained that it was still too early to set a date for a conference on the subject, lest such a confer-ence end in failure or in a treaty that never enters into force [see, e.g., comments by the French representative at the Sixth Committee, A/C.6/48/SR.29]. The Assembly, on the recommendation of the Sixth Committee, agreed to week-long consulta-tions in the Sixth Committee during the 49th Session of the Assembly, with the aim of determining whether there is sufficient agreement on the substance of the articles to proceed with the convening of a conference [A/Dec/48/413].

2. Peace and Security

The revitalization of the post-Cold War **Security Council** continues apace—at least in terms of the quantity of resolutions: nearly 100 between May 1993 and May 1994. Many of these resolutions bind all member gov-ernments to take or abstain from certain actions under Chapter VII or Article 25 of the U.N. Charter, while other decisions deal only implicitly with the legal obligations of states. What is becoming clear—at least to the Assembly, which is a keen observer of the Council's inadequacies—is that the Council's resolutions do not always, or even usually, have the desired effect. Indeed, in the past year, many of the states that were the targets of Security Council directives managed to disregard or otherwise avoid them, in breach of Charter obligations. Although the General As-sembly is in theory barred from considering peace and security issues that the Security Council is attempting to resolve, it has nonetheless taken up a good many of the items on the Council's agenda. The Council, despite its ability to sustain big-power unanimity in issuing resolutions and direc-tives, shows signs of becoming a paper tiger.

The clearest illustration of the Council's difficulties is presented by **the case of the former Yugoslavia,** and Resolution 824 of May 1993 offers a typical example of the kind of directives that tend to be ignored. That resolution, like many earlier and many since, condemned violations of humanitarian law in the region and demanded that the "taking of territory by force cease immediately" [for background, see *Issues/48*, pp. 283–84]. It reaffirmed the territorial integrity and political independence of a U.N. member—in this case the Republic of Bosnia and Herzegovina—and declared the city of Sarajevo and the towns of Tuzla, Žepa, Goražde, Bihać, and Srebrenica to be "safe areas," free from armed attack. And it demanded that all parties respect the rights of the U.N. Protection Force (UNPROFOR) and of the international humanitarian agencies to "free and unimpeded access" to all such safe areas. As subsequent newspaper headlines made abundantly clear, this resolution was generally ignored, and members were reluctant to commit more of the U.N.'s or NATO's resources to back up the demand for compliance [see also S/Res/836 (6/4/93), 838 (6/10/93), 844 (6/18/93), and 859 (8/24/93)].

Another resolution issued in the spring of 1993—this one calling on the **Democratic People's Republic of Korea** to comply with its obligations under the Treaty on the Non-Proliferation of Nuclear Weapons and commitments to the International Atomic Energy Agency (IAEA) [S/Res/825 (5/11/93)]—has little to show for itself a year later. More than two years have gone by in the case of its resolution on Libya [S/Res/731 (1/21/92)], which was asked to "cooperate fully in establishing responsibility for the terrorist acts . . . Pan American flight 103 and Union de transports aériens flight 772" (and has since become the target of equally unavailing Council sanctions) [see, e.g., S/Res/883 (11/11/83), and *Issues/47*, pp. 301–4]. Similarly ineffectual have been: Council and Organization of American States (OAS) demands, backed by sanctions, aimed at restoring to office Haiti's President Jean-Bertrand Aristide [see, e.g., S/Res/841, 861, 862, 867, 873, 875, and see *Issues/47*, p. 304]; Security Council efforts to achieve peace in **Angola** [see, e.g., S/Res/834, 851, 864, 890, 903]; and Council attempts to bring to justice those who launched armed attacks against U.N. personnel carrying out the U.N. operation in **Somalia** (UNOSOM II) [see, e.g., S/Res/837, 865, 885, 886, 897].

The Council continues to act inconsistently when it comes to enforcing Charter or customary international law obligations, as, for example, in respect to human rights. Thus, the Council did not respond to the Secretary-General's demand that it authorize a large peacekeeping operation to prevent further loss of life in **Rwanda** [see, e.g., *The New York Times*, 4/30/94; compare S/Res/846 (6/22/93), establishing UNOMUR, the U.N. Observer Mission Uganda-Rwanda) and S/Res/872 (10/5/93), establishing UNAMIR, the U.N. Assistance Mission for Rwanda)].

These and other ostensible failures tend to obscure the Council's achievements on behalf of restoring the rule of law, as through its electoral and other assistance to **Cambodia** [see, e.g., S/Res/826, 840, 880], its electoral assistance to still other countries [see, for example, S/Res/832 (5/27/93), El Salvador) and the "Other Legal Issues" section of the present chapter], and the Council's final demarcation of the territorial boundary between **Iraq and Kuwait** [S/Res/833 (5/27/93)].

The Council's failings may undermine the innumerable legal precedents it is setting—as when it established more direct **cooperative arrangements with regional organizations** (such as the OAS in connection with Haiti [S/Res/867 (9/23/93)], the CSCE and NATO in connection with Bosnia [S/Res/855 (8/9/93)], the Economic Community of West African States in connection with Liberia [S/Res/866 (9/22/93)], and the CSCE in connection with tensions in Azerbaijan [S/Res/874 (10/14/93)] and in the Republic of Georgia [S/Res/876 (10/19/93)]. The Council is also deploying its legal power to impose sanctions with greater sophistication, providing for unusually specific or targeted sanctions in some cases or adopting a gradualist approach in which different types of sanctions are imposed over time [see, e.g., S/Res/ 883 (11/11/93, tightening sanctions imposed on Libya and even containing an annex of newly prohibited items), S/Res/841 (6/16/93, imposing specific sanctions on Haiti), and S/Res/864 (9/15/93, imposing an arms embargo on Angola and threatening economic sanctions)].

International lawyers are only now beginning to notice another striking development: the Council's increasing propensity to **delegate authority,** including legal authority, to subbodies—whether sanctions committees, charged with the day-to-day oversight of various sanctions programs; international courts, such as the tribunal for the former Yugoslavia; Commissions of Inquiry, as in the case of crimes committed against U.N. personnel in Somalia [see, e.g., S/Res/885]; or even a Compensation Commission, such as the one created to deal with claims against Iraq resulting from the Gulf War. It is also becoming clear that these bodies, through their day-to-day activities and the decisions they make in carrying out their mandates, are contributing to the formation and interpretation of the Charter, to Council decisions, and even to general international law [for analysis of the legal precedents that these bodies have established to date or may yet establish, see, e.g., John R. Crook, "The United Nations Compensation Commission—A New Structure to Enforce State Responsibility," 87 *American Journal of International Law* (1/93), p. 144; Theodor Meron, "War Crimes in Yugoslavia and the Development of International Law," 88 *American Journal of International Law* (1/94), p. 78; and Michael P. Scharf and Joshua L. Dorosin, "Interpreting U.N. Sanctions: The Rulings and Role of the Yugoslav Sanctions Committee," 19 *Brooklyn Journal of International Law,* no. 3, p. 771]. These delegated organs of the Council are quietly creating institutional precedents in the peace and security area—without the direct application of the permanent members' veto.

Indeed, the Council's **Compensation Commission** is an unprecedented undertaking by the world community to adopt strategies from mass tort litigation in domestic courts to expedite the handling of millions of international claims. It is a novel dispute settlement forum that is neither a traditional arbitration tribunal nor a court of law but a unique melding of the two. To date 2,335,000 claims have been submitted by 78 governments on behalf of themselves, their citizens, and corporations for damages or harm arising from Iraq's invasion and occupation of Kuwait [see U.N. press release SG/SM/5197, 1/14/94]. (It remains to be seen, however, whether Council decisions that anticipate payment from Iraq's oil export earnings will actually produce the large sums of money required to pay these claims [for background, see *Issues/47,* pp. 298–300].

Further, for all of the Council's obvious failures regarding the former Yugoslavia, international lawyers may yet consider one of the Council's foremost achievements the establishment in May 1993 of an international criminal court to prosecute persons accused of committing war crimes there. The **ad hoc international war crimes tribunal for the former Yugoslavia,** established by the Security Council to prosecute "persons responsible for serious violations of international humanitarian law committed in the territory of the former Yugoslavia between 1 January 1991 and a date to be determined by the Security Council upon the restoration of peace" [S/Res/827 (5/25/93); see *Issues/48*, pp. 284–85], held its inaugural session on November 17, 1993 [U.N. press release SC/5751, 11/17/93], but to date no one suspected of carrying out the heinous crimes enumerated in the tribunal's statute has stood trial. It is charged that neither the United Nations nor certain important member states are enthusiastic about the tribunal's work and thus have refused to help with the gathering of evidence against suspects or to be more generous with financial support [see, e.g., Sadruddin Aga Khan, "War Crimes Without Punishment," *The New York Times,* 2/8/94; "U.S. Aide Assails Failure to Help Balkan Tribunal," *ibid.,* 1/16/94]. Further, the selection of judges dragged on for months, nominations for chief prosecutor deadlocked twice before agreement could be reached, and the individual eventually selected for the post resigned shortly thereafter.

On July 8 the Security Council approved the appointment of **Richard J. Goldstone of South Africa** to the chief prosecutor's post. Judge Goldstone, who headed an investigation into the sources of domestic violence in the period leading to the recent multiracial elections, will begin by "sift[ing] through thousands of pages of evidence" amassed by the Security Council's war crimes commission and by individual governments [*The New York Times,* 7/9/94]. His deputy, Graham T. Blewitt of Australia, had been serving as deputy prosecutor in the interim.

Despite its travails the tribunal has made measured progress since that inaugural session. Antonio Cassese of Italy was elected President of the tribunal; and on February 11, 1994, the judges released their long-awaited **Rules of Procedure and Evidence.** These rules—an experiment in the merging of common law and civil law prosecutorial methods—generally adhere to an adversarial procedure rather than to the inquisitorial one favored in continental Europe but display elements alien to both systems [see U.N. press release SC/5787, 2/15/94]: Defendants will be tried without a jury before a trial chamber of the full tribunal but will have a right to counsel, even in cases of indigence; presecutors will be able to question defendants only in the presence of counsel, and all interviews will be recorded or videotaped; trial chambers may order the pre-trial release of suspects in exceptional circumstances, but the defendant (and, in cases of the discovery of new evidence, the prosecutor), may appeal to an appeal chamber. Amicus briefs, from states, organizations, or persons, may be accepted at the discretion of the court; and a "victims and witnesses unit" under the authority of the registrar of the tribunal will be responsible for measures to protect these people and provide counseling and other support [International Tribunal (IT)/32, Rules of Procedure and Evidence, 2/11/94, 33 ILM 484 (1994)].

The tribunal's solicitude for victims, especially victims of rape and sexual assault, is clear in many other of its rules. Thus, although it is envisioned that all trial proceedings will be public, the press and public may be excluded from all or part (when it seems desirable) to protect the safety and security of witnesses and victims; still other methods are identified to the same end [rules 75 and 79]. The rules also provide that in cases of sexual assault there will be no need to corroborate the victim's testimony, that the prior sexual conduct of the victim will not be admitted in evidence, and that "consent shall not be allowed as a defence" [rule 96]. Evidently the judges decided that the usual definition of rape in domestic law—nonconsensual sexual intercourse—was inapplicable to the mass-rape charges. The judges also apparently rejected the possibility of trying individuals in absentia. Aware that concurrent national trials remain a possibility, the rules do anticipate requests to those courts to defer to the competence of the tribunal in some cases [rule 9; see discussion on Article 45 of the draft statute for the criminal court in the section on the ILC above].

The president of the tribunal has suggested that trials may commence by the end of 1994, but few states have passed the necessary implementing legislation to permit the transfer of individuals to The Hague (the seat of the tribunal) for an international trial; and most states question whether, with or without a peace settlement, the governments in control of the territory where the crimes were committed will cooperate with the tribunal. At the same time, many doubt that the Council will continue to press for trials if peace is achieved and trials of high-level government or military leaders of, for example, Serbia, are seen as a threat to that peace.

It has been suggested, however, that the very existence of the tribunal may lead governments outside the region to arrest those responsible for war crimes when such people come within their jurisdiction, say, as refugees, and the international tribunal itself could issue indictments that would at least restrict the ability of indicted individuals to travel outside the territory of the former Yugoslavia. (In February 1993 the Republic of Bosnia directed to be circulated as a U.N. document a list of 41 individuals it suspected of committing genocide [S/25205].)

Some international lawyers believe that the establishment of the tribunal and of the rules has already contributed to international criminal law and added to the legacy of the Nuremberg and Tokyo trials. For many, this is a genuine first: a really *international* criminal tribunal, not just a victors' court [see, e.g., *The New York Times*, 9/9/93].

Peace and security issues are also receiving unprecedented attention in the Assembly. The 48th Session, alike with the 47th, took a hard line, at least rhetorically, against **Serbia and Montenegro** and in defense of **the sovereignty and territorial integrity of Bosnia and Herzegovina,** once again affirming most of the relevant Security Council resolutions on point but going significantly beyond the Council in significant respects. The Assembly urged, as it had in 1992, that the Council exempt Bosnia and Herzegovina from the arms embargo imposed under Security Council Resolution 713 of 1991, condemning violations of human rights of the Bosnian people and of humanitarian law "committed by parties to the conflict, especially those committed as policy by Serbia and Montenegro and the Bosnian Serbs" [A/Res/48/88; vote: 109–0, with 57 abstentions; compare A/47/121 discussed in *Issues/48*, p. 289]. The Assembly cited in support of its stand the International Court of Justice's finding, in its order of September 13, 1993, in the Case Concerning Application of the Convention on the Prevention and Punishment of the Crime of Genocide (*Bosnia and Herzegovina v. Yugoslavia (Serbia and Montenegro)* [discussed in the section on the International Court of Justice, below]. And it had words of praise for the Council's establishment of the Yugoslav War Crimes Tribunal. Finally, the Assembly called upon the Security Council to ensure that proposals in the "Geneva peace package" conform to the Charter and other international law.

In this particular case the Assembly was interfering in a matter of peace and security that was clearly pending before the Council, and this may be questioned under Article 12(1) of the Charter. On the other hand, much of the resolution merely reaffirms what the Council itself has been saying and is directed at convincing members that they have a legal duty to comply with relevant Council decision. Further, the Assembly's putative interference with the Council's handling of the arms embargo or the peace process may well be justified by Articles 2 and 51 of the Charter; certainly, Assembly members could argue that Bosnian self-defense and its territorial integrity are nonderogable rights, part of *jus cogens,* which not even the Council can impair [compare Bosnian arguments to this effect before the ICJ, discussed in *Issues/47*, pp. 304–5, and the section on the ICJ below].

By separate resolution, the 48th General Assembly addressed the variety of legal issues raised by a number of individuals, regional organizations, and nongovernmental observers concerned about the **human rights situation in the former Yugoslavia** [A/Res/48/155]. After a recital of the many human rights and humanitarian law treaties contravened by certain practices alleged to be followed in that region, and after supplying considerable detail about these violations, the Assembly proceeded to condemn such practices "by all sides to the conflict" but added "that the leadership in territory under the control of Serbs in the Republics of Bosnia and Herzegovina and Croatia, the commanders of Serb paramilitary forces and political and military leaders in the Federal Republic of Yugoslavia (Serbia and Montenegro) bear primary responsibility for most of those violations" [ibid.]. This same resolution also focuses attention on the need for states and anyone else with information to present documentation of these violations to the Special Rapporteur charged with investigating human rights in the former Yugoslavia and as a priority to the Yugoslav War Crimes Tribunal so that responsible parties can be prosecuted [for other human rights resolutions targeting conditions in specific countries, see A/Res/48/142–47, 149–52, 154–55].

The Assembly's lengthy, complex resolution addressing the **question of peacekeeping operations in all their aspects,** adopted by consensus [A/Res/48/42], reflects concerns about the Council's attempts to implement many of the initiatives the Secretary-General outlined in his pathbreaking "An Agenda for Peace" [see *Issues/48*, pp. 281–83, 290–91]. This resolution puts the Assembly's imprimatur on recommendations made in various reports, including the Secretary-General's Report on the Work of the Organization [A/48/1, discussed in the next section], the report of the Special Committee on Peace-keeping Operations [A/48/173], and the report of the Joint Inspection Unit on Staffing of the United Nations Peace-keeping and Related Missions [A/48/421, Annex], which are intended to address concerns about the Organization's proliferating peace operations. While much of the resolution addresses operational improvements to peacekeeping operations and to the Organization's financing and administration [discussed elsewhere in this volume], it also reaffirms the important legal principle that members have a legal duty to finance peacekeeping in accordance with the collective responsibility of all members (Article 17[2] of the Charter).

The 48th Assembly's Resolution 42 also addresses an arguable gap in law (or at least an uncertainty) about **the extent to which U.N. peacekeepers are covered by existing rules on the conduct of war;** indeed, there is no specific treaty or other body of rules designed to protect U.N. personnel. The Assembly notes that the Sixth Committee is considering the creation of a treaty to safeguard the status and safety of U.N. personnel and, in the meantime, reminds states that the Charter assigns them responsibilities with respect to the U.N. personnel in their territory. In yet another resolution the Assembly established an ad hoc committee, with sessions scheduled from March through August 1994 and open to all members, to elaborate an **international convention dealing with the safety and security of U.N.-associated personnel** [A/Res/48/37]. A draft convention on this subject, proposed by New Zealand, would protect military, police, and civilian U.N. personnel as well as the staff of U.N. specialized agencies and of humanitarian groups working for the Organization, and it would commit states to "prosecute or extradite" individuals who carry out such actions as murder and kidnapping against protected persons [A/C.6/48/L.2; for justifications offered by New Zealand, see A/C.6/48/SR.13; see also draft convention on same subject submitted by Ukraine, A/C.6/48/L.3]. Attacks against peacekeepers in Bosnia and Somalia and threats to their safety elsewhere led to the Assembly's call for prompt action by member states "to deter and prosecute all those responsible for attacks and other acts of violence against all personnel of United Nations peace-keeping operations" [A/Res/ 48/42]. The Security Council dealt with similar issues in Resolution 865 [9/ 22/93] addressing attacks on U.N. peacekeepers in Somalia, S/26351 discussing law applicable to those guilty of such attacks, and Resolution 868 [9/29/93] on the need to secure the privileges and immunities of peacekeepers generally [see A/48/349 for the Secretary-General's report on the subject].

What the Assembly's resolutions on peacekeeping address only obliquely is another emerging problem arising from the allegation that peacekeepers themselves may violate human rights and must follow the rule of law as well as be protected by it [see, e.g., *The Christian Science Monitor*, 1/27/ 94]. One Assembly resolution requests that the Secretary-General include, as part of any status of forces agreements between the United Nations and host states, requirements that the U.N. forces "respect local laws and regulations" and the principles of the Charter; and it also asks the Secretary-General to include in agreements with troop-contributing states a "clause by which those states would ensure that the members of their contingents serving in United Nations peace-keeping operations are fully acquainted with the principles and rules of relevant international law, in particular international humanitarian law and the purposes and principles of the Charter" [A/Res/48/42; see also A/Res/48/43, calling upon the Secretary-General to strengthen the U.N. command and control capabilities]. It remains to be seen whether the domestic courts of host states can help to enforce such principles or whether the jurisdiction of the proposed international criminal court will have to be enlarged to accommodate a new need.

As in many years past, the "**question of Palestine**" was the focus of considerable Assembly attention, despite (or perhaps because of) ongoing peacemaking efforts between the PLO and Israel. The 48th Assembly adopted, over the dissent of a handful of members, including Israel and the United States, four resolutions on various aspects of a peaceful settlement in the Middle East [A/Res/48/158A-D]. While the Assembly "welcomed" the Declaration of Principles on Interim Self-Government Arrangements signed by Israel and the PLO, it outlined some controversial principles for inclusion in any "comprehensive peace" settlement, implying that these were required by consideration of international law. Among them were (1) the withdrawal of Israel from Palestinian territory occupied since 1967, including Jerusalem; (2) arrangements for the peace and security of all states in the region within secure and internationally recognized boundaries in accord with Resolution 181 (II) of 1947; (3) resolution of the problem of Palestinian refugees; (4) resolution of the problem of the "illegal" Israeli settlements; and (5) guaranteed access to all religious sites [A/Res/48/158D; vote: 92–5–51]. (A subsequent Assembly resolution praises the peace process and lends its support to bilateral negotiations [A/Res/48/58; vote: 155–3–1].)

Four more resolutions, unusually detailed, address concerns emerging from the **Report of the Special Committee to Investigate Israeli Practices Affecting the Human Rights of the Palestinian People and Other Arabs in the Occupied Territories** [A/Res/48/41A-D]. These legalistic resolutions, based on the Assembly's long-standing position that the Geneva Convention relative to the Protection of Civilian Persons in Time of War is applicable to all Occupied Territories, including Jerusalem, condemn Israel for violations of this convention "especially in the fields of collective punishment, closure of areas, annexation, establishment of settlements and mass deportation"; claim that all Israeli actions taken in violation of this convention and relevant Council resolutions are "illegal and have no validity"; demand that Israel facilitate the return of all deported Palestinians and put an end to Israeli settlements; call on Israel to respect all "fundamental freedoms of the Palestinian people, such as the freedom of education"; and condemn Israel for imposing its laws, jurisdiction, and administration on the Golan Heights, including its attempt to "forcibly . . . impose Israeli citizenship and Israeli identity cards on Syrian citizens" there, calling on other states not to recognize any of these legislative acts [A/Res/48/41C-D]. Israel was the sole dissenting vote on two of these resolutions; the United States joined a number of others in abstaining on two dealing with the applicability of the Geneva Conventions generally and with the Golan Heights. Sixty-five states abstained on the Assembly's demands that the Special Committee to Investigate Israeli Practices continue its work and that Israel be compelled to cooperate with it [A/Res/48/41; vote: 93–2]. (For related action in the Security Council, see Resolution 904 [3/18/94] condemning the massacre in the Mosque of Ibrahim in Hebron, calling on Israel to implement measures to prevent violence by Israeli settlers, and demanding other measures to protect Palestinians in the Occupied Territory. The United States abstained on two paragraphs dealing with the applicability of the Geneva Conventions to "occupied" territories, including Jerusalem [S/Res/904 (3/18/94].)

For the second year in a row the Assembly passed a controversial resolution, acting under a continuing agenda item, calling for **an end to the "economic, commercial and financial embargo imposed by the United States against Cuba."** This resolution condemns, as a violation of the Charter and of international law obligations concerning the "freedom of trade and navigation," the "unilateral application of economic and trade measures by one state against another for political purposes" [A/Res/48/16; vote: 88–4–57]. It also notes that since passage of its resolution of 1992 [A/Res/47/19], sanctions against Cuba have been not only strengthened but also extended, and it expresses concern about national laws "whose extraterritorial effects affect the sovereignty of other States and the legitimate interests of entities or persons under their jurisdiction." The Assembly passed a more general resolution to a similar effect. This one calls upon the international community to eliminate "the use by some developed countries of unilateral economic coercive measures against developing countries that are not authorized by the relevant organs of the United Nations or are inconsistent with the principles contained in the Charter of the United Nations, as a means of forcibly imposing the will of one State on another" [A/Res/48/168; vote: 116–32–16]. And the Assembly went on to ask the Secretary-General to monitor the imposition of such measures and produce a report for the 50th Session. The United States, not unexpectedly, voted against both resolutions relating to its Cuba embargo.

In a number of cases the 48th Assembly, usually following the Security Council's lead, continued its attempt to legitimize or delegitimize governments in different regions—without using its power under Articles 5 and 6 of the Charter to suspend or expel members. (The effect on the continuance of these regimes has yet to be determined.) As it has done since the 46th Session, the Assembly affirmed its support for the "constitutional President of **Haiti**, Jean-Bertrand Aristide," and condemned the delay in reinstating his government, expressing support for the many Security Council resolutions seeking the same goal [A/Res/48/47; see also A/Res/47/ 20; A/Res/46/7]. And as has been an annual occurrence since 1973, the Assembly reaffirmed the sovereignty of the Islamic Federal Republic of the Comoros over the island of **Mayotte,** urging France to act on the results of the referendum on the self-determination of the Comoro Archipelago conducted in 1974 [A/Res/48/56; vote: 91–2–36]. The French government continues to contest the interpretation of the results of that referendum; and France and Morocco supplied the 1993 resolution's two "no" votes (developed countries accounted for most of the abstentions) [for more on Mayotte, see *Issues/47*, p. 317].

Four other resolutions dealt with the transition to a "**united, democratic and non-racial South Africa,**" the Assembly expressing support for the April 1994 elections in that country, for the participation of U.N. observers during the implementation of the National Peace Accord, for the continuation of the Council's mandatory arms embargo and the monitoring of its effectiveness, and for the efforts, including legal assistance, of the United Nations Trust Fund for South Africa [A/Res/48/159A-D]. As South Africa continued its apparent transition to democracy, the Assembly abandoned its attempt to impose economic sanctions on that country, lifted its embargo on oil, and terminated the mandate of the Intergovernmental Group to Monitor the Supply and Shipping of Oil and Petroleum Products [A/Res/48/1 and A/Res/48/159C]. Elsewhere it condemned the military coup in **Burundi,** demanding the "immediate restoration of democracy and the constitutional regime" [A/Res/48/17].

The **right to self-determination** was the focus of a number of other resolutions, including one on **New Caledonia,** which urged French authorities to continue their efforts to promote political, economic, and social development on the island in the interest of progressing "towards an act of self-determination" and to "safeguard the rights" of all New Caledonians [A/Res/48/50]. With respect to **non-self-governing territories,** whose administering powers may be required to provide reports under Article 73(e) of the Charter, the Assembly affirmed the rights of local peoples to "determine freely their future political status" and called on all members to achieve the eradication of "colonialism" by the year 2000 [A/Res/48/51A; see A/Res/48/93, reaffirming self-determination as a "universal" right]. The Assembly considered individually the situations in American Samoa, Anguilla, Bermuda, the British Virgin Islands, the Cayman Islands, Guam, Montserrat, Tokelau, the Turks and Caicos Islands, and the U.S. Virgin Islands, and in each case called upon the administering power to undertake specific tasks (e.g., to assist the territory in increasing its agricultural output, in countering drug trafficking, in protecting against environmental degradation, or in restructuring the public schools). These resolutions, taken as a whole, suggest the international community's developing views concerning the contemporary duties owed by protecting powers "as a sacred trust" under customary international law or under Chapter XI of the U.N. Charter [A/Res/48/51B-X, by consensus; and see A/Res/48/46 (vote: 113–5–43), which, among other things, seeks cooperation from regional organizations, U.N. specialized agencies, the World Bank, and the IMF to provide "maximum" benefits to non-self-governing territories]. More controversial was another resolution condemning **"activities of foreign economic, financial and other interests"** that impede the exercise of self-determination for colonial, non-self-governing territories in the Caribbean, the Pacific, and other regions [A/Res/48/46; vote: 111–43–3]. This resolution proclaims that administering powers violate the Charter when they exploit the natural resources or "subordinate the rights and interests of those peoples to foreign economic and financial interests," and it calls on such powers to, among other things, "ensure that no discriminatory and unjust wage systems or working conditions prevail" in such territories. Alike with a resolution adopted by the 47th Session [A/Res/47/18], it conjures up the days of the Charter of Economic Rights and Duties of States and resurrects old North-South divisions on this issue [see Issues/48, p. 298].

Controversial too was the blanket resolution on the question of **self-determination and the speedy granting of independence to colonial countries and peoples**—one that, among other things, makes demands on France (with respect to Mayotte), Israel, and South Africa; condemns as "criminal" the use of mercenaries; and demands that all persons detained for struggling on behalf of their right of self-determination be immediately and unconditionally released [A/Res/48/94; vote: 101–26–36 (for the results of a similar effort, see Issues/47, p. 311)]. A related resolution urges ratification of the International Convention against the Recruitment, Use, Financing, and Training of Mercenaries and condemns states that violate it [A/Res/48/92; vote: 108–14–39].

As usual, the Assembly passed a series of resolutions relating to **arms control**. It called on the Conference on Disarmament to consider the best way to prohibit the development and manufacture of new types of weapons of mass destruction [A/Res/48/61], urged adherence to the U.N. standardized system for reporting military expenditures to advance transparency and the monitoring of such expenditures [A/Res/48/62], sought compliance with a number of arms control and disarmament conventions [A/Res/48/63, 65, 85], called for the conclusion of a multilateral and comprehensive test ban treaty for nuclear weapons [A/Res/48/70], and invited the establishment of nuclear-free zones in the Middle East [A/Res/48/71], in Africa [A/Res/48/86], and in South Asia [A/Res/48/72; see generally, *Issues/47*, p. 292, for prior consideration of these issues]. Over the dissenting vote of the Democratic People's Republic of Korea, the Assembly approved the report of the International Atomic Energy Agency, including its report on noncompliance with nonproliferation obligations by North Korea as well as by Iraq (Iraq abstained on this resolution, joined by Angola, China, Cuba, Ghana, Guinea, Mali, Senegal, and Vietnam).

More controversial, especially from the perspective of the United States, were Assembly moves favoring a far more ambitious agenda than at present to strengthen existing arms control regimes. Thus the Assembly: urged the Secretary-General to explore the development of "guidelines and principles" for U.N. verification of arms control agreements [A/Res/48/68; vote: 145–0–22]; sought to amend the Treaty Banning Nuclear Weapon Tests in the Atmosphere, in Outer Space and under Water to convert that agreement into a comprehensive test-ban treaty [A/Res/48/69; vote: 118–3 (Israel, the United Kingdom, and the United States), with 45 abstentions]; called upon states to attend a review conference for the Convention on Prohibitions or Restrictions on the Use of Certain Conventional Weapons Which May Be Deemed to Be Excessively Injurious or to Have Indiscriminate Effects and its Protocols to examine especially the regulation of anti-personnel land mines [A/Res/48/79, Georgia, the Russian Federation, and the United States abstaining]; urged early agreement to "assure non-nuclear-weapon States against the use of threat of use of nuclear weapons" [A/Res/48/73, the United States one of four abstainers]; and proclaimed that the Conference on Disarmament has the "primary" role in the negotiation of agreements to prevent an arms race in outer space and urged that the United States and the Russian Federation keep the Conference apprised of their bilateral negotiations on that issue [A/Res/48/74, the United States abstaining]. A number of other countries, but not the United States, had some qualms about the resolutions directed at encouraging enforcement action to end the illegal export of conventional weapons [A/Res/48/75H; 22 abstentions] or calling for regional and subregional conventional arms control [A/Res/48/75; 11 abstentions].

As in the past, the Assembly also welcomed the efforts of the Conference on Security and Cooperation in Europe (CSCE) and of the Secretary-General to withdraw "foreign military forces" [read: Russian] from Estonia and Latvia [A/Res/48/18].

The 47th Assembly had asked the Secretary-General to seek a report from the International Committee of the Red Cross on the protection of the environment in times of armed conflict, especially on the question of whether shortcomings in existing law call for new rules, perhaps a new treaty, on the subject [A/Res/47/37, see *Issues/48*, pp. 292–93], and the Sixth Committee and the 48th Assembly duly considered the issue. The Red Cross report came down essentially on the side of those states, the United States among them, that argue against any new attempt to codify rules on the subject, stressing that the result would be of dubious value and might even be counterproductive [see generally report at A/48/269 and the discussion in the Sixth Committee, A/C.6/48/SR.31-32]. The report summarizes the applicable international humanitarian law on the subject, including prohibitions on the destruction of civilian objects and relevant protections in Protocol I to the Geneva Conventions of 1949, including Articles 35(3) and 55 (which prohibit attacks agains the environment as such and the use of the environment as a means of warfare), and Articles 36 (regulating the use of new weapons), 52 (protecting civilian objects), 54 (protecting objects indispensable to the survival of civilians), 56 (protecting works and installations containing dangerous forces), and 57 (precautions to be taken in case of attack) [A/48/269]. The Red Cross, and ultimately the General Assembly, favored actions aimed at implementing existing law rather than at promulgating new standards. Thus, the Assembly endorsed the inclusion in military manuals of Red Cross-drafted guidelines for providing clear instructions to armed forces on protecting the environment, and asked states to comment on these guidelines by March 31, 1994 [A/Res/48/30].

3. Effectiveness of the Organization

The issue of the U.N.'s effectiveness—or, more accurately, many members' concerns about its *in*effectiveness, especially with respect to peace and security—was the subject of considerable discussion in both the Security Council and the Assembly during the 48th Session and will continue to spark discussion during the 49th. Protecting the U.N. peacekeepers and other mission personnel from violent attack, for example, is now a front-burner issue, whereas until recently the security of U.N. personnel was viewed as auxiliary to the issue of protecting diplomats and to the conventions related to such protection) [see also section on Peace and Security above]. Indeed, the personnel-security issue had a prominent place in Secretary-General Boutros Boutros-Ghali's second annual **Report on the Work of the Organization.**

The 1993 report on the Work of the Organization, lengthier than the first, provided a *tour d'horizon* of the U.N.'s myriad activities, though dealing only tangentially with legal issues other than human rights. Of particular interest to lawyers is the Secretary-General's theme, carried over from his first report, that the U.N.'s central, and interrelated, objectives are the promotion of peace, of development, and of democracy. The last, of these, he argues, requires efforts both within states and within the United Nations itself, since "democracy within States can be fully sustained over time only if it is linked to expanding democratization among States and at all levels of the international system" [A/48/1, par. 10; see also the Secretary-General's sppech on international law delivered in The Hague, 1/19/94, available in U.N. press release SG/SM 5202]. Of "crucial importance" to this process, the Secretary-General suggests, is reform of the Security Council membership, and he notes that relevant proposals "warranting serious study are now on the table."

Here, as in his first annual report, the Secretary-General provides concrete examples of the way in which the Organization has sought to promote peace—the first on his list of U.N. objectives—and specifically the efforts to implement Boutros-Ghali's own **"An Agenda for Peace."** He offers a summary of the expanding efforts to make Article 1(1) of the Charter effective through preventive diplomacy, humanitarian assistance, and the newly delineated forms of "peace-keeping," such as preventive deployments (in Macedonia), so-called "peace-keeping with teeth" (as through UNOSOM II in Somalia), and post-conflict peace-building efforts (as through electoral assistance) [compare *Issues/48*, pp. 293–94]. He indicates that traditional assumptions about peacekeeping have been under challenge ever since missions were sent to areas where there are no peace agreements, where governments do not exist or have limited authority, and where cooperation of the parties cannot be relied upon [A/48/1, par. 295]. And, in the course of a summary of U.N. activity in the former Yugoslavia, he notes that "serious questions" have been raised about the wisdom of deploying Blue Helmets in all such situations [ibid., par. 445]. The Secretary-General does not address the legality under the Charter of these activities—which Charter provisions are implicated by these actions, how these intrusive activities comport with Article 2(7) on noninterference, etc.—but simply alludes briefly to their controversial or unprecedented nature. Thus, the report indicates that the preelection deployment of civilian U.N. personnel to South Africa, sent with the consent of that government and the first-ever such deployment for the United Nations, is a "significant breakthrough and could serve as a useful precedent in similar situations elsewhere" [par. 282].

The Secretary-General's response to such issues as noninterference with domestic jurisdiction and the legitimacy of certain U.N. actions remains, presumably, a plea for flexibility and for some inventive lawyering. "Peace-keeping," he writes, is a United Nations invention. The concept is, however, not a static one, but is ever changing; in order to succeed, and to reflect the changing needs of the community of States, peace-keeping has to be reinvented every day. Each case in which United Nations peace-keepers are involved draws upon the fund of experience, imagination and professionalism of the Organization. It is not an exaggeration to state that today there are as many types of peace-keeping operations as there are types of conflict. [par. 293]

The question of whether the Organization should continue to rely on such inventive lawyering (in the belief that the Charter is a living and evolving instrument capable of creative reinterpretation to suit changing needs), or whether the Charter should be formally amended to address the challenges of the post-"Agenda for Peace" world, was the subject of general debate in the **Special Committee on the Charter of the United Nations and on the Strengthening of the Role of the Organization** [see its Report, A/48/33, p. 4]. In the Sixth Committee, the representative of the Czech Replubic argued for a "profound revision of the Charter," since his government "could not support attempts to interpret the Charter too broadly," in the belief that "creativity in that area might jeopardize legal certainty and predictability in international relations" [A/C.6/48/SR.7]. The representative of Colombia called attention to "a growing feeling that the Council had gradually and illegally extended its powers," and he proposed a "constitutional control body competent to decide on the legality of measures taken by United Nations organs" [ibid.]. The Colombian representative argued that, while U.N. organs needed some space for interpreting their powers, "they could not enjoy absolute sovereignty," adding that a review mechanism "would make it possible to strengthen the sense of responsibility of United Nations organs in exercising the powers delegated to them by all Member States and to avoid abuses of power while at the same time legitimizing the measures taken by the Council" [ibid.].

The Special Committee continued its discussion of member state proposals, many intended as Charter amendments. As in the committee's prior sessions, these proposals addressed (1) cooperative arrangements with regional organizations, (2) assistance to third states affected by U.N. sanctions, as anticipated in Article 50 of the Charter, (3) the role of the ICJ, (4) the effectiveness of the Security Council, and (5) the elaboration of rules for the conciliation of disputes [see *Issues/48*, pp. 294–96]. With respect to these issues, none of which led to consensus at this session, governments usually reiterated the positions of prior years. They demonstrated anew the existence of a clear division, usually along North-South lines, between those satisfied with the status quo (in whose view, the Charter and the Council are "finally working as intended") and those seeking sometimes radical changes. Developing and many formerly East-bloc states again pressed for formal measures to implement Article 50 of the

Charter—this through the establishment of a fund, drawn partly from assessed contributions, to **assist states injured as a result of the Council's Chapter VII sanctions** [see proposals by Bolivia, India, Nepal, and others, A/AC.182/ L.76/Rev.1 and A/AC.182/L.77, considered in A/48/33; for background, see *Issues/48*, p. 295]. Other states, in particular developed states, continued to oppose such a permanent mechanism as impractical and counterproductive, claiming it would lead to "false expectations" and "additional burdens" on major financial contributors [A/48/33, p. 37]. In the Sixth Committee the U.S. representative argued that the Council was sensitive to the impact of its sanctions on third countries and proposed, instead, "well-designed regional infrastructure projects," either by international financial institutions or on a bilateral basis, to promote trade with key markets [A/C.6/48/SR.8].

In the Sixth Committee the United States criticized as "overly ambitious and broad" the Russian delegation's **"draft declaration on the improvement of cooperation between the United Nations and regional organizations,"** which received considerable attention in the Special Committee as well [ibid.]. That declaration proposes a variety of formal mechanisms to implement Chapter VIII of the Charter (Regional Arrangements), including information exchanges, liaison meetings, and regular meetings between the U.N. Secretariat and officials of regional organizations [A/AC.182/L.72/Rev.1; see also *Issues/48*, p. 295]. As during prior sessions, this proposal was warily received by the members who saw a need for flexibility, since different regional organizations have different abilities to affect peace and security issues, and by other members who worried about preserving the autonomy of regional organizations [see, e.g., A/C.6/48/ SR.5, comments by the Chair of the Special Committee, proposing that the Committee continue discussing the topic in the form of "guidelines" for cooperation "possibly in the form of a handbook"].

Guatemala's revised draft **U.N. rules for the Conciliation of Disputes between States** was discussed at length at both the Special Committee and the Sixth Committee but was not uniformly praised. Some delegations questioned the need for such rules, given existing instruments on the topic; others argued that these could indeed serve as model rules [A/48/ 33]. Guatemala offered to undertake revisions for discussion at the Special Committee's next session [A/C.6/48/SR.5].

Other topics received only minimal consideration in both the Special Committee and the Sixth Committee. Among these were the proposals to **"strengthen" or "enhance the effectiveness"** of the Security Council submitted by Libya and Cuba [A/AC.182/1993/CRP.1 and 2, discussed in A/48/33]. Cuba recommended the preparation of reports addressing such basic issues as the structure and procedures of the Council, including the "special privileges" of permanent members, the need for "equitable geographical distribution," the application of the rules of procedure, and the scope and application of Articles 24 and 25 of the Charter [A/AC.182/1993/CRP.2]. It also proposed that the Council's actions be made more transparent through more detailed reporting, weekly press conferences, and advance identification of issues to be addressed. Libya echoed many of these concerns and highlighted the need to identify "those non-procedural matters in which the use of the veto can be suspended or restricted" [A/AC.182/1993/ CRP.1]. While some members thought more time should have been allocated to the study of these "timely" proposals, others, such as the Spanish representative to the Sixth Committee, argued that these issues were more appropriately considered in the Assembly plenary under the topic of equitable representation in the Council [A/C.6/48/SR.7; see below]. The 48th General Assembly, as was the case with the 47th, left all these issues on the Special Committee's agenda, indicating that there would be further discussion during the next Assembly session [A/Res/48/36].

Questions about relations between the Council and the Assembly and broad questions about the legitimacy of U.N. action in the peace and security area fueled discussions in the 48th plenary on the "**question of equitable representation on and increase in the membership of the Security Council.**" A resolution was passed, the product of intense debate, "recognizing the need to review the membership of the Council and related matters in view of the substantial increase in the membership of the United Nations, especially of developing countries, as well as the changes in international relations," and establishing an open-ended working group to develop the topic for further discussion at the 49th Session [A/ Res/48/26].

By now, most of the Organization's members have responded to the Secretary-General's request for views on restructuring the Council, with the vast majority calling for greater "democratization" of this body and proposing any number of ways to achieve it, including elimination of the veto, expansion of the veto to include at least one developing state, expansion of the Council's nonpermanent, non-veto-wielding membership to include more representatives of developing states, creation of new permanent seats without the veto power, and various combinations of these [see generally, Report of the Secretary-General, A/48/264 and additions thereto; for a summary of some of views, see *The InterDependent*, Winter 1993–94]. The two states most often suggested for a permanent seat on the Council, Japan and Germany, have contributed troops for U.N. peacekeeping for the first time, albeit in small numbers, but both continue to face internal opposition from those who claim that such action violates provisions of the German and Japanese constitutions, respectively [see, e.g., *The New York Times*, 9/28/93].

The **Committee on Relations with the Host Country**'s annual report to the Assembly raised virtually the same issues it had raised in its report to the 47th Session. And as in prior years, much of the discussion focused on the growing number of debt-ridden missions to the United Nations, the subject of scrutiny by a working group [A/48/26, pp. 11–14; see also *Issues/48*, pp. 297–98, and *Issues/47*, p. 316]. The United States reported that over $5 million was owed to such persons as landlords, and that this included what was owed by some 30 of the then 183 missions to the United Nations as well as what was owed (some $1.2 million) by members of missions and Secretariat officials who had left the country [A/48/26, p. 13]. The U.S. government also reported that, consistent with its treaty obligations, it continued to intervene in federal courts in defense of diplomatic privileges and to prevent evictions and attachments of bank accounts. It added, however, that it would take strong action when the pattern of indebtedness became "flagrant," noting that it had requested the departure of five diplomats over the previous year [ibid., p. 12].

The Host Country Committee heard renewed complaints from Cuba and Iraq with respect to alleged violations of the host country's responsibilities and then the U.S. responses [see, e.g., *Issues/47*, pp. 315–16]. The United States announced that it was removing all the travel restrictions that had been imposed on U.N. Secretariat staff of Afghan nationality and their dependents [A/48/26, p. 9]. Two of the newer issues raised in the Host Country Committee were crime in New York City and the inconvenience caused by many of the security precautions taken at U.N. Headquarters as a result of recent terrorist threats [A/48/26; see also the Assembly's approval of the Host Country Committee Report, A/Res/48/35].

A number of legal issues were also raised in connection with the mechanisms for dealing with U.N. member state **allegations of fraud, waste, and mismanagement** within the Organization, including demands that the United Nations establish a new Inspector General's office to deal with such charges [see Chapter VII, "Finance and Administration"]. In this connection, the Secretariat produced an overview of the existing legal mechanisms for dealing with allegations of this sort, featuring a short survey of the capacity of the Organization with respect to domestic courts, the U.N.'s regulatory powers, its standards of conduct and internal review mechanisms, and the role of the U.N. Administrative Tribunal [A/AC.243/1994/L.3].

4. Economic Relations

Discussions in the Sixth Committee concerning the need to "**develop principles and norms of international law relating to the new international economic order**," an item placed on the agenda of the 48th Session at the initiative of Cuba [see A/Res/46/52], split once again along North-South lines. Representatives of Cuba, Guyana, India, and Costa Rica all supported the initiative, arguing that the economic differences between rich and poor had become acute and needed legal attention, while representatives of the United States and Belgium (the latter speaking for the European Union) considered the debate anachronistic in the "new climate in international economic relations" evidenced by the turn toward "market-economy principles" [A/C.6/48/SR.30]. Guyana described its goals for the "progressive development" of this law in the most detailed fashion, arguing for a "creative, innovative approach to international law reform," an "attitudinal shift" resulting in new norms on the relationship between debt and development, equitable access to financial resources, the transfer of technology and know-how, and acceptance by creditor nations and multilateral financial institutions of an international legal regime for debt write-offs and debt forgiveness [ibid.]. The Assembly, withholding comment, decided simply to revisit the issue at its 51st Session [A/Res/48/412]. A related resolution (urging, among other things, the write-off of the bilateral debt of the least developed) passed with only one dissenting vote: that of the United States [A/Res/48/182]. Another resolution, a perennial attempt by the Assembly to give specific content to the amorphous "**right to development**" it has solemnly proclaimed on so many occasions [most recently in A/Res/48/130], was voted against by 34 states, representing most of the developed world. The resolution called attention to deteriorating living conditions in developing countries; sought equal attention to and consideration of economic, social, and cultural rights as against civil and political rights; and sought implementation of the right to development as an inalienable "human right" [A/Res/48/123; vote: 115–34–21]. At the same time, the Assembly achieved consensus on a resolution on "**entrepreneurship and privatization for economic growth and sustainable development**" [A/Res/48/180; see *Issues/47*, pp. 317–18, and *Issues/46*, p. 257, for prior efforts]. Designed to lend encouragement to those engaged in the difficult work of privatizing, demonopolizing, and deregulating industry, including the enactment of legal reforms, the resolution gives the Assembly's imprimatur to the

> important role of Governments in creating, through transparent and participatory processes, the enabling environment supportive of entrepreneurship and facilitative of privatization, in particular the establishment of the judicial, executive and legislative frameworks necessary for a market-based exchange of goods and services and for good management. [A/Res/48/180]

The resolution also endorses and encourages U.N. and other efforts toward the same end. A related resolution addresses the need to integrate "economies in transition" into the world economy [A/Res/48/181].

The most significant achievement of the 26th session of the **U.N. Commission on International Trade Law (UNCITRAL)**, held in Vienna in July 1993, was its adoption of the **UNCITRAL Model Law on Procurement of Goods and Construction** [A/48/17, Annex, reproduced at 33 ILM 445 (1994)]. The Model Law, accompanied by a Guide also adopted by the Commission, is intended to assist states in restructuring or improving their rules governing transactions with governmental agencies. It stems from awareness that, particularly in many developing countries, existing legislation is inadequate or outdated and results in inefficient procurement practices and the mismanagement of scarce public funds. The Model Law is also seen as vital to former East-bloc states, whose economic systems are in transition and where reform of the public procurement process is part of broader market-oriented reforms [see, e.g., "Introductory Note," 33 ILM 445]. Industrialized states benefit from the Model Law too, because inadequate legislation in countries with which they trade threatens a growing segment of world trade. And harmonization itself is seen as a desirable thing: Suppliers and contractors are more willing and able to sell to foreign governments when state practices are not at variance.

The Model Law, designed as a mere "framework" that must be fleshed out with appropriate regulations, is meant to be flexible enough that it can be adapted to different national circumstances and, to this end, offers governments a variety of options [ibid.]. The chapters, five in all, deal with "general provisions," "methods of procurement and their conditions," "tendering proceedings," "procedures for procurement other than tendering," and review procedures. The basic premise is that open public tendering (solicitation of proposals) is the preferred method of procurement, but there is a chapter on alternatives for situations in which tendering might be inappropriate. The Model Law sets out the procedures to follow in selecting the supplier or contractor with whom a contract will be concluded, but it leaves to the state the job of putting in place the bureaucratic procedures that will give effect to these rules. The intent here is to maximize economy and efficiency; foster and encourage participation in procurement by suppliers and contractors regardless of nationality; promote competition; promote the integrity and fairness of, and public confidence in, the procurement process; and achieve transparency throughout [preamble to the Model Law]. The 48th General Assembly endorsed the Model Law, urging states to consider it when they enact or revise their procurement law [A/Res/48/33]. During Sixth Committee discussions of the Model Law, the Chair of UNCITRAL indicated that the Commission could be expected to finalize work on related **rules for the procurement of services** at its next session [A/C.6/48/SR.3]. Some states had reservations about the desirability of setting such a goal, however, suggesting that UNCITRAL might be well advised to coordinate its efforts with those of GATT on the same issue to avoid incompatible or duplicative efforts [see, e.g., comments by representatives of Canada, Australia, and Japan, A/C.6/48/SR.3-4].

UNCITRAL's 1993 session made less progress on the Uniform Law on Guarantees and Stand-by Letters of Credit, with which it has been grappling since 1989 [see *Issues/47*, pp. 321–22]. Even as a working group continues its examination of the 27 articles already in draft, several issues have been reopened and new proposals have been submitted on questions that had been considered settled. This drew complaints, directed at the working group, from other members of the Commission about the rate of progress being made on a project that was to be completed in 1995 [A/48/ 17, p. 49]. Another UNCITRAL working group continues its efforts on behalf of a model law on **electronic data interchange** [see *Issues/48*, p. 302].

UNCITRAL's Report to the 48th Session of the General Assembly also described its progress with respect to establishing a system for collecting and disseminating information on court decisions and arbitral awards relating to the Conventions and Model Laws that have resulted from its efforts. The system, **"Case Law on UNCITRAL Texts" (CLOUT)**, relies on a network of national correspondents designated by parties to the relevant conventions and by the states that have enacted legislation based on an UNCITRAL model law. These correspondents collect the decisions and arbitral awards and abstract them. The abstracts are already published as part of the regular documentation of UNCITRAL under the identifying symbol A/CN.9/SER.C/ABSTRACTS. It is assumed that CLOUT will contribute to the awareness of UNCITRAL texts as well as to their uniform interpretation [A/48/17, pp. 50–51].

Finally, UNCITRAL decided to begin work on the preparation of **guidelines for prehearing conferences in arbitral proceedings**—a new topic, which had received the endorsement of participants at UNCITRAL's May 1992 Congress on International Trade Law. Participants in that Congress had observed that the predictability of arbitral proceedings would be enhanced if, at an early stage in such proceedings, there were prehearing conferences between the arbitrators and the parties to discuss and plan the proceedings. Pursuant to requests made at this Congress, the U.N. Secretariat prepared a note on the practice of such conferences and on the need for these guidelines. Although some of those present thought such proposed guidelines might make arbitral proceedings unduly rigid and could present an administrative burden, both the Commission and the Assembly endorsed the new topic, and the Secretariat was asked to prepare a draft for discussion at UNCITRAL's next session [A/48/17, p. 51; A/Res/48/32].

Acting upon a recommendation by UNCITRAL and the Sixth Committee, the Assembly also urged states, in the interests of progressive harmonization and unification of international trade law, to become parties to the **U.N. Convention on the Carriage of Goods by Sea (the Hamburg Rules)** [A/Res/48/34]. But the 48th Session put on hold, at least until the 50th, further plenary discussion of the long-dormant **Code of Conduct on the Transfer of Technology,** since the industrialized countries and developing countries still appear at a stalemate on outstanding issues [A/Res/48/167; see *Issues/48*, pp. 299–300].

An **International Convention on Maritime Liens and Mortgages** was adopted on May 6, 1993, by a joint U.N./International Maritime Organization Conference held at the Geneva headquarters of UNCTAD. Intended to improve conditions for ship financing and the development of merchant fleets, the Convention will enter into force six months after ten states have acceded to it [33 ILM 353 (1994)].

5. Space Law

The 48th General Assembly endorsed the 1993 Report of the **Committee on the Peaceful Uses of Outer Space** [A/48/20], including its Legal Sub-committee's long-standing agenda, namely: (1) the review and possible revision of the recently adopted principles relevant to the use of nuclear power sources in outer space, (2) the definition and delimitation of outer space, (3) the character and utilization of the geostationary orbit, and (4) legal applications of the principle that the exploration and utilization of outer space should be for the benefit of all states [A/Res/48/39]. As at its previous session, the Assembly urged consideration of the problem of space debris and of the possibility of holding a third U.N. Conference on the Exploration and Peaceful Uses of Outer Space (but noted that the goals of such a conference could also be met if the Outer Space Commit-tee intensified its efforts) [see *Issues/48*, p. 303]. Given their different economic concerns, member states divided along North-South lines on all these is-sues, and there was little discernible progress toward resolving perennial differences.

The 11 **Principles Relevant to the Use of Nuclear Power Sources in Outer Space,** which was adopted by the 47th Assembly after over a decade of discussion, establish criteria for the safe use of nuclear power sources, provide for publication of safety assessments of these sources, establish procedures for notification in case of reentry of radioactive ma-terials, and require states to provide clean-up assistance and pay compen-sation in cases of contamination or damage [A/47/68; see *Issues/48*, p. 303]. Under the terms set by these principles, they are to be "reopened for revision by the Committee on the Peaceful Uses of Outer Space no later than two years after their adoption" [A/47/68, principle 11]. Given concern that the "soft law" status of the principles might depreciate further as a result of overly hasty revisions, the Committee opted for caution: It decided at its 1993 session that the principles should now be reviewed only with an eye to whether future revision is necessary and that the Scientific and Technical Subcommittee would consider the need for revision before any drafting is undertaken by the Legal Subcommittee [A/48/20, p. 16].

Concerning the **definition and delimitation of outer space,** while delegates stated old positions on the need for a conventionally defined boundary between airspace and outer space, two developments provide hope for a possible break in the long-standing stalemate: a working paper on a legal regime for "aerospace objects" submitted by the Russians [A/AC.105/C.2/L.189] and a proposal, inspired by that paper, to canvass states and international organizations (including the International Civil Aviation Organization) about their views, current legislation, and practices on such matters as the upper limit of state sovereignty [A/48/20, pp. 16–17; see 1993 report of the Legal Subcommittee, A/AC.105/544, pp. 14–16]. Some states see the possibility of taking a less polemical approach to the subject based on the way states now handle aerospace objects (that is, aircraft capable of flying both in outer space or in airspace). Concerning **access to the geostationary orbit,** old North-South debates had a reairing in the comments to Colombia's working paper on the subject. The paper offers criteria for selecting among states in awarding orbital positions and would give preferential access to developing countries and to countries that have had no access to the geostationary orbit [A/AC.105/544, Annex IV(A)]. A more general debate has to do with the Outer Space Committee's competence to address proposals, such as Colombia's, for a discrete legal regime for the geostationary orbit. Industrialized countries tend to argue that, given the close link between use of the geostationary orbit and use of radio-frequencies by objects in that orbit, the entire issue is the preserve of the **International Telecommunications Union (ITU)**—which, in their view, has been allocating orbital positions rationally and equitably. Developing countries, for their part, start with the proposition that the geostationary orbit is an integral part of outer space, that it is thus subject to the entire regime of the Outer Space Treaty of 1967, and that the elaboration of rules on this issue by the Outer Space Committee need not work at cross purposes with the ITU. They also argue that the threats posed by space debris in the orbit underscore the need for a legal regime [A/AC.105/544, pp. 17–19]. The 48th Assembly kept the item on the Committee's agenda but indicated that this action was "without prejudice" to the role of the ITU [A/48/39; see also A/48/20, pp. 16–17].

The Outer Space Committee's 1993 session also saw extensive discussion of proposed Principles Regarding International Cooperation in the Exploration and Utilization of Outer Space for Peaceful Purposes, which took the form of a working paper submitted by a group of developing countries, among them Argentina, Brazil, Chile, Nigeria, and Mexico. These principles, intended to concretize in legal form the last topic on the Outer Space Committee's agenda—concerning the need to share the benefits of space exploration—suggest the Third World's sweeping agenda for legal reform of space law and these countries' frustration with the current pace of change. Under the proposed principles, "all" states would have access, on a nondiscriminatory, timely basis, to "knowledge and applications derived" from space exploration; the conditions offered to one state in cooperation programs "should, as appropriate, be extended to other countries," and the goal of such programs should be "the development by all states of indigenous capability in space science and technology and their applications"; and no "arbitrary or discriminatory conditions should be applied to exchanges of knowledge and applications" concerning the utilization of space [see A/AC.105/544, Annex IV(B) for other proposed principles].

As articulated most forcefully by Nigeria at the Outer Space Committee Legal Subcommittee's 1994 sessions, what the poorer nations are seeking is legally guaranteed access to that which has been denied them because of lack of resources and technology: "preferential rights of access to orbital positions and frequencies" within the geostationary orbit and a generally stricter regulatory framework for outer space, among other things [U.N. press release OS/1646, 3/24/94; see also views of Indonesia, Cuba, Colombia in OS/1593 and OS/1594; and see also *Issues/48*, pp. 303–4]. This has obvious implications for all the items on the Outer Space Committee's agenda. Some developing countries also favor a far more controversial broadening of the work of the Outer Space Committee—one encompassing disarmament issues as well [see, e.g., comments by China arguing that the principles on nuclear power sources be revised to cover "space weaponization and militarization" and attendant technology, U.N. press release OS/1591, 3/22/93; compare A/Res/48/74, discussed in the section on Peace and Security above].

Today's space powers, as might be expected, continue to resist what they see as a radical law reform agenda. France, Canada, and Russia, for example, have reservations about the proposed principles on "sharing" space benefits. They argue that some of these conflict with sovereignty—specifically, a state's right to choose its space partners, to set the terms of its programs of cooperation, to protect trade secrets and intellectual property, and to apply its own rules concerning the final use of any technology and equipment that is transferred to another state [see, e.g., U.N. press release OS/1652, 4/7/94].

6. International Court of Justice

On November 10, 1993, the General Assembly, in balloting held concurrently with the Security Council, elected five judges (reelected, in the case of two of them) to the International Court of Justice (ICJ, or World Court) to a nine-year term, beginning on February 6, 1994. The Court, as reconstituted, consists of Roberto Ago (Italy), Andrés Aguilar Mawdsley (Venezuela), Mohammed Bedjaoui (Algeria), Carl-August Fleischhauer (Germany), Gilbert Guillaume (France), Géza Herczegh (Hungary), Sir Robert Yewdall Jennings (United Kingdom), Abdul G. Koroma (Sierra Leone), Shigeru Oda (Japan), Raymond Ranjeva (Madagascar), Stephen M. Schwebel (United States), Mohamed Shahabuddeen (Guyana), Jiuyong Shi (China), Nikolai K. Tarassov (Russia), and Christopher G. Weeramantry (Sri Lanka) [U.N. press release GA/8585, 11/10/93]. Shortly after the new court met, the judges elected Bedjaoui as President and Schwebel as Vice President. The Court is probably busier than at any other time in its history, with eight contentious cases and one request for an advisory opinion pending. Over the year 1993–94 it rendered two decisions concerning the demarcation of territory and one dealing once again with the former Yugoslavia.

A second request for provisional measures by Bosnia and Herzegovina, as well as a first request by Serbia and Montenegro, forced the Court to revisit its order granting provisional relief in the **Case Concerning Application of the Convention on the Prevention and Punishment of the Crime of Genocide** of April 8, 1993. That order had, among other things, directed the latter state to "ensure" that its forces do not violate the Genocide Convention [see *Issues/48*, pp. 304–5]. This time Bosnia and Herzegovina claimed that Serbia and Montenegro had been violating the Court's earlier order in continuing its "campaign of genocide" against the Bosnian people. Bosnia, repeating the request contained in its first petition to the Court, made an additional one: that the Court order public officials in Serbia and Montenegro to cease and desist from any efforts to "partition, dismember, annex or incorporate the sovereign territory of Bosnia" and declare any annexation or incorporation "illegal, null, and void *ab initio.*" Further, Bosnia sought orders, directed at all contracting parties of the Genocide Convention, reminding them that they are obliged to prevent the commission of genocide and that they have the right "to provide military weapons, equipment, supplies and armed forces" to Bosnia for this purpose [ICJ Communiqué, 7/28/93]. Serbia and Montenegro filed its own request for provisional measures on August 10, 1993, claiming that the Bosnian authorities were responsible for genocidal acts against the Serbian people and seeking an order directed at Bosnia, pursuant to the Genocide Convention, directing it to "take all measures within its power to prevent commission of the crime of genocide against the Serb ethnic group" [ibid., 8/11/93]. The Court consolidated both requests, permitted the parties to appoint ad hoc judges (Elihu Lauterpacht for Bosnia, Milenko Kreca for Serbia and Montenegro), and conducted hearings on August 25–26, 1993.

The Court's order of September 13, 1993, reaffirmed its earlier order and declined both the far-reaching additional injunctions requested by Bosnia and the order sought by Serbia and Montenegro [Order, with Judges Tarassov and Kreca dissenting from all or part]. In declining Bosnian requests to interdict the partition of Bosnian territory, to declare the acquisition of its territory illegal, or to hold that Bosnia must have the means to prevent genocide, the Court found, as before, that it had only prima facie jurisdiction to determine issues within the scope of the Genocide Convention and could not address other parties, such as members of the Security Council, which had imposed an arms embargo in the region [see, e.g., Order of 9/13/93, par. 43]. Nonetheless, the new order shows considerable sympathy for Bosnia's arguments and the voluminous evidence of atrocities it submitted, and the Court notes that, despite Council resolutions, "great suffering and loss of life has been sustained ... in circumstances which shock the conscience of mankind and flagrantly conflict with moral law and the spirit and aims of the United Nations." The order goes on to declare that the "grave risk" it had apprehended in its earlier order "has been deepened by the persistence of conflicts" and the "commission of heinous acts in the course of those conflicts" [ibid., par. 52–53]. The Court also refused to give the provisional relief requested by Serbia and Montenegro, noting only that it did not find that the circumstances required a more specific order directed at Bosnia than the one it had issued earlier directing *both* parties to abide by their obligations under the Genocide Convention [par. 46]. The Court also stated that it was "not satisfied that all that might have been done has been done." What was called for, it indicated, was not any additional measure but "immediate and effective implementation" of its first order [par. 57, 59].

While the Court's decision might seem to go no further than its initial determinations in this case (and no further than prior instances in which the Court has refused to disturb a determination by the Council), the separate opinions appended to this latest order offer riches that legal scholars can mine for some time to come. One of the legal issues raised is the appropriateness of the Court's prompt dismissal of Serbia and Montenegro's claims [compare the brief declaration of Judge Oda, which sides with Serbia and Montenegro, to the lengthy individual opinion by Judge Shahabuddeen, which canvasses a number of reasons, both factual and legal, why the Court's dismissive tone toward this claim was appropriate]. Among the other legal issues are the evidentiary weight to be given materials from press, radio, and television and the Court's roles in documenting events for the sake of the historical record [see, e.g., the opinions of Judge Shahabuddeen and Judge Lauterpacht]; the binding nature of provisional measures and their enforcement [see, in particular, the opinions of Judges Weeramantry and Bola Ajibola]; the troubling possibility that the Security Council might be, perhaps inadvertently, violating Bosnia's *jus cogens* right to defend itself against genocide and serving indirectly as an accomplice to genocide [see, in particular, opinions by Judges Ajibola and Lauterpacht]; and, of course, the definition of "genocide" in the Genocide Convention requiring an "intent," which may be difficult to prove, especially in the context of "ethnic cleansing" directed primarily at the acquisition of territory [compare the opinion of Judge Lauterpacht to the dissents of Judges Tarassov and Kreca]. The case is proceeding on the merits, with Serbia and Montenegro's countermemorial to Bosnia's memorial due on April 15, 1995 [Order, 10/7/93].

On March 16, 1994, Serbia and Montenegro approached the Court again, this time with an application directed against the **members of NATO,** claiming that the NATO decisions threatening force constituted a breach of Articles 2(4) and 53(1) of the U.N. Charter. The claim was not registered on the Court's list of pending cases, since jurisdiction is being sought under Article 38(5) of the Court's statute, which provides that the Court may communicate applications to states that have not yet consented to the Court's jurisdiction [ICJ Communiqué, 3/21/94]. It is extremely doubtful that any NATO member will agree to the Court's jurisdiction for the purposes of this case.

The Court also issued a decision in the **Case Concerning the Territorial Dispute between Libya and Chad,** a long-festering dispute that has led to outbreaks of violence in the past. The two countries, entering into a special agreement, asked that the Court determine a boundary dispute between them. Libya proceeded on the basis that there was no existing boundary and sought a large swath of what is now neighboring Chad (totaling some 310,000 square miles) based on historical evidence; Chad asked that the Court merely recognize a boundary that Chad claims existed pursuant to treaty. The Court ultimately sided with Chad, deciding 16–1 (the sole dissenter was Judge ad hoc Sette Camara, appointed by Libya), that the boundary between the two states was defined by the Treaty of Friendship and Good Neighbourliness concluded in 1955 between France (the colonial power in Chad at the time) and the United Kingdom, which provides (Article 3) that the parties "recognize" that their frontiers would be determined by certain additional treaties listed in an annex [Opinion of 2/3/94, as summarized in Press Communiqué, 2/3/94; the order is yet to be issued]. The Court's judgment, which is likely to be seen as a precedent not merely for purposes of boundary demarcation but also as a matter of treaty interpretation, turns on its view of the "ordinary meaning" of the treaty, given its "object and purpose" and the "principle of effectiveness" [Judgment, par. 23–56]. Interestingly, the Court also declares that a boundary established by a treaty must be taken to be a permanent boundary, whether or not the treaty establishing it remains in force [ibid., par. 72–73]. A separate opinion by Judge Shahabuddeen argues that the Court did not need to reach the question of the permanence or stability of boundaries but should have based its decision solely on the normal rules of treaty interpretation.

The Court's judgment in **Maritime Delimitation in the Area between Greenland and Jan Mayen** (Denmark v. Norway), is, in some respects, almost the mirror image of its decision in the Libya-Chad case. Here Norway contends that a bilateral agreement of 1965 and the 1958 Geneva Convention on the continental shelf had already resulted in a border delimitation. It wanted the Court to declare that both the continental shelf and the fisheries zone between Norway and Denmark in the region between Jan Mayen and Greenland (an integral part of the Kingdom of Denmark but granted home rule in 1979) were to be delimited according to the median line [Judgment, par. 22–40]. Demark denied the existence of any such delimitation and asked the Court to declare that Greenland is entitled to a full 200-mile fishery zone and continental shelf area vis-à-vis the island of Jan Mayen, which would give Denmark the maximum extension of its claim and Norway merely the residual [ibid.].

The Court essentially "split the baby," giving neither party the full extent of its territorial claims. On the one hand, it rejected Norway's contention that either the 1965 agreement or the 1958 treaty had the effect of defining a median-line boundary, but it also found that Denmark's proposed alternative was "inequitable" and therefore contrary to the customary law requirement that such delimitations be based on an "equitable solution" [par. 33–48]. In drawing up such an equitable solution, the Court began with the median line, found "special circumstances" requiring an adjustment of that line (given the striking difference between the length of the coasts and the maritime areas that would be generated), and drew its own line (which, for the fishery zone, gives both states access to the capelin fishery resources in that area) [par. 72–78]. The many separate opinions in this case reflect differences about the justness of the line drawn by the majority of the Court, and there is a learned exposition, by Judge Weeramantry, on the role of equity in maritime delimitation.

On March 29, 1994, Cameroon instituted proceedings against Nigeria concerning the **Question of Sovereignty over the Peninsula of Bakassi,** requesting reparations for Nigeria's occupation of that peninsula and also asking the Court to determine the maritime frontier between the two states if that frontier has not already been established. Jurisdiction is based on Article 36(2) of the Court's statute. Cameroon is asserting, among other things, that Nigeria is committing "aggression," in violation of both customary and international treaty law, by deploying its troops at several "Cameroonian localities on the Bakassi peninsula" [ICJ Communiqué, 3/30/94]. Another new case was brought on July 2, 1993, by special agreement between Hungary and the Slovak Republic. This submits to the Court issues arising out of Hungary's suspension of its work on the **Gabcikovo-Nagymaros Projects**—a navigation program stemming from a treaty between Hungary and the Czech and Slovak republics [ICJ Communiqué, 7/5/93].

The dispute between Nauru and Australia, concerning **Certain Phosphate Lands in Nauru,** was settled by the parties and discontinued [Communiqué, 9/13/93; see *Issues/48,* p. 306]. (According to information supplied to *Issues/49,* Australia—trustee over the island from 1947 to 1968—will pay the Republic of Nauru A$107 million over 20 years to rehabilitate the land it had mined prior to Nauru's independence; New Zealand and the United Kingdom, the other participants in the British Phosphate Commission, will contribute A$12 million each to this sum.) Decisions on other contentious cases are expected soon: Public hearings on the U.S. objections to jurisdiction in the case brought by Iran, **Aerial Incident of 3 July 1988** [see *Issues/46,* p. 267], will open in September 1994; and in March 1994 there were public hearings in the **Case Concerning Maritime De-**

limitation and Territorial Questions between Qatar and Bahrain [see *Issues/48*, p. 307]. The Court's other pending contentious cases remain at the pleading stage: a second case brought by Iran against the United States, **Oil Platforms** [see *Issues/48*, p. 308]; **East Timor** (Portugal v. Australia) [see *Issues/ 46*, p. 269]; and Libya's claims against the United Kingdom and against the United States in **Questions of the Interpretation and Application of the 1971 Montreal Convention Arising from the Aerial Incident at Lockerbie** [see *Issues/47*, pp. 325–27].

In August 1993, acting on a resolution adopted by the World Health Organization, WHO's Director-General asked the Court for an **advisory opinion** on the following question: "In view of the health and environmental effects, would the use of **nuclear weapons by a State in war or other armed conflict** be a breach of its obligations under international law, including the WHO Constitution?" [ICJ Communiqué, 9/3/93]. Written statements by WHO, as well as by its members entitled to appear before the Court, were due on June 10, 1994. An answer to this extraordinary question is presumably intended to have dramatic impact on issues that go way beyond the jurisdiction of the WHO.

Acting on a recommendation from the Sixth Committee, the General Assembly again deferred consideration of a proposal, backed by the Latin American countries, to request an advisory opinion from the ICJ with respect to the **legality of extraterritorial arrests and apprehensions of criminal suspects** [A/Dec/48/414; see *Issues/48*, p. 308]. There is general agreement that the proposal was prompted by the U.S. Supreme Court's decision, in 1992, that the United States could try in U.S. courts a Mexican national who the U.S. government had kidnapped from Mexico [*United States v. Alvarez-Machain*, 112 S.Ct. 2188]. In the Sixth Committee, various representatives had urged ICJ consideration on the grounds that attempts at such extraterritorial jurisdiction were "not only contrary to the basic principles of international relations, but also detrimental to the proper functioning of the normal system of judicial cooperation and its future development and enhancement" [A/C.6/48/SR.34, comments by Brazil].

The Assembly's decision calling for **review of the procedure under Article 11 of the Statute of the Administrative Tribunal of the United Nations** [A/Dec/48/415] also relates to the jurisdiction of the ICJ. The U.N. Administrative Tribunal, a creature of the General Assembly, is charged with the adjudication of U.N. staff grievances; its opinions, along with those of comparable bodies of other international institutions, constitute precedents on the international law governing the international civil service. Under Article 11 of the Administrative Tribunal's statute, a Committee on Applications for Review of Administrative Tribunal Judgments, consisting of member state representatives, is authorized to request advisory opinions of the ICJ, as a kind of limited appeal from decisions of the Administrative Tribunal. Deep and widespread dissatisfactions with this procedure were canvassed in the Sixth Committee during the 48th Session. Representatives of various states, including those who had served on the Committee on Applications, argued that the arrangement was unsatisfactory for all concerned. And when only three advisory opinions had ever been requested of the ICJ in this area, it was noted, the claim to have instituted an appellate process was illusory, unfair (because it raised the expectations of staff), and costly to all concerned. Further, it was said to delay the finalization of Administrative Judgments, to place a politically constituted body in the position of making quasi-judicial judgments, and to force the ICJ to assume a role contrary to its central role as arbiter of interstate disputes [see, e.g., comments by the representative of the United Kingdom, A/C.6/48/SR.36].

Various reforms of the staff appeal scheme were suggested in the Sixth Committee, including abolition of the review procedure and use of an "ombudsman" in place of the present form of dispute settlement, but members also suggested that the issue be taken up by the Fifth Committee in the course of the comprehensive review of the administration of justice within the U.N. Secretariat requested in Resolution 47/226 [ibid.]. Accordingly, the 48th plenary asked the Secretary-General to undertake a review of the question and report to the 49th Session [A/Dec/48/415].

Making use of its power to form chambers for particular categories of cases [see ICJ Statute, Article 26(1)], the Court created a seven-member **Chamber for Environmental Matters** [ICJ Communiqué, 7/19/93]. The Court reports too that, as of July 1993, 57 states had made declarations accepting the so-called "compulsory" jurisdiction of the Court under Article 36(2) of the Court's statute [Report of the ICJ, A/48/4, p. 3].

7. Other Legal Developments

The U.N. role in promoting what some have called an "emerging right" to democracy [see, e.g., Thomas M. Franck, "The Emerging Right to Democratic Governance," 86 *American Journal of International Law* (1/92), p. 46] was either the explicit subject or the implicit subtext of a number of actions during the 48th Session of the General Assembly. As has been the case since its 45th Session, the Assembly adopted schizophrenic resolutions on the subject of **U.N. electoral assistance** [see, e.g., *Issues/48*, p. 309]. On the one hand, a majority of the membership voted in favor of a resolution proclaiming "respect for the principles of national sovereignty and non-interference in the internal affairs of states in their electoral processes" [A/Res/48/124; vote: 101–51–17]. This resolution, opposed by the United States and most of the developed world, affirms that electoral processes are solely an internal concern, to be determined by local laws and constitutions, that any activities directly or indirectly interfering in those processes violate the Charter, and that there is "no universal need" for the United Nations to provide electoral assistance. The Commission on Human Rights is asked to review the factors that have a negative impact on national sovereignty and on noninterference in electoral processes. On the other hand—and by an even larger margin [153-0-13]—the Assembly commended the use of U.N. electoral assistance (provided it is at the member's request), and more: It called upon states to contribute to a trust fund for this purpose, requested a focal point within the Organization to coordinate electoral activities, and asked the Secretary-General to provide a revised set of guidelines on the subject for consideration at the 49th Session [A/Res/48/131]. Lining up against greater U.N. involvement in the certification and observation of elections are, by tradition, Cuba, China, the Democratic Republic of Korea, Iraq, Libya, and Uganda.

In still other actions relating to the promotion of democracy, the Assembly praised the CSCE for its role in encouraging "democratic values" and the United Nations itself for cooperating with regional initiatives in Central America toward the same end [A/Res/48/19, A/Res/48/161].

Following up on the Vienna Declaration and Programme of Action adopted at the June 1993 World Conference on Human Rights, the Assembly requested that the Secretary-General prepare for the 49th Session some options for a comprehensive program for national and international action to "**promote democracy, development and human rights**" [A/Res/48/132]. The goal is to strengthen the rule of law and the capacity of the U.N. system to promote it. In another follow-up to the Vienna Conference, the Assembly created the post of **High Commissioner for Human Rights**—an office long sought by the international human rights community—and an Under-Secretary-General has since been named to fill it. The Commissioner is charged with the promotion and protection of all civil, cultural, economic, political, and social rights that are protected by international instruments [A/Res/48/141; see A/Res/48/119–20, 89–90, 148, and 156, urging effective ratification/implementation of various human rights conventions]. The Commissioner, based in Geneva, is charged too with the "rationalization, adaptation, strengthening and streamlining" of the U.N. machinery in the field of human rights, and may engage in "dialogue" with all governments to secure respect for human rights. The Assembly will receive an annual report of the progress made. It is expected that the Commissioner will emerge as the focal point for the Organization's efforts to "mobilize shame" against human rights violators; and human rights advocates hope that the office's power and impact will grow over time.

The Assembly continues at the forefront of the **progressive development of new human rights instruments and declarations.** During the 47th Session, it drew attention to the need for a compilation and analysis of existing rules to protect internally displaced persons [A/Res/48/135]; called attention to the plight of street children in light of the **Convention on** the Rights of the Child [A/Res/48/136]; encouraged the promotion of the Assembly's 1992 **Declaration on the Rights of Persons Belonging to National or Ethnic, Religious and Linguistic Minorities** [A/Res/48/138]; urged the convening of a U.N. conference for the "comprehensive consideration and review of the problems of **refugees, returnees, displaced persons and migrants**" [A/Res/48/113]; enunciated a new set of "**principles relating to the status of national institutions**" intended to describe the responsibilities of national entities in the protection of human rights [A/Res/48/134]; proclaimed a new **Declaration on the Elimination of Violence against Women** [A/Res/48/104]; asked the Secretary-General to appoint an expert to study ways of protecting **children affected by armed conflicts,** including a review of the relevance and adequacy of existing standards under humanitarian law [A/Res/48/157]; and adopted new, extremely detailed **Standard Rules on the Equalization of Opportunities for Persons with Disabilities** [A/Res/48/96].

The Assembly's now annual call for ratification and implementation of relevant **drug abuse and illicit drug-trafficking** conventions [see, e.g., *Issues/48*, p. 310] was issued as part of a broader appeal for a coordinated international program to combat these problems [A/Res/48/112]. That resolution stresses the central role of the U.N. International Drug Programme and asks that entity to report to the Commission on Narcotic Drugs on the Programme's experience to date concerning the implementation of the Convention against Illicit Traffic in Narcotic Drugs and Psychotropic Substances. As in prior years, the Assembly also called on states to adhere to the Charter and international law while engaged in combatting the drug trade, and, specifically, to refrain from violating the territorial integrity of other states or from using force [see also A/Res/47/98]. The growing importance of international criminal law was also demonstrated by the Assembly's consideration of legal methods to combat the smuggling of aliens, and the Assembly adopted a lengthy resolution reminding states of their obligations under relevant conventions, including the International Conventions for Safety of Life at Sea and Protocol of 1978 and relevant antislavery conventions [A/Res/48/102]. This last resolution also affirms that all states have the right to control their own borders, proclaims that alien smuggling violates international and national law and threatens lives, urges states to amend their national laws if necessary to enhance prosecution and discovery of alien smuggling, emphasizes that international efforts to combat this problem should not inhibit the freedom to travel or undercut the rights of refugees, and identifies relevant international organizations whose action could enhance international cooperation [for related Assembly action addressing the institutional capacity of the United Nations on crime prevention and criminal justice, see A/Res/48/103; see also *Issues/48*, pp. 309–10]. As it has done periodically, the Assembly also called attention to the need to protect human rights in the course of the administration of justice, enumerating the many international instruments on prisoners' rights, especially "soft law" principles, minimum rules, and guidelines that the Assembly has proclaimed over the years and appealing to governments to provide, for example, legal aid services to enforce and implement these rights [A/Res/48/137].

The Assembly recognized the approach of a milestone in international law: the entry into force on November 16, 1994, of the **U.N. Convention on the Law of the Sea,** including its controversial provisions proclaiming the resources of the deep seabed the "common heritage of mankind" and purporting to restrict the access of private investors to these resources [A/Res/48/28]. (The 60th instrument of ratification was deposited on November 16, 1993, and the Convention stipulates that it is to enter into force one year later.) While the vast majority of the membership joined in a call for universal participation in this Convention (144 in favor), there was lingering antipathy toward certain provisions, particularly those involving the deep seabed, as evidenced by 11 abstentions and one dissent (Turkey). An agreement resulting from consultations among the Secretary-General, such significant holdouts as the United States, and countries already party to the LOS Convention led the U.S. administration to announce in late June 1994 that it would sign the Convention as a first step toward ratification [for background on the issues, and the opposition to treaty ratification, see William Safire, "LOST at Sea," *The New York Times,* 3/31/94; and see "Global Resource Management: Law of the Sea," *Issues/47, 48, 49*].

Discussions about the possibility of convening an international conference to define **international terrorism** (prompted by a resolution passed at the 46th Session seeking members' views on the subject) was inconclusive [A/Res/48/411; see A/46/51]. While, as always, all members condemned "terrorism," there were different views about what actions were encompassed by the term as well as about the wisdom of even attempting to define the term or adding to the existing body of conventions that address the subject [for earlier views and background, see *Issues/47*, pp. 306–7]. During the 48th Session, the Sixth Committee reviewed the report of the Secretary-General on the subject containing the views of governments, canvassed the efforts of international organizations, and surveyed the status of all relevant international conventions [A/48/267 and additions thereto]. In the three years since the Committee considered the subject, two more antiterrorism instruments have entered into force: the Convention for the Suppression of Unlawful Acts against the Safety of Civil Aviation and the Protocol for the Suppression of Unlawful Acts against the Safety of Fixed Platforms located on the continental shelf. The Belgian representative, reflecting a view shared by many industrialized states, argued against the convening of a conference to define terrorism and in favor of the current pragmatic, ad hoc approach that focused on the outlawing of specific terrorist acts [A/C.6/48/SR.11]. Then, too, said the Swedish representative, convening such a conference might give the impression that the existing rules were not sufficient. Acts of terrorism were already punishable under existing national and international rules; the problem was that not all States were prepared to combat terrorism. The most fruitful approach would be to enhance adherence to existing international agreements aimed at preventing international terrorism and applying sanctions against perpetrators. . . . Unfortunately, the political will to implement existing conventions was lacking. [A/C.6/48/SR.12]

Canada's representative saw a conference on such a "divisive" issue simply "doomed to failure" [ibid.]. The representative of Syria, by contrast, stressed the need for "internationally agreed criteria to differentiate clearly between terrorism . . . and national struggles against foreign occupation, to which protection and support should be given" [ibid.; see also comments by the representative of Sudan, supporting the need for a "clear and precise definition," since "terrorism," like "human rights," "had become instruments which were used for dubious political ends," ibid., and of Cuba, condemning "state terrorism," A/C.6/48/SR.14, as well as the strident debate between the representatives of India and Pakistan on "state terrorism," ibid.]. The Assembly decided merely to continue requesting the views of governments on the subject but kept the item on the agenda for the 49th Session [A/Dec/48/411].

The Assembly continues to grapple with a sweeping environmental agenda, much of it prompted by the 1992 Rio Conference on Environment and Development and some of it directed at issues of great concern to developing states. At its 47th Session the Assembly decided to schedule for 1995 the first session of the conference of parties to the U.N. **Framework Convention on Climate Change,** as is anticipated by the Convention itself [A/Res/48/189]; urged governments to disseminate widely the Rio Conference's **principles for the achievement of sustainable development** [A/Res/48/190]; and approved the report of the Secretary-General concerning ongoing negotiations for an **international convention to combat desertification,** still expected to be concluded by the end of 1994 [A/Res/48/191 and 175; see *Issues/48,* p. 299].

The most significant development concerning the **U.N. Decade of International Law 1990–99** [proclaimed in A/Res/44/23 of 1989] was the Assembly's decision, taken upon the recommendation of a special working group of the Sixth Committee, to convene in 1995 a **U.N. Congress on Public International Law** [A/Res/48/30; for the Secretary-General's report on the Decade, see A/48/312]. While details of that conference have not been finalized, the working group proposed to include both governmental and NGO participants and speakers, who would be invited to U.N. Headquarters for five days (immediately after the 1995 session of the Special Committee on the Charter of the United Nations and on the Strengthening of the Role of the Organization) to express their views

on the codification, progressive development, and implementation of public international law, taking into account both theory and practice of international law, its teaching and dissemination, with a view to assisting the legal profession, States that have recently joined the international community, and the general public to meet the challenges and expectations of a new world order. The theme of the Congress would be "Towards the twenty-first Century: International Law as a Language for International Relations." [A/C.6/48/L.9; see also Report of the Secretary-General on the subject, A/48/435]

All who addressed the subject in the Sixth Committee supported the proposal for such a congress on the 50th anniversary of the United Nations, but there were different ideas about its focus and purpose. The Russian representative to the Sixth Committee expressed the hope that the congress would concentrate on developing peaceful means of settling disputes, especially the "development of the legal framework for peace-keeping operations," and on various means of protecting the environment [A/C.6/48/SR.31]. Representatives of certain developing countries sought to emphasize the means of avoiding "the imposition of international law on any particular group of States" and the need for changing the norms of international law that had been developed without their participation and failed to provide the "security which law was supposed to offer a community" [comments by Zaire, A/C.6/48/SR.31]. The representative of the Democratic People's Republic of Korea argued for a focus on the elimination of inequalities among nations, and the "fair and equitable" and impartial application of the law, including the principle of noninterference in internal affairs [A/C.6/48/SR.32]. Chile's representative expressed hope that the Congress would lay the groundwork for future legal developments to advance the cause of democracy and human rights, sustainable development, regulation of international trade, and cooperation between states [ibid.; for a related report by the Secretary-General on Secretariat activities intended to promote the teaching, study, dissemination, and wider appreciation of international law, see A/48/580 and the Assembly's resolution on point, A/Res/48/29].

VII
Finance and Administration

By Anthony Mango

1. The Fifth Committee's Agenda in 1994

The items that are likely to dominate the Fifth Committee's agenda in 1994 are personnel questions, the financing of peacekeeping operations, improving the financial situation of the Organization, and the review of the efficiency of the administrative and financial functioning of the United Nations. The Committee will also have to approve the scale of assessments for 1995–97.

The Committee's agenda will also include the financial reports and audited financial statements, together with the related reports of the Board of Auditors, the first performance report for the program budget biennium 1994–95, program planning, and interagency administrative and budgetary coordination, as well as items that come up every year, such as the pattern of conferences and appointments to subsidiary organs [A/Dec./ 48/458, Annex, Section A].

2. U.N. Finances

The Financial Situation Shows No Improvement

The account in *A Global Agenda: Issues Before the 48th General Assembly of the United Nations* of the discussion of the financial crisis in the Fifth Committee at the Assembly's 47th Session ended with the observation that it was clear that "the Organization is still facing a financial crisis, even though the agenda item has been renamed 'Improving the financial situation of the United Nations' " (p. 319).

That there had indeed been no improvement became patent at the end of August when, in a statement in the Fifth Committee at the resumed 47th Session, the Secretary-General announced that, given the cash flow difficulties, he had decided to curtail the conference services that would be provided to the Assembly at its 48th Session, which was due to begin in less than a month. The saving his decision was likely to yield was very small compared to the magnitude of the problem; the Secretary-General's intention, clearly, was to send a message to the member states. Predictably, their reaction was negative. The representative of Belgium, speaking on behalf of the 12 member countries of the European Union, said that "it was regrettable that Member States had been presented with a *fait accompli*. . . . [The economy] measures . . . indiscriminately penalized all Member States, and they were not commensurate with the magnitude of the crisis" [A/C.5/48/SR.22, par. 66]. A few weeks into the 48th Session the economy measures were rescinded. The General Assembly expressed "its deep concern regarding the economy measures announced . . . in the context of the financial crisis without prior consultation with Member States, those measures being in contradiction with the principle of equal treatment of the official languages of the U.N. . . . ." [A/Res/48/222 B, op. par. 8].

But while the approach taken by the Secretary-General was not particularly felicitous, his predicament was all too real. Introducing the agenda item in the Fifth Committee, the Controller said that as of November 17, 1993, outstanding contributions totaled $1.7 billion, of which $1,165 million was owed to the regular budget and $535 million to the budgets of peacekeeping operations; 42 countries had paid nothing in 1993 by that date and only 70 had paid their contributions to the regular budget in full [A/C.5/48/SR.20, par. 1].

The ensuing debate mainly dealt with the recommendations in the report of the **Independent Advisory Group on U.N. Financing,** cochaired by Shijuro Ogata and Paul Volcker [A/48/460]. As was pointed out by the representative of Botswana, many of those recommendations were not new [A/C.5/48/SR.25, par. 63]. They had been made by the Secretary-General at the Assembly's 46th Session, and had been discussed at the 47th Session, at which time views were divided and no action was taken [see *Issues/48*, pp. 314–15]. The recommendations met with the same fate at the 48th Session.

There was general acceptance of the Group's recommendation that all countries must pay their assessed U.N. dues on time and in full. It could hardly have been otherwise, but even here several delegations referred to the need to take into account the domestic budgetary procedures of member states.

No delegation dissented from the recommendations that the consensus procedure for approving the regular budget should be continued, and that the Organization's expenditures should continue to be financed in three ways, namely, by assessed contributions for the regular budget, by a separate assessment for peacekeeping operations, and by voluntary contributions for humanitarian and development activities.

By contrast, there was general reluctance to agree to additional assessments with a view to increasing the **Working Capital Fund** from $100 million to $200 million, and creating a $400 million revolving reserve fund for peacekeeping. It was pointed out in that connection that increasing the Organization's reserves in that manner would place an unfair burden on the member states that had been paying their assessments in full; if the member states in arrears paid off what they owed there would be no need to increase the reserve funds. As the representative of Japan pointed out, even if financial reserves were adequate and budgetary accountability and efficiency impeccable, it would be impossible to compensate for the failure of member states to pay assessed contributions in full and on time. The Japanese representative doubted whether member states that fulfilled their obligations would accept additional charges (such as interest on commercial borrowings) in order to compensate for the delinquency of other member states [A/C.5/48/SR.23, par. 101 and 107].

Several delegations blamed major contributors for the Organization's financial difficulties. The U.S. representative recognized that his government's failure to pay all its assessed contributions damaged the ability of the United Nations to carry out its responsibilities. He then went on to say that it was critical to keep the regular budget at zero growth. He also called for the establishment of the **Office of Inspector General** because, in the long run, it would produce cost savings that would help keep the size of the Organization's overall budget in check; it would also send a strong signal to the taxpayers of member states and their elected representatives that the United Nations was serious about rooting out waste and improving its effectiveness, and therefore deserved their financial support [A/C.5/48/SR.24, par. 8–10; see also below].

The representative of Malaysia considered it unacceptable for a member state to attach conditions to the fulfillment of its financial obligations to the Organization; funding mechanisms should be established to protect the United Nations from any pressures brought to bear by major contributors [A/C.5/48/SR.24, par. 2]. The representative of Argentina felt that it was necessary to eliminate the practice whereby some states exerted indirect pressure on the Organization by linking payment of their contributions to their own interests [ibid., par. 17], and the representative of Mexico said that defense of individual interests did not justify nonpayment of contributions [ibid., par. 19]. The representative of Namibia said that states must not evade their obligations under the Charter, and no conditions whatsoever should be attached to fulfilling them [ibid., par. 29].

The representative of Latvia proposed that "instead of asking for the impossible, namely that dues should be paid on time and in full," an effort should be made to find out the actual reasons why member states were in arrears; new states sometimes lacked the necessary infrastructure for revenue collection [ibid., par. 33]. In the same vein, the representative of Cuba pointed out that, in most cases, failure to pay their contributions was due to the countries' acute economic difficulties and not to any lack of political commitment [A/C.5/48/SR.25, par. 42]. Similarly, the representative of Cameroon said that very few of the member states that failed to fulfill their financial obligations had deliberately withheld their assessed contributions; they had had no choice; the time had come for an end to insistence on the need for member states to pay in full and on time without consideration of whether they were able to do so [A/C.5/48/SR.23, par. 58]. By contrast, the representative of Mexico said that it had become less and less acceptable for countries to use domestic economic conditions as a pretext for not honoring their international commitments [A/C.5/48/SR.24, par. 19].

The consensus resolution that emerged following informal consultations, recognizing the need for a continuing dialogue at the intergovernmental level to analyze possible solutions for the improvement of the financial situation of the Organization, reaffirmed the obligation of member states to pay assessed contributions promptly and in full and recognized that nonpayment and delays in payment have damaged and continue to damage the ability of the Organization to implement its activities effectively. It was also decided to continue consideration of the item at the resumed 48th Session [A/Res/48/220]. As of the time of writing no further action was taken by the Fifth Committee to improve the financial situation of the United Nations.

In the meantime, 1993 ended with member states owing a total of $478 million in unpaid assessments to the regular budget (as against $501 million on December 31, 1992). The list of debtors was headed by the United States which, once again, was responsible for more than 50 percent of the arrears. The changes in the arrears owed by the largest five debtors between the beginning and the end of 1993 are summarized in Table VII-1.

Of the arrears owed by the United States as of December 1993, an amount of $48.4 million was attributable to unilateral withholdings. The amount requested by the Clinton administration in respect of the regular budget assessment for 1994—and approved by Congress in April 1994—provides for a further withholding of $3.7 million, consisting of $1.1 million for programs related to the Palestine Liberation Organization, $2.2

Table VII-1
Arrears of Five Largest Debtors, 1993 (in millions of US $)

	Arrears 12/31/93	Arrears 12/31/92	Increase/ (Decrease)
United States	260.4	239.5	20.9
South Africa	53.2	49.0	4.2
Russian Federation	43.5	96.0	(52.5)
Ukraine	29.3	17.3	12.0
Brazil	12.4	29.0	(16.6)

million for the construction of a conference center for the Economic Commission for Africa at Addis Ababa, Ethiopia, and $0.4 million for the Preparatory Commission on the Law of the Sea [*Washington Weekly Report,* XX-3, 2/11/94, and XX-11, 4/29/94]. The repayment of other arrears owed by the United States will also be slowed down; the process will now be completed in 1997 and not in 1995 [ibid., XX-3]. Furthermore, there is a difference of opinion between the United States and the United Nations concerning the amount standing to the credit of the United States in the Tax Equalization Fund, from which Americans employed in the U.N. Secretariat are reimbursed for taxes levied on them by the United States. This difference, which relates to the methodology of reimbursement, amounted to $75.5 million as of December 1993 and a further $8.5 million for 1994.

As of December 31, 1993, only 75 of the 184 member states had no arrears to the regular U.N. budget. Among them were some of the poorest countries, such as Albania, Bangladesh, and Ethiopia.

In January 1994 assessed contributions in a total amount of $1,061.9 million became payable in respect of the 1994 regular budget. Seventeen countries paid their assessments in full by the end of January 1994. These countries are Australia, Canada, Denmark, Finland, Iceland, Ireland, Liechtenstein, Luxembourg, Malaysia, the Federated States of Micronesia, Netherlands, New Zealand, Norway, Pakistan, Singapore, Slovakia, and Sweden. On the other hand, a considerable number of countries paid little or nothing. As of the end of February 1994, 23 countries were in arrears under the terms of Article 19 of the Charter, i.e., the amount owed by them equaled or exceeded their contributions for the preceding two years and they were liable to lose their vote in the General Assembly. Nineteen of those 23 countries are assessed at the floor rate of 0.01 percent and two at 0.02 percent; the remaining two countries were South Africa and Yugoslavia [A/48/853/Rev.1]. Faced with the loss of their vote, countries usually make a payment on account that reduces their indebtedness to below the two-year trigger point.

As of December 31, 1993, member states owed a total of $992.8 million for peacekeeping operations (after deducting $12.8 million in credits for two completed operations), of which $473.6 million was owed by the Russian Federation. Four operations accounted for the bulk of the arrears, namely, those in the former Yugoslavia ($268.2 million), Cambodia ($221.8 million), Somalia ($98.4 million), and Lebanon ($207.7 million). Assessment letters for five new operations were sent out in January 1994, totaling $95 million; these operations are the U.N. Observer Mission in Georgia (UNOMIG), the U.N. Mission in Haiti (UNMIH), the U.N. Observer Mission in Liberia (UNOMIL), the U.N. Assistance Mission for Rwanda (UNAMIR), and the U.N. Military Liaison Team in Cambodia (UNMLTIC). Member states were also assessed in January 1994 for several ongoing operations. The total amount owed as of January 31, 1994, for peacekeeping operations was approximately $1.43 billion.

The U.S. administration's requests for funds for U.N. peacekeeping operations have been encountering growing resistance in Congress. In 1993, Congress failed to approve the entire amount requested by the administration. In February 1994, President Clinton asked Congress for nearly $1 billion for new U.N. peacekeeping assessments in 1994 (the requests were contained in supplemental appropriations for Fiscal Year 1994 and in appropriations for Fiscal Year 1995) [*Washington Weekly Report*, XX-3, 2/11/94]. In April 1994, Congress authorized $510.2 million in Fiscal Year 1995 funds, and $670 million in supplemental Fiscal Year 1994 funds; however, half of the latter amount will be made available only upon certification by the Secretary of State that the United Nations has created an independent Office of Inspector General (see below) [ibid., XX-11, 4/29/94]. At the time of writing, Congress had not completed action to appropriate the funds approved in the authorizing legislation.

The practice of the General Assembly to authorize the Secretary-General to enter into commitments in respect of peacekeeping operations, without simultaneously approving additional assessments, aggravates the financial situation of the Organization. While not all commitments involve immediate outlays, the practice nonetheless does have an impact on the cash flow situation.

Scales of Assessments

Approval of a scale of assessments for the *regular budget* for the years 1995–97 will be one of the major items on the Fifth Committee's agenda at the 49th Session.

Two issues dominated the discussion of this question in recent years. One of them was the assessment rates of the states admitted to membership in the United Nations following the dissolution of Czechoslovakia, the USSR, and Yugoslavia (the so-called "22 States"). The other was whether to change the methodology used by the Committee on Contributions in constructing the scale, and if so in what way. On both issues the same arguments were stated and restated both in the Committee on Contributions and in the Fifth Committee itself at the 47th [see *Issues/48*, pp. 319–21] and 48th sessions.

At the 48th Session there was no disagreement with the arguments advanced by the "22 States" that their assessments must be reviewed, but at the same time there was general reluctance to do so before the end of the triennium 1992–94, for which a scale had already been approved. There was no desire to invoke Rule 160 of the General Assembly's Rules of Procedure, which permits the revision of the scale if "substantial changes in relative capacity to pay" had occurred since the scale was approved.

By contrast, there were sharp disagreements on the various aspects of the methodology (see below). The last statements by delegations were delivered on November 1, 1993, but it was only on December 21 that, following extensive informal consultations, a consensus text could be submitted to the Fifth Committee for approval; even then 11 delegations felt it necessary to make statements in explanation of their positions.

The consensus resolution reaffirmed in its preamble that **capacity to pay is the fundamental criterion for determining the scale of assessments** [A/Res/48/223 B]. There had been virtually no disagreement in the debate as to that principle, the only reservation having been voiced by the U.S. delegation [A/C.5/48/SR.7, par. 28]. However, differences arose when it came to deciding how capacity to pay should be determined.

In operative paragraph 1 of the consensus resolution the Assembly gave the Committee on Contributions very specific and detailed instructions on how it should construct the scale for 1995–97, which clearly reflected the results of hard bargaining. The criteria laid down by the Assembly were as follows.

1. *The scale is to be based on the average of two separate scales, one of which would have a seven-year statistical base, and the other an eight-year base.* The current scale has a ten-year base. The delegations of countries with growing economies, and of those that were opposed to any change in the current methodology (Bangladesh, Chile speaking on behalf of the 12 members of the Rio Group, Japan, Malaysia, Oman, and Saudi Arabia), had argued that the ten-year base should be retained in the interest of greater predictability and stability. By contrast, the delegations of countries whose economies have contracted and of those that are likely to benefit from heavier assessment of countries with growing economies had sought a shorter base, on the grounds that a ten-year base reflected a member state's past rather than current capacity to pay. Thus, Algeria and Ukraine advocated a three-year base, which was also favored by the Independent Advisory Group on U.N. Financing [A/48/460, par. 50–51]; Nigeria suggested a base of three to five years; Hungary, of three to six years; Iran, of five to seven years. Australia (on behalf also of Canada and New Zealand), Belgium (on behalf of the European Union), Croatia, Kazakhstan, Kyrgyzstan, Latvia, Poland, Slovenia, Sweden (on behalf of the Nordic countries), and the former Yugoslav Republic of Macedonia said that they favored a shorter base, without specifying its length. Bangladesh, India, Pakistan, Uganda, and Uruguay saw merit in a nine-year base for the technical reasons advanced by the Committee on Contributions, namely, that the length of the base period should be a multiple of three, since a scale was adopted for a three-year period.

2. Uniform exchange rates should be used for converting local statistical data into U.S. dollars. There was general agreement in the Fifth Committee in support of the conclusion of the Committee on Contributions that market exchange rates (MERs) should continue to be used wherever possible; in exceptional circumstances price-adjusted rates of exchange (PAREs) would be used.

3. The adjustment for external indebtedness used in the preparation of the 1992–94 scale would also be used in the 1995–97 scale.

4. The low per capita income allowance would also be retained. It would be applied in calculating the assessments of countries with a per capita income below the average world per capita income for the statistical period (as in the existing scheme), and a "gradient" of 85 percent. In the debate, some developing countries had sought a 100 percent gradient (i.e., full compensation).

5. There would be no change in the existing ceiling rate of 25 percent (which is applied to the assessment of the United States) *and the floor rate of 0.01 percent.*

6. The scheme of limits would be phased out in two equal steps over the scale periods 1995–97 and 1998–2000. The Assembly thus confirmed its earlier decision [A/Res/46/221 B] to abolish the scheme of limits, the purpose of which is to prevent excessive fluctuations in assessment rates between one scale and the next. The Independent Advisory Group on U.N. Financing had recommended that the scheme of limits be retained for the time being in order to ease the impact on the assessment rates of individual countries of the adoption of a three-year base [A/48/60, par. 51].

The degree of detail in Resolution 48/223 B suggests that—unless attempts are made to undo the package—the scale for 1995–97 should be adopted without too many difficulties. While its impact on individual states will become known only after the Committee on Contributions has held its 1994 session and issued its report, it is already clear that the member states that used to be parts of the former Czechoslovakia, USSR, and Yugoslavia will have their assessments lowered considerably, and that countries with growing economies, particularly those that had benefited most from the scheme of limits, will see their assessments increase; several developing countries are likely to fall into the latter category. The number of countries assessed at the floor rate of 0.01 percent is likely to decline (the 1992–94 scale contains 87 such countries), but the least-developed countries are guaranteed that their rates will remain at 0.01 percent [A/Res/48/223 B, operative par. 4]. Adoption of the scale for 1995–97 will not mean, however, that all the contentious issues will have been resolved.

In operative paragraph 1 of Resolution 48/223 C, the General Assembly requested the Committee on Contributions "to undertake a thorough and comprehensive review of all aspects of the scale methodology with a view to making it stable, simpler and more transparent while continuing to base it on reliable, verifiable and comparable data, and to report thereon to the General Assembly at its 50th session" in 1995. Operative paragraph 2 of the same resolution again reaffirms the fundamental nature of the capacity to pay criterion. In the same paragraph the Assembly—responding to a suggestion by the Japanese delegation—decided "in principle" to set up an ad hoc body to study the implementation of that criterion. Decision on the mandate and modalities of that body was postponed until the resumed 48th Session (as of the time of writing no action had been taken in this regard).

While the length of the base period will naturally be one of the issues to be considered as part of the "thorough and comprehensive review," the main point at issue will be whether—and if so, to what extent—factors other than a country's national income (which has been defined as its GDP plus or minus the net income from the rest of the world, and minus consumption of fixed capital) should be taken into account in constructing future scales of assessments; these factors are a country's debt burden and low per capita income.

The material submitted by the Committee on Contributions in its report to the Assembly at the 48th Session included an illustrative scale for 1992–94 using only each country's national income and the 0.01 percent "floor"—the so-called "clean slate" approach [document A/48/11, annex V]. Assessment rates using base periods of ten years (1982–91), three years (1989–91), and one year (1991) were provided. The figures for the three-year base show that the number of countries assessed at the floor rate of 0.01 percent would decline from 87 to 73. The assessments of 45 countries currently assessed at more than the floor rate would rise—dramatically so in the case of populous countries (Brazil from 1.59 to 2.34, China from 0.77 to 2.74, Egypt from 0.07 to 0.21, India from 0.36 to 1.39, Indonesia from 0.16 to 0.52, Iran from 0.77 to 2.64, Morocco from 0.03 to 0.13, Pakistan from 0.06 to 0.25, Philippines from 0.07 to 0.22, Thailand from 0.11 to 0.42, Turkey from 0.27 to 0.52). The assessment of the United States would be increased from 25 to 26.14 percent under the "clean slate" approach if the ceiling were abolished. It is, of course, unlikely that the United States would agree to that; if the ceiling were retained, the extra 1.14 percent would have to be distributed among other countries.

The assessments of 46 countries would decline. The 15 member states (including Belarus and Ukraine) that used to be part of the USSR would see their assessments lowered by more than two-thirds—from a total of 10.90 percent under the current scale to 3.27 percent. The total assessment of the 12 members of the European Union would decline from 30.22 percent to 28.15 percent (eight members' assessment would decline, three would increase, and one would remain unchanged).

The first speaker in the debate on the report of the Committee on

Contributions, the representative of Belgium, speaking on behalf of the members of the European Union, endorsed the "clean slate" approach. The contributions of member states should be based solely on national income, he said; the scale of assessments could not be regarded as an instrument for income redistribution among states [A/C.5/48/SR.5, par. 33 and 37]. Support for the "clean slate" approach was also voiced by the representatives of Australia (who spoke also on behalf of Canada and New Zealand), Belarus, and Hungary. The United States supported the "clean slate" concept in principle, provided the "ceiling" rate was also retained [A/C.5/48/SR.7, par. 29].

The "clean slate" approach was opposed by the representatives of Bangladesh, China, Cuba, Egypt, India, Iran, Malaysia, Nigeria, Oman, Pakistan, Qatar, Republic of Korea, Saudi Arabia, Slovenia, and Uganda.

Several delegations who did not endorse the "clean slate" approach did so on the grounds that it was too extreme. Sweden said that the Nordic countries had studied that approach with interest; they favored a simple transparent methodology based on reliable, verifiable, and comparable data, particularly if the change was accompanied by a shortening of the statistical base period [A/C.5/48/SR.7, par. 14]. Thus, while the member states are at present clearly divided in their views, some move away from the current methodology should not be ruled out.

The *scale of assessments for peacekeeping operations* is derived from the scale for the regular budget. Although this special scale has been in use for over 20 years, since the adoption of Resolution 3101 (XXVIII) of December 11, 1973, it is applied each time as "an *ad hoc* arrangement." For purposes of the special scale, member states are divided into four groups: (a) the five permanent members of the Security Council; (b) countries that, as a group, pay a percentage of the expenses of a peacekeeping operation equal to their total assessment rates for the regular budget; (c) countries that, as a group, are assessed 20 percent of their aggregate rates for the regular budget; and (d) countries that, again as a group, are assessed 10 percent of their aggregate regular budget rates. The shortfall attributable to the lower assessments of countries in groups C and D is added to the assessments of the five permanent members in group A, because of their special responsibilities—and powers—under the Charter [see *Issues/48*, pp. 321–23].

Reservations about the special scale have been voiced by member states ever since the adoption of Resolution 3101 (XXVIII), which is why it has been applied on each occasion as an ad hoc arrangement. At the 47th Session the General Assembly decided to request the Chairman of the Fifth Committee to convene an open-ended working group, which was to study the question and report back at the Assembly's 48th Session [A/Res/47/218, Section II]. As of the time of writing, the working group had not submitted its report, and in all likelihood the matter will be deferred to the 49th Session.

One of the points at issue is the placement of member states into particular groups. A country that is moved from group B to group C (as Belarus and Ukraine have insistently sought for the past two years) would have its rate of assessment for peacekeeping operations reduced from 100 percent of the regular budget rate to 20 percent. Conversely, a country moved from group C to group B would experience a fivefold increase in its contribution to peacekeeping operations.

Furthermore, the United States has been pressing for its assessment to be reduced to 25 percent (i.e., to the ceiling rate under the regular budget scale). The granting of permanent-member status in the Security Council to Germany and Japan, and moving some more highly industrialized developing countries such as Brazil and India from group C to group B, have been discussed in this connection.

The United States has been assessed for 1994 at a rate of 31.7 percent for peacekeeping operations. The increase from the earlier rate of 30.4 percent was due to two factors: the fact that the regular budget rate of assessment of one permanent member of the Security Council, namely, the Russian Federation, is lower than that of its predecessor, the USSR (because a portion of the USSR's assessment is now assessed on the new member states that used to form part of the USSR); and the fact that the Czech Republic and Slovakia have not yet been assigned to any particular group for purposes of assessment for peacekeeping operations. (For a description of how the peacekeeping scale is derived from the scale of assessments for the regular budget see *Issues/48*, p. 322.)

Congress has refused to permit authorization of assessments in excess of the earlier rate of 30.4 percent and, moreover, has put the United Nations on notice that the United States will reduce its peacekeeping assessment to 25 percent effective in Fiscal Year 1996 [*Washington Weekly Report,* XX-11, 4/29/94]. This unilateral action is inconsistent with Article 17, paragraph 2, of the U.N. Charter, which provides that it is the General Assembly and not individual member states that decides on the apportionment of the expenses of the Organization; and it bodes ill for the latter's financial stability.

3. The Expenses of the Organization

The Program Budget for 1994–95

At its 49th Session the Fifth Committee will consider the Secretary-General's proposals for revisions to the program budget for 1994–95. The amount approved for the biennium at the 48th Session was nearly $2.6

billion gross ($2.1 billion net). The final budget appropriation for 1992–93, as approved by the General Assembly in Resolution 48/219 A and B, was $2.4 billion gross ($2.0 billion net).

The estimates for 1994–95 as originally submitted by the Secretary-General, the recommendations thereon of the **Advisory Committee on Administrative and Budgetary Questions (ACABQ)**, and the appropriations as approved in Resolution 48/231 A and B (which also incorporate additional requirements related to various decisions taken by the Assembly at its 48th Session) are summarized in Table VII-2.

Thus, for the biennium 1994–95 the General Assembly at its 48th Session appropriated approximately $257.4 million for political activities and international justice, $761.3 million for economic, social, and humanitarian activities, and $1,156.6 million for administration, common services, and public information.

For several reasons—in particular because of the uncertainties surrounding the drawn-out restructuring of the Secretariat—the Secretary-General's program budget proposals for 1994–95 were submitted in November, i.e., seven months late, in violation of Financial Regulations 3.4 and 3.5. They were introduced in the Fifth Committee by the Secretary-General himself on November 24, and the general debate began a week later, without waiting for the ACABQ report. The latter was introduced on December 8. Because of the very short time available to the ACABQ in which to consider the Secretary-General's proposals, its report was not as detailed as customary, and the requirement in rule 157 of the Rules of Procedure of the General Assembly that "at the beginning of each regular session at which the proposed program budget for the following biennium is to be considered [the ACABQ] shall submit to the General Assembly a detailed report on the proposed program budget for that biennium" could not be respected.

Several points clearly emerged from the debate in the Fifth Committee. Regarding the allocation of resources to programs, there was a clear division between North and South. Whereas the former agreed with the growth in resources proposed for peacekeeping, human rights, and humanitarian activities—and some delegations even felt that the increase had been inadequate—the latter, while not disputing the importance of those three areas, argued that the resources allocated to economic and social development were not commensurate with the priorities attached to those programs in General Assembly decisions.

The developing countries' suspicion that the Secretary-General might use his authority under the Financial Regulations to reallocate resources within appropriation lines in a manner that might be inconsistent with mandates approved by the General Assembly also underlay the decision to approve separate appropriations for budget sections 11A (U.N. Conference on Trade and Development), 11B (International Trade Cen-

Table VII-2
Program Budget, 1994–95

	Secretary-General's Estimates, $	ACABQ Recommendations, $	Appropriations, $
Expenditure sections			
1. Overall policy-making, direction, and coordination	42,219,300	36,605,000	37,049,800
2. U.N. integrated offices	3,604,900	0	(see below)
3. Political affairs	72,870,500	67,707,000	67,923,600
4. Peacekeeping operations and special missions	92,886,700	86,834,600	101,573,200
5. International Court of Justice	19,427,900	18,336,800	18,329,400
6. International War Crimes Tribunal	pro memoria		(see below)
7. Legal activities	34,297,700	32,507,700	32,490,000
8. Dept. for Policy Coordination and Sustainable Development	52,155,500	47,848,100	50,355,600
9. Dept. for Economic & Social Information and Policy Analysis	49,821,500	46,554,000	46,815,700
10. Dept. for Development Support and Management Services	30,130,200	28,078,200	29,385,800
11A. U. N. Conference on Trade and Development	133,302,500	127,803,100⎤	108,296,400
11B. International Trade Centre		⎦	19,982,200
12A. U.N. Environment Program			
12B. U.N. Centre for Human Settlements (Habitat)	28,884,700	23,250,100⎤	11,384,500
		⎦	11,854,300
13. Crime control	4,918,400	4,639,600	4,638,200
14. International drug control	14,832,400	14,004,900	13,998,700
15. Economic Commission for Africa	83,835,600	77,921,000	78,020,100
16. Economic and Social Commission for Asia and the Pacific	64,699,300	59,911,000	59,846,200
17. Economic Commission for Europe	46,289,400	44,740,400	44,684,500
18. Economic Commission for Latin America and the Caribbean	90,001,100	80,024,700	79,992,600
19. Economic and Social Commission for Western Asia	43,227,500	38,245,300	38,226,600
20. Regular program of technical cooperation	45,371,000	42,910,000	42,910,000
21. Human rights	38,465,000	35,544,300	36,063,300
22A. Office of the U.N. High Commissioner for Refugees	69,998,800	66,402,700⎤	45,329,400
22B. U.N. Relief and Works Agency		⎦	21,007,900
23. Dept. of Humanitarian Affairs	20,306,300	18,461,200	18,541,200
24. Public information	135,789,100	131,050,100	133,145,300
25. Common support services	927,013,500	889,151,900	876,856,000
26. Jointly financed administrative activities	27,050,300	26,204,600	26,192,800
27. Special expenses	37,664,300	31,780,400	31,780,400
28. Staff assessment	448,196,900	402,925,000	404,949,000
29. Technological innovations	19,096,100	18,841,500	18,841,500

Table VII-2 (continued)

		Secretary-General's Estimates, $	ACABQ Recommen-dations, $	Appro-priations, $
30.	Construction, alteration, major improvements, and major maintenance	72,707,600	64,306,900	58,306,900
31.	Office for Inspections and Investigations	0	0	11,429,100
	Total, expenditure sections	2,749,064,000	2,562,590,200	2,580,200,200
Income sections				
1.	Income from staff assessment	454,711,900	409,340,200	411,364,200
2.	General income	59,258,800	59,258,800	59,258,800
3.	Services to the public	6,297,100	6,778,700	6,778,700
	Total, income sections	520,267,800	475,377,700	477,401,700
	Total, net	2,228,796,200	2,087,212,500	2,102,798,500

tre), 12A (U.N. Environment Programme), 12B (U.N. Centre for Human Settlements/Habitat), 22A (Office of the U.N. High Commissioner for Refugees), and 22B (U.N. Relief and Works Agency, which aids Palestine refugees in the Middle East)—this despite assurances by the Secretariat that the presentation of consolidated amounts for sections 11, 12, and 22 in the proposed program budget was not motivated by any desire to be able to move resources from one subsection to another [see, for example, the statement by India, A/C.5/48/SR.27, par. 30, and by the Controller, A/C.5/48/SR.31, par. 86].

Regarding other issues, there was general condemnation of the late submission of the proposed program budget. Many delegations were not convinced that the cost increases built into the proposals were justified. And there was widespread dissatisfaction with the perceived failure of the Secretary-General to carry out specific requests by the Assembly, and to consult adequately with member states.

The General Assembly's decisions on these and other matters were embodied in two resolutions on "Questions relating to the proposed program budget for the biennium 1994–95," which contain a total of 87 operative paragraphs [A/Res/48/228 and 230]. Thus, in operative paragraph 2 of Resolution 48/228, the Assembly *"deplores* the extraordinary and unacceptable delay in the submission of the proposed program budget for the biennium 1994–95 by the Secretary-General, which compelled the General Assembly and its subsidiary organs to conduct a review on the basis of incomplete and inadequately transparent proposals."

On the question of the allocation of resources, operative paragraph 3 of Resolution 48/228 *"stresses* that the activities included in the proposed program budget must be derived from the medium-term plan for the period 1992–97 as adopted by the General Assembly . . . and other relevant

intergovernmental decisions, and should be aimed at the full implementation of the mandates, policies and priorities previously established." In
operative paragraph 21 of the same resolution, the Secretary-General is
requested "to respect fully the rules and regulations governing program
planning in the presentation of future proposed program budgets." This
point had been stressed by several speakers, including the representative
of India, who said that the budget "was not a mechanism for the announcement of policy proposals" by the Secretary-General [A/C.5/48/SR.27,
par. 32].

Similarly, the representative of Cameroon said that "there appeared
to be an increasing tendency for the Secretariat to use program budget
proposals to introduce activities that had no approval from substantive
bodies [ibid., par. 52]. One such proposal was for $3.6 million under Section
2 of the program budget for U.N. integrated offices. ACABQ recommended that this amount be provisionally deleted pending action by the
General Assembly. Although the question was considered by the Second
Committee, no decision had emerged by the time the Assembly adopted
the appropriation resolution; therefore, the latter contains no funding for
the integrated offices.

The proposed program budget for 1994–95 included *pro memoria*
Section 6 for the International War Crimes Tribunal. The representative
of India recalled in that connection that in Resolution 47/235 the General
Assembly had requested that the budget of the tribunal be presented outside the framework of the regular budget [A/C.5/48/SR.27/, par. 32]. By contrast,
the representative of Sweden, speaking on behalf of the Nordic countries,
said that the tribunal should be funded under the regular budget [ibid., par.
38]. No decision on the mode of financing was taken by the time of the
adoption of the appropriation resolution. Discussion of the question was
continued at the resumed session in 1994; there were major differences of
opinion among delegations, and no consensus was reached. The General
Assembly authorized the Secretary-General to enter into commitments
for the tribunal in an amount not exceeding $11 million for 1994 without
specifying whether the expenses would be apportioned in accordance
with the regular budget scale or with the special scale for peacekeeping
operations.

Cost increases, in an amount of $256.3 million, accounted for some
90 percent of the growth in dollar terms in the estimates for 1994–95 over
appropriations for 1992–93. Although the recosting methodology had, by
and large, been applied for several years, there was a widespread feeling in
the Fifth Committee that it was not sufficiently transparent. In operative
paragraph 7 of Resolution 48/228 the Assembly *"stresses the need for full
and comprehensive information regarding the costing parameters applied
in the program budget, including instructions to program managers on
the preparation of the budget, and requests the Secretary-General to en-

sure that the proposed program budget for the biennium 1996–97 contains a clear indication of all the cost elements, including inflation, exchange fluctuations and others." In operative paragraph 8 the Board of Auditors was requested "to review the development of the assumptions used in the presentation of the program budget and performance reports with a view to suggesting improvements."

In operative paragraph 17 of Resolution 48/228 the General Assembly reaffirmed "the need for a comprehensive, substantive and timely dialogue between Member States and the Secretary-General on administrative and budgetary matters." The resolution also contains paragraphs expressing the Assembly's regret at the failure of the Secretary-General to comply with requests contained in earlier resolutions.

Several delegations sought additional information on how extra-budgetary resources (which were estimated at $3.4 billion in the proposed program budget for 1994–95) are expended. In operative paragraph 9 of Resolution 48/228 the Secretary-General is requested to present in future documents the actual regular budget and extrabudgetary expenditure by section for the prior and current biennia, with appropriate forecasts to the end of the current biennium, for the sake of comparison with the request contained in the proposed program budget.

In other action related to the regular budget, the General Assembly noted that a balance of $16 million remained in the Contingency Fund as at December 23, 1993 [A/Res/48/230, section VIII]; and it kept the size of the Working Capital Fund at $100 million [A/Res/48/232, par. 1]. It authorized the Secretary-General to enter, without seeking the ACABQ's prior concurrence, into commitments not exceeding a total of $5 million in any one year of the biennium, that related to the maintenance of peace and security [A/Res/48/229 on unforeseen and extraordinary expenses for the biennium 1994–95]. In the same resolution it decided that if a Security Council decision gives rise to the need for commitments in an amount exceeding $10 million, the matter would be submitted to the General Assembly, if need be at a resumed or special session.

In Decision 48/459 the Assembly deferred to its resumed 48th Session in 1994 consideration of 22 reports and notes by the Secretary-General. In subsequent decisions, several of them have been further deferred to the Assembly's 49th Session.

The Budgets of Peacekeeping Operations

The report of the Independent Advisory Group on U.N. Financing, co-chaired by Shijuro Ogata and Paul Volcker, contained several recommendations on the financing of peacekeeping operations [A/48/460, par. 52–88]. The Group recommended that the **international community be prepared to accept significantly increased peacekeeping costs in the next few years** and that, because peacekeeping is an investment in security, governments **consider financing its future cost from their national defense budgets.** The group also recommended that the U.N. establish a revolving fund, set at $400 million, to be financed by three annual assessments, to meet the costs of operations pending receipt of assessed contributions; and it supported a regular appropriation for peacekeeping training. The Group saw merit in a unified peacekeeping budget, to be financed by a single annual assessment, and it believed that the Secretary-General should be permitted to obligate up to 20 percent of the initial estimated cost of a peacekeeping operation once it has been approved by the Security Council.

The delegations that addressed the Group's recommendations at the 48th Session were reluctant to endorse them. Thus, the representative of Thailand said that while his country supported peace and stability in the world, it was not in favor of increasingly frequent resort to peacekeeping operations, because equal priority should be given to the economic, social, and development sectors [A/C.5/48/SR.14, par. 41]. The representative of Brazil also expressed reservations concerning the ever-expanding scope of peacekeeping operations. Such operations were not necessarily the most appropriate mechanism for humanitarian and developmental assistance, he said; there was need for a thorough reassessment of peacekeeping operations in the light of the experience gained with the recent multipurpose operations. His delegation believed that the peak in peacekeeping costs had been reached and that, at most, member states would have to meet only incrementally higher costs [A/C.5/48/SR.20, par. 35 and 43].

Only one delegation, Bulgaria [A/C.5/48/SR.24, par. 25] supported the establishment of a $400 million revolving reserve fund. The Nordic countries, the members of the European Union, and Malaysia were opposed [A/C.5/48/SR.20, par. 29, SR.22, par. 71, and SR.24, par. 5]. The unwillingness to pay up-front assessments (which the creation of the revolving reserve fund would have involved) outweighed the current disadvantages to member states of having to face multiple assessments for peacekeeping operations in the course of the year, in a manner inconsistent with their own domestic budgeting processes.

The delegations of Australia, Canada, New Zealand, and Botswana favored a unified peacekeeping budget [A/C.5/48/SR.20, par. 9; SR.25, par. 64], and those of Austria, the Nordic countries, the United States, and Uganda expressed interest in it [A/C.5/48/SR.20, par. 17 and 29; SR.24, par. 14; SR.25, par. 62]. On the other hand, outright opposition or reservations were voiced by the delegations of Brazil, the members of the European Union, China, Singapore, Malaysia, and Egypt [A/C.5/48/SR.20, par. 44; SR.22, par. 71; SR.23, par. 66 and 80; SR.24, par. 6; SR.25, par. 59].

The Group's recommendation that the Secretary-General be permitted to obligate up to 20 percent of the estimated cost of a peacekeeping operation once it has been approved by the Security Council was supported by the delegations of Australia, Canada, New Zealand, the Nordic countries, the United States, and Botswana [A/C.5/48/SR.20, par. 10 and 29; SR.24, par. 14; SR.25, par. 64]; but opposed by the delegations of Austria, Brazil, the members of the European Union, and Japan [A/C.5/48/SR.20, par. 18 and 44; SR.22, par. 72; SR.23, par. 107].

The main ground for the opposition to or reservations about the unified peacekeeping budget and the obligating authority was concern about loss of control by the General Assembly over the costs of peacekeeping operations.

Because of the very late submission of documentation, the Fifth Committee could not begin consideration of the budgets of the 17 ongoing peacekeeping operations before the very end of the first part of the 48th Session. Even then, what it received was a consolidated document covering all the operations. The Secretariat attributed the delay to changes by the Security Council in the mandates of some of the operations and the late receipt at U.N. Headquarters of information from the field.

The **current operations financed by assessments in whole or in part** are the U.N. Disengagement Observer Force (UNDOF); the U.N. Interim Force in Lebanon (UNIFIL), the U.N. Angola Verification Mission (UNAVEM); the U.N. Iraq-Kuwait Observation Mission (UNIKOM); the U.N. Mission for the Referendum in Western Sahara (MINURSO); the U.N. Observer Mission in El Salvador (ONUSAL); the U.N. Transitional Authority in Cambodia (UNTAC—this mission is being wound up); the U.N. Protection Force (UNPROFOR—in the former Yugoslavia); the U.N. Operation in Somalia (UNOSOM); the U.N. Operation in Mozambique (ONUMOZ); the U.N. Peacekeeping Force in Cyprus (UNFICYP—prior to mid-June 1993 this operation had been financed entirely from voluntary contributions); the U.N. Observer Mission in Georgia (UNOMIG); the U.N. Mission in Haiti (UNMIH); the U.N. Observer Mission in Liberia (UNOMIL); the U.N. Assistance Mission for Rwanda (UNAMIR); the U.N. Observer Mission in Uganda-Rwanda (UNOMUR); and the U.N. Military Liaison Team in Cambodia (UNMLTIC).

Delegations in the Fifth Committee were highly critical of the late submission and the form of presentation of the Secretary-General's report. The representative of France said that the late submission of documentation was intolerable. It was unacceptable for the Committee to be put in the position of having to make decisions, in just a few hours, on proposals involving more than $1 billion. The process of budgeting for peacekeeping operations required more transparency [A/C.5/48/SR.44, par. 39].

In its related report, ACABQ recommended that the Secretary-General be granted commitment authority until March 31, 1994, in most cases (i.e., one month less than requested by him); it also recommended assessments for several peacekeeping operations.

In a series of decisions worked out in informal consultations, the General Assembly decided to approve assessments in a total amount of $585.3 million gross ($577.9 million net) for 12 operations [A/Dec.463–71 and 473–80].

The Secretary-General was also authorized to enter into commitments for all the operations. The commitment authority expired on February 28, 1994, for five operations, and on March 31, 1994, for eight operations. In the case of three operations, commitment authority expired on dates in March and April 1994 that were linked to the duration of their mandates. No commitment authority was deemed necessary for one operation. For all the operations taken together, the Secretary-General was authorized to enter into commitments totaling approximately $200.3 million gross ($197.2 million net) a month.

In a separate decision, the General Assembly was strongly critical of the delays in submission and of the form of presentation of the budgets of peacekeeping operations, and decided that such budgets will continue to be considered on an individual basis until such time as the General Assembly decides otherwise [A/Res/48/227].

The General Assembly's decision at the end of the first part of its 48th Session to extend commitment authority for five peacekeeping operations only until Feburary 28, 1994, meant that the Fifth Committee had to reconvene at the beginning of March 1994 to extend that authority by one month. The total commitments authorized for the five operations was $198.7 million gross ($196.1 million net).

The budgets of the peacekeeping operations were revisited in late March, early April, and May 1994. The action taken by the General Assembly on these occasions involved the levying of additional assessments for peacekeeping operations in a total amount of $708.4 million gross. The Secretary-General was also given commitment authority as shown in Table VII-3.

Further discussion of the administrative and financial aspects of peacekeeping operations and of the budgets of individual operations was scheduled for July 1994. At the 49th Session the Assembly will be called upon to approve additional assessments on member states and to authorize the Secretary-General to enter into further commitments for peacekeeping operations.

The backstopping at U.N. Headquarters, New York, of the Organization's peacekeeping operations is done by staff, most of whom are financed from a special support account, and not from the regular program budget. In Resolution 48/226 the General Assembly authorized the Secretary-General to enter into commitments related to the support account of up to $16,376,250 for the first six months of 1994. The 342 posts fi-

Table VII-3
Peacekeeping: Commitment Authority

Operation	$ (gross)	Period
UNAMIR	9,082,600 per month	4/5/94–10/31/94
UNIFIL	11,857,000 per month	8/1/94–1/31/95
UNAVEM	2,098,700 per month	6/1/94–9/30/94
UNIKOM	1,833,300 per month	5/1/94–3/31/95*
ONUSAL	3,895,900	6/1/94–9/15/94
UNFICYP	11,950,000	6/16/94–12/15/94**
UNOMIG	600,000	4/1/94–5/31/94
UNMIH	44,200 per month	7/1/94–12/31/94
UNOMIL	4,359,100 per month	4/22/94–7/21/94
UNDOF	2,680,000 per month	4/1/94–11/30/94
ONUMOZ	26,900,000 per month	5/1/94–7/31/94
UNPROFOR	15,900,000 per month	4/1/94–7/31/94
UNOSOM	77,442,517 per month	6/1/94–9/30/94

* Net of voluntary contributions; the authority covering the period 11/1/94–3/31/95 has been granted "on an experimental basis."
** Net of voluntary contributions.

nanced from the support account are located in the Department of Peacekeeping Operations, the Field Operations Division, the Internal Audit Division, the Peacekeeping Financing Division, and the Purchase and Transportation Service of the Department of Administration and Management. In June 1994 the Secretary-General requested 92 additional posts [A/48/470/Add.1].

Program Planning

The Regulations and Rules Governing Program Planning, the Program Aspects of the Budget, the Monitoring of Implementation, and the Methods of Evaluation, which have been in force for over a decade, provide for a medium-term plan covering a six-year period. The current plan is for the period 1992–97. Like its predecessors, it is a bulky and very detailed document whose preparation, consideration at the intergovernmental level, and periodic updatings consumed much time and labor. But given the need for the United Nations to react to rapidly changing situations in the world, much of the detail is irrelevant, and the actual outputs often differ from what had been planned. For that reason, the medium-term plan has been the object of increasing criticism on the part of delegations and within the Secretariat.

At the 47th Session the General Assembly requested the Secretary-General to submit a prototype of a new format for the plan to the **Committee for Program and Coordination (CPC)** in 1993. The Secretariat proved unable to comply with that request. Instead, it submitted a report to the CPC in which it proposed that future plans consist of a "Perspective" and a four-year program of work. The Perspective, which would replace the current Introduction, would be a forward-looking document designed to inspire member states to seek solutions to future problems and challenges. It would contain broad directions for U.N. action, but would not address resources, priorities, and sectoral strategies [A/48/277, par. 15]. The narrative in the four-year program of work would be at the program level, which corresponds to the level of divisions in the Secretariat.

The CPC noted that the effectiveness of the medium-term plan in its current form was increasingly being called into question, and that the plan was little used. The Committee did not go along with the view of a few delegations that medium-term planning be abandoned altogether. Instead, it recommended that consideration be given to a new form along the lines proposed by the Secretary-General. The Perspective would contain an analysis of persistent problems and challenges and of emerging trends, and of the role of the United Nations, and would indicate broad priority areas. The program framework, which would reflect existing mandates and would be reviewed every two years to reflect new mandates, would list only major programs and subprograms; it would provide guidelines against which the preparation and implementation of the biennial budgets would be assessed [A/48/16, par. 232–34].

In the discussion in the Fifth Committee there was general endorsement of the CPC's observations and recommendations. Several delegations were critical of the current form of the plan. In the opinion of the representative of the Russian Federation, for instance, it was a flagrant example of the squandering of resources [A/C.5/48/SR.18, par. 40].

At the same time, several delegations said that they were not in favor of rushing to a decision. Thus, according to the representative of Brazil, the Perspective should be the final product of intense discussions among member states and between them and the Secretariat; while he endorsed CPC's approach, he did not think that all the criticism of the current plan was valid; a hasty decision should be avoided [A/C.5/48/SR.10, par. 6–8]. The Cuban delegation also advocated caution: The Assembly must be quite clear as to the advantages the new format would offer before any decisions were taken [A/C.5/48/SR.14, par. 3]. The representative of Mexico likewise felt that to take a final decision would be premature: The document that would be adopted at the end must support the mandates of member states [ibid., par. 6]. The representative of Algeria said that a change in the plan's format must not be allowed under any circumstances to question the priorities determined by member states [A/C.5/48/SR.22, par. 55]. Similarly, the Cuban representative was of the view that the CPC proposal for a Perspective should be interpreted to mean a statement of mandates authorized by member states embracing recurrent and existing as well as new problems and challenges; otherwise there was a risk that economic and social issues would be overlooked [A/C.5/48/SR.26, par. 5].

The representative of Denmark, speaking on behalf of the five Nordic countries, said that the current approach to planning was unrealistic; the ultimate goal of planning should be to be prepared for changes rather than define activities in detail several years in advance. Unlike the Secretary-General, he felt that the Perspective should set out broad priorities and resource levels. The Perspective should be supplemented, when the need arose, by separate plans dealing with specific ad hoc issues on which more precise intergovernmental guidance was needed [A/C.5/48/SR.14, par. 28–29].

The General Assembly decided to give the issue of program planning in-depth consideration at the 49th Session, and it requested the Secretary-General to submit at that time a prototype of a new format of the plan that would take account of the views expressed at the 48th Session [A/Res/48/218 I.B].

4. Staffing and Administration

In line with the General Assembly's decision to biennalize to the extent possible the work of its main committees, personnel questions were not considered by the Fifth Committee at the 48th Session. These questions, which include the composition of the Secretariat, geographical distribution, recruitment and career development, and the issue of women in the Secretariat, will be on the Fifth Committee's agenda in 1994.

Restructuring of the Secretariat

The restructuring of the Secretariat figured prominently in the deliberations of the Fifth Committee at both the 47th and 48th Sessions. At the 49th Session the Committee should have before it "an analytical report on all aspects of the restructuring . . . and its effects on the programs, including UNCTAD and Transnational Corporations" that has been requested by the General Assembly upon the recommendation of the Committee for Program and Coordination [A/Res/48/218 I.C operative par. 4]. The CPC recommendation received broad support in the Fifth Committee at the 48th Session on the ground that the Secretary-General's report on restructuring and efficiency of the Secretariat [A/48/428] had merely described earlier action [for which see *Issues/48*, pp. 332–39].

The documentation available to the Fifth Committee on this question at the 48th Session included, in addition to the report on restructuring, a report on high-level posts and the related comments by ACABQ, and additional proposals contained in the Secretary-General's program budget for 1994–95. While all delegations agreed on the need to restructure the Secretariat, there was widespread unhappiness over the lack of prior consultations with member states, the seeming absence of a comprehensive approach to restructuring, the length of time the process was taking, and failure on the part of the Secretary-General to heed the requests of the competent intergovernmental organs.

The representative of Japan said that the Secretary-General had failed to justify some of the important changes proposed in his restructuring plan. No specific proposals had been made with regard to decentralization. No persuasive reasons had been advanced for the transfer of the Office of Outer Space Affairs to Vienna, the restructuring of UNCTAD, or the future administrative framework at Nairobi. The confusion engendered by restructuring was a serious matter, and certain current problems might not be temporary [A/C.5/48/SR.13, par. 1–5]. The representative of China wondered whether restructuring was actually achieving the desired results and leading to greater efficiency [A/C.5/48/SR.14, par. 14]. The representative of Tunisia called for an overall approach and a clear vision of the future, as well as a timetable for the implementation of the major proposals [ibid., par. 16]; the latter point was also mentioned by the representative of Ukraine [ibid., par. 21].

Among the issues discussed in the context of restructuring were the structure of the Department of Administration and Management (DAM), the Secretary-General's proposal that the Office of Project Services (OPS) of UNDP be merged with the Department for Development Support and Management Services (DDSMS) of the U.N. Secretariat, and the special identity of the International Trade Centre (ITC) and the U.N. Centre for Human Settlements (Habitat).

The integration of OPS within DDSMS had been originally proposed by the Secretary-General at the Assembly's 47th Session in his revised budget estimates for 1992–93. The question was subsequently discussed in the UNDP Governing Council in June 1993. A further report by the Secretary-General was before the Fifth Committee at the 48th Session [A/48/502]. Noting that several matters related to the proposed merger were still under discussion, ACABQ called for an additional report before any action was taken [A/48/7/Add.1]. At the 48th Session the proposed merger was criticized by both developing (Bangladesh, Cuba, Pakistan) and developed countries (Canada, European Union, Japan, Nordic countries). In the Canadian delegation's view, the proposal "went against all the improved practices which Member States had been seeking" [A/C.5/48/SR.12, par. 6]. The matter was deferred for further consideration in 1994, including in the UNDP Executive Board. The latter received a revised proposal from the Secretary-General.

The Executive Board decided to recommend to the General Assembly that OPS "should become a separate and identifiable entity," with its own Management Coordinating Committee to be chaired by the Administrator of UNDP and having as members the Under-Secretaries-General for DAM and for DDSMS. The modalities of establishing OPS as a separate and identifiable entity will be determined at the Board's session in October 1994 [UNDP Executive Board decision 94/12].

Following restructuring in 1992 and 1993, the Department of Administration and Management currently includes four Offices, one of which (Office of Conference Services) had previously been a separate department headed by an Under-Secretary-General (USG). The Secretary-General originally envisaged the elimination of that USG post and of the three Assistant Secretary-General (ASG) posts of the heads of the other three Offices. It was proposed that each Office be headed by a D-2 level official. (As each Office consists of several Divisions, each of which is headed by an official at the D-2 level, the Secretary-General's proposal meant that the D-2 level heads of Offices would be supervising officials at their own level.) The General Assembly requested the Secretary-General to review his proposal [A/Res/47/212B, Section I; see *Issues/48*, p. 339]. In response to that request, the Secretary-General revised his proposal and restored the post of Controller to the ASG level. Subsequently, in introducing his program budget proposals for 1994–95, the Secretary-General said that he now envisaged that the USG for Administration and Management would be assisted by two ASGs, one of whom would supervise budgetary and personnel activities and the other Conference Services and General Services [A/C.5/48/SR.24, par. 53]. In his report on high-level posts, the Secretary-General indicated that the second ASG in DAM would also be responsible for the Secretariat services to the General Assembly and the Security Council, services formerly provided by the Department of Political Affairs [A/C.5/48/9, par. 13]. ACABQ had reservations about that transfer and also about the proposed amended senior structure of DAM; the Committee recommended that the Secretary-General be requested to resubmit his proposal [A/48/7/Add.2]. Although the General Assembly has requested such a report for its 49th Session [A/Res/48/228, section II, par. 69], a report by the Secretary-General, adding a third ASG post in DAM (for the head of the Office of Human Resources Management), was submitted to the Fifth Committee in June 1994 [A/C.5/48/72].

As for the U.N. Centre for Human Settlements (Habitat), the Secretary-General, in the revised estimates submitted to the Assembly at the 47th Session, proposed the elimination of the USG post of the head of the Centre. In section I of Resolution 47/212B the General Assembly asked him to reconsider that proposal [see *Issues/48*, p. 339]. In his statement to the Fifth Committee at the 48th Session, the Secretary-General proposed that the head of the Centre be an official at the ASG level [A/C.5/48/SR.24, par. 52]. The developing countries were not placated by that concession. In Resolution 48/228, section II, operative paragraph 53, the Assembly "reiterates its request in resolution 47/212B, section I, paragraph 3(c) and stresses the need for the Secretary-General to implement fully and promptly the decisions of the General Assembly contained therein." A virtually identical paragraph is also contained in Resolution 48/218 C. The General Assembly decided to maintain the current approved senior management arrangement for the U.N. Centre for Human Settlements (Habitat)—i.e., the USG post [A/Res/48/218 D, par. 3].

In Resolution 47/212 B, section I, the General Assembly also requested the Secretary-General to agree with the Director-General of GATT on the prompt appointment of the Executive Director of the UNCTAD/GATT International Trade Centre at the ASG level. The Secretary-General had proposed that the post be downgraded to D-2 [see *Issues/48*, p. 339]. A year later the post remained unfilled. The CPC regretted that the Assembly request had not been complied with [A/48/16, par. 118], and its recommendation that the post be filled without further delay was endorsed by the Nordic countries [A/C.5/48/SR.34, par. 7]. In Resolution 48/228, section II, paragraph 52, the General Assembly reiterated its request for the prompt appointment of the Executive Director.

In a report on high-level posts, the Secretary-General proposed the downgrading of one USG post in the Department of Political Affairs to the ASG level, and the redeployment of the ASG post of Chef de Protocol to accommodate the **new post of head of the Office for Inspections and Investigations** [A/C.5/48/9 and Add.1]. There was no objection to this proposal. However, the European Union expressed concern at the apparently ad hoc approach to the management of high-level posts [A/C.5/48/SR.28, par. 7].

In Resolution 48/218 C the General Assembly decided to keep under review the number and distribution of high-level posts, including those financed from extrabudgetary resources, and requested the Secretary-General to provide a clear rationale for the establishment of such posts in the context of future proposals he might make. It also stressed that, once approved by the General Assembly, high-level posts should be filled promptly [par. 1 and 2]. The Assembly also decided to consider at its resumed 48th Session the Secretary-General's report on the high-level posts of special representatives, envoys, and related positions [A/Res/48/230, section V, par. 3].

As has been stated above, several delegations indicated at the 48th Session that the restructuring process has gone on for too long. The hope of the European Union was that restructuring, which had been rather turbulent so far, would now enter into a phase of consolidation so that its impact could be analyzed [A/C.5/48/SR.28, par. 6]. The General Assembly took note of "the indication by the Secretary-General in his statement to the Fifth Committee that the Secretariat can now enter into a phase of consolidation" [A/Res/48/218 I.C, par. 2].

Questions of Audit and Control

The Fifth Committee devoted considerable time at the 47th and 48th Sessions to questions of audit and control. Their consideration will be continued at the 49th Session.

The United Nations has two external bodies in this field: the **Board of Auditors,** which consists of the Auditors General of three member states chosen by the General Assembly, who then designate members of their national audit staffs to carry out the audit operations; and the **Joint Inspection Unit,** whose writ runs throughout the U.N. system and whose members are elected by the General Assembly.

The General Assembly has been satisfied, on the whole, with the work of the Board of Auditors. Criticism has been directed at the dilatoriness or the outright failure of U.N. programs and other organizational units to carry out the Board's recommendations. In Resolution 48/216 B the General Assembly again urged compliance with the Board's recommendations.

At the 48th Session the General Assembly had before it the Board's reports on the financial reports and statements of only two bodies: the U.N. Institute for Training and Research (UNITAR) and the voluntary funds administered by the U.N. High Commissioner for Refugees. At the 49th Session the General Assembly will consider the Board of Auditors' reports on the U.N. regular program budget for 1992–93 and the biennial budgets of various programs associated with the United Nations. Pursuant to operative paragraph 6 of Resolution 48/216 B the Board must give particular attention in its audits to procurement, the employment of consultants, and property accountability in field missions. One area of concern is departures from the requirement in the Regulations mandating competitive bidding for supplies and services.

In recent years the effectiveness of the Joint Inspection Unit and the relevance of its reports was questioned by delegations [*Issues/48*, p. 342]. A much more positive attitude prevailed at the 48th Session, when the Unit was praised for its reports on several issues of concern to the Fifth Committee. The Committee was informed by the Chairman of the Unit that a study commissioned by the Unit showed that during the eight-year period January 1, 1985, to December 31, 1992, savings resulting from the implementation of JIU recommendations had amounted to more than $75 million, while the cost of operating the Unit during that period had been $24 million [A/C.5/48/SR.11, par. 13].

The representative of the United States asked how those figures had been arrived at. He criticized the way in which organizations sometimes completely ignored the JIU recommendations and referred to the observation of the ACABQ that it was virtually impossible to quantify the rate of implementation of the recommendations, partly because of the vagueness and generality of many of them. Member states bore a share of the blame for the situation. In his opinion, not all the inspectors appeared to meet the qualifications laid down in the Unit's statute [A/C.5/48/SR.15, par. 9–14].

The representative of Poland said that while there was no need to change the regulations governing the appointment of inspectors, the requirements concerning professional competence, knowledge of the U.N. system, and drafting ability could be made more demanding; in this connection he referred to the holding of public hearings in the Fifth Committee of candidates for appointment as inspectors [ibid., par., 20]. The representative of Belgium, speaking on behalf of the European Union, also favored paying more attention to the appointment of members of the Unit. Despite the uneven quality of its reports, it would be unacceptable to abolish what was the only system-wide body with powers to investigate the administrative efficiency and financial management of the United Nations [A/C.5/48/SR.25, par. 13]. Several delegations praised the JIU and called for its strengthening.

In Resolution 48/221 the General Assembly was appreciative of the work of the Unit. The Unit was invited to put more emphasis in its future work program on inspection and evaluation to ensure optimum use of funds in order to enhance the efficiency of the administrative and financial functioning of the U.N. system; to indicate the estimated financial implications or possible cost-savings of its recommendations; and to follow up on the implementation of the latter. The participating organizations were asked to make extrabudgetary resources available to the Unit. At the same time the Secretary-General was requested to submit to the Assembly at its 49th Session proposals regarding the procedure for selecting inspectors, with a view to improving the selection process, with due regard to the principle of equitable geographical distribution.

The discussion at the 48th Session centered around the questions of the accountability and responsibility of program managers, the setting up of the Office for Inspections and Investigations for which $11.4 million was appropriated in the program budget for 1994–95, and the **proposal by the United States for the setting up of an Office of Inspector General.**

In response to requests by the General Assembly, the Secretary-General submitted a report on the accountability and responsibility of program managers in which he described the existing procedures. He promised to carry out a thorough review of those procedures and also of the relevant financial and personnel regulations and rules so as to give program managers sufficient discretion in conducting their work, while preserving adequate central control and oversight. Managers now claimed that often they were not delegated enough authority to manage their programs [A/48/452].

The CPC found that the report was not responsive to the requests of the General Assembly. What was needed was a transparent and effective system, to be set in place not later than January 1, 1995, which would provide, as a minimum, unmistakable allocation of responsibilities among staff members, particularly program managers, including clear supervisory responsibilities and mechanisms for performance assessment and remedial action [A/48/16, par. 241–46].

The representative of Canada, speaking also on behalf of Australia and New Zealand, was critical of the current situation. He said that managers must be given the freedom to act within a set of rules that facilitated program delivery and reduced any tendency toward defensiveness. The rules now in place were sufficient to ensure that funds were spent for the purposes approved by the General Assembly. If applied positively, they permitted considerable freedom of action. However, a large body of prescriptive rules and procedures had come into being that stifled initiative and led to loss of control. What was needed was not more rules but a commitment to good management [A/C.5/48/SR.12, par. 3–4].

The representative of Denmark, speaking on behalf of the Nordic countries, advocated training in financial and administrative issues and management techniques, and asked for a transparent link between good performance and reward [A/C.5/48/SR.14, par. 33]. The representative of the Republic of Korea asked for a report that would describe why program managers now felt that the existing regulations and rules were too rigid [ibid., par. 46].

The question of staff accountability was also considered by the Joint inspection Unit in a report whose main thrust was the existing internal oversight machinery and how it should be improved [A/48/420, Annex]. They found that the existing oversight units (Internal Audit Division, Central Evaluation Unit, Central Monitoring Unit, Management Advisory Service) lacked the necessary resources and support and were seriously understaffed. In his related comments the Secretary-General ascribed that situation to the zero-growth approach by member states to the U.N. budget over four biennia and by the post reduction exercise mandated by General Assembly Resolution 41/213 [A/48/420/Add.1, par. 5]. The JIU believed that accountability and oversight control could not be established on the cheap: Instead of the current staff strength of 90, there would be need, depending on the yardstick chosen, for 217 to about 800 staff [A/48/420, Annex, par. 60].

While recognizing that the Secretary-General, as the Chief Administrative Officer of the Organization (under Article 97 of the U.N. Charter), is alone accountable to member states, the JIU report went on to say that the record of management in the U.N. did not instill confidence in the managerial capacities of the kind of individual whom member states persisted in selecting as Secretary-General [ibid., par. 166–67].

The solution proposed in the JIU report is the establishment of an Office of Accountability and Oversight, which would absorb the four existing oversight units. Two alternatives are discussed.

Under one of them, the Office would be headed by an ASG, who would serve under the direct authority of the Secretary-General and would have ready access to him; he or she would be chosen and appointed by the Secretary-General in consultation with member states. The staff of the Office would form part of the Secretariat, and its funding would be through the normal U.N. budget process. The annual report of the Office would be submitted to the General Assembly through the Secretary-General.

Under the second option, the head of the Office would be at the USG level, and would be selected by the Secretary-General from a short list of candidates proposed by the International Organization of Supreme Audit Institutions. He or she would have delegated authority for the recruitment and personnel administration of the Office staff. The Office would be financed through a mix of voluntary contributions, if available, and a fixed percentage (at least 1 percent) of the financial resources available to the activities for which the Office would have oversight responsibilities [ibid., par. 171–75].

While the JIU report was in preparation, the Secretary-General decided to amalgamate the four existing oversight units in a new Office for Inspections and Investigations, headed by an official at the ASG level.

The U.S. delegation did not submit in an official document its proposal for the establishment of an Office of Inspector General, but it made an outline available to delegations. The United States proposed that the Inspector General be selected from a list of candidates drawn up by the International Organization of Supreme Audit Institutions; the Inspector General would be an internationally recognized expert in accounting, auditing, financial or management analysis, law, public administration, or investigations. The appointment would be made by the Secretary-General and approved by a two-thirds majority for one six-year term; he or she could be removed only by a two-thirds majority vote in the General Assembly.

The Office of Inspector General would have an inspection function (enabling it to examine all aspects of an operation, identifying problems, and suggesting solutions), an audit and program evaluation function (assessing the efficiency and effectiveness of individual programs with a view to recommending improvements in management or functioning), a compliance capacity (monitoring of the measures taken to implement its recommendations), and an investigations function (acting on reports of misconduct and malfeasance). The recommendations of the Office must be accepted and implemented by the program manager; if there was disagreement, the matter would be referred to the Secretary-General for resolution.

The Office would be set up using resources deployed from existing U.N. oversight bodies. The Board of Auditors would no longer undertake detailed management audits, and the JIU's remit would be limited to system-wide issues and to activities of the specialized agencies. It will be noted that there are many similarities between the U.S. proposal and the second option in the JIU report, but there is a major difference between the two when it comes to the volume of resources that would be made available to the proposed Office.

A call for the establishment of the Office of Inspector General was included in the statement by President Clinton in the General Assembly on September 27, 1993, and in several statements by representatives of the United States in the Fifth Committee.

In the discussion at the 48th Session several delegations welcomed the action taken by the Secretary-General in creating the Office for Inspections and Investigations. The representative of Canada, speaking also on behalf of Australia and New Zealand, said that the Office should have a clear mandate to promote a culture of performance and accountability and not merely to delve into lapses of probity and instances of noncompliance. Staff members should not have to follow unwieldy rules and procedures, which inhibited innovation, and the success of the Office should not be measured by the number of mistakes it found; its relationship with the staff should not be adversarial. Unless the Office was neutral it could not serve as a guide to managers, and the whole purpose of the internal audit and evaluation function would be lost [A/C.5/48/SR.12, par. 7].

While welcoming the establishment of the Office, the representative of Bangladesh said that its work must not degenerate into a witch-hunt and that it should not stifle genuine innovative initiatives [A/C.5/48/SR.14, par. 52].

The representative of Cameroon, on the other hand, felt that the problem of fraud, mismanagement of resources, and inefficiency would not be resolved by consolidating the existing oversight units into a single unit or by creating a new unit. What was needed was simply to enhance the authority and resources of the existing oversight mechanisms; to be effective, the oversight units must have the power to impose penalties [A/C.5/48/SR.15, par. 6–7]. The representatives of Egypt and Austria also believed that consolidation of existing mechanisms would be preferable to creating new ones [ibid., par. 35 and 37; A/C.5/48/SR.18, par. 54]. The representative of Sierra Leone said that while in many countries, including his own, the office of Auditor-General was provided for under the Constitution, there was no strict analogy between such models and the U.N. Charter, under which member states were sovereign participants to whom only the Secretary-General was answerable for the proper management of the Organization [A/C.5/48/SR.22, par. 61].

The representative of Belgium, speaking on behalf of the members of the European Union, said that the new Office for Inspections and Investigations should form the nucleus of a new structure that must be given adequate staff and financial resources to become an effective instrument for the Secretary-General. The investigative functions of the new Office should be very precisely defined and they should not include the power to decide penalties. A presumption of innocence and respect for the right of defense must be guaranteed and investigations should not be based solely on reports of alleged wrongdoing. They should be part of regular inspection activities that would make it possible to uncover irregularities and identify the persons responsible. Internal auditing and evaluation were distinct but complementary processes; both should be considerably strengthened. The members of the European Union agreed with the principle of establishing an Office of Inspector General, subject to a number of safeguards. The reform should not generate a costly new bureaucracy disproportionate to any benefits that might accrue from it [A/C.5/48/SR.25, par. 10, 14–16].

The U.S. proposal was supported by the Russian Federation. The Nordic countries agreed in principle with many of the U.S. suggestions, but felt that further discussions were needed on certain aspects of the relationship or balance between the Inspector General, the Secretary-General, and the General Assembly, and also on the division of labor between internal and external audit and oversight activities. If an area of responsibility was excluded from the Secretary-General's remit, there might be ambiguity as to where the ultimate responsibility lay. There were arguments in favor of making the Office of Inspector General a part of the Secretariat, but its effectiveness would really depend on an independent and impartial status. The establishment of the Office must be in accordance with Article 100 of the Charter. The oversight responsibility of the General Assembly should still be discharged by the Board of Auditors without any weakening of its mandate [ibid., par. 19–24]. Support for the principle of establishing an Office of Inspector General was also voiced by the representatives of France and of Brazil.

At the end of the first part of the 48th Session the General Assembly adopted Resolution 48/218, in section I.E of which it requested the Secretary-General to report to the 49th Session on a system of accountability and responsibility to cover program delivery, including performance indicators as a measure of quality control; effective management of personnel and financial resources; performance evaluation of all officials, including senior officials, with objectives and performance indicators; and training for staff in financial and management responsibilities.

In section II of the same resolution, the Assembly reaffirmed the role and mandates of the Board of Auditors, of the JIU, and of its own subsidiary organs in the field of administration, budget, and management. It decided to continue discussions at the resumed 48th Session with a view to making a decision to establish an additional independent entity, taking into account Article 97 of the Charter, to enhance oversight functions, in particular with regard to evaluation, audit, investigation, and compliance, subject to the definition of the related modalities, including the entity's relationship with existing control mechanisms.

In section III of Resolution 48/218, responding to a proposal by the French delegation, the Assembly decided to establish an ad hoc intergovernmental working group of experts to study the possibility of setting up a new jurisdictional and procedural mechanism, or extending the mandates of existing such mechanisms to deal with alleged cases of fraud in the United Nations in an impartial manner, in accordance with due process of law and full respect for the rights of each individual concerned, especially the rights of defense.

At the resumed 48th Session the Fifth Committee approved the redeployment of resources from the budget section for Common Support Services (Section 25) to a new section for the Office for Inspections and Investigations (this redeployment was implicit in the decision on budget appropriations for 1994-95, A/Res/48/231 A). It also decided to continue the current arrangements pending review later in the resumed 48th Session (not completed at the time of writing).

While the question was being discussed in the General Assembly, the U.S. Congress was considering ways to bring pressure to bear on the United Nations so that it would adopt the U.S. proposal for the establishment of the Office of Inspector General. A Senate bill sought to reduce the payment in 1993 of U.S. arrears to the U.N. regular budget by some $53 million unless an independent internal auditing office were established [*Washington Weekly Report,* XIX-25]. Another proposal, which the Senate did not accept, was that two-thirds of the U.S. voluntary contributions to the United Nations be withheld pending the appointment of an independent auditor [ibid., XIX-30]. A provision in the Fiscal Year 1994 appropriations bill for the Department of State (Public Law 103-121 of November 11, 1993) withholds 10 percent of the U.S. contribution to the U.N. budget for 1993 (i.e., approximately $29 million) until the Secretary of State has certified that an independent Inspector General has been appointed [ibid., XIX-31, XIX-32 and XIX-38]. In January 1994 the Senate decided by an overwhelming majority that the withholding would be increased to 20 percent if the appointment of an independent Inspector General has not occurred by Fiscal Year 1995. The decision also calls for a system of review of the U.N.'s internal audits by member states [ibid., XX-1]. In February 1994 the Senate approved its version of the State Department authorization bill for Fiscal Years 1994–95, which also provides for a withholding of 20 percent of U.S. contributions to U.N. peacekeeping operations in Fiscal Year 1995 and thereafter until an independent Inspector General is appointed in the United Nations [ibid., XX-2]. The House and Senate conferees to the State Department authorization bill for Fiscal Years 1994-95 decided that half of the $670 million in supplemental U.S. contributions to U.N. peacekeeping operations would be made available to the United Nations only upon certification by the Secretary of State that an independent Office of Inspector General has been established [ibid., XX-10].

The Senate also went on record that the position of Under-Secretary-General for Administration and Management should be held by a citizen of the United States, and that the U.S. contribution would be withheld if that position is not held by an American after October 1, 1994. The withholding could be waived if there is a non-American appointee who is committed to efficient management practices and restrained budgets for the United Nations, provided there is a justification for the appointment of a non-American [ibid., XX-2]. The Senate's position was at variance with the conclusion of the U.S. Commission on Improving the Effectiveness of the United Nations that the practice of reserving top U.N. Secretariat posts for certain nationals should be eliminated [ibid., XIX-27].

Respect for the Privileges and Immunities of International Officials

This was the only subitem on personnel questions that was considered by the Fifth Committee at the 48th Session. The Committee had before it a report by the Secretary-General, which contained a consolidated list as of June 30, 1993, of staff members under arrest and detention or missing with repsect to whom the United Nations and the specialized agencies and related organizations had been unable to exercise fully their right to protection [A/C.5/48/5]. The list contained 44 names (one less than the previous year). Of the individuals involved, 36 were staff members of UNRWA (nine of them had been released after the end of June); three had been detained in Afghanistan, two were missing or detained in Somalia, two had been detained in Ethiopia, and one had been abducted in Pakistan. Since the beginning of 1993, 19 staff members belonging to different organizations had lost their lives because the organizations were now operating in extremely dangerous situations.

The delegations that took part in the debate deplored the loss of life and conveyed their condolences to the families of the deceased. In Decision 48/462 the General Assembly took note of the information furnished by the Secretary-General.

The Common System

The reports of the **International Civil Service Commission (ICSC)** and the **U.N. Joint Staff Pension Board** were considered jointly by the Fifth Committee at the 48th Session.

In its resolution on the ICSC report the General Assembly approved, with effect from March 1, 1994, a revised scale of gross and net salaries for staff in the Professional and higher categories and a revised staff assessment scale, as recommended by the ICSC. It endorsed the ICSC decision to reject the view of some organizations in the common system that have longer working hours than the United Nations that they should pay their staff at correspondingly higher rates. It welcomed the action taken by the World Health Assembly and the Governing Body of the International Labour Organisation to discontinue gradually the extra step increments above the common system salary scale. And it requested that procedures be established whereby the views of the ICSC would be made know to the U.N. Administrative Tribunal and the Administrative Tribunal of the ILO before they issued their judgments on matters within the mandate of the ICSC [A/Res/48/224].

In its resolution on pension matters, the General Assembly approved a new methodology, based on the income replacement approach, for determining the pensionable remuneration of staff in the General Service and related categories. The new methodology is intended to reduce—but not to eliminate entirely—the income inversion anomaly, which resulted in higher pensions being paid to some former General Service staff than to former staff in the Professional category with the same period of pensionable service and higher remuneration while in service. The Assembly noted that further attention will need to be given to this problem, which arose because of differences between the methodologies used for calculating the pensionable remuneration of the two categories [A/Res/48/225].

Index

An invitation from thousands of your fellow citizens

Do you feel powerless to deal with terrorism, AIDS, hunger, human rights violations, drug abuse? Do you wish there was a way you, as an individual, could help international efforts to address these global problems?

There is a way! Join with thousands of your fellow citizens in an effort to make the United Nations even more effective. Join the United Nations Association.

UNA-USA is a nonpartisan, nonprofit organization working in Washington, at U.N. Headquarters in New York, and in thousands of communities across America to build public understanding of, and support for, international cooperation through the United Nations.

■ *Get the inside story*

Founded a quarter-century ago, UNA boasts a membership of more than 20,000 Americans—citizens who want to get beyond the headlines of the popular media.

As a UNA member you will receive the Association's acclaimed news journal, *The InterDependent,* with expert analysis of the global issues that affect our lives. You will learn from UNA's Policy Studies reports the latest in Soviet policy toward the

United Nations, the newest thinking on Third World debt, and the future of U.N. reform as the world body prepares to enter the 21st century.

■ *Be a part of it all*

You are invited to participate in your local UNA Chapter to whatever degree your schedule permits: planning U.N. Day observances (October 24); sponsoring Model U.N. conferences for local high school and college students; attending lectures and conferences, often with the participation of senior U.N. officials and representatives of U.N. member governments; and setting up seminars for educators, the media, and elected officials—all aimed at shaping a U.S. agenda for a stronger and more effective U.N.

■ *Sign up and receive . . .*

• One year's subscription to the *Inter-Dependent.*
• A membership kit, containing UNA Fact Sheets, *ABCs of the U.N.,* and other vital information on global issues.
• Discounts on all UNA materials.
• The opportunity to become active in your local UNA-USA Chapter.

$35 ☐ Individual $20 ☐ Limited income (individual) $500 ☐ Patron
$40 ☐ Family $25 ☐ Limited income (family) $1,000 ☐ Ambassador
$10 ☐ Student $100 ☐ Sponsor

☐ Additional contribution for my local chapter $_____
☐ Additional contribution for UNA's national programs $_____

Contributions are tax deductible. **Total enclosed $_____**

Please make checks payable to UNA-USA.

Name_____

Address_____

City_____ State_____ Zip_____

Mail this form and check to: UNA-USA Membership Dept. 485 Fifth Avenue New York, N.Y. 10017